The Catholic Biblical Quarterly
Monograph Series
29

Wisdom, You Are My Sister

Studies in Honor of
Roland E. Murphy, O.Carm.,
on the Occasion of His
Eightieth Birthday

EDITED BY

Michael L. Barré, S.S.

The Catholic Biblical Quarterly
Monograph Series
29

©1997 The Catholic Biblical Association of America,
Washington, DC 20064

Produced in the United States of America

Library of Congress Cataloging-in-Publication Data

Wisdom, you are my sister : studies in honor of Roland E. Murphy, O. Carm.,
on the occasion of his eightieth birthday / edited by Michael L. Barré.
   p.   cm. — (The Catholic Biblical quarterly. Monograph series ; 29)
Includes bibliographical references and indexes.
ISBN 0-915170-28-0
1. Wisdom literature.   I. Murphy, Roland Edmund, 1917–   .
II. Barré, Michael L.   III. Series.
BS1455.W564   1997
223'.06–dc21
97-16060
CIP

Contents

Foreword

It has been truly said that it is of little use to live long without living well. Roland E. Murphy, O.Carm., at the age of eighty, has done both. Though perhaps not old by modern standards, he certainly has lived well, and present indications are that he will continue to lead a good and productive life for many years to come.

He is, first of all, a faithful Carmelite religious (since 1935) and priest (since 1942), a widely renowned Scripture scholar, author, and teacher of a multitude of students. He is loved and admired by his Carmelite brothers and sisters, his colleagues in Scripture studies, and that multitude of students just referred to.

Most of those who pick up this book will need no introduction to Fr. Murphy, but it is appropriate in a work intended to honor him that some mention be made of his accomplishments. But first, a note about the title of this book. Many years ago, sometime after the publication of *Seven Books of Wisdom* (1960), I remember Fr. Murphy saying that he had wanted to title that book *Wisdom, You Are My Sister,* but the publisher had other ideas. It seemed a good idea to give that name to this collection for a couple of reasons: first, because it would assuage that earlier disappointment; but, perhaps more importantly, because his life-long interest in Old Testament wisdom literature and his quest for true wisdom make it particularly appropriate.

The fourteen-page bibliography in this volume indicates something of Fr. Murphy's prolific career as an author, of both scholarly and popular writings, beginning in 1943. Though it documents his particular interest in wisdom literature, it also illustrates the variety of his interests and competencies, including Qumran, seminary instruction, Church documents, eschatology, biblical theology, prophecy, exegesis, inclusive language, and so much more. Among his most significant publications projects has been the editing, along with

Raymond E. Brown, S.S., and Joseph A. Fitzmyer, S.J., of *The Jerome Biblical Commentary* (1968) and *The New Jerome Biblical Commentary* (1990).

Fr. Murphy has been a highly respected member of the Catholic Biblical Association of America. He functioned as General Editor of *The Catholic Biblical Quarterly* from 1959 to 1965 and Associate Editor from 1953 to 1971 and again from 1977 to 1984; he was Associate Editor of *Old Testament Abstracts* from its inception in 1978 to the present and a member of the Editorial Board of the Catholic Biblical Quarterly Monograph Series from 1971 to 1984. He was a member of the board of editors responsible for revising the Psalter of the New American Bible. He is one of the tiny number of elect scholars who has been President of both major U.S. biblical societies, the Catholic Biblical Association (1968–1969) and the Society of Biblical Literature (1984). He was also a Fellow of the American Schools of Oriental Research, Jerusalem (1950–1951).

The expertise demonstrated in these publications and activities had its beginnings in education pursued at the Catholic University of America, where he obtained degrees in both theology (S.T.D.) and Semitics (M.A.), and the Pontifical Biblical Institute in Rome (S.S.L.). His distinction as a teacher has put him in demand at many institutions, including Whitefriars Hall (Washington, DC), the Catholic University of America (in the Department of Semitic and Egyptian Languages and in the School of Theology), Pittsburgh Theological Seminary, Yale University Divinity School, Princeton Theological Seminary, and Duke University; he retired from the last-named as G. W. Ivey Professor, Emeritus. Of course he's not *really* retired, from teaching or anything else. Among other things, he is currently on the faculty at the Washington Theological Union and a member of the board of editors charged with revising the Old Testament for the New American Bible.

To this illustrious member of the Catholic Biblical Association of America we gladly dedicate this volume in his eightieth year.

JOSEPH JENSEN, O.S.B.
Catholic University of America
CBA Executive Secretary

PART ONE

Job and Psalms

Psalm 36

Psalm 36 contains both typological and textual problems. The textual problems in vv 2–3 (and the meaning of *šām* in v 13) will be discussed below, in the exegesis section of this paper. As to typology, Psalm 36 eludes exact classification, exhibiting as it does a hymnic section (vv 6–10) framed by two sections with characteristics of wisdom (vv 2–5; 11–13); the last three verses have also been considered to manifest characteristics of lament.[1] Given the connection of Psalm 36 with the wisdom tradition, a treatment of this psalm seems appropriate to a Festschrift for Roland Murphy, who has devoted his scholarly career to the study of the sapiential literature.

Noting that Psalm 36 has been variously classified as an individual lament, a national lament, and a wisdom poem, a recent commentator concludes:

> The psalm must be viewed primarily as a literary and devotional composition, in which the poet has blended different literary types in his creative purpose. Against this background the psalm should be set in the wisdom tradition, though it does not adhere to any distinctive literary form.[2]

---

[1] M. Dahood, *Psalms I* (AB 16; Garden City, NY: Doubleday, 1966) 218; G. Ravasi, *Il libro dei Salmi I°* (Lettura pastorale della Bibbia 12; Bologna: Dehoniane, 1986) 651 (who describes Psalm 36 as "una composizione irriducibile ad uno schema unico").

[2] P. C. Craigie, *Psalms 1-50* (WBC 19; Waco, TX: Word, 1983) 291. See also A. A. Anderson, *Psalms 1* (NCB; Grand Rapids, MI: Eerdmans, 1981) 285–86: "If we emphasized the Wisdom elements of this poem, it could be classed, with certain reservations, as a Wisdom Psalm...." The psalm's sapiential tone has been noted also by D. G. Castellino, *Libro dei Salmi* (La Sacra Bibbia;

Provisionally, taking into account the sapiential tone of vv 10–13, the structure of Psalm 36 can be analyzed as containing a hymnic section on the Temple framed by two wisdom sections (vv 2–5; 11–13)[3]:

Part I, vv 2–5: description of the wicked, in wisdom language

Part II, vv 6–10: subdivided into:

   (a) vv 6–7: the grandeur and extent of Yhwh's *ḥesed* (covenant love)

   (b) vv 8–10: the Temple as the preeminent place for the experience of this divine love

Part III, vv 11–13: concluding prayer (in wisdom language) that God will continue his love toward the faithful and will destroy the wicked

Note that the first lines of each of the subdivisions of Part II (vv 6, 8) and the first line of Part III (v 11) feature the key word *ḥesed*.

Literary devices employed by the poet include an inclusio that frames the whole poem: *rāšāʿ* in v 2, and *rĕšāʿîm* in v 12. Similarly, there are other instances of inclusio, or inclusio-like structures that mark off the individual sections. In Part I (vv 2–5), the oracle of sin in the heart (i.e., the mind) of the wicked in v 2 corresponds to the thinking or planning of iniquity by the wicked in v 5. In Part II (vv 6–10), the upward direction of Yhwh's *ḥesed* to the clouds of heaven and the towering mountains of v 7 contrast effectively with Part III, which concludes with the downward movement (falling into Sheol) of the wicked in v 13. The second subsection of Part II (vv 8–10) is marked off by a wordplay: *mâ yāqār* in v 8, and *māqôr* in v 10. In Part III, *yišrê lēb* ("upright of heart") is balanced by its antonym *pōʿălê ʾāwen* ("evildoers") in v 13.[4] In addition to the two clear examples of merismus in vv 7 (human being and sub-human animal) and 8 (gods and humans), there is also a more subtle example

---

Rome: Marietti, 1955) 798; Ravasi, *Salmi I°, 652*; F.-L. Hossfeld and E. Zenger, *Die Psalmen I* (Die Neue Echter Bibel; Wurzburg: Echter V., 1993) 213.

[3] The presence of cultic material in a wisdom psalm need occasion no surprise, since L. G. Perdue's exhaustive examination of the issue in his dissertation, *Wisdom and Cult* (SBLDS 30; Missoula, MT: Scholars, 1977); and more recently R. Davidson, *Wisdom and Worship* (London: SCM; Philadelphia: Trinity Press International, 1990). Two other psalms which similarly join didactic characteristics with praise are Pss 33 and 92.

[4] *Yišrê lēb* and *pōʿălê ʾāwen* recall *lēb* in v 2 (the heart of the wicked, as the antonym of "the upright of heart") and *ʾāwen* (the plotting of evil by the wicked) in v 5; thus elements that occur at the beginning and end of Part I (vv 2–5) are matched by elements at the beginning and end of Part III (vv 11–13).

in v 5: here the wicked are described both as "on their beds," i.e., lying prone, in a horizontal posture, and as "standing in the way," i.e., standing erect or upright, in a vertical position. The first activity ("on their beds") takes place in private; the second ("in the way") occurs in public. The point made by this merismus is that the wicked are always involved in evil, in private and in public, whether lying down or standing upright.

The framing Parts I and II are further linked by the use of parts of the body: the heart, eyes (twice), and mouth of the wicked in vv 2–4, dealing with damaging speech, are balanced by the heart (of the upright), and the foot and hand of the wicked in vv 11–12, dealing with sinful deeds. Further there is an effective chiasmus that connects vv 5 and 12: in v 5, "malice on their beds" (A) and "way not good" (B) is matched by the inversion "the foot of the arrogant" (B′) and "fall (lie prostrate), unable to rise" (A′) in v 12. The AA′ parallelism involves the way (*derek*) and the foot (*regel*) of the wicked; the BB′ elements involve the law of talion: those who lie on their beds plotting evil will fall into the underworld and be unable to rise.[5]

Finally, worth noting are the wordplays of *ʿên, ʿāwōn,* and *ʾāwen* in vv 2–4, and, as mentioned above, the wordplay of *mâ yāqār* in v 8 and *māqôr* in v 10.

Little can be said about the time and place of the psalm's composition. Rendsburg has pointed to several features of Psalm 36 that he believes indicate its origin in the North.[6] If Rendsburg is right about the Northern provenance of the poem, the the time of composition of Psalm 36 would be between the tenth and the eighth centuries B.C.E. In a Northern poem, the Temple referred to in vv 8–10 could be one of the Northern temples. However, given the pro-Zion bias of the Northern Deuteronomistic source and D's argument for unity of sanctuary, with the Jerusalem Temple as the dwelling-place of the divine name and as the only legitimate place for worship, one might detect in a Northern poem like Psalm 36 a similar bias on the part of the poet for the cultic establishment in Jerusalem.

---

[5] Note too that *miškāb* can mean both "bed" and "grave"; see BDB 1012b, and N. J. Tromp, *Primitive Conceptions of Death and the Nether World in the Old Testament* (BibOr 21; Rome: Biblical Institute, 1969) 156–57, 183.

[6] G. A. Rendsburg, *Linguistic Evidence for the Northern Origin of Selected Psalms* (SBLMS 43; Atlanta: Scholars, 1990) 39–43: (1) the use of *nĕʾum* ("oracle") for a non-divine speaker in v 2; (2) the non-elision of the article in *bĕhaššāmayim* ("in the heavens") in v 6; (3) the reduplicative plural *harĕrê* ("mountains") in v 7; (4) the retention of *yod* in the III-y verbs *yeḥĕsāyûn* ("they take refuge") in v 8, and *yirwĕyûn* ("they feast" [lit., "they are drenched"]) in v 9. C. A. and E. G. Briggs, *The Book of Psalms* (ICC; Edinburgh: T. & T. Clark, 1906) 1. 315 also believed Psalm 36 (or at least vv 6–10) to be of Northern origin.

Translation of Psalm 36

1. To the leader; of David, the servant of Yhwh
2. An oracle of sin to the heart of the wicked one,
   in whose sight there is no fear of God.
3. For he flatters himself in his own eyes,
   before the One who finds out his iniquity and hates it.
4. The words of his mouth are malice and deceit;
   he has ceased to act wisely and to do good.
5. Malice he plots on his bed;
   he takes his stand in a way that is not good;
   evil he does not reject.
6. O Yhwh, in the heavens is your love;
   your fidelity reaches to the clouds;
7. your righteousness is like the highest mountains;
   your justice, like the Great Deep;
   humankind and beast you save.
8. O Yhwh, how precious is your love!
   Gods and mortals take refuge in the shadow of your wings.
9. They feast on the rich food of your house;
   from the stream of your delights you let them drink.
10. For with you is the fountain of life;
    in your light we see light.
11. Extend your love to those who know you,
    and your righteousness to the upright of heart.
12. Let not the foot of the proud come near me,
    and let not the hand of the wicked drive me away.
13. There, let evildoers fall;
    thrust down, let them never be able to rise.

Commentary

2. "An oracle of sin to the heart of the wicked one, in whose sight there is no fear of God." The opening words of Psalm 36 (after the superscription in v 1) contain an ambiguity. Of the many suggestions and emendations that have been proposed for the meaning of *něʾum pešaʿ*, two proposals make the best sense of the problematic words. M. L. Barré understands the phrase to be a parody of an oracle; he notes that the structure of Ps 36:2 ("An oracle of sin to the wicked one") is exactly the same as Ps 110:1 ("An oracle of Yhwh to my lord"). As Barré understands the phrase, rather than heeding the voice of

God in his life, the wicked person heeds the voice of evil.[7] Note the parallel in Zech 5:8.

One problem with this understanding is the absence of the oracle referred to. In Ps 110:1, the "oracle of Yhwh" to the Davidic monarch follows: "Sit at my right hand." In light of this difficulty, another possibility may be proposed for the ambiguous words: "An utterance about sin, which comes from the heart of the wicked person" (lit., "an utterance about sin [which belongs] to the wicked person, [which is] from his heart").[8] In this understanding, the "utterance about sin" from the heart of the wicked person is his boast that "there is no fear of God in his sight."

While this second proposal is attractive, I provisionally accept here the analysis of Barré; perhaps we are to think of personified Sin as something akin to the rabbinic *yēṣer hārāʿ* ("evil impulse"), directing the course of those who are evil.[9]

One final observation can be made on the connection of these opening words with the hymnic section of the psalm. If, as Barré suggests, v 2 is an oracle parodied, then there is set up here an opposition to the Temple (vv 6–10) as the place where authentic oracles are given.[10]

The noun *pešaʿ* ("rebellion") is a term regularly used for breach of covenant or political revolt, the diametric opposite of the theme word *ḥesed* in vv 6, 8, and 11, the essence of the covenant bond.

The only emendation proposed in v 2 is the commonly accepted change of *libbî* ("my heart") to *libbô* ("his heart").[11] In addition to some versional evi-

---

[7] J. S. Kselman and M. L. Barré, "Psalms," *The New Jerome Biblical Commentary* (ed. R. E. Brown, J. A. Fitzmyer, and R. E. Murphy; Englewood Cliffs, NJ: Prentice Hall, 1990) 532. Tournay would seem to be in agreement: "Far from being an oracle of the Lord, the oracle with which Ps xxxvi begins is a blaspheming and sacrilegious word, uttered by Sin personified" (R. J. Tournay, "Le psaume XXXVI, structure et doctrine," *RB* 90 [1983] 7).

[8] For this sense of the construct chain, cf. *šîrat dôdî* ("a song about my friend") in Isa 5:1 (J. A. Emerton, "The Translation of Isaiah 5,1," *The Scriptures and the Scrolls* [FS A. S. van der Woude; VTSup 49; ed. F. García Martinez et al.; Leiden: Brill, 1992] 18–30). I owe this understanding of *nĕʾum pešaʿ* to an oral suggestion of Peter Machinist to an earlier form of this paper.

[9] J. Levy, *Wörterbuch über die Talmudim und die Midraschim* (Darmstadt: Wissenschaftliche Buchgesellschaft, 1963 [orig. publ. 1924]) 2. 258–59.

[10] J. Levenson, "The Jewish Temple in Devotional and Visionary Experience," *Jewish Spirituality* (ed. A. Green; London: Routledge & Kegan Paul, 1986) 56.

[11] On the parallelism in v 2 of "within his heart" and "before his eyes," see W. G. E. Watson, *Traditional Techniques in Classical Hebrew Verse* (JSOTSup 170; Sheffield: Sheffield Academic Press, 1994) 284–301.

dence summarized in *BHS,* this 3d-pers. masc. sing. suffix coheres with the five 3d-pers. masc. sing. verbs in vv 2b–5.[12]

3. The obscurities continue in v 3. We will begin our analysis with what is clear in the verse, the idiom *māṣāʾ ʿāwōn* ("find out the iniquity/guilt") at the end of v 3. The same idiom occurs in Gen 44:16: *hāʾĕlōhîm māṣāʾ ʾet ʿăwōn ʿăbādékā* ("God has found out the guilt of your servants"). I tentatively suggest understanding *lmṣʾ* as a qal participle (*mōṣēʾ*) referring to God (as in Gen 44:16) with the preposition *lĕ-* meaning here "before"[13]: "For he flatters himself in his own eyes, before the One who finds out his guilt." This leaves the difficult *lśnʾ.* The association of the verb *ḥlq* ("flatter") with *lāšôn* ("tongue"), as in Ps 5:10,[14] might suggest taking them together to mean "flatter with his tongue." However, it would be difficult to explain how *lĕšônô* could have been changed to *lśnʾ,* which should be retained as the lectio difficilior. I propose rather that, like its parallel *lmṣʾ, lśnʾ* is also prep. *lĕ-* and qal participle *śōnēʾ*: "He flatters himself in his own eyes before the One who finds out his iniquity (and) hates it."[15]

Finally, if the idiom *mṣʾ ʿwn* does refer to God (*hāʾĕlōhîm*), as in Gen 44:16, then an effective chiasmus is revealed:

v 2 *ʾĕlōhîm*   (A)   *lĕneged ʿênāyw*   (B′)
v 3 *bĕʿênāyw*   (B)   *lĕmōṣēʾ ʿăwōnô*   (A′).

4. "The words of his mouth are malicious lies; he has ceased acting wisely and doing good." "Malicious lies" is a hendiadys (lit., "malice and lies"). The theme of deceitful speech, begun in v 3 with the self-congratulation of the wicked, is common in the wisdom literature.[16] Also noteworthy is the similar language in Psalm 14, considered by some commentators[17] to be a wisdom

---

[12] Tournay, "Le psaume xxxvi," 8, makes two points in support of this emendation: the similarity of Ps 36:2 to Ps 14:1 (= 53:2): "The fool says in his heart (*bĕlibbô*), 'There is no God'"; and MT *libbî* as the result of a *relecture,* linking Ps 36 to David, who is the speaker in the final verse of Psalm 35.

[13] For *lĕ-* = *lipnê,* see BDB 511b.

[14] See also Pss 12:3–4; Prov 6:24; 26:28; 28:23.

[15] See Prov 6:16–19, a wisdom text on the things Yhwh hates (*śānēʾ*), which contains a number of parallels to Psalm 36; note especially *lēb ḥōrēš maḥšĕbôt ʾāwen* ("a heart plotting malicious schemes" and "proud eyes, a lying tongue ... feet running to evil." See also Prov 8:13. The two qal participles could be related asyndetically; or one could imagine a haplography of *waw: ʿwnw* [*w*]*lśnʾ.*

[16] Prov 12:17,19,22; 14:5,25; 17:4; 19:5,9; 26:24; Job 3:7; 27:4; 31:5.

[17] Dahood, *Psalms I,* 80; Craigie, *Psalms 1-50,* 145–46.

psalm. Parallel to the wicked one ceasing to do good (*lĕhêṭîb*) is "There is no one doing good" in Ps 14:1,3; and echoing "he has ceased acting wisely (*lĕhaśkîl*)" is 14:2: "Yhwh looked down to see if there was anyone who was wise (*maśkîl*)."

5. "Malice he plots on his bed; he stands in a way that is not good; evil he does not reject." V 5 is a tricolon, the only one in the poem. "In his bed" is taken to mean "in private" (Pss 4:5; 149:5).[18] There is an effective merism in v 5: on his bed, where he lies for sleep, he plots evil in private. When he rises in the morning he stands on a way (in public) that is not good.[19] It may be worth pointing out that the meristic description of the wicked one constantly involved in evil, in private on his bed, and in public on the road, contrasts with the meristic description of the Torah-observant Israelite in Deut 6:6–7: "Keep these words which I am commanding you today *in your heart;* recite them to your children, and talk about them when you are *dwelling at home* (i.e., in private) and when you are *walking in the way* (i.e., in public), when you *lie down* (verb related to *miškāb*, "bed," in Ps 36:5) and when you *rise* (verb *qûm*, equivalent to *yityaṣṣēb*, "stand"; see Ps 94:16, where they are in parallelism). In place of an oracle of sin in the heart of the wicked, the Torah-observant Israelite has the words of Yhwh's law in his heart. Whether lying in bed or walking on the road, the wicked one is always engaged in evil, while the righteous Israelite is engaged in constant study of the Torah of Yhwh.

Vv 4 and 5 are constructed with the antonyms *ʾāwen* ("malice," in both verses) and *rāʿ* ("evil" in v 5) and *lĕhêṭîb* ("do good") in v 4, and *ṭôb* ("good") in v 5. This is the same kind of unifying repetition as the linking *lĕneged ʿênāyw* ("before his eyes") and *bĕʿênāyw* ("in his sight") in vv 2–3.

6. "O Yhwh, in the heavens is your love; your fidelity (reaches) to the clouds." See similar Ps 57:11. The heavens constitute the highest point of the three-level universe in Hebrew cosmology; the towering mountains are part of the second level, the earth; and the "Great Deep" in v 7 is the lowest level. The sequence of "heavens/clouds," then "mountains" (as a synecdoche for the earth), and the deep, subterranean sea shows the reach of God's love and

---

[18] A. R. Ceresko, "Psalm 149: Poetry, Themes (Exodus and Conquest), and Social Function," *Bib* 67 (1986) 186–87.

[19] For *yityaṣṣēb/niṣṣāb badderek* ("stand in the way") see Num 22:22,23,31. For "standing" (*ʿāmad*) in the way (*bĕderek*), see the opening of the wisdom psalm that prefaces the Psalter (Ps 1:1). For taking a way that is not good, see Prov 16:29 and especially Isa 65:2: "walking in a way that is not good, after their own plans" (*hahōlĕkîm hadderek lōʾ ṭôb ʾaḥar maḥšĕbōtêhem*). For plotting evil on their beds, see Mic 2:1.

fidelity (i.e., his reliable love) and the extent of the divine righteousness and justice throughout the whole three-story universe.

7a. "Your righteousness is like the highest mountains; your justice, like the Great Deep." The phrase rendered "highest mountains" is literally "the mountains of God," a not uncommon way of expressing the superlative in Hebrew.[20] The meaning of "righteousness and justice" is something like "social justice," with more specific meanings dependent on context (e.g., social justice toward the oppressed could mean salvation or deliverance).[21] The comparative particle *kĕ-* is double-duty, governing *tĕhôm rabbâ* ("Great Deep") in v 7b, as well as *harĕrê* ("mountains") in v 7a. Worth noting is the balancing of a vertical image (the high mountains) with a horizontal (the wide expanse of the sea).

7b. "Humankind and beast you save." In this verse, the psalmist's gaze now moves from the heavens, the earth (the mountains), and the sea to the inhabitants of the earth, human and subhuman, in the merism "humankind and beast."[22] In this merism we may hear an allusion to the Priestly creation account which describes the creation of beasts (*bĕhēmâ*) and human beings (*ʾādām*) on the sixth day (Gen 1:24–27). The allusion may be significant, given the wisdom cast of Psalm 36, and the often documented connection between wisdom and creation.

While most commentators and translations take the vocative "O Yhwh" in v 7b as closing off vv 6–7, forming an inclusion with the vocative "O Yhwh" in v 6 that begins this subsection, I follow here Dahood, who takes it as the first word of the subsection made up of vv 8–10.[23]

Vv 8–10 form the center of the three sections of the poem (vv 6–7, 8–10, 11–13) that deal with *ḥesed*, divine covenant love. To know Yhwh's life-giving presence in the Temple is the supreme experience of his love, indeed of life

[20] See P. Joüon and T. Muraoka, *A Grammar of Biblical Hebrew* (Subsidia Biblica 14; Rome: Biblical Institute, 1991) 525, and the literature cited there.

[21] For exhaustive discussion, see M. Weinfeld, *Social Justice in Ancient Israel and in the Ancient Near East* (Jerusalem: Magnes; Minneapolis: Fortress, 1995) 179–214.

[22] J. Krašovec, *Der Merismus im Biblisch-Hebräischen und Nordwestsemitischen* (BibOr 33; Rome: Biblical Institute, 1977) 65–66, 75 (#6). The use of merisms in v 7b ("humankind and beast") and in v 8 ("gods and humans"; Krašovec, 78 [#20]) gives some support to the interpretation of v 5 as meristic; see above. Krašovec also takes "mountains and sea" in v 7a as a merism (97 [#77]), but this ignores the fact that these are part of a tripartite structure.

[23] Dahood, *Psalms I*, 221.

itself (Ps 63:3). The language of banquet or feast is appropriate in a meditation on Yhwh's covenant love: see Exod 24:9–11 for the meal at the end of the Sinai covenant.[24] To be noted is the effective contrast between the private plotting of the wicked and the psalmist's public proclamation of the extent of God's *ḥesed*, between the pettiness and ephemerality of human evil and the grandeur of God's enduring, reliable love, extending from the heavens to subhuman creatures.

8. "O Yhwh, how precious is your love! Gods and mortals take refuge in the shadow of your wings." Recent translations and commentaries translate this verse as "How precious is your love, O God! All humankind takes refuge in the shadow of your wings," taking *ʾĕlōhîm* as a vocative. Dahood dissents, attaching the vocative "O Yhwh" of v 7 to v 8, and takes *ʾĕlōhîm ûbĕnê ʾādām* to mean "gods and humans," i.e., a merism including all rational creatures.[25] In defense of Dahood's reading are the other merisms in the poem, the conjunction *waw* ("and") with "humankind," and the chiasmus that this reading produces: v 7 (A): *ʾādām* ("man, human being"); (B): *ûbĕhēmâ* ("beast" [subhuman])//v 8 (B'): *ʾĕlōhîm* ("gods" [superhuman]); (A'): *ûbĕnê ʾādām* ("sons of man, human beings"). For the parallelism of *ʾādām // ben/bĕnê ʾādām*, see Pss 8:5; 80:18.

The association of the verb *ḥāsâ* ("take refuge") with the Temple, and perhaps with asylum there, is present in a number of texts (Pss 5:12; 57:2; 61:5; 142:6). The image of the "shade/shadow of your wings" could refer to the outstretched wings of the Cherubim in the sanctuary (Pss 17:8; 52:7; 63:8).[26] Alternatively it could refer to the outstretched wings of the solar disk, an ancient Near Eastern symbol of deity applied to Yhwh (Ps 84:12; Mal 3:20).[27] See the Appendix below.

---

[24] For the language of feasting associated with the Temple, see Pss 63:5–6; 65:5; 132:13–15; Isa 25:6. On the covenant banquet, see G. E. Mendenhall and G. A. Herion, "Covenant," *The Anchor Bible Dictionary* (6 vols.; ed. D. N. Freedman; New York: Doubleday, 1992), 1. 1194. This tradition is echoed in Isa 55:1–3, where the Davidic covenant, democratized and extended to Israel, is associated with feasting.

[25] Dahood, *Psalms I*, 221. Dahood pointed out the parallel in the wisdom fable of Jotham in Judg 9:13, "wine that gladdens gods and humans" (*ʾĕlōhîm waʾănāšîm*). He neglected to point out that the idiom of taking refuge in the shade (*ḥāsû bĕṣillî*) occurs in the fable as well (Judg 9:15).

[26] C. Meyers, "Cherubim," *Anchor Bible Dictionary*, 1. 899–900.

[27] K. van der Toorn, "Sun," *Anchor Bible Dictionary*, 6. 239; M. S. Smith, *The Early History of God: Yahweh and the Other Deities in Ancient Israel* (San Francisco: Harper & Row, 1990) 115–24.

"They feast on the rich food of your house; from the stream of your delights you let them drink." The Temple language that began in v 8 with refuge under the deity's wings continues in vv 9–10. There is a close parallel to v 9 in Ps 65:5: "May we be sated with the goodness (i.e., good things) of your house, your holy Temple." "The stream of your delights" recalls Gen 2:10, where the river springing from Eden (Hebrew *ʿēden*, "delight") provides water (*lĕhašqôt*) to the garden and to the whole earth.[28]

10a. "For with you is the fountain of life." V 10 continues the theme of the Temple as the source of life, appropriately symbolized by a fountain of life-giving water in arid Palestine.[29] Dahood has pointed out that in some cases "with X" can mean "in the house of X"; that may be the nuance of *ʿimmĕkā* ("with you") here.[30] Besides Ps 36:10, the only other places where the expression "fountain of life" occurs are in Proverbs, where it is a synonym for the words of the righteous (10:11), the instruction of the wise (13:14), the fear of Yhwh (14:27), and wisdom (16:22).[31] Thus, the wisdom character of Psalm 36, present in vv 2–5 and 10–13, extends to the hymnic section as well.

10b. "In your light we see light." The meaning of this sentence is not immediately apparent. We shall begin our consideration of it with the idiom, "to see light," which in some contexts can mean "to live" (Ps 49:20; Job 3:16).[32] Kraus, followed by Anderson and Craigie, plausibly suggests that "in your light" is an

---

[28] The vocable *ʿdn* in Ugaritic and in the Aramaic inscription of Tel Fekherye means "irrigate, provide with water"; see M. Weinfeld, "Kuntillet ʿAjrud Inscriptions and their Significance," *Studi Epigrafici e Linguistici* 1 (1984) 127 n. 4; he translates v 9 as: "Let them drink at your stream of abundance (of water)." On the association of the Temple with Eden, see J. Levenson, *The Theology of the Program of Restoration of Ezekiel 40–48* (HSM 10; Missoula, MT: Scholars, 1976) 28: "In both the Garden of Eden and the Temple, the great fecundity is associated with a marvelous stream . . . issuing from the cosmic mountain beneath the Temple. Note that this stream appears also in Ps. 36. . . ."

[29] On the basis of the expression *mĕqôr mayim ḥayyîm* ("fountain of living [fresh, flowing] water") in Jer 2:13 and 17:13, perhaps we are to understand *mĕqôr ḥayyîm* here as an abbreviation of this phrase.

[30] Dahood, *Psalms I*, 242.

[31] In Prov 10:11 ("The mouth of the righteous is a fountain of life; but the mouth of the wicked conceals violence") one finds the same opposition occurring in Psalm 36, where vv 2–4 speak of malice and deceit coming from the mouth of the wicked, while v 10 speaks of the (divine) fountain of life.

[32] Cf. the similar expressions "know the light" in Job 25:16; "give light (and life)" in Job 3:20; and the phrase "the light of life" in Ps 56:14; Job 33:30.

abbreviated form of "in the light of your face" (Pss 4:7; 44:4; 89:16).[33] The verse then means something like "Under your benevolent gaze, we live our lives."

11. "Extend your love to those who know you, and your righteousness to the upright of heart." God's *ḥesed* ("covenant love") and *ṣĕdāqâ* ("righteousness") first occurred in the four-member sequence of God's covenant love, fidelity, righteousness, and justice in vv 6–7. The "upright of heart" creates an inclusion by recalling and reversing the sin-directed heart of the wicked in v 2.

The idiom "continue/extend your covenant love" occurs in Ps 109:12; Jer 31:3; and the prepositional phrase "to those who know you" has interesting parallels in Deuteronomy and in Qoheleth; these parallels underline the sapiential character[34] of the poem: in Deut 1:13 and Qoh 9:11 *layyōdĕ'îm* ("to those who know") is paralleled by *laḥăkāmîm* ("to the wise") and *lannĕbōnîm* ("to the understanding/perceptive").[35] Secondly, in a poem which uses *ḥesed* ("covenant love") three times, the covenantal sense of the verb "know" (the mutal acknowledgement and recognition of suzerain and vassal) may be hinted at here.[36]

12. "Let not the foot of the arrogant come near me nor the hand of the wicked put me to flight." The verb *tĕnidēnî* ("put to flight") may be more exactly rendered as "expel/drive away (from the Temple)."[37] This interpretation connects v 12 thematically with the Temple hymn in vv 6–10; both refuge in the shadow of Yhwh's wings in v 8 and the petition not to be driven away from the Temple speak of the sanctuary as a place of asylum. For the term *ga'ăwâ* ("arrogance, pride") in the wisdom literature, see Prov 8:13; 14:3; 16:18; 29:23; Job 35:12. The use of the abstract "arrogance" for the concrete "arrogant ones" is a common feature in Hebrew poetry.[38]

---

[33] H.-J. Kraus, *Psalms 1–59: A Commentary* (Minneapolis: Augsburg, 1988) 400; Anderson, *Psalms 1*, 290; Craigie, *Psalms 1–50*, 292. Dahood typically goes his own way, emending *'ôr* to *'ûr*, which he understands to mean "field," translating v 10b as "in your field we shall see the light." His emendation and his identification here of the motif of the Elysian Fields, the abode of the blessed after death, have not convinced many (*Psalms I*, 222–23).

[34] On the sapiential character of Deuteronomy, see M. Weinfeld, *Deuteronomy and the Deuteronomic School* (Oxford: Clarendon, 1972) 244–81.

[35] Similarly *yāšār* ("upright") is a common term in wisdom literature (Prov 2:21; 3:32; 11:3). Note especially Prov 11:6 which speaks of "the righteousness of the upright," and Prov 21:29, where the upright gives thought (reading *yābîn* [qere] for *ykyn* [ketib]) to his ways.

[36] H. Huffmon, "The Treaty Background of Hebrew *Yāda'*," *BASOR* 181 (1966) 31–37.

[37] This is the interpretation of Kraus, *Psalms 1-59*, 400, accepted by Anderson, *Psalms I*, 291. For the idiom *hēnîd regel* ("cause the foot to wander"), see 2 Kgs 21:8.

[38] On the root *g'h* in wisdom, see D. Kellermann, *TDOT*, 2. 349–50. For the use of an abstract

13. "There, the evildoers fall; thrust down, they will never be able to rise again." The verse describes the descent of the evildoers into the world of the dead, from which they will never return.[39] Significantly, some striking parallels to this conception are found in wisdom:

Prov 14:32: "By his evil the wicked one is thrust down (to Sheol: *yiddāḥeh*); but the righteous will take refuge (*wĕḥōseh*). . . ."[40]

Prov 24:16: "Though the righteous fall seven times he will get up (*yippôl ṣaddîq wāqām*); but the wicked will stumble (and fall) into/because of evil."[41]

Prov 26:28: "A flattering mouth (*peh ḥālāq*) will bring about downfall (*midḥeh*)."

And the contrast between the righteous (*yišrê lēb*) in v 11 and the wicked evildoers (*rĕšāʾîm . . . pōʿălê ʾāwen*) in vv 12–13 is typically sapiential.

Problematic is v 13's initial *šām*, seemingly without antecedent. A number of interpretations have been put forward.[42] Two possibilities deserve further consideration. Barré revocalizes *šām* as *śîm* (imperative of *śûm/śîm*, "place, put"), here with the specific meaning "determine one's fate" (like the Akkadian cognate *šiāmu/šâmu*). Barré translates v 13 thus: "Decree that evildoers fall (dead), thrust down (to Sheol), never to get up again."[43] The attractiveness of this proposal is that it requires only a minimal change in vocalization, and that it locates the verse in a known ancient Near Eastern context, the determining/decreeing of the fates of human beings by the gods.

But there is another interpretation that requires no emendation or revocal-

---

noun with concrete meaning, see W. G. E. Watson, *Classical Hebrew Poetry: A Guide to its Techniques* (JSOTSup 26; Sheffield: JSOT, 1984) 314–16.

[39] Tromp, *Primitive Conceptions of Death*, 189–90.

[40] Dahood, *Psalms III* (AB 17A; Garden City, NY: Doubleday, 1970) xliii, 253: "But the righteous will find refuge at his death (*bĕmōtô*)." This is emended by many (with the LXX) to *bĕtummô* ("But the righteous will find refuge in his integrity").

[41] The verb *kšl* ("stumble") is regularly asociated with *npl* ("fall"); see Y. Avishur, *Stylistic Studies of Word-Pairs in Biblical and Ancient Semitic Literatures* (AOAT 210; Kevelaer: Butzon & Bercker; Neukirchen-Vluyn: Neukirchener V., 1984) 268.

[42] E.g., Kraus, *Psalms 1–59*, 397, followed by Craigie, *Psalms 1–50*, 290, emend *šām* to *šāmēmû* ("they are ruined, desolate"). Dahood, *Psalms I*, 224, translates it as "See how," on the basis of Amarna *šumma*.

[43] I am grateful to M. L. Barré, who suggested this orally to me; see *CAD* Š/1, 358–60.

ization. One can understand *šām* in its basic meaning ("there") as a euphemism, a veiled allusion to the world of the dead. Several authors have pointed to instances of this usage in Job (1:21; 3:17,19; 34:22) and Ezekiel (32:22,24,26,29,30).[44] While either of these last two proposals is possible, understanding *šām* as a circumlocution for the world of the dead seems to me the simplest and most satisfying solution.

There are a number of connections between the concluding v 5 of the first section and vv 11-13. "Malice . . . on his bed" and "a way not good" in v 5 are matched by "the foot of the arrogant" in v 12 and the fall of the evildoers into the nether world (v 13). The law of talion is operative here: those who lie plotting on their beds will lie prostrate in their graves/in the nether world, unable to rise. Note the chiastic arrangement of the terms: v 5: "malice in their beds" (A); "a way not good" (B) // vv 12–13: "the foot of the arrogant" (B′); evildoers fall (into their graves, into Sheol) (A′). Finally, note the allusions to v 5 in the concluding verse of the psalm, where "plotters of evil" have become "doers of evil"; described in v 5 as "standing on the way" in v 5, their fate in v 13 is to fall into the nether world, never to rise.[45]

We conclude this discussion of Psalm 36 by returning to the issue of genre. At the beginning of this essay, I noted the fairly common classification of the poem as a wisdom psalm. As we have seen, there are enough instances of wisdom language and themes to sustain this classification, especially but not exclusively in the framing vv 2–5 and 11–13. Without denying the wisdom character of the psalm, I believe that one can be more specific and identify the main issue of the psalm as the access to the Temple offered to the righteous and denied to the wicked. Psalm 36 begins with a description of the sin-directed wicked one, his sins of speech and his furtive plotting; it ends with a prayer (v 11) that the divine *ḥesed*, associated with the Temple in vv 8–10, be bestowed on the upright, on those covenanted with Yhwh. The end of the evildoers is death and descent into the world of the dead (v 13), the polar opposite of the Temple, the source of life.

This analysis aligns Psalm 36 with the so-called "entrance liturgies" (Psalms 15; 24:3–6), as well as with other psalms concerned with access to the Temple:

---

44 N. Habel, *The Book of Job* (Philadelphia: Westminster, 1985) 43, 93, 110; G. Vall, "The Enigma of Job 1,21a," *Bib* 76 (1995) 326. Vall indicates (n. 5) that M. Buttenwieser, G. Fohrer, F. I. Andersen, and R. Gordis had earlier identified this euphemistic use of *šām*.

45 For *yityaṣṣēb* ("stand") in parallelism with *yāqûm* ("rise"), see Ps 94:16; for *niṣṣab* + *yāqûm*, see Exod 33:8.

Psalm 5,[46] Psalms 16 and 17,[47] and echoes of these rituals in the prophets (Isa 33:14–16; Jer 7:1–15; Ezekiel 18). This is not to deny the relationship of Psalm 36 to the wisdom tradition. Several scholars have pointed out the didactic propensities of Psalms 15 and 24.[48]

In light of this discussion, it is suggested that Craigie's statement (quoted at the beginning of this paper) that Psalm 36 "does not adhere to any distinctive literary form" may need to be modified: Psalm 36 can be classified as an entrance liturgy, with strong sapiential content.

Appendix

In the discussion of v 10b ("In your light we see light") above, it was proposed that the meaning of the prepositional phrase was derived from the full expression "the light of your face," an idiom for a bright happy, smiling face.[49] Even in English one can speak of a face brightening or lighting up with joy. So the meaning of the prepositional phrase in v 10b proposed above was: "Under your benevolent gaze (= "in your light," i.e., in the light of your shining, happy face).

There is another possibility that understands v 10 in connection with v 8, also part of the hymnic extolling of the Temple. As mentioned above, "in the shadow of your wings" could refer to the outstretched wings of the solar disk, an ancient Near Eastern iconographic symbol of the manifestation or epiphany of the deity in solar imagery.[50] The presence of this symbol in Israel

[46] L. Krinetzki, "Psalm 5: Eine Untersuchung seiner dichterischen Struktur und seiner theologischen Gehaltes," *TQ* 142 (1967) 23–45, identified Psalm 5 as an entrance liturgy (pp. 34–35).

[47] E. Beaucamp, *Le Psautier: Ps 1–72* (SB; Paris: Gabalda, 1976) 83: "Le psaume *15* est le premier d'une série de trois psaumes, Ps *15; 16; 17* . . . qui possèdent en commun l'idée d'une entrée dans le sanctuaire."

[48] J. T. Willis, "Ethics in a Cultic Setting," *Essays in Old Testament Ethics: J. Philip (In Memoriam)* (ed. J. L. Crenshaw and J. T. Willis; New York: Ktav, 1974) 156; M. Greenberg, *Ezekiel 1–20* (AB 22; Garden City, NY: Doubleday, 1983) 345–47; W. Beyerlin, *Weisheitlich-kultische Heilsordnung: Studien zum 15. Psalm* (Biblisch-Theologische Studien 9; Neukirchen-Vluyn: Neukirchener V., 1985) 51–60.

[49] For the expression, "the light of the face of X," denoting a shining, happy face, see M. I. Gruber, *Aspects of Nonverbal Communication in the Ancient Near East* (2 vols.; Studia Pohl 12; Rome: Biblical Institute, 1980) 557–64.

[50] The most recent treatment of this phenomenon is J. G. Taylor, *Yahweh and the Sun: Biblical and Archaeological Evidence for Sun Worship in Ancient Israel* (JSOTSup 111; Sheffield: JSOT/Sheffield Academic Press, 1993).

is witnessed to by such texts as Mal 3:20 and Ps 84:12. This transfer of the iconography of the solar disk to Yhwh does not assume that Yhwh is a solar deity, any more than the epithet "rider of the clouds" identifies Yhwh with Canaanite Baal.

The proposal is this: the expression "in the shadow of your wings" in v 8, in the Temple context suggested by the verb *ḥāsâ* ("find refuge"), is parallel to, even equivalent to "in your light" in v 10.[51] In this interpretation, the "light" is the refulgence shining forth from the deity; it is shared with or bestowed on everything endowed with divine power or sanctified by divine presence (e.g., weapons, symbols, temples).[52] In Hebrew theology, this is what is meant by *kābôd* ("glory") and a number of related terms. In Mesopotamian theology, this is the *melammu,* the aureole or nimbus of light surrounding and streaming from the deity.[53] Against this background, v 10 might then be understood thus: "In/by your light (the luminous refulgence of Yhwh, the divine *kābôd*), we see light" (i.e., we experience a theophany in the Temple). The sense is the same as Ps 63:3: "Thus I look to you in the sanctuary, to see your glory and power."[54]

There is a parallelism, then, between refuge in the Temple under the outstretched wings of Yhwh (v 8), represented by the solar disk, and the rich feasting and abundant life in the Temple, where the worshipper is blessed with a theophany of divine light (v 10).[55]

[51] A structural point: in this interpretation, the subsection of the hymn in vv 8–10 is framed by the parallel phrases "in the shadow of your wings" in v 8 and "in your light" in v 10.

[52] N. M. Waldman, "Hebrew עז and the Divine Aura," *Gratz College of Jewish Studies* 1 (1972) 7–13; M. Weinfeld, *TDOT,* 7. 28–29.

[53] See the fundamental study of A. L. Oppenheim, "Akkadian *pul(u)ḫ(t)u* and *melammu,*" *JAOS* 63 (1943) 31–34.

[54] See G. E. Mendenhall, "The Mask of Yahweh," *The Tenth Generation: The Origins of the Biblical Tradition* (Baltimore/London: The Johns Hopkins University, 1973) 32–66. Mendenhall understands the winged sun disk as the external manifestation, the "sacrament" of the divine glory, the *melammu:* "This *melammu* is the word label for a most complex conceptualization of divine and royal glory that is realized in the art motif of the winged sun disk" (p. 53).

[55] I am grateful to Peter Machinist, who suggested this line of interpretation to me.

J. CLINTON McCANN

Wisdom's Dilemma: The Book of Job, the Final Form of the Book of Psalms, and the Entire Bible

As Roland Murphy recognizes in *The Tree of Life: An Exploration of Biblical Wisdom Literature,* the traditional scholarly appropriation of the Book of Job is not wrong, but neither is it entirely sufficient:

> Scholars often speak of a crisis of wisdom in connection with Job and Ecclesiastes. Job is seen as an iconoclastic attack on the traditional ideas of divine justice and retribution, which are so firmly upheld in the Book of Proverbs. Such a reading is not mistaken, but at the same time the problem of retribution has to be viewed in the perspective of the entire Bible . . . . The book's most positive teaching is at the same time negative: the application to Job of the traditional theory of divine retribution is not relevant.[1]

This essay takes Murphy's balanced judgment about the Book of Job as a point of departure; and it will attempt to achieve the following: (1) To offer an assessment of Wisdom's dilemma, without being unfair to the Book of Proverbs; (2) to demonstrate how the Book of Job's rejection of the traditional theory of divine retribution inevitably invites the reader to hear Job in the context of the entire Bible, especially the Book of Psalms; and (3) to consider the importance of the rejection of the theory of retribution for Biblical Theology.

---

[1] R. E Murphy, O. Carm., *The Tree of Life: An Exploration of Biblical Wisdom Literature* (Anchor Bible Reference Library; New York: Doubleday, 1990) 34.

Wisdom's Dilemma

As Murphy implies, the frequent scholarly reading of the Book of Job is not fair to the Book of Proverbs. The traditional theory of divine retribution held that God rewards the righteous and punishes the wicked in a tangible way in this life. To be sure, there is much in the Book of Proverbs that supports this understanding (see Prov 2:20–22; 3:33–35; 6:12–15; 10:3–4, 7–8, 24–25, 27–31; 11:6–8, 18–19, 21, 30; etc.). Furthermore, *in some sense* at least, the traditional theory is true; the righteous in all times and places have and do testify to experiencing life as more abundant and "rewarding" precisely as a result of their faith in God.

The problem arises, however, when the theory of divine retribution is understood as a mechanistic system, a sort of "religion machine."[2] In this view, every event or experience must be understood directly and unambiguously as the reward or punishment of God. If a person is wealthy, for instance, his or her wealth is to be interpreted as a reward from God. And, if a person is poor, then poverty is to be viewed as punishment from God. While the Book of Proverbs *appears* to support such conclusions, it also very clearly *undermines* such a simplified moral calculus, especially, in fact, in its treatment of wealth and poverty. As K. M. O'Connor points out, the Book of Proverbs "appears cruel and heartless," portraying the poor as lazy (19:24), blaming them for being victims (19:15), and even suggesting that wealth is a divine reward (22:4). At the same time, however, the Book of Proverbs "presents an alternative portrait of the poor," counseling compassion and generosity toward the poor (13:8; 21:26) and providing a rationale for such caring (11:24–25; 21:13; 22:9; 28:27).[3]

According to O'Connor, the tension between these alternative portrayals of the poor is most evident in those sayings which assert the equality of rich and poor in God's sight (22:2) and which identify God with the poor (14:31; 19:17). As she concludes:

> These astonishing sayings contradict the notion that wealth is equivalent to righteousness. In them the poor are raised to the highest dignity. They and the rich are regarded as equals, but the poor alone are identified with God. God's relationship with them is so complete that actions toward the poor are indistinguishable from actions toward God. No such claim is made for

---

[2] T. G. Long, "Job: Second Thoughts in the Land of Uz," *TToday* 45 (1988) 13.

[3] K. M. O'Connor, *The Wisdom Literature* (Collegeville: Liturgical Press, 1988) 53, 55.

the rich. God's identification with the poor is unique. Consequently, the wealthy and the powerful are warned that to violate or oppress the poor is equivalent to blaspheming against the Creator.[4]

In short, neither poverty nor any other misfortune should be interpreted as divine punishment. What this means, of course, is that the mechanistic understanding of the theory of retribution does not properly derive from the Book of Proverbs. In short, Wisdom's dilemma is not the fault of the Book of Proverbs.

Nevertheless, it seems that in ancient Israel some persons derived from the Book of Proverbs (or from somewhere—the Book of Deuteronomy is another possibility) support for the traditional theory of retribution—for instance, Job's friends (and Job himself initially). After Eliphaz's rather polite introduction of the dialogues (chapters 4–5), Bildad is quick to apply the theory of retribution to condemn Job's children (8:4), and Zophar uses it to condemn Job himself (11:6), even though both the narrator *and God* have told the readers that Job is "blameless" (see 1:1, 8). But this problem is not confined to ancient Israel. Many contemporary Christians, especially relatively well-to-do ones, regularly appeal to the traditional theory of retribution (although they may not name it as such) to congratulate themselves that God has rewarded them for their righteousness and to blame, at least implicitly but often very explicitly, victims for their victimization—for instance, the poor for being poor. *This* is Wisdom's dilemma!

But, in fact, Wisdom's dilemma is the dilemma *of all theology.* It seems that human beings, including those who explicitly identify themselves as God's people, have an inevitable propensity to want to tame God, to contain God in neat and tidy retributional schemes—in short, to turn theology into anthropology. For this is precisely what the traditional theory of retribution does. Ironically, in attempting to assert God's sovereignty, it removes the necessity of talking about God at all, since everything is really determined finally by *human* behavior. God loses God's freedom, and it simply becomes impossible to speak of anything like *grace*—a major dilemma! It is precisely this dilemma which makes the Book of Job profoundly and perennially important.

The Book of Job

Roland Murphy is undoubtedly correct when he states that the Book of Job's

---

[4] Ibid., 57–58.

"most positive teaching" is that "the application to Job of the traditional theory of divine retribution is not relevant." While this teaching may, in some sense, be a "negative" one, as Murphy suggests, it also has some extraordinarily positive and positively extraordinary implications. In this essay, I shall focus primarily on one of these implications: By its rejection of the traditional theory of retribution, the Book of Job reveals a God whose essence is love, and thus a God who suffers with, for, and on account of humankind and the world.

In this regard, it is crucial to notice that the question raised at the beginning of the Book of Job, the question on which the whole plot turns, is essentially a lover's question: "Does Job fear God for nothing?" (1:9 [NRSV]). To be sure, the question is raised by the satan; but the satan is one the heavenly beings, one of God's own, and God readily agrees to explore this crucial question.[5] In other words, God wants and needs to know if love between humanity and God is really possible, or whether humanity simply acknowledges God because it pays off. From God's side, the question can be paraphrased, "Does humanity really love me?"

By simultaneously asserting his own integrity and clinging to God in the midst of incomprehensible suffering, Job helps God by answering God's question (see especially 19:23–27; 27:1–6). What God learns is that Job, representing humanity, does love God even when there is no pay-off. Job, by his witness and his words, has thoroughly obliterated the traditional theory of retribution. While the Book of Job does not directly state that God is grateful to Job for his help, such is at least implied by 42:7. This implication makes Robert Frost's imaginative sequel to the Book of Job a cogent and compelling interpretation. In his "A Masque of Reason," Frost has God address Job as follows:

> I've had you on my mind a thousand years
> To thank you someday for the way you helped me
> Establish once for all the principle
> There's no connection man can reason out
> Between his just deserts and what he gets.[6]

Of course, it is precisely this lack of connection between just deserts and what we get that makes love a possibility. Otherwise, the relationship between God

---

[5] See G. Janzen, *Job* (Interpretation; Atlanta: John Knox, 1985) 37–42. I am particularly indebted to Janzen throughout this essay.

[6] Robert Frost, "A Masque of Reason," *Robert Frost: Poetry and Prose* (ed E. C. Lathem and L. Thompson; New York: Holt, Rinehart and Winston, 1972) 176.

and humanity would be simply a transaction in which pay-off is pre-eminent—in short, no *relationship* at all! Job has spoken of God "what is right" (42:7 [NRSV]), because Job has shown that he really does love God. Anything other would be intolerable to God, because God's essence is love.

But to love is to suffer, even for God—indeed, especially for God! In his book, *Narratives of a Vulnerable God,* W. C. Placher quotes C. S. Lewis, as follows:

> To love at all is to be vulnerable. Love anything, and your heart will certainly be wrung and possibly be broken. If you want to make sure of keeping it intact, you must give your heart to no one . . . . It will not be broken; it will become unbreakable, impenetrable, irredeemable. The alternative to tragedy, or at least to the risk of tragedy, is damnation. The only place outside Heaven where you can be perfectly safe from all the dangers and perturbations of love is Hell.[7]

If there's anything the biblical story asserts from beginning to end, it is that God was not content to confine the divine self to heaven. The very act of creation involved, in effect, God's decision to give God's heart to humanity, which, if genuine relationship was to exist, had to be free. And, as the opening chapters of Genesis relate, the act of creation risked tragedy, because humanity could choose not to respond to God's love. Indeed, because this is exactly what happened according to Genesis 3, T. Fretheim aptly concludes, "The very act of creation thus might be called the beginning of the passion of God."[8]

Given the paramount significance of Genesis 1–3 for comprehending the love, vulnerability, and suffering of God, it is revealing that this passage is alluded to frequently in the Book of Job. Of special importance is the fact that, excluding the folktale, the first and last speeches focus squarely upon creation. Job's opening soliloquy is a chilling reversal of the imagery of Genesis 1; Job suggests that God's "creative" purposes really serve darkness and death rather than light and life. The divine speeches in chapters 38–41 are, on the other hand, an effusive celebration of creation. Because Job has begun by criticizing creation, the divine speeches are *not* the divine *non sequitur* which many scholars have taken them to be. Rather, they are right to the point.

---

[7] W. C. Placher, *Narratives of a Vulnerable God: Christ, Theology, and Scripture* (Louisville: Westminster/John Knox, 1994) 20. The quote is from C. S. Lewis, *The Four Loves* (New York: Harcourt, Brace, 1960) 169.

[8] T. E. Fretheim, *The Suffering of God: An Old Testament Perspective* (Philadelphia: Fortress, 1984) 58.

Granted, the divine speeches do not mention Job's suffering nor do they even touch upon humanity's role in the creation. This makes sense, however, if the speeches are heard not as an evasion of the issue nor a sarcastic put-down of Job. Rather, God speaks to Job, representing humanity, in order to challenge him to understand creation differently, to view God's role in creation differently, and thus to accept the God-given vocation of dominion that is articulated in Genesis 1. Actually, by the time God begins to speak, Job has already significantly modified his understanding of God's role in creation, because Job's experience has already led him to reject the traditional theory of retribution. What Job has not been able to fathom is that creation is so structured that God is vulnerable and that God inevitably suffers! There are two aspects of the divine speeches that apparently bring Job to this realization. First, God suggests to Job that the creation itself retains a certain randomness or freedom, in that while chaotic forces have been bounded and ordered, they have not been eliminated (38:8–11). This means that the sheer vitality of creation itself will produce situations and results beyond God's control. Second, by focusing on creation and thus recalling Genesis 1–3, God reminds Job of one particular situation beyond God's control and of its tragic results—the choice of humankind to disobey God and thus to fail to properly exercise dominion.

But, the evocation of Genesis 1–3 and thus humanity's failure, comes as a challenge to Job to "gird up your loins like a man" (38:1, which is reminiscent of 3:3!). In other words, God says to Job, "Accept the God-given gift and vocation of dominion over this marvelous creation, even in the midst of your abysmal suffering." God will not let Job be put down. When Job initially reacts as if humiliated, God re-issues the challenge (40:7)! The remainder of the divine speeches focus on Behemoth (40:15–24) and Leviathan (41:1–34), two mythical creatures often representing chaotic forces. Of course, Job cannot control them. But, in view of 38:8–11, neither can God, at least not completely! Job has apparently gained a new understanding of creation (one in which the traditional theory of retribution does not fit) and of God, and the way is open for a new understanding of human vocation.

This is precisely what Job finally arrives at in 42:6. Job had helped God learn something; in chapters 38–41, God helps Job learn something too. If *God* suffers, then Job's own suffering need not be understood as punishment from God. Rather, it can be interpreted now as simply one of the conditions for participation in creation. In my view, this is the new understanding Job articulates in 42:6. To be sure, 42:6 is difficult, perhaps even intentionally ambiguous, according to W. Morrow, who quite rightly points out that one's translation of 42:6 will be affected by how one understands the whole Book of Job.[9] In keeping with my construal of the whole book, I prefer to translate 42:6 as Janzen does:

> Therefore I recant
> and change my mind concerning dust and ashes.[10]

Obviously, this differs significantly from the *NRSV*, in which the translators have supplied a direct object, "myself," in 42:6a, and in which they have translated the verb and preposition in 42:6b as "repent in." But from the beginning (1:8) and again at the end of the book (42:7), the divine voice makes it clear that Job has done nothing for which to "repent," insofar as repentance involves sin. This makes it far more likely that *nḥm ʿal* has the sense which it also has elsewhere, "change one's mind about." In short, as suggested above, Job has learned something about "dust and ashes," a phrase which denotes humanity (see 30:19; Gen 18:21).

What Job has learned is that humanity will inevitably suffer as it fulfills the God-given vocation of dominion, just as God suffers. Clearly, Job's new understanding of humanity follows from his new understanding of God and creation. That Job has needed to learn this lesson has been signaled throughout the book by way of several allusions to Psalm 8, which, very revealingly, is another text about creation that explicitly cites Genesis 1. The first allusion to Psalm 8 is in 7:17, where Job echoes the psalmist's question about human identity (see Ps 8:5 [4]). Whereas the psalmist had answered this question positively (Ps 8:6–9 [5–8]), Job answers it negatively. The royal imagery of Psalm 8 ("crowned," "glory," "honor," "dominion") will recur throughout the Book of Job (see 29:25; 31:36–37), signaling a growing understanding on Job's part that culminates in 42:6, where Job finally "gets it." That is, the royal vocation of dominion is not incompatible with suffering. Indeed, it inevitably involves suffering, for humanity as much as for God. Or, to use a phrase from Genesis 1 that Psalm 8 and Job do not use, humanity fulfills the "image of God" precisely by way of a dominion that is exercised by way of suffering love.

To say both that God rules the world and that God suffers seems contradictory to many persons, but it is precisely this tension which characterizes

---

[9] W. Morrow, "Consolation, Rejection, and Repentance in Job 42:6," *JBL* 105 (1986) 212, 223–25.

[10] Janzen, *Job*, 251.

the entire Bible. The perspective is what I call *eschatological*—the affirmation that God reigns amid circumstances which seem to deny it. It means that the people of God live always in "the already" and "the not–yet," perpetually in waiting.[11] It is the Book of Job's eschatological perspective which especially invites the reader to hear it along with the Book of Psalms, and indeed, the entire Bible.

The Book of Psalms

Given that it is a wisdom work, the Book of Job, which directly confronts the dilemma of all theology, it is interesting to note that at least some scholars have suggested that the Book of Psalms shows evidence of a final wisdom editing. G. H. Wilson, for instance, citing the key positions of Psalms 90, 107, and 145, suggests that Books IV (Psalms 90–106) and V (Psalms 107–150) have been edited with the concerns of wisdom in mind. Furthermore, Wilson also points out that Psalms 1 and 73, often classified as wisdom psalms, open Books I (Psalms 1–41) and III (Psalms 73–89); and he thus concludes that the Psalter has received "a final wisdom frame."[12] According to Wilson, the effect of the final form of the Psalter is to counsel trust in God alone as ruler of the world (see Psalms 93–99), in response to circumstances that seemed to deny God's rule—the exile and ongoing oppression of God's people in the postexilic era (see Psalm 89). In short, this is precisely what I call an eschatological perspective; and again, it invites the reader to consider together the Book of Psalms and the Book of Job. Not surprisingly, a growing number of scholars in recent years have suggested that the Book of Job was an instrumental resource in assisting Israel to respond to the crisis of exile and perhaps even was composed in response to the exile.

Even apart from Wilson's thesis, however, the final form of the Book of Psalms creates an eschatological perspective. Psalm 1 begins the book by presenting what sounds like the traditional theory of retribution—the righteous will "prosper" (v 3 [*NRSV*]) and "the wicked will perish" (v 6 [*NRSV*]).

---

[11] For a similar conclusion about Job, but based primarily upon chapters 32–37, which I have not examined, see J. D. Pleins, "'Why Do You Hide Your Face?': Divine Silence and Speech in the Book of Job," *Int* 48 (1994) 233–36.

[12] G. H. Wilson, "Shaping the Psalter: A Consideration of Editorial Linkage in the Book of Psalms," *The Shape and Shaping of the Psalter* (ed. J. C. McCann, Jr.; JSOTSup 159; Sheffield: JSOT, 1993) 80; see 78–82. It should be noted too that Psalm 73 is particularly reminiscent of Job.

Indeed, many scholars label Psalm 1 as naive and unrealistic, linking it to the kind of perspective created by a superficial reading of Proverbs or to the Deuteronomists. Psalm 2 seems to reinforce in corporate terms what Psalm 1 has presented in individual terms; that is, the opponents of God "will perish in the way" (2:12; see 1:6) but those who "take refuge in" God will be "happy" (2:12; see 1:1). That these two psalms cannot be construed as support for the traditional theory of retribution, however, is indicated by their juxtaposition with Psalm 3 and the preponderance of laments or complaints which follow, especially in Book I.

If the wicked are blown away, as Psalms 1 and 2 suggest, then it becomes impossible to understand why the righteous psalmists are regularly located in the midst of painful and powerful opposition by the wicked. Psalm 3:1–2 is paradigmatic; the psalmists are persistently surrounded by persons who are their enemies and enemies of God. Indeed, the psalmists, especially in the laments of Books I and II, regularly characterize themselves not only as the "righteous" but also as the "afflicted," the "oppressed," the "poor," the "needy," the "meek," and so on. It is clear that they do not subscribe to the traditional theory of retribution. Rather, like Job, whose friends acted more like enemies (see Pss 35:11–21; 55:12–15), the psalmists are convinced that God stands with them in the midst of their suffering. Indeed, three of the four words or phrases which describe Job in Job 1:1 also frequently describe the suffering psalmists—"blameless"/"integrity" (see Pss 25:21; 26:1, 11; 37:18), "upright" (see Pss 7:11[10]; 32:11; 36:11[10]), "fear God" (Pss 22:24[23]; 25:12; 34:10[9]). The psalmists knew what Job eventually came to understand—that is, their suffering was not divine punishment. Convinced of this, they continued to look to God and affirm God's sovereignty (see Ps 22:28–32 [27–31]) in the midst of difficult circumstances which made it appear that God did not reign. In short, like the Book of Job, the fundamental perspective of the Book of Psalms is eschatological. It is this perspective which invites the reader to hear Job and the Psalms in the context of the entire Bible.

The Entire Bible

Of course, our consideration of the entire Bible must be illustrative and suggestive, not exhaustive. Even so, given the diversity of the biblical material, such a consideration may seem hazardous. On the other hand, it is the task of Biblical Theology to discern threads of unity amid the diversity; and the more recent tendency toward canonical, synchronic readings of the Bible makes the risk worthwhile. In any case, I want to suggest modestly that the eschatological perspective found in the Books of Job and Psalms is a pervasive biblical perspective; and I shall illustrate by referring briefly to the Deuteronomistic History, Isaiah, and the preaching of Jesus.

1 and 2 Kings anchor the Deuteronomistic History, which offers an interpretation of Israel's history from the perspective of the Book of Deuteronomy, which in turn is generally taken to be one of the sources supporting the traditional theory of retribution. It is likely that the Book of Deuteronomy and the Deuteronomistic History are intended in their final forms to respond to the crisis of exile. But therein lies their dilemma; that is, what can be said *after* the conclusion that God has duly punished a sinful people? According to the traditional theory of retribution the answer may well be: "Nothing! They got what they deserved, and that's it!" But, as Richard Nelson points out, this is *not* what the Book of Kings says. In particular, the good King Josiah is unexpectedly killed, and the exiled Jehoiachin is described in a manner which leaves the future surprisingly open-ended. As Nelson concludes:

> In the end, the story that the narrator has told actually undercuts the theology that it [the Deuteronomistic History] is explicitly intended to support.
> . . . In the case of Josiah, this unpredictable God undercuts Deuteronomistic principles to punish the people in outraged wrath . . . .
> The first exilic readers were to remain open to whatever future God might send them. Once false hopes had been put behind them, they could wait in obedient and repentant faith, open to the sort of amazing grace discovered by Jehoiachin in the thirty-seventh year of his exile . . . .
> Kings concludes with God's option held wide open. In this, the book is a paradigm of all biblical faith.[13]

In short, even the Deuteronomistic History finally finds that the traditional theory of retribution is insufficient for comprehending who God is and what it means to be God's people. Only when the traditional theory is abandoned can God be known as gracious and can a sinful people be truly hopeful. Thus, the Deuteronomistic History finally shares the eschatological perspective of Job and Psalms; it too is "a paradigm of all biblical faith."

The same could be said about the Book of Isaiah. When the book is read as a unity rather than as three separate works, the eschatological perspective

---

[13] R. Nelson, *First and Second Kings* (Interpretation; Atlanta: John Knox, 1987) 268–69.

comes into focus. As E. W. Conrad has pointed out, the situation of the implied audience of the book is best reflected in chapters 1–5, 40–66. It is a situation in which the monarchy has disappeared, and the people await deliverance by God. In historical terms, the situation could have been the Babylonian exile; but Conrad argues that Babylon may be a symbol and should not be understood merely historically. In any case, the promise of deliverance is reliable, according to the book in its unity. As God had once delivered Jerusalem in accordance with the word of the prophet (chapters 36–39), so God will deliver God's people again from the "Babylonian" oppression. But, as Conrad rightly points out, the book ends before this deliverance is recounted; so the effect is to leave the people awaiting God's new activity, even as they proclaim God's present and world-wide sovereignty (see Isa 52:7–10). In Conrad's words:

> ... the setting that the book provides for the reception of the vision of Isaiah is an imagined world in which the conventional ideologies of kingship and community have been replaced, a world that never was but is filled with the possibility of what might be. To enter into that world does not require a journey into the past but contemplation of a future.[14]

In other words, the perspective again is eschatological.

Jesus also imagined a world "in which the conventional ideologies of kingship and community have been replaced," a world "filled with the possibility of what might be." Jesus called this world "the reign of God," and remarkably, he proclaimed it as a present reality, even though he himself was persistently opposed and finally crucified on account of what he had proclaimed and embodied. This paradoxical perspective—a present reality which is also to be anticipated and awaited—is eschatological, for Jesus proclaimed the reign of God amid circumstances that seem to deny it. Indeed, Jesus taught that the reign of God belongs to those who, according to the traditional theory of retribution, appeared to be experiencing divine punishment—the poor, the grieving, the humbled, the persecuted (see Matt 5:1–11). Like the Book of Job, Jesus obliterated the traditional theory of retribution. If his teaching did not do it sufficiently, then his whole life did. In particular, the cross is the definitive rejection of the traditional theory. Jesus taught and embodied what Job had learned—namely, that suffering love is constitutive of God's fundamental identity and the identity of those created in the image of God. The

---

[14] E. W. Conrad, *Reading Isaiah* (Minneapolis: Fortress, 1991) 161.

one whom Christians profess is the very incarnation of God is the crucified one, the one who invited his followers to "take up their crosses and follow" (Mark 8:34 [*NRSV*]).

Implications For Biblical Theology

For the academic discipline of Biblical Theology, the preceding analysis and conclusions suggest the paramount importance of the Book of Job, since it confronts directly the traditional theory of retribution. In its forceful rejection of it, the Book of Job opens the way for what I have called an eschatological perspective—the affirmation of God's reign amid circumstances which seem to deny it. This perspective truly protects the sovereignty of God, a sovereignty manifest as suffering love. As Murphy has suggested, the Book of Job should be heard in the context of the entire Bible; and as I have suggested, its eschatological perspective is an invitation to do just that, thus furthering the primary task of Biblical Theology to discern a unity among the diversity of the Bible's witness.

For the communities of faith that profess to take seriously the results of the academic discipline of Biblical Theology, the Book of Job offers both challenge and encouragement. The challenge is to proclaim and embody the message that the fullness of human life is realized in suffering love for each other and the whole creation. This would be a challenge in any place and time; but it is a monumental one in a thoroughly narcissistic North American culture in which people generally attempt to avoid suffering at all cost. On the other hand, the eschatological perspective of Job and the entire Bible can perhaps serve to prevent what is popularly known as "burn-out." Or, in the more eloquent words of H. H. Schmid, to live as people who simultaneously experience and await the reign of God "could free us from dogged striving toward the realization of the ultimate righteousness at any cost and from the frustration that necessarily arises from it." Schmid calls such freedom "courage for the fragmentary."[15]

Courage for the fragmentary may become increasingly important as we approach the twenty-first century, since we appear to be witnessing a worldwide resurgence of fundamentalism among a variety of world religions.

---

[15] H. H. Schmid, "Creation, Righteousness, and Salvation: 'Creation Theology' as the Broad Horizon of Biblical Theology," *Creation in the Old Testament* (Issues in Religion and Theology; ed. B. W. Anderson; Philadelphia: Fortress, 1984) 114.

Because Christian fundamentalists at least have not done well with the ambiguous and the fragmentary, they have frequently been inclined to uphold the traditional theory of retribution, often with dangerous and violent consequences such as blaming victims for their victimization and responding with further oppression that is supposedly justified by God. In other words, Christian fundamentalists have been inclined to do what R. Girard suggests that Job's friends were compelled to do—namely, to blame the "victim in order to feel good, in order to live more harmoniously with one another, in order to feel established in their faith."[16] This fundamentalist inclination may explain why the Book of Job has recently become particularly important among liberation theologians; that is, its obliteration of the traditional theory of retribution means that there is no biblical justification for blaming victims for their victimization.[17] What all this means, unfortunately, is that the contemporary scene may well present to us another version of Wisdom's dilemma. In facing this dilemma, the Book of Job will again be a major biblical and theological resource, as it has been for centuries.[18]

[16] R. Girard, "Job as Failed Scapegoat," *The Voice from the Whirlwind: Interpreting The Book of Job* (ed. L. G. Perdue and W. Clark Gilpin; Nashville: Abingdon, 1992) 196.

[17] See, for instance, G. Gutiérrez, *On Job: God-Talk and The Suffering of the Innocent* (Maryknoll: Orbis, 1988) 22, 87–92.

[18] It is a joy and a privilege to contribute this essay in honor of Fr. Roland E. Murphy, O.Carm., whose wisdom has been, is, and always will be a source of inspiration, motivation, and instruction for my scholarship and my life.

Psalm 119
Profile of a Psalmist[1]

The first thing that strikes a reader of this psalm is its remarkable elaboration of form: an eightfold alphabetic acrostic employing eight key terms, each intended to be synonymous and, taken together, occurring 176 times—the exact number of cola (verses) in the work. The next thing to be observed is the very large element of repetition of thought and language (e.g., "I do not forget your word" with variations occurs eight times: vv 16, 61, 83, 93, 109, 141, 153, 176).

What do these features tell us about the author? It is clear that he lays claim to superior literary skill,[2] since he has deliberately chosen—indeed, he has

---

[1] In this article no attempt is made to discuss many of the aspects of this psalm that have been abundantly treated by earlier scholars such as the identity of the author, the historical situation that inspired the psalm, the significance of the eightfold acrostic form, and the meaning of the term "torah" and its concomitant terms. The article is solely concerned with the author's spirituality and literary skill.

[2] This claim has been rejected by a number of commentators, though rarely as decisively as by B. Duhm, *Die Psalmen* (Kurzer Handcommentar zum Alten Testament; Tübingen: Möhr, 1899) 268, who described the psalm as "the most meaningless product that ever blackened paper"; but it has frequently been dismissed as "monotonous" and "tedious." A very different view has been expressed by several recent writers including M. J. Dahood, *Psalms 3: 101–150* (AB17A; New York: Doubleday, 1970) 172; J. W. Rogerson and J. W. McKay, *Psalms 101–150* (Cambridge Bible Commentaries; Cambridge: Cambridge University, 1977) 89; L. C. Allen, *Psalms 101–150* (WBC; Waco, TX: Word, 1983) 139; J. H. Eaton, *Psalms of the Way and the Kingdom* (JSOTSup 199; Sheffield: Sheffield Academic Press, 1955) 52; W. Soll, *Psalm 119: Matrix, Form and Setting* (CBQMS 23; Washington: The Catholic Biblical Association of America, 1991).

himself created—a poetical form and structure that are exceptionally difficult to master, much more so than any other acrostic in the OT. And this pattern he has executed with perfect precision, unlike some other OT writers
who have attempted much simpler types of acrostic.[3] Further, this author has
expounded his personal faith with great intensity and concentration. Whatever may be said about his failure to produce a connected sequence of
thought—a failure frequently consequent on the choice of the acrostic
form—his total concentration on a single topic and his avoidance of any kind
of digression from it have given the poem an impressive unity. There is no
room here for theories that have sometimes been advanced of a combination
into a single poem of a series of originally separate poems,[4] or of a gradual
expansion of a single, much simpler and less repetitive poem.[5]

This is as personal a piece of literature as is to be found anywhere in the
OT: "I" and "me" occur in it more than 240 times. The constant repetition of
the same thought—albeit with frequent variations, sometimes very minor
ones, of language—has often been found tedious; but this could equally be
said of much ancient Hebrew and Semitic poetry, for example of the frequently repeated imagery of the Song of Songs, which is generally highly
regarded for its poetical qualities. The language of Psalm 119 is the language
of *devotional* poetry: the outpouring of the most intense religious feeling.

What is the nature of this spirituality? The psalm is, of course, apart from a
short introduction (vv 1–3), throughout a *prayer* of the most personal kind,
addressed wholly to God. The introductory verses are composed in exactly
the same style and express the same thoughts as the rest of the poem, but are
not addressed to God. It has often been observed that they are strongly reminiscent of Psalm 1.[6] Both texts are impersonal and expressed in general

---

3 For example, the alphabetic sequence is defective in Psalms 9–10, 25, 34, 37, and 145.

4 As proposed by A. Deissler, *Psalm 119 (118) und seine Theologie* (Münchener Theologische Studien 1/11; Munich; Zink, 1995) and S. Bergler, "Der längste Psalm—Anthologie oder
Liturgie?" *VT* 29 (1979) 257–88.

5 This also applies to the view that the psalm is a collection of originally independent
proverbs and/or other material held, e.g., by H. J. Kraus, *Psalmen* 2 (BKAT 15/2; Neukirchen-
Vluyn: Neukirchener V., 1961) 819–20; R. E. Murphy, "A Consideration of the Classification
'Wisdom Psalms'" (VTSup 9; Leiden: Brill, 1963) 156–67; J. L. Mays, "The Place of the Torah
Psalms in the Psalter," *JBL* 106 (1987) 6–7. The consistency of the style, despite the use of dif-
ferent *Gattungen,* tells against this view.

6 C. Westermann, "Zur Sammlung des Psalters," *Forschung am Alten Testament* (TBü 24;
Munich: Kaiser, 1964) 336–43, suggested that Psalms 1 and 119 had at one stage in the compo-

terms. Like Psalm 1, Ps 119:1–3 pronounces "happy" (*ʾašrê*) those who are sincerely devoted to the observance of God's law. This similarity perhaps suggests the kind of readership for whom Psalm 119 was composed. The use of the term *ʾašrê* in vv 1 and 2 implies that the kind of spirituality displayed in the rest of the psalm is not something that is exclusive to the psalmist: that the psalm is, in a real sense, addressed to others who, whether or not they have reached the "happy" state of the author, "seek him (sc. Yahweh) with their whole heart" (v 2b). The purpose of the author is to encourage them in that search.

However, vv 1–3, like the rest of the poem, provide very little information about the identity of the psalmist or about the circumstances in which the psalm was composed. The psalmist admittedly speaks of himself as one whose devotion to God's will has exposed him to opposition and even to persecution. The psalm is in fact replete with an astonishing variety—evidently this was a special characteristic of this author's literary style—of references to enemies (*ṣārîm*, v 57), wicked persons (*rĕšāʿîm, mĕrēʿîm*, vv 61, 115), oppressors (*ʿōšĕqîm*, vv 121, 134), even "princes" (*śārîm*, vv 23, 161) who taunt, humiliate, persecute (*rādap*, vv 84, 161) the psalmist and even seek to kill him (v 87), so that he feels that he is an "alien upon the earth" (*gēr . . . bāʾāreṣ*, v 19). There is no reason not to take these references to opposition and persecution literally; but they are so devoid of specificity that attempts to define the historical situation have been unconvincing, apart from a general agreement that the absence of any allusion to *foreign* enemies suggests that all the psalmist's troubles are caused by internal enemies—that is, fellow-Israelites.[7]

There can be no doubt that the psalm ought to be counted among the "wisdom psalms," however that category may be defined.[8] This is indicated,

---

sition of the Psalter been set as a framework to the then Psalter (which had concluded with Psalm 119) in order to detract from its cultic importance and to give it the character of a manual of law piety. This hypothesis has been reiterated by Westermann in subsequent studies and has been taken up by some other scholars.

[7] The great majority of commentators have placed the composition of the psalm in the post-exilic period; Dahood is an exception (*Psalm 3*, 173). Suggestions (e.g., by C. A. Briggs, *Psalms* 2 [ICC; Edinburgh: T. & T. Clark, 1907] 417, and by W. E. Barnes, *The Psalms* 2 (Westminster Commentaries; London: Methuen, 1931) 567) that the author was a Pharisee or proto-Pharisee are over-precise. Fierce disputes over the right interpretation of the traditional Israelite faith began soon after the Exile as is attested, for example, in Isaiah 56–66, and may have persisted throughout the post-exilic period.

[8] Murphy ("A Consideration") made a notable and influential contribution to the subject; but no two scholars have been able to agree about the question or even about the criteria to be

among other characteristics, by the psalmist's repeated appeals to God to be his teacher (e.g., vv 12, 26, 33, 68, 124, 135, 171) and other statements asserting the supreme value to him of the *knowledge* that God imparts to him (e.g., vv 27, 29, 32, 34, 73, 99, 100, 104, 125, 144, 152, 169). A formidable array of verbs denoting knowledge, teaching and learning is deployed in these verses: *lmd, byn, yrh, śkl, ydᶜ*. The thought of God as teacher, perhaps rather surprisingly, is rarely found in the OT outside the wisdom books, although his knowledge of the human heart as of his created world as a whole is often presupposed. Requests for instruction are most frequently found in the so-called wisdom psalms. In Proverbs 1–9, where great emphasis is laid on education as the means to success and well-being, this is mainly imparted by human teachers; but in some passages the teacher is personified Wisdom who is the wisdom of God himself (Prov 2:1–6, 8). That Psalm 119 is a wisdom psalm is further confirmed by the frequency of the occurrence the verb *byn* (in the forms *hēbîn* and *hitbônān*), a verb that is extremely characteristic of, if not exclusive to, the wisdom books, and of some other characteristic terms. In v 98 the author specifically states that God's commandments confer exceptional wisdom on him (*tĕḥakkĕmēnî*).

Nowhere else in the OT is there such a constant appeal to God to instruct the writer as in this psalm. But the nature of the teaching that the psalmist is requesting is not clearly defined. The meaning of *tôrâ* and its synonyms here is an old and unsolved question (it may be significant that whereas the other equivalent terms used in the psalm appear in the plural, *tôrâ* is always referred to in the singular). It has frequently been noted that, although the psalm makes much use of the language of Deuteronomy, the author never refers specifically to any of the Pentateuchal laws. The "torah" and its equivalents,[9] whether in the singular or the plural, are apparently regarded as a single entity to be honored and obeyed—or disobeyed—as a whole. However, of the many verses in which the psalmist speaks of this "law" of Yahweh and of his personal relationship to it, some make it plain that it is a written document

---

employed. See also *inter alia* J. K. Kuntz, "The Canonical Wisdom Psalms of Ancient Israel: Their Rhetorical, Thematic and Formal Dimensions," *Rhetorical Criticism: Essays in Honor of James Muilenburg* (PTMS 1; ed. J. J. Jackson et al.; Pittsburgh: Pickwick, 1974) 186–222; A. Hurvitz, "Wisdom Vocabulary in the Hebrew Psalter: A Contribution to the Study of 'Wisdom psalms'," *VT* 38 (1988) 41–51; R. N. Whybray, "Wisdom Psalms," *Wisdom in Ancient Israel: Essays in Honour of J. A. Emerton* (ed. J. Day et al.; Cambridge: Cambridge University, 1995) 152–60.

9 These words are taken in this article to be synonymous.

(or documents). He frequently states that he has "kept" it or will keep it, does not forget it or does not turn away from it (the temporal significance of the verbs employed is not always clear).[10] He speaks of his delight in it,[11] his love of it,[12] and his trust in it (v 66). He declares or recounts (*sippēr*) it (v 13); he clings (*dābaq*) to it (v 31); he has chosen it (v 173). He seeks guidance from it (*dāraš*, vv 45, 94). That it is, at least sometimes, a written document of which he has access to a copy is also probably implied by the use of the word *śîaḥ*, "meditate" (vv 15, 23, 48, 78, 99).

On the other hand, another set of expressions gives a somewhat different impression about this "law" and the psalmist's relationship to it. He states that he waits or hopes for Yahweh's law (vv 43, 81, 114—*yiḥaltî*) and that he longs for it (*tā'ab, yā'ab, ta'ăbâ*, vv 20, 40, 131, 174). He also asks God not to hide it from him (v 19). These lines give the impression that it is something that is not, or not yet, familiar to him, but that he recognizes its supreme importance and is eager to know it.

This impression is confirmed by the number of places in which he asks God to teach him his law (e.g., vv 12, 26, 33, 64, 68, 108, 124, 135). The apparent inconsistency may perhaps be resolved by a number of other lines which make similar requests but do not employ the technical vocabulary of instruction (*limmad, hôrâ*). From these it appears that what the psalmist is requesting is not a knowledge of the law in a literal sense but a deeper understanding of that law, with which he is already familiar. There are at least seven of these:

27 Make me understand (*hăbînēnî*) the way (*derek*) of your precepts,
      and I will meditate on your wonders.
34 Give me understanding, that I may keep your law.
35 Lead me in the path (*nātîb*) of your law, for I delight in it.
36 Turn my heart to your decrees, and not to unjust gain (*beṣaʿ*).
73 Give me understanding, that I may learn your commandments.
104 Through your precepts I get understanding: therefore I hate every
      path (*'ōraḥ*) of falsehood.

These petitions provide an insight into the core of the psalmist's inner life—his spirituality. This is a spirituality of wisdom piety, as is indicated by

---

[10] So, e.g., vv 5a, 7a, 10a, 22b, 32a, 44a, 55, 56, 60a, 61b, 129b, 134b, 145, 146, 153b, 157b, 166a, 167a, 168a, 176b.

[11] Vv 14, 16, 24, 27, 70, 77, 92, 144, 174.

[12] E.g., vv 47, 48, 96, 113, 119, 127, 159, 163.

the use of the three words *derek, 'ōraḥ* and *nātîb*. The first two of these, used here in a metaphorical and ethical sense of a way of life, are characteristic of wisdom teaching; the third, *nātîb*, is exclusively so; it occurs only five times in the OT: here, three times in Job and once in Psalm 78:50. These are all prayers for illumination: not for the knowledge of the letter of God's law, but for God to impart to the psalmist the deeper meaning of his law, which can come neither from the unaided study of that law nor from any institutional form of theophany or cultic performance, but only from a silent, private communication from God himself to the individual believer. It is this for which he is waiting and longing.

In this prayer, then, the psalmist is sure that he is in direct communication with God. This gift of illumination will, he is convinced, provide the means fully to understand the meaning of God's law and, through that, to appreciate, by meditation, the wonder of his operations (v 27). It will lead him to live as God wills him to live (vv 34, 35) and so to abstain from base and fraudulent behavior (v 36). The psalmist already *knows* the letter of the law, but only through divine illumination will he learn its true implications (vv 73, 125)—that is, that it requires him to live an honest life (v 104). These petitions thus encapsulate the essence of true wisdom and torah piety: a moral life based on a true knowledge of God. With this in mind we are in a position to examine the spirituality of the psalm more closely.

The situation in which the psalmist finds himself is very different from that confidently predicted in the other great torah psalm, Psalm 1. In that cold and entirely impersonal psalm there is no recognition whatever that those who delight in God's Torah and meditate continually on it will encounter trouble of any kind: one verse suffices to describe their reward (v 3). They will be "like trees planted by streams of water that yield their fruit in due season, whose leaves do not wither": in plain language, "in all that they do, they prosper." If that is wisdom teaching, it is a bland and unrealistic wisdom. Not so in Psalm 119: its author, who is equally devoted to God's torah, displays his wisdom in the real world, where he encounters opposition, persecution and even threats to his life. His situation may be compared to that of the Servant of Yahweh in Deutero-Isaiah[13] and, in a somewhat different way, to the figure of Job in the book of Job, or to Jeremiah: all three are "suffering servants" of God, and in each case their suffering, whether inflicted by human agents (Deutero-Isaiah), by God himself (Job), or by both (Jeremiah) causes them to

---

[13] So also, for example, Kraus, *Psalmen 2,* 829.

reflect on its purpose: is it meaningless, simply due to the malice of their persecutors (human or divine), or has it some deep and positive significance in
the gracious but hidden purposes of God?

In the case of Psalm 119—and this is also true of Jeremiah—the author's
distressful situation leads him to express his sentiments in a series of paradoxes. On the one hand he reminds God of his extreme anguish: his life
clings to the dust (v 25); it melts away (if that is the meaning) in tears (v 28); he
is like a wineskin shriveled in the smoke (v 83); he is overwhelmed by his distress (v 143). His enemies have brought him close to despair. Yet in these very
same verses he recognizes that God has promised to save his life and to give
him strength, and he still trusts in his laws and delights in them. He frequently
implores God to rescue him, yet he knows that his "humbling" was for his
good (v 71), and that it was in faithfulness (ʾĕmûnâ) that God humbled him
(v 75)—that is, that in so doing God was faithful to his own nature and to his
promises.

Paradoxical also is the psalmist's understanding of his relationship with
God. This varies from a real terror (paḥad) of God (v 120) to a confident feeling of intimacy with him (qārôb ʾattâ yhwh, v 151). Again, on the one hand he
has exhausted himself in fruitless expectation that God will intervene on his
behalf (vv 82, 84, 123), while on the other he speaks of maintaining an inti-
mate dialogue with him: God has spoken to him directly in answer to an earlier prayer (v 26), and he expects once more to receive an answer from him
(v 145). His description of his own situation is also paradoxical: he speaks of
himself as insignificant (ṣāʿîr) and despised (nibzeh, v 141), yet claims that he
will speak (or speaks) before kings and not be ashamed (v 46). When he
speaks of God as creator he does so in personal terms ("Your hands made and
established me"—yĕkônĕnûnî, v 73), implying that God is especially concerned with him as an individual. Similarly, his statement that "all my ways are
before you" (negdĕkā, v 168) reflects a more personal relationship than in
such general statements as are found, for example, in Proverbs: that "Yahweh
tests the hearts" (Prov 17:3); or that the hearts of men are neged yhwh (Prov
15:11).

Such paradoxes are consistent with, and even characteristic of, a person in
spiritual turmoil. They testify to the reality of the psalmist's faith, not to spiritual uncertainty and vacillation. They can be closely paralleled with the utterances of many spiritual and mystical writers throughout the ages, who also
experienced the "dark night of the soul." They attest the genuineness of this
writer's outpouring of his soul. The constant reiteration in almost every verse

of the psalmist's devotion to God's law acts as a kind of refrain expressing an underlying confidence in God despite all adversities that never varies, and which is the real theme of the psalm.

This confidence is further expressed in passionate terms that show the reader something of the character of the psalmist. He is an extremely passionate person. He is seized with raging fury (*zalʿāpâ*) against the wicked who forsake God's law (v 53), and weeps floods of tears over their apostasy (v 136). He is consumed with zeal (*qinʾâ*) for God (v 139) and filled with disgust for those whom he dubs "traitors" (*bōgĕdîm*) (v 158). God's teaching, on the other hand, fills him with joy and delight (vv 14, 35, 70, and especially v 162: "I rejoice in your word like one who finds great spoil"). But he is also capable of bold (and passionate) address to God, telling him that "It is time to act," because his enemies have broken his law (v 126). He expresses the completeness of his own devotion to the law by the employment of a device used elsewhere in the OT for other purposes,[14] of recounting those bodily organs that serve this end: eyes (vv 18, 37, 82, 123, 136, 148), mouth (vv 13, 43, 103, 108, 131), tongue (v 172), lips (vv 13, 171), and above all, the heart (vv 7, 10, 11, 32, 34, 36, 58, 69, 80, 111, 112, 145, 161)—the last of these especially in the phrase "with my whole heart." He does not specifically mention the organ of hearing, which plays such an important role in Proverbs 1–9, but this is probably implied in those verses that speak of a dialogue with God.)

From all this it may be deduced that Yahweh is regarded by the psalmist as in a special sense his personal God;[15] this is evident in almost every line of the psalm. There are even lines that imply that the rest of the world is totally hostile to him and that he alone enjoys this privilege: in v 19 he claims, "I am an alien (*gēr*) on earth (*bāʾāreṣ*)." However, it appears from other passages that he belongs to a company of likeminded persons. These are those who "fear Yahweh" (vv 63, 74, 79) and observe Yahweh's teachings and are consequently "blameless" *(tĕmāmîm,* v 1), seeking him with their whole heart. They are probably the persons for whom the psalm was composed. The psalmist distinguishes himself from them, claiming a knowledge of God that they do not yet possess, and appealing to them to "turn," or possibly "return" (*yāšûbû*), to

---

[14] E.g., Pss 115:5–7; 135:15–17; Prov 6:16–19.

[15] See especially R. Albertz, *A History of Israelite Religion in the Old Testanent Period* 2 (London: SCM, 1994) 556–60. There are traces of the notion of a personal God (an important feature of Mesopotamian religion) in pre-exilic times in Israel, notably in the stories of the patriarchs in Genesis and in the case of King David in 1 and 2 Samuel.

himself so that they may learn from him (v 79). (The reading *wĕyēdĕ'û* [v 79b, Kethib] is preferable to Qere's *yōdĕ'ê,* "those who know.") This is an indication of the purpose for which he has composed the psalm: to show how his own experience and knowledge of God have strengthened his faith, and to encourage his readers to share these experiences. He claims that meditation on God's law has made him wiser, not only than his enemies (v 98a) and his elders (v 100a) but also than his orthodox teachers *(mĕlammĕday,* v 99a). He is indeed an outstanding example of a suffering but ultimately victorious servant of God. He is not, in fact, entirely alone: he is supported by companions *(ḥābēr,* v 63) who share his devotion to Yahweh and his laws and with whom he is eager to share his acquired wisdom.

The psalmist does not, however, claim to be perfect. He admits that his understanding of the divine will is imperfect and that he needs to perfect it; and twice he refers to his failings. In v 67, "Before I was humbled I was going astray *('ănî šōgēg),* but now I keep your law," he is referring to the past, before he had experienced God's loving discipline; but in v 176, despite the perfect tense *(tā'îtî),* he is apparently speaking of the present: he confesses that he is "like a lost sheep" *(kĕśeh 'ōbēd)* that has gone astray, and appeals to God to "seek him out" *(baqqēš)*—a final appeal to God the good shepherd to rescue him and bring him to safety.

What is the psalmist's relationship to the traditional faith of Israel? Like other wisdom psalmists he makes no direct reference to Israel or to its special status; but he is clearly familiar with its traditional faith and with much of its literature—a topic that cannot be discussed in this article, but one that has been frequently noted. He employs several of the literary forms which occur in other, non-wisdom psalms, especially the individual lament, which is particularly suited to his purpose. He does not speak of the "covenant" *(bĕrît);* but the "law" *(tôrâ)* with its various equivalents, though its contents are not specified, is clearly related in some way to the written laws of the Pentateuch: this is indicated *inter alia* by the occurrence of words characteristic of Deuteronomy and the priestly laws: *tôrâ, dĕbārîm, miṣwôt, mišpāṭîm.* Yet, as has been concluded above, the psalmist knows that those laws do not comprise the whole of God's will for him: God speaks directly to him, rather as to a prophet.

The psalmist's references to *worship* are restricted to his own private prayer and direct communication with God. He uses only one word, *nĕdābâ,* "gift, freewill offering," that is used elsewhere as a technical term of the temple cult; and he uses it in a special sense, of *prayer* as an offering to God:

he asks God to accept the "offerings of my mouth" (*nidĕbôt pî*, v 108)—that is, his verbal offering of praise. It is in this sense that he speaks of the frequency of his times of worship: he remembers Yahweh's name (that is, he prays to him) in the night (v 55), he rises at midnight to praise him (v 62), he rises at dawn to cry for his help (v 147) and is awake to meditate in the watches of the night (v 148). He praises God seven times a day (v 164).

The terms in which the psalmist speaks of God—that he is creator and eternal, faithful, reliable, just, loving, merciful, lifesaving, gracious, shepherd, and savior—appear, like almost everything else in this psalm, to spring at least as much from his personal experience of God as from a knowledge derived at second hand from the corporate faith of Israel. The sincerity of these statements cannot be missed: this is no formal exercise of conventional piety. Yet these divine attributes do in fact correspond closely to the corporate experience of the people of Israel reflected in the OT. The psalmist has become intensely aware of them in his own person.

Has the psalmist been successful in his aim to instill in his readers his own conviction that total devotion to the will of God is the only sure route to happiness in this world (vv 1–3)? That he considered himself to be an outstandingly skillful writer is obvious: no one who did not possess such confidence would have dared to choose a literary form of such complexity as his medium.[16] No doubt the element of frequent repetition which is inherent in the twenty-twofold structure helped to serve his purpose, conveying as it does an impression of completeness, of totality, and of regularity. Formally, then, the psalm has a structural unity. Can it also be said that it has a thematic one?

A number of themes are endlessly repeated: the psalmist makes it clear that God, whose will is expressed in his torah or teaching, is the sole guiding principle of his life: he loves and delights in this law, which is eternal and righteous, saves him, gives him life, freedom and superior wisdom. He studies it and meditates on it and so receives illumination. Yet he recognizes that his understanding of it is incomplete, and he desperately longs for a deeper knowledge. He also recognizes the danger of being led astray by a desire for

---

[16] Eaton (*Psalms of the Way and the Kingdom,* 51–52) argues that the acrostic scheme enhances rather than detracts from the contemplative purpose of the psalm: "From the letters which are the primal elements of all utterance unfolds a yet richer alphabet of communion—from each letter in turn eight sayings that draw to God. It is precisely this 'disjointed' nature of the sayings that is their strength, intentionally so. Each has its own completeness as a link to God, spokes in a wheel of communion. The various names for God's healing word . . . reveal new facets, like stones ever moved to new settings."

wealth and unjust gain, and prays that he may avoid this. He feels isolated from society and prays to be delivered from his tormentors who seek his life. He prays for life, help, comfort and grace, and speaks of his frequent turning to God in prayer and praise.

The very pervasiveness of these themes and the close relationship between them give the psalm a massive thematic unity. The psalmist rings the changes on the themes like a change-ringer: he does not sound the carillon always in the same order. It is this that has led to the charge of incoherence. In fact there is evidence of an attempt at structural coherence: the psalmist has frequently linked adjacent stanzas by the principle of repeated key words—a device not uncommon in Hebrew poetry. At least sixteen of the twenty-one intervals between the twenty-two stanzas have such links.[17] Repetition has also been used as a linking device *within* some sections.[18]

There is much more thematic consistency of theme and sense within individual stanzas than has been commonly supposed. Indeed, some sections have quite definite sequences of thought. Thus in vv 33–40 (*he*) every verse except the last begins with a prayer: prayers for instruction and understanding, for guidance and avoidance of sin, for deliverance from disgrace. The stanza also ends with a prayer, for life (v 40b). Vv 49–56 (*zayin*) begin, after an initial prayer for the fulfilment of God's promises, with references to the comfort (*nḥm*) that God gives (vv 50, 52), and continues with an assertion of the psalmists zeal in celebrating this in song, worship and obedience (vv 54–56). Vv 81–88 (*kaph*) consist almost entirely of lamentation: the psalmist has been disappointed in his expectations from God, and prays for consolation and satisfaction.

Verses 89–96 (*lamed*), which begin with praise of God for the establishment of his word in heaven and earth (vv 89–91), continue with the psalmist's assurance that he does not forget these benefits and will keep Yahweh's teaching (vv 92–96). Vv 137–144 (*ṣadhe*) affirm the righteousness of God and his

---

[17] So *lēb/lēbāb*, vv 7, 10 and *šāmar*, vv 8, 9; *dēbārĕkā/dēbārĕkā*, vv 15, 17; *dbr*, vv 23, 25 and *ḥuqqĕka*, vv 23, 26; *lēb*, vv 32, 34; *ḥrp*, vv 39, 42; *šāmar*, vv 55, 57; *'elmād*, vv 71, 73; *lēb*, v 80 with *nepeš*, v 81 and *ᶜayin*, v 82; *'ereṣ*, vv 87, 90; *lî*, vv 95, 98; *nāḥaltî*, v 111 with *yiḥāltî*, v 114 (paronomasia); *mišpāṭ*, vv 120, 121; *ᶜal-kēn*, vv 127, 123, 129; *ᶜēdôtékā*, vv 145, 146; *dēbārĕkā*, vv 160, 161.

[18] *Lēb/lēbāb*, vv 2, 7; *'ôraḥ*, vv 9, 15 and *dēbārĕkā*, vv 9, 16; *dbr*, vv 17, 23; *dābaq*, vv 25, 31 and *derek*, vv 26, 32; *zākar*, vv 49, 55; *šāmar*, vv 57, 63; *ṭôb/ṭûb*, vv 65, 66, 71, 72; *yĕrĕ'êkā*, vv 74, 79; *kālâ*, vv 81, 82 with *killâ*, v 87; *'āhab*, vv 113, 119; *ṣaddîq*, v 137 with *ṣedeq*, vv 138, 144 and *ᶜēdôtêkā*, vv 138, 144; 146, 152; *rĕ'êh*, vv 153, 159; and *ḥayyēnî*, vv 154, 159.

law (*ṣedeq, ṣaddîq*) both in the first and last verses (137–138, 144) and also in the middle of the stanza (*ṣidqātĕkā ṣedeq lĕʿôlām*, v 142)—affirmations no doubt influenced by the need to begin each verse of the stanza with *ṣadhe*. In vv 145–152 (*qoph*) the psalmist moves from one topic to another, but in logical progression. In 145–147 he prays for an answer, for help. Verse 147 is pivotal: in that verse and v 148, which form a pair, he reinforces the urgency of his prayer by mentioning the danger from his persecutors and asking that Yahweh preserve his life; vv 150b and 151a then contrast these persecutors, who are far (*rāḥāqû*) from the law, with Yahweh, who is near (*qārôb*) to him and so able to intervene on his behalf. Finally, the affirmation in v 151b that Yahweh's commandments are true (*ʾĕmet*) is supported in v 152 by the psalmist's statement that he has long known this through his study of them.

In addition to these examples of connected or consecutive thought covering entire stanzas there are numerous smaller groups of two or more consecutive verses that pursue a particular thought, or pairs of which the second verse completes the thought of the first. Thus vv 5 and 6 together express a single thought: a wish is followed by a statement of the expected result if or when (*ʾaz*) the wish is granted. The declarations in vv 14 and 16 of delight In God's laws form an enclosure within which (v 15) the psalmist speaks of his meditation on and close attention to them. Vv 41–42, somewhat similarly to vv 5–6, consist of a prayer followed by a statement about the consequence of that prayer's being granted. Again, v 45 sets out the consequence of continual obedience to the law promised in v 44. Vv 98–100 together state the consequences of the psalmist's love of and meditation on the law proclaimed in v 97; they also share a common motif, that of wisdom or divine illumination: the law makes the psalmist wiser (*tĕḥakkĕmēnî*) than his enemies and gives him more understanding (*hiśkaltî*) than his teachers and more discernment (*ʾetbônān*) than his elders. Vv 116 and 117, in which the psalmist prays to be supported (*somkēnî*) and sustained (*sĕʿādēnî*) also form an obvious pair. Vv 121b and 122b, in which the psalmist prays not to be abandoned to his oppressors, echo one another; similarly vv 169a and 170a. In vv 174–76, finally, there was apparently an attempt to round off the whole psalm by referring back to the initial verses of the psalm proper (vv 4–6).

These signs of structural activity both formal and material cannot all be dismissed as due to coincidence. Indeed, they may be examples of a wider phenomenon which modern scholars have not yet had the wit to perceive. Yet, so far as our modern understanding of the poem goes, it must be concluded that the author has been only partially successful in his attempt to produce a poem that would be entirely coherent as a literary work. The links between and within stanzas that have been identified are sufficient to show that this was his intention; but the immense difficulties presented by the literary medium that he had imposed on himself seem ultimately to have defeated him, or at least to have impaired his grand plan. On the other hand, there can be no doubt that the psalm was remarkably successful in its day both as a personal testimony and as a commendation of a law-centered piety which could elicit, through meditation, direct, unmediated communication and dialogue with God himself; and as such it has retained its effectiveness to this day, when it is still used in liturgical and private devotion.[18]

18. It is both a pleasure and an honor to have been given the opportunity to participate in this tribute to Roland Murphy, from whose many writings on the wisdom literature, not least on the "wisdom psalms," I have learned more than I can say.

PART TWO

Proverbs

Observations on the Text and Versions of Proverbs

Enormous strides over have been made over the last half century in understanding the history of the Hebrew text and its versions. This article will bring to bear some of this new knowledge on the Book of Proverbs, in the process illustrating how the text of each biblical book is unique. It will examine the Hebrew text of Proverbs and the approaches and techniques of its major versions—the Septuagint, Peshitta, Targum, and Vulgate. The article is the fruit of several years' work on the entire Hebrew text of Proverbs and all the ancient versions in the course of preparing a commentary. The complexity and sheer mass of Proverbs forbid an exhaustive treatment, but it is possible to note some characteristics and provide examples. It is a pleasure to dedicate this study to Roland Murphy, O. Carm., who has contributed so judiciously over so many years to the interpretation of Proverbs and other wisdom literature on both a scholarly and popular level.

Three preliminary remarks must be made. First, apart from chaps. 1–9, and a few poems in the later chapters, Proverbs consists of two-line epigrams of six to eight words, many elliptical and indirect, each complete in itself. No narrative or thematic context aids the interpreter; the meaning is entirely within the verse. Before one can judge the soundness of a text, one must have at least a provisional grasp of the epigram. Words and meaning are fused. The ancient versions are invaluable, for each is not only a textual witness but an early interpretation.

Second, the ancient translators, with the possible exception of Jerome, found much of Proverbs exceedingly difficult. Modern scholars, aided by concordances, lexica, and commentaries, may fail to appreciate the puzzlement of the ancients before Proverbs' indirect and elliptical style. Their puzzlement explains why the Syriac Peshitta (S), the Vulgate (V), and the Targum (T) keep one eye on earlier versions as they translate the proto-masoretic or Masoretic Text (MT). Third, the specific genre of Proverbs affected its textual transmission. As a collection of (mostly) epigrams, the book attracted additional sayings as correction or commentary. No narrative plot or extended rhetorical logic "protected" the book from glossators. Who can resist topping a proverb? Many apparently could not, especially Greek speakers, for LXX has many sayings not in MT. Even MT has suffered some additions though they are more difficult to discern.[1]

The Hebrew Text

The Masoretic Text traces its origins to the scrolls chosen by the rabbis around 100 C.E. as the standard. The rabbis did not "establish" the texts in a modern critical sense but simply chose one scroll over others. In the course of the first millennium C.E., the texts were copied, edited, and written with vowels. The rabbinic action ended the period of live texts and creative pluriformity of the late Second Temple period.[2]

Any evidence of pre-masoretic Hebrew readings is obviously of great value to the text critic. There are two sources of evidence: the Hebrew text used by the LXX translators of the third or second century B.C.E. (G^V) and the Qumran biblical texts. The latter range in date from ca. 250 B.C.E. to 68 C.E., and some are of recensions different from the rabbinic recension that became the Masoretic Text.

What does Qumran tell us about the early Hebrew text of Proverbs? Two fragmentary manuscripts are preserved at Qumran, 4QProv^a (= 4Q102) and

[1] MT 1:16, "for their feet run to evil and they hasten to shed blood," is a gloss to supplement the enigmatic v 17. It was taken from Isa 59:7 and is not in B and S (first hand).

[2] For general orientation, see F. M. Cross, "The Text behind the Text of the Hebrew Bible," *Approaches to the Bible: A Collection of Articles from* Bible Review *and* Biblical Archaeology Review (2 vols.; ed. M. Minkoff; Washington: Biblical Archaeological Society, 1995), 1. 148–61, and E. Ulrich, "Pluriformity in the Biblical Text, Text Groups, and Questions of Canon," *The Madrid Qumran Congress: Proceedings of the International Congress on the Dead Sea Scrolls Madrid 18–21 March, 1991* (STDJ; ed. J. T. Barrera and L. V. Montana; Leiden: Brill, 1992), 1. 23–41.

4QProv^b (= 4Q103) in addition to a quotation of 15:8 in CD 11:20–21.[3] 4QProv^a contains 1:27c–2:1 and can be dated from its script to the middle of the first century B.C.E. It differs from the rabbinic recension only in the reading *mwškt* in 1:32, where MT has *měšûbat pětāyim tahargēm*, "for the turning aside of the simple will kill them." The word *mšwbt* may well have troubled a copyist, for it seemed to say that conversion (a good thing) kills! It is conceivable that the copyist substituted a verse from elsewhere in the Bible that provided better sense; G. W. Nebe suggests the copyist borrowed *mwškt* from Job 38:31b (MT *mōšěkôt kěsîl*, "Orion's bands"). Another possibility is that the scribe simply confused the letters *b* and *k* (similar in some Hebrew scripts); at some point *waw* was inserted as a vowel letter. Vowel letters were often added by Qumran scribes. If Job 38:31b were the source of the reading, it would be evidence of a live text, one still open to alterations. It is interesting to note that the Qumran manuscript offers no support for the LXX interpretation of v 32, *exetasmos asebeis olei*, "(divine) inquisition[4] destroys the impious."

4QProv^b (= 4Q103) contains the vestiges of two columns, 13:6–9, 14:5–10, 12–13; 14:31–15:8; 15:20–31. Paleographically, it is mid-first century C.E. It is identical to MT except for its omission of *yhgh* in 15:28 through haplography (*yod*), its spelling *ḥwnn* for MT *ḥnn* in 14:31; *bṣ^c bṣ^c* for MT *bwṣ^c bṣ^c* in 15:27a, and *wśn^ʾ* for MT *wśwn^ʾ* in 15:27b. The vowel letter *waw* marks the word as a qal participle. In the first case, the Qumran manuscript has *waw* and in the latter two, does not. 4QProv^b follows the MT rather than the LXX sequence of verses in chap. 15, i.e., it does *not* have 16:6 (Rahlfs "27a") after 15:27 nor 16:7 (Rahlfs "28a") after 15:28 nor 16:8, 9 (Rahlfs "15:29ab") after 15:29. It also contains a verse missing in LXX, MT 15:31. On the basis of this admittedly meager evidence, 4QProv^b can be called proto-rabbinic.

The second source of evidence for the early Hebrew text of Proverbs had always been available to scholars: the second-century B.C.E. *Vorlage* of LXX. Evidence from this source is indirect, requiring the subjective process of retroversion from Greek to Hebrew. For several biblical books, LXX reflects

---

[3] G. W. Nebe, "Qumranica I: Zu unveröffentlichen Handschriften aus Höhle 4 von Qumran," *ZAW* 106 (1994) 308–9, describes the texts, lists variants from MT, and gives references to the photographs in *A Facsimile Edition of the Dead Sea Scrolls* (ed. R. Eisenman and J. M. Robinson; Washington: Biblical Archaeology Society, 1991). I am indebted to Prof. Eugene Ulrich for sharing with me his readings of 4QProv^{a,b}.

[4] LXX seems to read Hebrew *šlwt* instead of MT *šʾlt*, possibly a quiescing of *aleph + waw* vowel letter. Suggestion of E. Ulrich, private communication.

a different and earlier Hebrew text than MT, e.g., Jeremiah,[5] Joshua, the story of David and Goliath in 1 Samuel, and Ezekiel. Is the Hebrew *Vorlage* of LXX Proverbs a different recension than the rabbinic? Emanuel Tov argues the *Vorlage* differs recensionally from MT and has gathered all the possible arguments: (1) the different sequence in LXX of the major sections of Proverbs after 24:22[6] and of verses in chaps. 15–16, 17, 20, and 31; (2) pluses in LXX (e.g., 3:16; 3:22a; 27:1) that likely arose from a different *Vorlage* rather than from inner-Greek causes; (3) minuses in LXX, which are too many to be attributable to parablepsis in a translator.[7] The LXX of Proverbs has not hitherto been discussed extensively as evidence for a recensional stage

> not only because the text is difficult and cannot be assessed easily, but also because scholars tended to ascribe its deviations from the MT to inner-translational factors rather than to its Hebrew *Vorlage*. As long as these deviations are ascribed to the translator's whims, they are irrelevant to the textual criticism of the Hebrew Bible, and their main importance lies in the realm of exegesis. However, if at least some of these deviations of the LXX derived from a different Hebrew *Vorlage*, that Hebrew text would have differed recensionally from the MT.[8]

Tov's arguments are essentially arguments *against* inner-Greek explanations for the differences between LXX and MT. Not all are persuasive. *LXX pluses*. The vocabulary of several LXX pluses (3:16; "3:22a"; 27:1) differs from that in similar verses. True, but LXX Proverbs suffered additions at different periods and such additions would likely have a distinctive vocabulary. They need not have come from a different *Vorlage*. *LXX minuses*. In a number of instances, the text of LXX is shorter than MT, i.e., LXX does not have MT: 1:16; 4:7; 7:25b; 8:29a, 33; 11:4, 10b, 11a; 15:31; 16:1, 3; 18:23–24; 19:1–2; 20:14–19; 21:5, 18b; 22:6; 23:23. The number is too large to attribute

---

[5] The LXX text of Jeremiah, one-eighth shorter than MT and with a different placement of the oracles against the nations, is found in 4QJer[b, d].

[6] The Greek order of sections after 24:22 is (to use MT verse numbers) 30:1–14 + 24:23–34 + 30:15–33 + 31:1–9 + 25:1–29:27 + 31:10–31.

[7] E. Tov, "Recensional Differences between the Masoretic Text and the Septuagint of Proverbs," *Of Scribes and Scrolls: Studies in the Hebrew Bible, Intertestamental Judaism, and Christian Origins Presented to John Strugnell* (ed. H. W. Attridge, J. J. Collins, and T. H. Tobin; College Theology Resources in Religion 5; New York: University Press of America, 1990) 43–56.

[8] "Recensional Differences," 43–44.

all of them to a scribal phenomenon (parablepsis); it must have come from the *Vorlage*. This argument has some probability. *The different sequence in LXX of sections after 24:22.* Whoever rearranged the sections was likely aware that 24:23, 30:1, and 31:1 were section titles, but the translator was not, for he failed to understand they were titles and mistranslated them. Tov is thus correct in presuming the *Vorlage* already had the rearrangement, for translator and rearranger seem to have been different people. *The different order of verses in LXX in chaps. 15–16, 17, 20, and 31.* The argument is not persuasive, for no logic is discernible in the sequence of verses in either LXX or MT. There is no way of knowing whether the distinct sequence was in the *Vorlage* or introduced by the translator. Taken as a whole, the evidence suggests that G^V was a recension distinct from the proto-rabbinic recension that became MT. The shape of that recension is difficult to imagine, however: probably it had a different sequence of the final sections; probably it did not have some verses that the proto-rabbinic recension had, and had others not in that recension; possibly it had a different order of verses in chaps. 15–16; 17; 20; 31. No Qumran manuscript reflects G^V.

We turn now from the pre-rabbinic Hebrew texts of Proverbs to MT. How is the MT of Proverbs to be characterized? Is it expansionistic like the Hebrew text of Jeremiah, or shortened by haplography like sections of MT Samuel? One measure of quality is the number of corruptions from haplography and dittography. Instances of haplography are relatively few: 5:4 (*pîpîyôt*); 7:10 (*ha'iššâ*); 11:9 (*tikkōn*); 19:6 (*ûbōzēh*); 20:18 (*tēʿăśēh*); 23:32 (*yaprîś rōʾš*, cf. LXX and Deut 32:32). Instances of dittography are also relatively rare: 2:14 (second *raʿ*); 5:2 (*śĕpātêkā* from v 3); 5:18a (*yĕhî . . . bārûk* from v 17a); 6:5a (*miyyad*); 14:21 (*lĕrēʿēhû* from v 20); 16:11 (*mišpāṭ* from v 10); 21:11b (*l* before *ḥkm* from *hśkyl*); 21:21b (*ṣdqh* from v 21a); 22:27b (*lāmmâ* from v 27a); 25:20a (corrupt dittography from v 19). There are some obviously corrupt verses—at least twenty-two in my very minimal count[9]— but this does not seem large in a book of the size of Proverbs. One cannot say for sure that MT is slightly expansionistic, but the numerous LXX minuses do not always prove MT additions.

[9] 6:26; 7:22c; 8:13a; 10:10b, 11b; 11:7; 12:28; 13:8, 15; 14:7b; 16:27; 18:19; 19:7; 20:30; 22:11, 21; 24:10, 27b; 26:10; 27:9, 16; 31:31.

The Greek Version

The Greek text has been the object of much study,[10] though recently attention has shifted away from textual matters to ideology.[11] The Proverbs volume in the Göttingen series was never published though Joseph Ziegler collated the manuscripts, which are available in Göttingen. One must use the edition of Alfred Rahlfs, based mainly on B, S, and A, and supplement it with Field's collection of hexaplaric readings[12].

The Greek translator renders his *Vorlage* in a free and sometimes paraphrastic style. On the LXX spectrum of free and literal, Proverbs is near Isaiah and Job. The translator does not seem to have had the help of an interpretive tradition, for he misses the nuance of many sayings even when his rendering is technically correct.

As S. Brock points out, the earliest Greek translators had no model as they began their unprecedented translation of a great body of sacred texts. In the course of their work, a new ideal of translation came into being for biblical translators: *verbum e verbo*, "word for word," replacing the classical ideal of *sensus de sensu*, "sense for sense." People were aware, however, that the translations did not represent the Hebrew originals with sufficient accuracy at least by the time of the preface to Sirach (ca. 130 B.C.E.). The dissatisfaction set in motion a series of corrections to the Greek text to bring it more into line with the Hebrew text (itself still developing), culminating in the "sophisticated literalism of Aquila in the second century A.D."[13]

---

[10] P. de Lagarde, *Anmerkungen zur griechischen Übersetzung der Proverbien* (Leipzig: Brockhaus, 1863); A. J. Baumgartner, *Etude critique sur l'état du text du Livre des Proverbes d'ápres les principales traductions anciennes* (Leipzig: Drugulin, 1890); G. Mezzacasa, *Il libro dei Proverbi di Salomone: studio critico sulle aggiunte greco-alessandrine* (Rome: Pontifical Biblical Institute, 1913); G. Gerleman, "Proverbs," *Studies in the Septuagint III* (LUÅ N.F. Avd. 1. Bd 52, No. 3; Lund: Gleerup, 1956) 1–63; W. McKane, *Proverbs: A New Approach* (OTL; Philadelphia: Westminster, 1970) 33–47.

[11] M. B. Dick, "The Ethics of the Old Greek Book of Proverbs," *Studia Philonica Annual: Studies in Hellenistic Judaism* (ed. D. T. Runia; Atlanta: Scholars, 1991) 20–50; J. Cook, "Hellenistic Influence in the Septuagint Book of Proverbs," *VII Congress of the International Organization for Septuagint and Cognate Studies Leuven 1986* (SBLSCS 31; ed. C. Cox; Atlanta: Scholars, 1989) 341–53; "The Septuagint Proverbs as a Jewish-Hellenistic Document," *VIII Congress of the International Organization for Septuagint and Cognate Studies* (SBLSCS 41; ed. L. Greenspoon and O. Munnich; Atlanta: Scholars, 1995) 349–65.

[12] F. Field, *Origenis Hexaplorum quae supersunt sive veterum interpretum Graecorum in totum Vetus Testamentum Fragmenta* (Hildesheim: Olms, 1964 [reprint]).

[13] S. P. Brock, "Translating the Old Testament," *It is Written: Scripture Citing Scripture:*

Some characteristics of LXX Proverbs can be assigned to a stage in its history. Its free translation style is the work of the first translators in the early second century B.C.E. (Old Greek = OG). The compressed epigrammatic Hebrew invited paraphrase; a Proverbs type (singular) such as *ṣaddîq*, "the righteous person," *rāšāʿ*, "the wicked person," became a generalizing plural in Greek idiom, *hoi dikaioi* and *hoi asebeis*; Semitic sentences were recast for Greek style; irony and wordplay sometimes fell victim to the *verbum e verbo* ideal. Only after the original translation had circulated for a time, perhaps by the end of the second century B.C.E. (preface to Sirach), could the next stage have occurred: correcting verses and half-verses toward the Hebrew. The major result of this corrective process is the famous LXX doublets, some seventy-six in C. T. Fritsch's count. These are double translations of entire verses (1:7; 2:21; 3:15; 6:11; 14:22; 15:6, 18; 18:22; 22:8; 29:25), of single cola (1:14, 27; 2:2, 3, 19; 4:10; 5:23; 6:25; 8:10; 9:10; 14:35; 16:17, 26; 29:7; 31:27, 29, 30), and of phrases and words.[14] The more literal rendering is generally judged to be later, a correcting of the free or inaccurate earlier rendering, according to Lagarde's widely accepted axiom.[15] Unlike the practice of modern text criticism, LXX scribes copied the original rendering as well as its correction. The LXX habit of incorporating new and old verses may account for the presence of verses for which there is no Hebrew counterpart, e.g., 3:22a; 4:10b, 27ab; 6:8abc; 8:21a; 9:8abc, 10a, 12abc, 18abcd; 15:27ab; 16:11; 25:10a; 26:11.

We now turn LXX Proverbs' translation techniques. One must know how a LXX book ordinarily translates before one can retrovert from Greek to Hebrew. It is well known that the Greek translator of Proverbs was often at a loss before the Hebrew but never lacking in ingenuity. When puzzled, the translator used a number of techniques, six of which are noted here: (1) borrowing from another verse; (2) metathesis (partial or full); (3) changing the

---

Essays in Honour of Barnabas Lindars, S.S.F. (ed. D. A. Carson and H. G. M. Williamson; Cambridge: Cambridge University, 1988) 90. Brock notes the other important ancient attitude toward LXX, represented by the Letter of Aristeas and Philo: the LXX was inspired and had an independent value.

[14] "The Treatment of the Hexaplaric Signs in the Syro-Hexaplar of the Proverbs," *JBL* 72 (1953) 170.

[15] *Anmerkungen*, 20. For further reflections, see Z. Talshir, "Double Translations in the Septuagint," *VI Congress for Septuagint and Cognate Studies* (SBLSCS 23; ed. C. E. Cox; Atlanta: Scholars, 1987) 21–63.

tri-consonantal root; (4) switching graphically similar consonants; (5) double translation; (6) inventing or heightening antithetic parallelism.[16] Regarding the second, third, and fourth technique, one cannot know with certainty if a particular example was already in G^V or the work of the Greek translator. The techniques are not mutually exclusive.

(1) *Borrowing from another verse*. In 10:32, to avoid an unseemly phrase (Hebrew *yēdĕ'û*, "[lips] know!"), the translator borrowed the verb *apostazō*, "to drip," from the previous verse to get, "the lips of the just drip grace." Other examples of borrowing scriptural verses: 1:16 (from Isa 59:7); 2:22 (from Ps 1:6b); 3:16 (from Isa 45:23 and Prov 31:26); 10:6b (from v 11b); 10:10b (from v 8b).

(2) *Metathesis* is the partial or full transposition of consonants in the Hebrew *Vorlage*. 11:27, Hebrew: "Whoever quests (*šḥr*) after good seeks favor"; LXX: "Whoever devises (*tektainomenos* = *ḥrš*) good things seeks good favor." 26:13, Hebrew: "A lazy person says, 'There's a lion (*šḥl*) in the road'"; LXX: "A lazy person having been sent (*šlḥ*) into the road says . . ." Other examples of full metathesis are: 11:9 (*ṣlḥ* for Hebrew *ḥlṣ*); 12:21 (*n'wh* for Hebrew *y'nh* + *y/w* confusion); 14:7 (*kl* for Hebrew *lk*); 14:16 (*mt'rb* for Hebrew *mt'br*); 14:32 (*btwmw* for Hebrew *bmwtw*); 20:29 (*ḥkm* for Hebrew *kḥm*); 28:20 (*ḥrš'* for Hebrew *h'šr*); 28:23 (*'rḥy* for Hebrew *'ḥry*); 30:3 (*'l* to Hebrew *l'*). Examples of partial metathesis are: 11:30 (*ḥāmās* for Hebrew *ḥākām*); 12:24 (*bḥwrym* for Hebrew *ḥrwṣym*); 13:8 (*'md* for Hebrew *šm'*); 13:23 (*yšrym* for Hebrew *r'šmym*); 14:15 (*ybw 'l šwb* for Hebrew *ybyn l'šrw* + *b/r* and *y/w* confusion); 15:30 (*r'h* for Hebrew *m'wr*); 21:21 (*drk* for Hebrew *rdp*); 25:27 (*dbrym* for Hebrew *kbdm*); 26:10 (*bśr* for Hebrew *śkr*); 30:10 (*šlm* for Hebrew *lšn*).

(3) *Change of the triliteral root*. 15:4 "but a crooked [tongue] breaks the spirit (*šbr brwḥ*)" is rendered by LXX, "but the one who guards it will be full of the spirit" (*yśb' brwḥ*). Other examples: 11:26 (*yqbrh* for Hebrew *yqbh*); 15:33 (*'ānîḥâ* for Hebrew *'ānāḥâ* + *w* for *y*); 17:1 (*'rbh* for Hebrew *ḥrbh*); 21:6 (*mwqšy* for Hebrew *mbqšy*; *rdp* for Hebrew *ndp*); 21:12 (*lbwt* for Hebrew *lbyt*), 21:26a.

(4) *Switching graphically similar consonants*. One can never be certain if a particular case is unintentional or a technique for solving a problem. The consonants most commonly confused in LXX Proverbs are *d* and *r*. Examples are

---

[16] S used analogous techniques; see H. Pinkuss, "Die Syrische Übersetzung der Proverbien," *ZAW* 14 (1994) 114–18. The article is in two parts, pp. 65–141, 161–222.

14:34 (*ḥsr* for Hebrew *ḥsd*); 15:10 ([y]*dᶜ* for Hebrew *rᶜ*); 22:8 (*ᶜbdtw* for Hebrew *ᶜbrtw*); 27:13 (*zēd* for Hebrew *zār*). Switching of the graphically similar *b* and *k* occurs in 14:7b: LXX reads *kly dᶜt*, "instruments of knowledge," for Hebrew *bl ydᶜt*, "you surely do not know." Another example is 11:19 (*bēn* for Hebrew *kēn*).

(5) *Double translation of words or phrases.* This technique differs from retranslation toward the Hebrew mentioned above, for it is a device to make sense of a difficult Hebrew text. 11:13a: "A two-tongued man reveals *counsel* (*sôd*) in *the assembly* (*sôd*)." In 14:30a, *ḥyy bśrm lb mrpʾ*, "a tranquil heart is life for the body," the translator did not read the first two words and double translated the final two to get "a gentle man is a physician of the heart." LXX rendered Hebrew *lēb marpēʾ* once as if from √*rpʾ*, "heal" = *iatros*, and once as if from √*rph*, "relax," = *prauthumos anēr*. Other examples: 11:3a (*tnḥm*); 21:26a; 25:13; 30:14 ("so as to consume *and devour*"), 16 ("water and water").

(6) *Invention or heightening of antithetic parallelism.*[17] Hebrew 14:9: *ʾwlm ylṣ ʾšm wbn yšrm rṣn*, "The wicked scorn a guilt offering[18] / but among the upright is acceptance." Evidently puzzled, the translator invented an antithesis by altering two Hebrew words: "Houses (reading *ʾhlym*, "tents," for Hebrew *ʾwlym*) of the lawless will owe a sacrifice, / houses (reading *byt* for Hebrew *bên*) of the just are acceptable." Hebrew 15:32: "Whoever lets go of discipline rejects his very self, but whoever heeds reproofs gets wisdom." LXX: "Whoever thrusts away discipline hates himself, but whoever keeps reproach loves his soul." Other examples: 5:16 (adds a verb in colon B), 17 (adds a verb in colon B), 21 (takes *mpls* as "see"); 10:10, 18; 11:2, 7, 15; 14:20; 26:20.

In summary, LXX is a relatively free translation of a recension different from the proto-rabbinic. Though the translator's own culture and interests are reflected in his rendering, he was primarily interested in rendering the text as accurately as he could. The *Vorlage* cannot be described in detail. It probably had its own sequence of sections after 24:22 and possibly of verses in chaps. 15–16, 17, 20, and 31. It is uncertain whether its many pluses and minuses are to be attributed to its *Vorlage* or are the result of a long and uncontrolled transmission history up into the late second or third century

---

[17] Gerleman discusses the predilection of LXX for antithetic parallelism and gives many examples, "Proverbs," pp. 18–24.

[18] The simplest solution to the problem of a singular Hebrew verb and a plural subject is to posit *yālîṣū*, the plural not being marked by a vowel.

C.E. Its numerous double translations are the result of a process in which original translations were later judged unfaithful to the Hebrew and retranslated
closer to the Hebrew. The phenomenon reflects the growing authority of the
Hebrew text in the eyes of some tradents. Though the original was judged
unsatisfactory, it was nonetheless copied along with its correction. Faced
with difficult verses, the translator found meaning in the Hebrew text by a
variety of techniques.

The value of the Greek version has been judged variously by scholars. F.
Delitzsch, who combined great respect for the Masoretic Text with exact
knowledge of the versions, is positive: "Along with the Books of Samuel and
Jeremiah, there is no book in regard to which the LXX can be of higher significance than the Book of Proverbs."[19] This is not the view of the *Preliminary
and Interim Report on the Hebrew Old Testament Text Project* (New York:
United Bible Societies, 1979), which seldom recommends emendations on
the basis of LXX. In the present writer's opinion, LXX has an important role
in Proverbs text criticism. Its occasional mangling of the Hebrew and obfus-
cation should generally be attributed to the enigmatic Hebrew; one should
not dismiss the whole. LXX contains a number of superior readings and can
offer much help to the commentator.[20]

The Syriac Version or Peshitta

There is a critical edition of the Peshitta Proverbs in the series The Old Testament in Syriac of the Peshitta Institute.[21] The Peshitta Old Testament is a
Christian work generally dated to the second century C.E.[22] It was a tightly

---

[19] *Commentary in the Old Testament in Ten Volumes* (Grand Rapids, MI: Eerdmans, 1993
[reprint]) 48.

[20] The present writer proposes the following superior readings in G: 3:3, 24; 5:18; 6:2, 5, 24;
the original placement of MT 6:22 after 5:19 (see P. W. Skehan, "Proverbs 5:15–19 and
6:20–24," *Studies in Israelite Poetry and Wisdom* [CBQMS 1; Washington: The Catholic Biblical Association of America, 1971] 1–8); 8:24, 33; 9:1; 10:10; 12:16; 13:11, 15; 14:21; 20:28; 21:21;
22:17; 24:5; 25:4, 18, 20; 26:26; 31:21. In its Proverbs apparatus *REB* explicitly adduces LXX to
support twenty-two emendations, and *NRSV*, thirty-three emendations.

[21] Part I, fascicle 5, prepared by A. A. Di Lella, O.F.M.

[22] Joosten proposes a slightly later date for Proverbs on the grounds that the Syriac New Testament does not cite it, "Doublet Translations in Peshitta Proverbs," *The Peshitta as a Translation* (Monographs of the Peshitta Institute Leiden 8; ed. P. P. Dirksen and A. van der Kooij;
Leiden: Brill, 1995), 66. The fact that the New Testament does not cite it is an argument for its
being a Jewish work.

controlled text, by the fifth or sixth century reaching the form it was always to retain.[23]

S is a simple, literal, but not slavish translation of MT into clear and idiomatic Syriac. Frequently S finds MT difficult, in which case he turns to LXX as a "trot." Ordinarily, S keeps an eye on LXX to check his own translation, in the way that T translates MT with an eye on S, and V translates MT with an eye on LXX. Though following LXX dozens of times,[24] S nonetheless regards MT as the authoritative text and aims to translate it. There are many proofs: when MT is clear, S translates it straightforwardly; S follows LXX with a certain freedom and sometimes corrects it in the light of the Hebrew;[25] S rarely translates LXX doublets; S follows the MT rather than LXX order of sections after 24:22 and of verses in chaps. 15–16, 17, 20, and 31.

Two recent articles have examined the relationship of S and LXX Proverbs. J. Joosten supports Pinkuss's conclusions that the Peshitta was neither a conflation of distinct translations nor subject to extensive later editing by analyzing its seven doublet translations. They illustrate the working method of the translator, i.e., refusing to choose between MT and LXX but trying to preserve the gist of both. But Joosten's conclusion that "Doublet translation might be called an epitome of the translational procedure found in Peshitta Proverbs"[26] seems to me to slight somewhat the general Peshitta preference for MT. As Pinkuss has demonstrated in his study of the whole of Peshitta Proverbs, S regards MT as authoritative and always aims to translate it even though it sometimes relies on LXX for sense. J. Cook goes in the opposite direction on the relation of S to LXX. After examining the LXX and S handling of the phrase *ʾiššâ zārâ* in Proverbs 1–9, he concludes, "The answer to the question of whether the Peshitta was dependent on the Septuagint must be negative," and applies Goshen-Gottstein's judgment on Isaiah to Proverbs: "I myself am still in doubt as to whether there are even five to ten such possible instances [of dependence of S on LXX] in the whole book of Isaiah. . . ." In my view, Cook's formulation understates the general reliance of S upon LXX.[27]

---

[23] Patristic citations suggest unusual conservatism as early as the fourth century; see H. Pinkuss, "Die Syrische Übersetzung," 107–8.

[24] Pinkuss, "Die Syrische Übersetzung," gives a complete list of the dozens of agreements of S and G on pp. 96–102.

[25] For examples, see Pinkuss, "Die syrische Übersetzung," 104–5.

[26] J. Joosten, "Doublet Translations," 72.

[27] J. Cook, "Are the Syriac and Greek Versions of the *ʾšh zrh* (Prov 1 to 9) Identical (On the Relationship between the Peshitta and the Septuagint)?" *Textus* 17 (1994) 117–32. The quotations are on pp. 131–32.

A long-standing scholarly problem is the relationship of the Peshitta to the Targum. They are obviously closely related but which is prior and the source of the other? In all biblical books except Proverbs, the Peshitta draws on the Targum. In the case of Proverbs, however, the Targum draws on the Peshitta in the view of most scholars, among them T. Nöldeke,[28] H. Pinkuss,[29] S. P. Brock,[30] and R. Déaut.[31] The chief arguments are: (1) the artificial language of the targum—Jewish Aramaic with many Syriacisms—is best explained by the hypothesis of heavy borrowing from a Syriac exemplar; (2) T's more than one hundred agreements with G, where S = G;[32] (3) T's partial agreement with S *and* partial correcting of S to MT in the same verse.[33]

A minority reject the priority of S but their arguments are not persuasive. A. Kaminka and M. Black argue that no targumist would have chosen a Christian text,[34] but it is quite possible that S Proverbs was written by a Jew. J. F. Healey hypothesizes that "in Tg we have a reworking in the light of the Hebrew of an older Jewish Aramaic or Syriac translation of the book which was also used by the compilers of the Peshiṭtā."[35] Such a hypothesis, however, is unable to explain T's partial correcting of S to MT.

A good example of the Peshitta's reliance on LXX for sense is 21:13. The verse also has the advantage of illustrating T's partial reliance on S and partial correcting back to MT. MT: "The one who blocks his ears from the cry of the poor / will himself call but go unheard." LXX: "Whoever blocks his ears from hearing the weak, / will himself call and there will be none who hearkens." S follows LXX in dropping "cry" and adding the verb "to hear": "The one who blocks his ears so as not to hear the weak. . . ." T retains "to hear" of S but corrects to MT with "the cry of the poor": "The one who blocks his ears so as not to hear the cry of the poor."

---

[28] "Das Targum zu den Sprüchen von der Peschita abhängig," *Archiv für wissenschaftliche Erforschung des Alten Testaments* 2 (1871) 246–49.

[29] "Die Syrische Übersetzung," 113.

[30] *The Anchor Bible Dictionary* (6 vols.; ed. D. N. Freedman; New York: Doubleday, 1992), 6. 794.

[31] *Introduction à la littérature targumique* (Rome: Biblical Institute, 1966) 136–39.

[32] Pinkuss, "Die syrische Übersetzung," 109.

[33] Some examples are 1:12, 20; 2:11, 13, 14, 16; 4:26; 6:2, 25; 10:28; 11:21, 22, 24, 26, 27, 28; 12:10, 14, 25; 13:2, 5, 10, 14, 20, 22; 14:12; 15:2, 6, 7, 9; 17:4, 7; 20:4; 24:33, 34; 26:18–19; 29:14, 16.

[34] Healey, "The Targum of Proverbs" (The Aramaic Bible 15; Collegeville: Liturgical Press, 1991) 3, 9.

[35] "The Targum of Proverbs," 9.

In summary, S translates MT into transparent Syriac using LXX as a help to understand MT. S is valuable as an interpretation and witness of MT, an independent witness of the LXX text, and a critique of the latter's rendering.

The Targum

There is no critical edition of the Proverbs targum and the printed texts leave something to be desired. Critical study requires work with manuscripts. Printed texts include P. de Lagarde's *Hagiographa Chaldaice*[36], the Zamora manuscript published by L. Díez Merino[37], and Walton's London Polyglot of 1675. J. F. Healey's English translation in The Aramaic Bible series uses Lagarde as its base, collating Zamora and Walton and noting disagreements with MT and the versions.[38]

T renders MT in concise Jewish Aramaic mixed with many syriacisms. In the manner of S with MT and LXX, T translates MT with an eye on S. At times, and not simply when MT is difficult, T seems inexplicably to "coast," leaning on S not only for sense but for phraseology, even to the point of incorporating Syriac words and grammatical forms. From his practice of correcting S to MT, it is clear that for T MT is the authoritative text.

The targum to Proverbs is completely lacking in haggadic and midrashic expansions (except for minor ones in 28:14 and 28:1) even in Prov 8:22 where Jewish speculation on wisdom was available. As noted in the previous section, it is the only targum that drew on the Peshitta. Nöldeke in particular has underscored its character as a *Mischsprache* combining Syriac and Jewish Aramaic, e.g., the third-person prefix *y-* and *n-* coexist throughout and in 9:11 occur in the same verse![39] Healey suggests it might be Eastern Aramaic but allows the possibility it is a hybrid from the desk of a scholar.

The function of the Targum to Proverbs is not clear. Targums are unlike the other versions in being read publicly *with* the Hebrew text. In the reading of

---

[36] (Leipzig, 1873 [reprint: Osnabrook: Zeller, 1967]). Lagarde is a transcript of the consonantal text of the first Bomberg Bible of Felix de Prato with a large number of his own emendations.

[37] *Targum de Proverbios. Edición Principe del Ms. Villa-Amil nº 5 de Alfonso de Zamora* (Madrid: Consejo Superior de Investigaciones Cientificas, 1984). Díez-Marino provides an extensive survey of scholarship.

[38] "The Targum of Proverbs." See also E. Z. Melammed, "Targum Mišlê," *Bar Ilan* 9 (1972) 18–91.

[39] "Das Targum."

the Pentateuch, for example, one scriptural verse was read and then its targum. For the reading of the prophets, three scriptural and three targum verses were read in conjunction. It was forbidden to read the targum alone in the synagogue.[40] Proverbs was not part of the synagogue service and thus its targum had no liturgical function. Lack of liturgical status may explain the non-haggadic and non-midrashic character of the Targum to Proverbs.

In conclusion, T is a literal translation of MT, occasionally relying on S for comprehension and for phrasing. It nonetheless gives priority to MT, for it often corrects back to the Hebrew and follows the MT sequence of sections and verses. Its text-critical usefulness lies chiefly in its reading of MT in the light of S and its implicit assessment of the S interpretation. Its function, date,[41] and provenance are unclear.

The Vulgate

Sometime after 387, Jerome revised the Old Latin version of the LXX of Proverbs, but that Latin translation is no longer extant. In 398 he translated Proverbs from the Hebrew into a literarily polished Latin. As was his custom, he took account of the Greek versions and followed them when he considered them superior.[42] He knew the Peshitta but rarely followed it independently.[43] He did not know T. A few Vulgate verses make no sense, e.g., 17:14; 19:25a; 20:26b; 22:6a; 30:33, but his achievement, especially when compared to the other versions, is impressive. Jerome was an extraordinary scholar for his time, proficient in Greek, Latin, Hebrew, and Aramaic, and to some extent in Syriac. He knew the Hebrew text, LXX in its *trifaria varietas,* the Old Latin, and had access to Aquila, Symmachus, and Theodotion through Origen's Hexapla at Caesarea. His writings in fact are a source of Hexaplaric readings.

The text-critical value of the Vulgate is three-fold: (1) Jerome had direct access to important textual witnesses (some no longer extant) and had the training and talent to use them properly; (2) he was heir to ancient interpretive traditions, especially Jewish lore from his rabbi teachers; (3) as an educated man, he was familiar with the genres of Proverbs from the Hebrew

---

[40] Brock, "Translating the Old Testament," 92.

[41] There is no internal or external evidence for the date. Dates from the third century B.C.E. to the eighth century C.E. have been proposed. See Healey, *The Targum of Proverbs,* p. 10.

[42] E.g., 11:2, 8, 13, 15; 14:4, 25; 15:5; 17:1, 3, 4, 11; 18:3, 17, 19; 20:11; 21:6; 31:21.

[43] E.g., 17:26; 20:18b, for LXX is missing; 25:11.

wisdom tradition and the Greek aphorists. Jerome is able time and again to make sense of what the versions mangle. One example out of scores is 14:16: MT: "A wise person fears and turns from evil / but a fool goes right on and is confident." All the versions adopt the LXX metathesis of Hebrew *mit'abbēr*, "to pass by or over," to *mit'arab*, "to get mixed up in," but V renders *transilit*, "to spring over, to pass on," catching the Hebrew perfectly.

The Vulgate is a literal translation of MT with an occasional look at the Greek versions. It reflects early Christian and Jewish interpretations of the turn of the fifth century C.E.

Conclusions

Proverbs has a unique textual history, largely shaped by its genre of epigrams, which are self-contained and invite additions that are usually undetectable. There are about twenty-five verses in MT that are not in LXX but there is no general way of knowing if MT added them. LXX, on the other hand, surely added many in the long course of its transmission, most visibly in its doublets and in chaps. 6 and 9.

All the versions without exception aim to translate MT (or G^V in the case of OG) as accurately as they could. Though cultural factors undoubtedly influenced the translators, one must emphasize that each intended to render the Hebrew *verbum e verbo*. It is possible that some Greek *additions*, especially in chaps. 6 and 9, were intended to support a particular interpretation but the fact remains that the translator aimed to render the Hebrew exactly. Apart from OG, each version translated MT with the help of another version. S used LXX and T used S. Jerome is a watershed in Proverbs translation, for he not only drew on LXX in its several varieties to translate the Hebrew but brought to bear the Hexapla (esp. Symmachus), Old Latin, Syriac, and interpretive traditions some of which would later appear in the targum, the midrash, and in the Masoretic vocalization.

MICHAEL V. FOX

Who Can Learn?
A Dispute in Ancient Pedagogy

The authors of Wisdom Literature were teachers, whether in the school or the home,[1] and as such they gave thought to the means and possibilities of education. This essay examines three ideas on innate learning ability and its relation to learning, as these are expressed in Proverbs and in Egyptian Wisdom Literature. The Egyptian-Israelite comparison is not intended to demonstrate influence or a direct transmission,[2] but to clarify the intellectual context of the pedagogical ideas of Proverbs. At issue is the way the ancient sages defined the scope of god-given (in modern terms, innate) learning

---

[1] The *Sitz im Leben* of Wisdom Literature is a matter of considerable scholarly debate. Professor Murphy surveyed and evaluated some of the theories and added weight to the view that the origin of Wisdom teachings is the family in "Israelite Wisdom and the Home" (*"Où demeures-tu?" (Jn 1,38): La maison depuis le monde biblique* [FS Guy Coutourier; ed. J.-C. Petit; Montreal: Fides, 1994], 199–212).

I agree that the locus of wisdom instruction was usually the home. In any case, the setting in which Wisdom instructions locate *themselves* is paternal instruction, though that does not mean that they are essentially oral or "folk" literature. The family setting was, in certain cases, the actual one. See M. V. Fox, "The Social Location of the Book of Proverbs" (*Texts, Temples, and Traditions: A Tribute to Menahem Haran* [ed. M. V. Fox et al.; Winona Lake, IN: Eisenbrauns, 1996] 227–39).

Modern sages teach both in the classroom and in writing. Though I did not have the privilege of absorbing Roland Murphy's teachings in the university *Sitz*, I have learned much from his extensive written wisdom in the study of both Wisdom Literature and the Song of Songs.

[2] Or to deny it. There is some evidence that some sayings in Proverbs were derived from Anii; see H. Washington, *Wealth and Poverty in the Instruction of Amenemope and the Hebrew Proverbs* (SBLDS 142; Atlanta: Scholars, 1994) 142–45.

capacity. In both traditions, opinions varied as to who is capable of learning and how moral education can best be pursued.

Three views are come to expression in both Wisdom traditions:

(1) Some people cannot learn;
(2) Everyone can be taught, given sufficiently stringent methods; and
(3) Teaching is fundamentally possible and generally effective but requires the right approach.

These three views do not follow in historical progression but emerge at various stages in the history of Wisdom Literature and can coexist in a synchronic dialectic.

I will focus on two passages in which the debate is sharply defined by the clash of diverging viewpoints: Prov 9:7–10 and the epilogue of the Instruction of Anii (22.13–23.17).

I. The Dialectic in Israelite Wisdom

1. Some People Cannot Learn

a. Prov 9:7–10: Prov 9:7–10 is a later addition to the chapter. "Later additions," as Bible scholars have come to realize, are not extraneous accretions to the "real" biblical text but contributions to the growing biblical tradition through a process of exegesis, expansion, and counterstatement. Prov 9:7–10, a self-contained epigram wedged between the speeches of two personifications, Lady Wisdom (9:1–6 + 11) and Lady Folly (9:13–18), is one such counterstatement.

7   He who chastises an impudent man receives insult,
       he who reproves an evildoer gets hurt.
8   Don't reprove an impudent man lest he hate you;
       reprove the wise man and he'll love you.
9   Give (reproof) to the wise, and he'll grow even wiser.
       Instruct the righteous man and he'll enhance his learning.
10 Wisdom begins with the fear of the Lord,
       and understanding—with the knowledge of the Holy One.

b. The Growth of Proverbs 9: The epigram in Prov 9:7–10 responds to its context but is distinct from it. Verse 7 follows awkwardly upon the injunction of v 6 ("Abandon callowness and live; walk in the path of understanding"). It interrupts Lady Wisdom's summons, and it does not serve the purpose of her invitation, which is to convince everyone to join her banquet.

Almost all modern commentators remove vv 7–12 as secondary and regard these verses as a mixed collection.[3] In my view, the original conclusion of Lady Wisdom's speech is v 11 ("for through me your days will increase, and years be added to your life"). This verse provides an appropriate motivation for v 6 ("Abandon callowness and live . . ."), not for v 10 ("Wisdom begins with the fear of the Lord . . ."). Verse 12 too is later, but it stands alone, belonging neither to Lady Wisdom's speech nor to the epigram in vv 7–10. Whereas that passage addresses the question of who is capable of learning, v 12 identifies the recipient of wisdom's benefits, which is a separate issue.

c. Comments on the Epigram: The inserted epigram does not directly repudiate the invitation to the callow (*pty*) and mindless (*ḥsr lb*), but it does sound a cautionary note, as if Lady Wisdom were casting too wide a net in including such people in her summons.

The epigram begins by warning that "he who chastises an impudent man [*lṣ*] receives insult" (7a). The *lṣ*, arrogant and contemptuous of others, cannot tolerate rebukes.[4] He will react with ire and contempt to any affront to his

---

[3] For example, C. H. Toy (*The Book of Proverbs* [ICC; Edinburgh: T. &. T. Clark, 1899 (repr. 1959)], ad loc.) describes 9:7–12 as a "little group of aphorisms" comprising four independent units: vv 7–9, 10, 11, and 12. W. McKane (*Proverbs* [OTL; London: SCM, 1970] 360) believes that vv 7–12 were added to expand the role of Wisdom as a teacher, which is otherwise confined to v 6. A. Meinhold (*Die Sprüche* [Zürcher Bibelkommentare 16; Zurich: Theologischer V., 1991] 155–57) maintains that vv 7–12 is a compound of several sayings appended as a conclusion to the first division of Proverbs, chapters 1–9. These verses, he says, provide a transition to the rest of the book by pointing back to chapter 1 while previewing the following collections. However, no transitional function is evident in 9:7–12. On the contrary, chapter 8 would have served that purpose more effectively, if the first division of Proverbs had ended there.

[4] The *lṣ*, commonly translated "scoffer" or the like, is arrogant and, consequently, scornful. As Yosef ibn Kaspi says (commenting on Prov 1:4), "The *lṣ* is the haughty man; he is wise in his own eyes and so mocks whomever rebukes him" (*ḥṣwṣrwt ksp* [ed. I. Last; Pressburg: Alkalay, 1903 (repr. Jerusalem 1969–70)]). Prov 21:24 defines his character: "The arrogant insolent man [*zd yhyr*]–*lṣ* is his name; he acts in the rage of insolence [*ʿbrt zdwn*]." The essence of *lṣwn* is hybris, a quality which naturally reveals itself in expressions of contempt and derision. I discuss the semantic field of folly in "Words for Folly," forthcoming in *Zeitschrift für Alt-Hebraistik*, 1997.

self-image. Acceptance of criticism requires the wisdom of humility, which is the awareness of one's limitations. The callow and mindless are not necessarily "impudent" (*lṣym*). The epigram intensifies the issue by referring to a more malevolent kind of fool, the arrogant and scornful *lṣ*.

Verse 7b, bringing the *rš'* into the picture, sharpens the danger even further, for an evildoer, a *rš'*, who is guilty in deeds, is worse than a *lṣ*, whose offenses may be confined to thoughts and words. Hence chastening an evildoer may bring upon the rebuker not only verbal but also physical abuse (*m'wm*).[5]

Verse 8 is a transition to the topic of wisdom and the wise in v 9: "Give (reproof)[6] to the wise . . . instruct the righteous man." Teaching must be directed to those who are by nature open to improvement, namely, the wise and righteous. The equation of these two is a peculiarity of Proverbs.[7] In that book, wisdom is a matter of moral character, which is the *sine qua non* of intellectual and personal growth. Such a person will take a rebuke seriously and "enhance his learning" (v 9b), which the prologue designates as one of the book's goals (1:5).

Verse 10 situates the observations of vv 7–9 in a larger conceptual framework. Verses 7–9 speak about chastisement (a frequent topic in Proverbs). Verse 10 broadens the entire passage into a statement on the religious relationship between intellect and moral character.[8]

Verse 10 reiterates the great principle of Prov 1:7, "The fear of the Lord is

---

[5] In 18 of 20 occurrences, *mwm* (= *m'wm*) refers to physical blemish or injury, in animals or man. A *mwm* may be damage caused (*ntn*) by another (Lev 24:19–20). When *mwm* refers to moral blemish (Deut 32:5 and Job 11:15 only), it means *guilt*, which is not something caused by a hostile act of another. Hence in Prov 9:7, *mwm* should be understood as a physical wound, such as a broken tooth (cf. Lev 24:20).

[6] "Give" lacks a direct object in the Hebrew, but a noun such as *twkḥh* "reproof" or *mwsr* "discipline" (R. Moshe Qimḥi) can be inferred from v 8.

[7] While no one would deny that the righteous are wise and that it is wise to be righteous, Proverbs goes farther and assumes that a *ḥkm* (which lexically means smart and knowledgeable but not necessarily virtuous) is ipso facto righteous. See my article "What the Book of Proverbs is About" (section III, §2), forthcoming in VTSup, Congress Volume.

[8] Although v 10 now concludes the epigram, the verse may have originated separately from vv 7–9. If 9:7–10 is read without its present context, v 10 seems abrupt and isolated, for the practical advice in vv 7–9 does not prepare the way for the definition of wisdom in v 10. In the context of Wisdom's summons, however, v 10 converts the entirety of vv 7–10 into a comment on the moral-religious preconditions of education. Thus I surmise that v 10 is a citation of a principle appended to vv 7–9 by the scribe who inserted those verses after 9:6.

the beginning of knowledge." Here the principle provides the rationale for the foregoing counsel: It makes sense only to educate the righteous (9:7–9), because wisdom can grow only on the fertile soil of conscience and piety (v 10). The starting point of education is an awareness of God's will (*d'ct qdwšym*[9]) and the fear of the Lord (*yr't yhwh*), which is a concern for what God wants—or at least a fear of his anger.[10] Intellectual growth issues in a divine grant of wisdom (2:6) and a deeper form of fear of the Lord (2:5). But the goal, wisdom, must be latent in the beginnings, imbedded in the child's untutored attitudes and qualities.

d. The Message of Prov 9:7–10: The inserted epigram reacts to Wisdom's call to naive, mindless people to partake of her repast, that it to say, to learn wisdom. It comments on this invitation not by disputing it so much as by cautioning against the unrealistic expectations it might arouse.[11]

The epigram insists that the proper recipients of wisdom are those who are already "wise," in the sense defined in v 10, namely, those who possess religious awareness and moral conscience. No one is born wise, but some are born with a predisposition to wisdom, and they alone can absorb its teachings.[12]

The author of the epigram does not believe that fools *can* be educated, at least not if their ignorance is rooted in arrogance and vice. The types of fools he refers to are worse than those addressed by Wisdom, as if to say: You might attempt to educate the naive and mindless (though this too is probably a

[9] *qdwšym*, plural in form, is a crux, but probably it is an epithet of God. A comparison with Prov 2:5, in which *yr't yhwh* strictly parallels *d'ct 'lhym*, "knowledge of God," shows the equivalence of *qdwšym* and *'lhym* in this locution. Compare also *'l qdwšym//* in Hos 12:1.

[10] The phrase *d'ct qdwšym*, in synonymous parallelism with "fear of the Lord," designates an attitude or aptitude—religious awareness—rather than cognitive knowledge *about* deity. "Fear of the Lord" is minimally fear of the consequences of disobedience, but it may include a more sophisticated attentiveness to God's will. As such, fear of the Lord is both the starting point and the culmination of wisdom.

[11] Similarly B. Gemser (*Sprüche Salomos* [HAT 1/16; 2d ed.; Tübingen: Mohr, 1963]) and H. Ringgren (*Sprüche* [ATD 16; Göttingen: Vandenhoeck & Ruprecht, 1962]).

[12] This predisposition would probably be called *ḥkmt lb* and its possessor designated a *ḥkm lb*. God puts wisdom in the heart of all who are "wise of heart" (Exod 31:6). A woman can be "wise of heart in her hands" (Exod 35:25), meaning that she has talent (not knowledge) in her hands. One who is "wise of heart" can absorb the precepts (Prov 10:8). According to Prov 16:21, one who has this endowment will come to be called a *nbwn*, "an understanding man," a status that presumes learning and experience.

hopeless task), but if you go further and try to straighten out a *lṣ* or (even worse) a *ršᶜ*—the very ones who most need correction—you will only bring harm upon yourself.

e. *Elsewhere in Proverbs:* The epigram agrees with a number of proverbs (Prov 13:1b; 15:5a, 12; 23:9; 27:22) that insist on the futility of reprimanding or otherwise attempting to educate fools, in particular the *lṣ*, who is impudent, and the *ʾwyl*, who is morally perverted.[13] Ben Sira shares the sentiment: "Teaching a fool is like gluing a broken pot" (Sir 22:9).

Prov 19:25 grants that the *pty* can learn from the beating the *lṣ* receives, but it allows no hope for the *lṣ* himself: "Smite an impudent boy (*lṣ*)[14] and the callow (*pty*) will gain cunning. Rebuke an astute man, and he will gain knowledge" (similarly 21:11). In other words, if you smite an impudent lad, not he but others—*even* the callow naïf—will get the point. But you need merely scold the wise person and he will learn better.

According to Prov 14:6, even if an impudent man seeks wisdom, he cannot acquire it. (*ḥkmh* in this case means *learning*, since one who desired moral-religious sagacity could not be impudent and cynical, whereas even such a one as this might wish for the trappings and privileges of learning.) The *ksyl* too cannot acquire learning, even if he is willing to pay for it, because he lacks "heart"—that is, intelligence (17:16).

The practical purpose of the sayings that assert the ineducability of fools is to admonish the reader against the folly of resisting chastisement, but in so doing, they imply a psychological principle: some people are beyond redemption.

Proverbs divides the world into two categories, but it does so along three different axes. One dichotomy contrasts the wise and the foolish. A second (probably a later stratum) contrasts the righteous and the wicked and applies to this dichotomy much that is said about the first pair.[15] The third major

---

[13] An *ʾwyl* is not inevitably stupid, but he is morally obtuse. A number of verses show this. For example, in Isa 19:11, the princes of Zoan are called both *ḥkmym* (that is, "expert") and *ʾwylym*, because, however erudite and clever they may be, they are blind to God's plans (vv 12–15).

[14] *lṣ*, like most terms for the wise and the foolish, is indifferent as to age. But when it comes to smiting one, a translation "boy" is called for, rather than "man," which would imply a street brawl. For the most part, the teachings of Proverbs are directed to youths perched between adolescence and adulthood.

[15] Wickedness and folly are not exactly equated, for the fool may not yet have slid into active sin. But wickedness and folly have much the same symptoms and effects and are for practical

dichotomy places the fault line between the teachable and the obtuse. The teachable may not yet be wise, but they *can* progress in learning. Ingrained fools are incapable of learning. The exception is the *pty*. In his present condition, he is foolish and empty-headed (Prov 7:7), but he is still malleable and *can* learn (1:4; 19:25; etc.). There may be marginal hope for the mindless and the ignoramus (*b'r*) too. Other types of fools are blind to moral demands and are almost never addressed. There is no expectation that they can repent and change their ways.

2. *Everyone* Can *be Taught*

In the personification interludes (1:20–33; 8:1–36; 9:1–6, 11, 13–18), Wisdom summons fools as well as the wise. In 8:5, she urges both the callow and dull-minded (*pt'ym* and *ksylym*) to "get smart" (*hbynw lb, hbynw 'rmh*). In 1:22 she addresses not just the callow, but also the impudent and the dull-minded (*lsym* and *ksylym*). In 1:22, she addresses them in order to excoriate them, but in 1:24 we learn that she had earlier appealed to them to repent.[16]

Wisdom's calls to the foolish (1:22; 8:5; 9:4) are not necessarily a theoretical assertion of the educability of such types. When Wisdom speaks in 1:22, she already knows that the fools have ignored her call. Nevertheless, in 8:5 the callow and the dull-minded, and in 9:4 the callow and the mindless, are being invited to learn wisdom. The call to the callow is not problematic, because the *pty* is defined as the primary audience of the book in 1:4; the mindless are similar. As for the pernicious sorts of fools—the *lsym* (1:22) and the *ksylym* (8:5)—the author may believe that the wise has a duty to urge them to repent and gain wisdom, just as the prophets preached to the wicked with little expectation of success.

No saying in Proverbs asserts programmatically that everybody can learn, but Prov 22:15 declares confidence in the efficacy of beatings to purge a lad of folly: "Folly [*'wlt*] is bound to the heart of a lad, but the rod of discipline will

---

purposes identified. Though the *ksyl* is not inevitably or inherently wicked, his smug and loutish nature closes him to reason and impels him to sin (10:23; 13:19). The *b'r*, animal-like in his ignorance, is impervious to the insights of chastisement and thus one step away from moral debasement (Prov 12:1; but Agur [30:2] would disagree).

[16] Earlier, that is, in mythic time. In linear time, Wisdom is "always" calling on fools to repent and "always" being rebuffed.

remove it from him." A young person starts with a measure of folly, though he is not necessarily a dyed-in-the-wool fool, an *ʾwyl* whose perversity is probably indelible.[17]

3. Teaching Requires the Right Approach

Even for the educable, the path to wisdom is a difficult one. The learner, after all, does not really know the benefits of what he is supposed to strive for, and he cannot even be certain of attaining the goal. Proverbs 2 encourages the learner in this task. This chapter goes beyond the all-or-none dichotomy. Without disputing either side, it examines how the difficult process of moral education can succeed.

Education, it says, begins with the father's teaching and its rote incorporation by the child (2:1–2), but this must be complemented by the learner's own thought and inquiry—"calling," "digging," and "seeking" (vv 3–4). *Then* God steps into the picture and grants wisdom (v 6)—not the words or propositions of wisdom teaching, but the faculty of wisdom, realized as moral character. But this is a long process, and its endpoint is not evident to the neophyte. Proverbs 2 assures the pupil that if he seeks wisdom earnestly he will surely find it. In this way, the teacher and God collaborate with the youngster himself in the shaping of moral character, which will provide sure guidance and protection throughout his life.[18]

II. The Dialectic in Egyptian Wisdom

The dispute about the possibilities of learning emerged first among Egyptian sages, in a dialogue extending through many centuries. This dispute has invariably been construed as the clash between determinism and free will—the "nature or nurture" debate[19]—but the argument is more nuanced than

---

[17] As a constitutional character trait, *ʾwlt* is persistent and irremediable in an *ʾwyl* (Prov 27:22). Others, however, may suffer from a measure of *ʾwlt* periodically. A psalmist confesses to his *ʾwlt* (Ps 69:6), which a true *ʾwyl* would not do.

[18] See M. V. Fox, "The Pedagogy of Proverbs 2," *JBL* 113 (1994) 233–43.

[19] The standard study of the issues discussed here is H. Brunner's *Altägyptische Erziehung* (Wiesbaden: Harrassowitz, 1957), esp. pp. 112–16: "Das Bewusstsein von Möglichkeiten und Grenzen der Erziehung." See also idem, "Die menschliche Willensfreiheit und ihre Grenzen in ägyptischen Lebenslehren," *Biblische und ausserbiblische Spruchweisheit*" (ed. H. J. Klimkeit;

that. There are three viewpoints, and although one of them can be called "deterministic," this is not meant as a philosophical or theoretical category but as a label for the implications of the attitude in question.

The clash between views 1 and 2 in Egyptian Wisdom is well recognized, but the place of view 3 has been overlooked. The third view emerges most clearly in the epilogue of Anii. and is a profound innovation in pedagogical thought.

1. Some People Cannot Learn

Some Egyptian sages believed that obtuseness is innate and indelible. This belief was born not of theory or a deterministic philosophy, but of a teacher's frustration at the impenetrability of some pupils, who may be intellectually capable of improving but refuse to do so.[20] This frustration is revealed in the exclamation of the teacher of the New Kingdom Pap. Lansing,[21] stymied by his inability to force his pupil to learn: "If only I knew another way of doing it! Then I would do it for you and you would listen" (2.8). But he cannot think of one.

The most elaborate exposition of the deterministic viewpoint is in the Instruction of Ptahhotep, from the Old or Middle Kingdom,[22] mainly in the conclusion (lines 534–607). Ptahhotep contrasts two types of people: those who listen and those who do not. "Listening" or "hearing" is the precondition and means of moral growth. Ptahhotep's purpose is to encourage the reader to be a "listener," but in doing so, he reveals his assumption that this crucial faculty must be infused in an individual's character at birth:[23] "He whom god hates does not listen" (line 546). The morally deaf man, Ptahhotep says earlier, has a congenital inability or "impediment" (*sḏb*): The hateful son is "one for whom an impediment was assigned (already) in the womb"

Wiesbaden: Harrassowitz, 1991) 35–36. Similarly J. F. Quack, *Die Lehren des Ani* (OBO 141; Göttingen: Vandenhoeck & Ruprecht, 1994) 186–93, though he translates the passage quite differently.

[20] Brunner, "Willensfreiheit," 32–33.

[21] A. H. Gardiner, *Late-Egyptian Miscellanies* (Bibliotheca Aegyptiaca 7; Brussels: La Fondation Egyptologique, 1937) 101–2.

[22] Ž. Zába, *Les Maximes de Ptahhotep* (Prague: Editions de l'Académie Tchécoslovaque des Sciences, 1956).

[23] The predetermination of character is discussed by S. Morenz, *Untersuchungen zur Rolle des Schicksals in der ägyptischen Religion* (Abhandlungen des Sächsischen Akademie des Wissenschaft zu Leipzig, Philologisch-historische Klasse 52/1; Berlin: Akademie, 1960) 8–9.

(line 217). (A later manuscript [L₂] reformulates this as "one into whom God has driven an impediment [already] in the womb"). The handicap is virtually physical: "It is the heart [the mentality, we might say] that makes its possessor into a listener or a non-listener" (lines 550–51). Within the "hearing" group, there is still much scope for wisdom and ignorance, but nothing can be done for the congenitally obtuse man other than to reject him—as the gods manifestly have done—and make him into a virtual slave, whose every action is commanded by others (lines 206–19).

About a millennium later, O. Petrie 11 echoed this opinion: "Do not straighten out what is crooked; then you will be loved [compare Prov 9:8b!]. Every man is compelled [lit., "dragged"] by his character just as by his limbs" (rto. 4).[24]

In Pap. Lansing, a teacher castigates his pupil for his refusal to listen and for his dull heart. Even animals, the writer says, can learn, but "even if I beat you with a stick of whatever kind, you do not listen" (2.4–3.3). The rod *should* be effective in enforcing education, so when it fails to do so, one looks for an explanation in prior disposition.

This view comes to clear expression in Pap. Beatty IV (New Kingdom), which quotes it so as to repudiate it:

> Beware of saying,
> "Every man is in accordance with his character,
> The ignorant and the wise are the same thing.
> Shay and Renenet[25] are engraved on one's character
>   with the writing of God himself.
> Every man is as he is made,
> and his lifetime is (run) within an hour" (vso. 6.5ff.).

The belief that character is predetermined was maintained into Hellenistic times. Pap. Insinger urges the reader to persist in instructing his son, yet recognizes that "It is the god who gives the heart, gives the son, and gives the good character. The fate and the fortune that come, it is the god who determines them" (9.19 f.)[26] From the same period, Anchsheshonq (in language

---

[24] J. Černý and A. H. Gardiner, *Hieratic Ostraca* (Oxford: Oxford University, 1957), pl. I, rto.

[25] The gods who determine an individual's destiny.

[26] M. Lichtheim, *Late Egyptian Wisdom Literature* (OBO 52; Göttingen: Vandenhoeck &

strongly resembling Prov 9:8) warns: "Do not instruct a fool, lest he hate you. Do not instruct him who will not listen to you" (7.4–5).[27]

The epigram in Prov 9:7–10 and the other proverbs mentioned above (§I.1.e) express similar pessimism (or realism) about the universal malleability of character.

2. *Everyone* Can *be Taught*

One way of conceiving of education is as the imposition of the teacher's will on the student, a process epitomized in images of forcing and bending. The practical motive for this view is to rebut a pupil's excuse that he *cannot* learn, that the task is beyond him. Model letters addressed to students and copied in the schools dismiss this rationalization, using, among other arguments, the cliché that even animals can be trained: "Pay attention and listen to what I have said, that it may be of use to you. Apes can be taught to dance; horses can be tamed; a kite can be put in a nest; a falcon can be pinioned. Persevere in seeking advice and do not weary of it" (Pap. Anastasi III, 4.1–4[28]; cf. Pap. Sallier I, 7.1–8.2[29] and Pap. Bologna 1094, 3.9–10[30]).

The author of Pap. Beatty IV (quoted above) rejects the view that one's character is fixed at birth and that his life is too short to allow significant change. But this author does not assume that the cure for sluggish learning is simply greater rigor in the teaching. Rather:

> Instruction is good, without (the pupil) wearying of it,
> (and then) a son will speak out
> with the saying of his father (vso. 6.7–8).[31]

This sentence has some ambiguity, but I take it to mean that instruction is good and pleasant and does not require the pupil to weary himself. When it succeeds, the son can respond in conformity to what he was taught—unlike Anii's son, described below.

Ruprecht, 1983) 206. Lichtheim shows that Western Asian influence on Egyptian Wisdom is likely in the Hellenistic period, and this saying in Anchsheshonq seems to be one such case.

[27] Ibid., 72.

[28] *Late Egyptian Miscellanies,* 24.

[29] Ibid., 85.

[30] Ibid., 3–4.

[31] The relation between the two clauses is ambivalent. It may be: "... *when* a son answers..." or "... let a son answer...."

The issue of predetermination of character is not raised in Proverbs, but the background assumption, described above (§I.1), is that certain types of people are impervious to instruction.

3. Teaching Requires the Right Approach

One Egyptian thinker rejected the pessimism implicit in the belief that learning ability is predetermined. Rather than asserting that the teacher's mold can be forcibly impressed on the pupil's raw material (view 2), he holds that gentler methods alone can influence him (view 3). This view emerges in the epilogue of the New Kingdom Instruction of Anii (22.13–23.17), in a lengthy debate between view 2, represented by Anii, and view 3, advocated by Anii's son Khonsuhotep, the recipient of the instruction.[32]

The epilogue is probably a later addition to Anii's instruction. First of all, it differs from the epilogues of other Wisdom instructions by recording a debate of principle rather than reporting the reception and transmission of the instruction. Moreover, the scribe of the instruction proper (Anii) would not compose a dialogue in which he himself was effectively challenged and possibly bested, or at least not decisively victorious. Since Wisdom instructions were sometimes transmitted within the family,[33] the epilogue may have been appended by Khonsuhotep himself to express his own ideas on learning and teaching. He does seem to get the better of the argument.

Khonsuhotep protests that Anii's teachings are too difficult for him to master. He quotes the proverb, "Every man is compelled by his personality [*inw*, lit., "complexion"]" (22.14f.).[34] Anii assumes that Khonsuhotep is reiterating the deterministic axiom that one who lacks the right predisposition *cannot* learn (= view 1), and he disputes this by insisting that education can indeed be imposed on anyone, for the teacher's willpower can subdue inborn refractoriness (= view 2). But Anii has not heard his son correctly and does not understand what he is really saying. The dispute proceeds through four exchanges of opinion.

Though sounding deterministic at first hearing, Khonsuhotep in fact believes that everyone *can* learn. At issue is method, not metaphysics. As the

[32] Text in Quack, *Ani* (above, n. 19). References are to Pap. Boulacq IV.

[33] See Ptahhotep lines 30–32, 590–96; Duachety (§ XXXg; Pap. Sallier II, 11.4); and the ending of Kagemeni, in which the old vizier gives his teaching in writing to his children.

[34] Or, "toward [*r*] his personality," that is, "after it," as if on a rope.

means of overcoming barriers to learning, Khonsuhotep advocates pleasant-
ness and moderation in teaching rather than mere pressure to memorize and
recite, for the ability to iterate the teachings does not assure their performance: "A youth does not carry out the ethical instructions [*sbȝyt mtrt*] (if)
books have (merely) appeared upon his tongue" (22.17). The books must also
be *received* (*šsp* = Hebrew *lqḥ*) in the heart, to which end they must be delivered pleasantly and in right measure (22.16).

Anii replies by reiterating the tiresome commonplace that everyone can be
compelled to learn: Education "conquers" character: Wild animals can be
tamed, dogs and geese trained, foreigners taught Egyptian (22.17–23.7).

Khonsuhotep's reply (23.7–11) is an extraordinary move in the history of
educational thought:[35]

> (7) Do not make your strength overbearing. (8)
> I am wronged by your arguments.[36]
> Has there never arisen a man who relaxed his arm,
> so as to hear an appropriate response?
> Men are the likenesses [*snw*] (9) of God:
> their practice is to hear a man with his statement.[37]
> It is not the wise man alone who is his (God's) likeness,[38]

---

[35] There are a number of uncertainties and textual corruptions in this passage and the translations differ. Quack's rendering (*Ani*, 123–27) differs from the above in several respects. He
translates *sn* as "Gefährte" rather than "image" (of God).

The present translation assumes the emendation of *ˤš* to *nˤš* in line 7 and *ḏˤd* to *wˤd* in line 11
(for which see Quack, ibid.), and implicitly supplies some determinatives. Some pronouns have
been replaced by their referents in translation.

[36] *sḥrw*; apparently referring to Anii's comparison of Khonsuhotep to animals and foreigners.

[37] *ḥr wšbt.f*, "with his statement," or "response," or perhaps "charge." Man is godlike when
he listens patiently to another person, in particular a pupil, who has something to say. The verb
wšb usually means "answer, response" but, like Hebrew *ˤnh* sometimes means "speak up"—
responding not to a question but to a statement or situation (cf. Job 3:2). Khonsuhotep has himself in mind in the first instance. His statements, as well as his father's, are introduced by *wšb*,
"responded."

Learning to give the right "response" is a goal of Wisdom instruction. Anii teaches that
excelling in one's "responses" protects him from punishments (15.8f.), and that one should
choose the right "response" from the ones stored in his belly (20.10). P. Beatty IV says, "Instruction is good, without wearying of it, (and then) a son responds (or "speaks out," *wšb*) with the
saying of his father" (vso. 6.7–8). Good "responses" are often praised elsewhere.

[38] *sn* means "likeness" or "second," not (physical) "image." ("Gefährte," as Quack prefers to

while the masses have all become cattle.[39]
It is not the wise (man) alone (10) whom (God) teaches,
so that only one man becomes a possessor of a heart,
while all the multitude are stupid.
All you say is excellent indeed. (11)
It is judged (so?) by the spirit (?).
Say to the God who gave you understanding:
"Set them (sc., my children) upon your path" (23.7–11).

The old analogy of animal training fails, Khonsuhotep says, because to teach is to be like God[40] and it is godly to listen before answering. Thus not only should a son listen to his father, as all the sages said, but *a father should listen to his son.* Moreover, it is not only the elite who are able to learn. The mass of men can do so, given the right approach, for the real teacher of all is God. So, Khonsuhotep urges his father, give instruction in gentle, moderate words, and ask God for help in setting your children on the right path.

Anii, unmoved, comes back with another analogy: straight sticks can be bent into an axle (23.14).[41] Why, then, does Khonsuhotep resist? "Do you desire to comprehend,[42] or are you corrupt?" (23.15).

Khonsuhotep answers:

> "See," he said, "(you) [God's] likeness,[43]
> wise man with strong arm:

---

translate *sn,* places man and God too much the same plane.) Humans are God's *snw* by virtue of resembling him, in particular in the possession of reason (B. Ockinga, *Die Gottebenbildlichkeit im alten Ägypten und im Alten Testament* [Ägypten und Altes Testament; Wiesbaden: Harrassowitz, 1984] 139). Khonsuhotep relates wisdom to divinity when he calls his father *pʾy.f mitt pʾ rḫ tnr m ḏrt.f,* "[God's] semblance, wise man strong of arm" (23.15f.; ibid., 87f.).

[39] Quack (*Ani,* 123) reads this as an affirmative: "Der eine entsteht mit einem hervorragenden Verstand, / Während die grosse Masse töricht ist." But Anii elsewhere uses *nn* as a negative, not as a writing for *in.* Quack understands Khonsuhotep as a rigid determinist who says that for most people it is *impossible* to grasp another's teaching. This reverses Khosuhotep's intention and makes little sense of the analogy to God as the *listener* par excellence. Also, if man is God's likeness, why would the majority of humans be considered brutish?

[40] See also 23.11, quoted below.

[41] See Quack, *Ani,* 125.

[42] *ʿrq* basically refers to full proficiency in some area. N. Shupak (*Where Can Wisdom Be Found?* [OBO 130; Göttingen: Vandenhoeck & Ruprecht, 1993] 62–63) understands *ʿrq* as "mastery" or "full knowledge," gained either by study or (cf. Anii 23.11) divine gift.

[43] *mitt,* a synonym of *sn,* is used.

The infant who is in his mother's bosom (16),
his desire is to suck" (23.15f.)

Of course he wishes to learn—even an infant in arms craves what nourishes him.[44] The desire to learn is innate; the question is how to stimulate and satisfy it.

The final sentence reads:

"Look," said he, "when [the child] finds his mouth [= learns how to
    speak],
what he says is, 'Give me food'" (23.16f.).

It is probably Anii speaking here, since there is a new *verbum dicendi* (though indefinite), and the preceding sentence, though it too lacks specification of speaker, is clearly Khonsuhotep's. If so, Anii has in the end been persuaded, though he might be understood as saying that Khonsuhotep should use his mouth to ask for intellectual nutrition rather than complaining that he cannot digest it.

Throughout the epilogue, Anii's response to his son's modest demurral sounds harsh, but in fact Anii is insisting on a democratic notion, that all are educable, no one is beyond hope. The contrary opinion, which insisted that only those endowed with the right character can learn, is, in fact, the more pessimistic.

Khonsuhotep takes a new tack, denying that learning can be *imposed*, but not because character is predetermined and unalterable. Rather, pushing the pupil too hard is self-defeating. Better to respond to the innate desire to learn and to choose methods that nurture it.

The author of Proverbs 2 saw the learning process in much the same way as Khonsuhotep: the combined efforts of parent, child, and God bring one to wisdom. Education commences with the father's teaching and its rote incor-

---

[44]Quack (*Ani*, 193) understands this to mean that the teaching is *inappropriate* to an infant interested only in his mother's milk. Hence, by analogy, it is too hard for Khonsuhotep himself. But it would not be reasonable for Khosuhotep, who is at least an adolescent, to compare himself to a baby who is oblivious to wisdom. Khonsuhotep never says that he lacks a desire to learn, but only that he finds it impossible to do so under the present conditions. The sentence must mean that just as a babe desires nutrition, so anyone (Khonsuhotep, in this context) naturally craves (intellectual) nutrition.

poration by the child, but this must be complemented by the learner's own thought and inquiry. *Then* God steps into the picture and grants wisdom.

The similarity in the formulation of the three viewpoints in Egypt and Israel is not sufficient to show a direct or genetic connection. It does, however, present a significant analogy: both Wisdom traditions deliberated on and debated basic questions of the potentials and processes of education. There was, and could be, no simple resolution of the dispute in ancient Wisdom, nor is there one today.

Wisdom Theology and Social History in Proverbs 1–9[1]

Introduction: The Date of the Collection

Old Testament theology has traveled many paths since the end of the late eighteenth century when Johannes Gabler gave his famous inaugural lecture in 1787 at the University of Altdorf.[2] In more contemporary times, approaches have varied from salvation history issuing from positivistic history and a rather naive view of archaeology as confirming biblical narrative or at least provided a context for understanding the Bible, to salvation history as the history of traditions, to narrative theology and close readings, to feminist and third world liberation theology, to the Old Testament as canon, and to Old Testament theology as the ideology of social groups vying for wealth, power, and/or status.[3] In a recent volume, I suggest that the extended family provided the major categories and conceptualities for understanding God, the world, Israel, humanity, the nations, and social ethics.[4] My first point, then, is and continues to be that theology eventually emerges out of the social

---

[1] This essay is dedicated to Professor Roland Murphy whose elegance of speech, keen mind, depth of knowledge, and personal warmth have embodied for so many of us the most noble traits of the sages whose literature he has spent a lifetime interpreting.

[2] For the text, see O. Merk, *Biblische Theologie des Neuen Testaments in ihrer Anfangszeit* (Marburger Theologische Studien 9; Marburg: Elwert, 1972) 273–84.

[3] L. G. Perdue, *The Collapse of History* (OBT; Minneapolis: Fortress, 1994).

[4] L. G. Perdue, C. Meyers, J. Blenkinsopp, and J. Collins, *Families in Ancient Israel* (Louisville: Westminster/John Knox, 1997). See especially chapter 5.

life of ancient Israel and then, once conceived while constantly evolving, tends to exert a formative influence on the same social institutions that gave it birth. My second point is this: theology should not be construed as ideology, for the first is self-transcendent, i.e., it requires even demands that the interests of the group, and even more important, the demands of Transcendence take precedence over self-interest. Indeed Transcendence even becomes a critical force in challenging and at times negating both self-interest and group interest. Ideology, in its basest of understandings, is radically geared to the philosophy of self or group promotion.

This said, the following essay is an initial attempt to provide a sociohistorical setting to Proverbs 1–9 in general and to the Prologue (1:1–7) and first speech of Woman Wisdom in 1:20–33 as examples. I suggest that too long we have allowed the various sapiential forms in Proverbs to exist as pithy sayings that have no concrete basis in Israelite social life. As a result, the book is perhaps the most ignored and unengaging in all of Scripture, with the exception of the poems on or by Woman Wisdom in chapters 1, 8, and 9. Any attempt to provide some social and historical background to Proverbs is fraught with peril. The few scattered references to historical data are themselves ambiguous, while concrete mentionings are absent from most of the collections. Yet there are intriguing hints that perhaps are suggestive of the churning and turmoil of Israelite social history. With these caveats duly mentioned, let us turn to the "Proverbs of Solomon, Son of David, king of Israel."

Proverbs 1–9 is the most elegantly composed and theologically astute of the collections in the Book of Proverbs. Many of the lengthy instructions and most of the didactic poems in the Book of Proverbs are assembled and arranged here. Conventional scholarly wisdom has concluded that the first collection is not only the latest redactional compilation in Proverbs, but also consists of various materials largely deriving from the early post-exilic or Persian period.[5] This proposal is based on several hypotheses. First of all, in the variety of wisdom's literary forms, brief sayings incorporating human obser-

---

[5] For example, see Roland Murphy, *The Tree of Life: An Exploration of Biblical Wisdom* (Anchor Bible Reference Library; New York: Doubleday, 1990) 19. Professor Murphy has written many other pieces on Proverbs in general and this collection in particular. Among his most insightful writings on this first collection are "The Kerygma of the Book of Proverbs," *Int* 20 (1966) 3–14; "Wisdom and Creation," *JBL* 104 (1985) 3–11; and "Proverbs and Theological Exegesis," *The Hermeneutical Quest* (ed. D. G. Miller; Allison Park: Pickwick, 1986) 87–95. For a detailed study of wisdom theology, see my *Wisdom and Creation: The Theology of Wisdom Literature* (Nashville: Abingdon, 1994).

vations suggest a more archaic genre than do lengthy instructions and didactic poems that require greater intellectual and literary sophistication. Second, the detailed theologizing and nationalizing of wisdom leading to its incorporation of the definitive religious traditions of Israel (e.g., the exodus from Egypt, the law and covenant at Sinai, and the dwelling place of Yahweh in the temple at Jerusalem) are not evidenced in the sapiential corpus until Ben Sira in the early second century B.C.E. The climate for the sages' strong impetus towards theological and religious wisdom may have been provided by the dramatic turn of events and challenging circumstances of the early Persian period. Third, the personification of wisdom occurs elsewhere in sapiential literature in the Persian and Hellenistic periods (cf. Job 28; Sirach 24; and Wisdom 6–9). Fourth, the closest literary parallels to the Book of Proverbs are found in literature from the late sixth and fifth centuries B.C.E. These include Deuteronomic, Deuteronomistic, and late prophetic literature (cf. Jeremiah, Deuteronomy, Second Isaiah, and Malachi).[6] Finally, the absence of the legitimation of wisdom by reference to the Torah suggests that the latter had yet to achieve its central position in Jewish piety that originated especially with Ezra in the fourth century B.C.E. The dating of the materials and redaction of Proverbs 1–9 in the early Persian period (late sixth and fifth centuries B.C.E.) appears to be the most plausible possibility from the very limited evidence we possess. The interpretation that follows, then, understands this initial collection as deriving from sages working in early post-exilic Yehud, a colony in the Persian empire for a period of just over two centuries (538–332 B.C.E.).

The Sages in the Persian Period:
The Emergence of Religious and Social Parties

Post-exilic Judah and second-temple Judaism did not represent a homogenous society and unified religion.[7] Geographically, major Jewish communities developed not only in Judah, but also in various regions of the Diaspora,

---

[6] A. Robert, "Les attaches littéraires biblique de Prov. I–IX," *RB* 44 (1935) 44–65; and S. L. Harris, *Proverbs 1–9: A Study of Inner-Biblical Interpretation* (Alpharetta, GA: Scholars, 1996). Harris also argues that the Joseph Story is a source used by the sages who wrote Proverbs 1–9.

[7] For historical and social overviews of the Persian period, see J. L. Berquist, *Judaism in Persia's Shadow* (Minneapolis: Fortress, 1995).

including in particular Egypt and Babylon. In Judah, the major challenge was to reshape in vital and effective ways the restored Jewish community's social institutions and religious expressions in view of the political, economic, and religious collapse occasioned by the Babylonian exile and captivity (586–539 B.C.E.) and the new opportunities and constraints presented by the later inclusion in the expanding Persian empire. However, this challenge was met in many, often conflictive ways.

In the colony of Yehud, where times were hard during Persian rule, significant tension developed between the indigenous population who remained during the Babylonian exile and the Jewish exiles who, leaving Babylon, returned to Judah and sought to reclaim and then rebuild the country as a Persian colony. The returnees eventually were to prevail in this struggle to shape the identity of the Jewish community largely because they enjoyed the support of the Persian authorities, but competing factions and dissension continued throughout the post-exilic period.

The Persian authorities maintained political control over the colony of Yehud and prompted peaceful stability through the appointment of governing officials who carried out Persian policy by the combined means of loyalty to the ruling Achaeminian family, the collection and payment of taxes to the empire, and the creation of local social and economic stability. Persian authorities also allowed the colony to shape its own social and religious institutions with their own values and beliefs as long as the empire's political control and interests were duly acknowledged and supported. Temples like the one that was rebuilt in Jerusalem provided not only ideological legitimation of Persian rule and the colony status of the province, but also made significant economic contributions to the empire through the collection of taxes, tithes, and offerings. Persian support for the rebuilding of the temple was not an expression of religious tolerance, but rather a means by which local stability, the collection of resources, and social construction could be achieved in the interests of the empire. If tolerance and local support did not materialize, the Persian rulers could and would resort to more brutal means to achieve their ends, as they did in some of their other colonies.[8]

The great majority of Jews living in post-exilic Judah, whether returnees or indigenous natives, did not belong to any of the major political and religious

---

[8] See the *Cambridge History of Judaism* 1 (ed. W. D. Davies and L. Finkelstein; Cambridge: Cambridge University, 1984).

movements, though their lives and fortunes were shaped by them. These unnamed Jews carried on their lives largely within the social contexts of extended families that comprised the village clans of rural life.[9] However, Jewish leaders, including intellectuals we commonly call the sages, formed competing groups that contended for influence and power, socially and religiously, in the colony of Yehud during the Persian period.

While significant religious, political, and social diversity developed among the Jews in Judah during the post-exilic period, one may identify on the whole two major social and religious movements that formed, strove to increase their power and influence, and finally separated into opposing, even hostile camps.[10] The first and eventually more powerful, politically and religiously speaking, of the two was the hierocratic party of Zadokite priests who were aligned with Persian appointed governors, centrist prophets, and traditional sages. The social groups who comprised the hierocratic party, at least in the early years of the return, were largely immigrants from Babylonian captivity. The other movement consisted of the "visionaries" that included early apocalypticists, peripheral prophets, and critical sages. While some of the leaders of the visionaries originally came from Babylonian captivity, they were not among the prominent exiles. They were among the marginalized in Babylon and in Yehud following the return.

Both movements relied upon Second Isaiah's (Isaiah 40–55) vision of restoration and new creation as the future to be realized. Second Isaiah clearly pointed to Cyrus, the Persian emperor conquering the Babylonian empire, as the "anointed one" (messiah) who was establishing a new political order under the direction of Yahweh, the one true God who created and continues to direct the course of the world, and not one of the false idols worshipped by pagan nations. This prophet of the exile saw the expanding Persian empire as the opportunity for the deportees to reestablish themselves as the leaders of a restored Jewish community in Jerusalem. However, the pressing question was whether this vision was realized by the early restoration in Judah or was yet to be realized sometime in the future.

---

[9] See L. G. Perdue, et al., *Families in Ancient Israel* (Louisville: Westminster/John Knox, 1997). For the second temple period, see the essay in this volume by J. Collins.

[10] P. Hanson, *The Dawn of Apocalyptic* (Philadelphia: Fortress, 1975). While reductionistic, Hanson's bifurcation of Jewish parties into two major, contending groups is a useful heuristic tool in unpacking the significant expressions of Judaism in the Persian period.

[11] Hanson, *The Dawn of Apocalyptic,* 310–14.

The Hierocratic Party

The important religious and social features of the hierocracy that shaped the major contours of second temple Judaism initially focused on Second Isaiah's vision of a transformation of creation and culture, initiated by the conquest of Babylon by Cyrus, the "messiah" appointed by Yahweh. The absence of the former ruling house of David in this vision of the future allowed people to rethink the role of governmental leadership in the restored community. Early messianic hopes seem to have been pinned on descendants of the house of David (see 1 and 2 Chronicles, Haggai, and the early redaction of Zechariah 1–8). This is possible for Sheshbazzar and likely for Zerubbabel (Hag 2:20–23), who appear to have been the first two Persian appointed governors to preside over the colonial province of Judah. However, after early messianic expectations concerning a descendant of the house of David did not materialize, many in the hierocratic movement moved away from hopes of restoring the Davidic monarchy and allied themselves with Persian appointed Jewish governors even without royal connections. Central to the hierocratic vision was the emphasis placed on establishing and maintaining cosmic, social, and religious order through the Torah, the central focus on Jerusalem as the sacred city of Yahweh, the ritual of the temple cult that theologically was understood as legitimating and sustaining creation and society as well as projecting an ordered and harmonious world yet to be realized,[12] creation theology and providence, and the moral life centered in the ethical and judicial principle of retributive justice (see Ezra, Nehemiah, and the Priestly Code in the Torah).[13]

The significant elements of the ideology of this hierocratic group, led by exiled Jerusalem priests (Aaronides and Zadokites), the descendants of the old royal house of David and other governmental officials of the former state, and centrist prophets (esp. Haggai, Zechariah 1–8)[14] included several related

---

[12] See J. Levenson, *Creation and the Persistence of Evil* (San Francisco: Harper & Row, 1988); and F. Gorman, *The Ideology of Ritual: Space, Time, and Status in Priestly Theology* (JSOTSup 91; Sheffield: JSOT, 1990).

[13] For detailed studies of priests and Levites, see A. H. J. Gunneweg, *Leviten und Priester* (FRLANT 89; Göttingen: Vandenhoeck & Ruprecht, 1965); and A. Cody, *A History of Old Testament Priesthood* (AnBib 35; Rome: Pontifical Biblical Institute, 1969). A detailed summary with a substantial bibliography is found in H. D. Preuss, *Old Testament Theology* 2 (OTL; Louisville: Westminster/John Knox, 1995), 2. 52–66.

[14] R. R. Wilson, *Prophecy and Society in Ancient Israel* (Philadelphia: Fortress, 1980) 39–41, 83–85.

features. First, this ideology was shaped by both a social conservatism and an increasingly realized eschatology that expressed the view that the future restoration was largely realized with the rebuilding of the temple assisted by Persian aid and the institution of the political order of Persian hegemony actualized largely through the appointment of Jewish governors. Creation theology and divine providence were the theological traditions drawn upon to legitimate and sustain this existing social and religious order. Second, the city of Jerusalem in political affairs and sacral thinking and practice achieved the dominant place in Jewish life. Third, the hereditary Zadokite priesthood achieved increasing religious and political prominence. More and more they came to be seen as the representatives of God, while the roles and influence of the other orders of Levites continued to diminish. Fourth, major emphasis was placed on the centrality of the Jerusalem temple for Jewish life through pilgrimage festivals, offerings, and tithes. These sacral events, sacrifices, and tithes (e.g., Neh 10:32–39) increased dramatically the economic support for the priesthood and the city of Jerusalem and even its non-priestly population who derived major economic benefits from its presence (from "tourism," to jobs for temple maintenance, to merchandising, and so forth).[15] Fifth, this movement achieved the codification and canonization of the Torah and in particular the Priestly Code that provided the major lens through which to read and understand this early collection of sacred texts that became authoritative for shaping Jewish religious and social life. Sixth, the alignment of centrist prophets (e.g., Haggai and Zechariah) with the temple priesthood at least in the early Persian period was likely due to the hope for a restored Davidic monarchy. Seventh, however, there developed among this hierocratic movement a subsiding expectation concerning a restored Davidic monarchy, coupled with the high priesthood steadily assimilating much of the pomp and ceremony as well as some limited authority originally associated with royal leadership in earlier times.[16] Eighth, and finally, one of the

[15] See W. G. Dever's suggestive essay on the merging of royal and priestly interests in the temple that included the areas of economics, the subsidizing of public works, the payment of tribute, various administrative tasks, the collection of archives, the pursuit of charitable work, and the providing of jobs both as a center for pilgrimage festivals and tourism as well as renovation and expansion ("Palaces and Temples in Canaan and Ancient Israel," *Civilizations of the Ancient Near East* [5 vols.; New York: Simon and Schuster, 1995], 1. 611–12).

[16] In the post-exilic period, the Aaronide priests become the only "true" priests (Exodus 28–29; Leviticus 8–10; and Numbers 16–18); Aaron became the first "high priest" (Ezra 7:1–5)

profound economic changes involved the re-establishment for the exiles and their family and the tenure rights of family households that were largely patrimonial and patrilineal in nature. The hierocratic movement endorsed the claims of extended families whose land was lost in the captivity, thus negating the inheritance of foreigners, including children of mixed ethnic (i.e., Jewish and non-Jewish) parentage (Ezra 9–10). Along this line, this party attempted at least to establish Levitical cities that would provide property rights and claims for priests left largely destitute by Josiah's centralization of worship in Jerusalem in the latter part of the seventh century B.C.E. and by the later destruction of the temple by the Babylonians in 586 B.C.E. This predominantly Zadokite movement, aligned with Persian appointed political leaders, some centrist prophets, and traditional sages formed an aristocratic party that maintained social and religious power throughout the period of Persian rule. This party practiced a pragmatic politics of accommodation with Persian authorities.

The Party of the "Visionaries"

Other political, economic, and religious expectations gave rise to a second movement that challenged the reconstituted social order achieved following the return of the exiles. This movement of "visionaries" especially opposed the hierocracy of the Zadokite priests, their "allies," and their control of second temple Judaism. Jewish apocalypticism first distinctly manifests itself in the Hellenistic period, although several of its major features originated in earlier Israelite religion and society, including, e.g., the prophetic emphasis on the "day of the Lord" that points to a coming time of judgment and the notion of a heavenly council of supernatural beings presided over by Yahweh (Job 1–2; Psalm 82). Paul Hanson has argued that the early roots of Jewish apocalyptic eschatology are traceable to the first part of the Persian period and may be found in Isaiah 56–66, Zechariah 9–14, Isaiah 24–27, Malachi, and perhaps Joel.[17] Whether the social groups behind these texts are best classified as early apocalypticists or later, peripheral prophets from whom apoca-

---

who had royal rank and vestments (Exodus 28–29); and the Zadokites came to control the office of high priest (1 Chr 24:3–19) as descendants of Eleazar (Exod 6:23 [P]; cf. Num 20:25–26) and Phinehas (Num 25:11) who were the son and grandson of Aaron (Ezra 7:5; 1 Chr 5:30–34; and 6:35–38).

[17] *The Dawn of Apocalyptic.*

lypticism would largely develop is an historical question that will not be addressed here. However, Hanson's major thesis is a cogent and supportable one. According to Hanson, the Persian period witnessed a power struggle involving, on the one hand, the hierocratic party led by the Zadokite priesthood, Persian appointed governors, centrist prophets, and traditional sages who acquired the dominant political power, were able to shape the prevailing world view and practice of second temple Judaism along the lines of a theocracy, and controlled the ritual practices and economic resources of the temple in Jerusalem In this struggle for at least local power that still yielded to foreign domination, the hierocratic movement prevailed, at least politically, through the Persian period and much of the time that followed, until the Great Revolt against Rome led to the destruction of Jerusalem and the Temple in 70 C.E. This did not lead, however, to the silencing of the visionaries who continued as political marginals to articulate their contrasting world view for the Jewish community in Judah which, shaped by future eschatology, was yet to be realized.

This second group, the "visionaries," consisting of peripheral prophets,[18] critical sages (Job, Agur, and Ecclesiastes), and some of the Levitical families[19] dominated by the Zadokite priestly hierarchy and the Aaronide priests, developed a more inclusive view of second Temple Judaism. This party also focused its future expectations on Second Isaiah's (Isaiah 40–55) vision of the cosmic and social transformation of reality. However, the visionaries in the Persian period regarded this vision as largely unfulfilled. This prophetic vision, emanating from the community in Babylonian captivity, regarded the collapse of the Babylonian empire as the act of Yahweh through his "anointed one" Cyrus. These visionaries shaped a future eschatology in which the final restoration would be rendered by a miraculous act of God that would culminate in a new sacral and social order ruled over by the messiah, who would be a descendant of David and presided over by a legitimate priesthood that would conduct proper rituals in a purified temple cult. This eschatological act of God thus would bring about salvation for the faithful and righteous remnant who would be honored and held in esteem in the time of the new

---

[18] See R. Wilson, *Prophecy and Society in Ancient Israel*, 69–83.

[19] The functions of the Levites were those of minor servants in the temple (Gen 49:5–7; Num 1:47ff.; 3; 4; 8:24ff.; 18:2ff.; and 35:2ff.; and Ezek 44:6–14). The Chronicler seems to give them additional status by making them teachers (2 Chr 17:8–9; 35:3), singers (1 Chr 16:4; 23:5); and "servants before the ark" (1 Chr 16:4; 2 Chr 35:3).

order. This largely disenfranchised group came to regard the existing temple cult as defiled and its priesthood as corrupt, pronounced judgment on Jewish civic leaders appointed by the Persians, argued that Yahweh would break the power of foreign tyranny and establish a new political order, and challenged the dissolving of marriages and families comprised of Jewish men, non-Jewish women, and their offspring (Malachi 2). The visionaries also were more inclined to support the land tenure of families of mixed races who, faithful to God, could be included within the community of the restored Israel (Ezek 47:21–23). As things developed during the Persian period, this group of visionaries was largely disenfranchised and held only a secondary status in the new order dominated largely by the hierocratic party that cultivated and enjoyed the support of the Persian government. However, the leaders of the "visionaries" were not themselves poor, dispossessed, uneducated, and socially on the fringe of Jewish culture and politics. Rather, they came from socially respectable families with means if not power and were well educated intellectuals. However, they were not among the Jews who comprised the political and religious aristocracy in the colony of Yehud that recognized and made their bed with the Persian authorities. This collection of "visionaries" became increasingly pessimistic about the transformation of the current cosmic and social order and finally concluded that every vestige of present reality must either be radically reshaped or even destroyed by a cataclysmic act of God before the creation of a "new heaven and new earth" could occur.

The sages were active participants in this struggle for power, influence, and the opportunity to shape second temple Judaism in the Persian period. Theologically, the sages joined with Second Isaiah in articulating a theology of Yahweh's creation of the world and sustaining of the orders that made life possible.[20] However, from the extant wisdom literature, it is clear that two distinct camps of sages emerged during the post-exilic period: traditional sages who aligned themselves largely with the increasingly dominant hierocratic party of the Zadokite priests (Proverbs 1–9; Sirach), and critical teachers who, in challenging many of the conventions of the conservative wise and the priests with whom they were aligned, reached rather pessimistic or even skeptical conclusions about the evils of the current cosmic and social order (Job, Agur, and Qoheleth). While religiously and perhaps socially compatible with the party of "visionaries," these critical teachers did not share the hopeful anticipation of God's dramatic ending of the current reality and reshaping

---

[20] See my detailed study, *Wisdom and Creation*.

of a new social and political order. Indeed, G. von Rad may be at least partially correct in his argument that the failure of a righteous order to prevail in cosmic and social life led to the emergence of Jewish apocalyptic.[21]

The Sages and Proverbs 1–9

Following the return from exile, the religious and social parties that emerged in the early Persian period included the sages whose literary artistry and editorial activity are represented by Proverbs 1–9.[22] Finding their primary locus of activity in Jerusalem, these sages and their descendants quickly allied themselves with the hierocratic party of second temple Judaism that would become the dominant political and religious group in the post-exilic period.

Although this alignment would not reach its full realization until the time of Ben Sira in the early second century B.C.E., there are elements in the thinking of the sages already recognizable in the first collection of Proverbs that are compatible with the agenda of the hierocratic party. These compatible elements included the theme of a largely static and just cosmic order that is universal (3:19–20); the implication at least that Yahweh is the one true God (1:7, 29; 2:6; 3:5, 9, 11, 19, 26, 32, 33; etc.); the insistence that justice is largely retributive and dispensed by a righteous deity (3:6, 9–12, 26, 32–35; etc.); divine providence expressed through the theory of retribution as the justification for the possession of wealth and power by the dominant social group (e.g., 3:9–10, 13–18; 8:18, 21); the legitimation of wisdom teachings by grounding them in the just order of creation and by personifying the tradition as the daughter of God (Prov 1:22–31; 8:1–9:6); the authentication of the rule of the kings of the earth by reference to their selection by Wisdom, the queen of heaven, who embodies God's creative power and providential rule (8:15–16); the warning against the dangers of extra-Israelite culture and religion personified by the metaphor of the "strange woman" (2:16–19; 5:1–14, 20; 6:20–35; 7:1–27; and 9:13–18); the affirmation of the social features of the traditional extended household (3:33), including the authority of the senior male and

---

[21] G. von Rad, *Old Testament Theology* (2 vols.; New York: Harper & Row, 1965), 2. 303–8.

[22] For detailed social descriptions of the sages in ancient Israel and early Judaism, see J. Blenkinsopp, *Sage, Priest, Prophet* (Library of Ancient Israel; ed. D. A. Knight; Louisville: Westminster/John Knox, 1995) 9–65; and *The Sage in Israel and the ancient Near East* (ed. J. G. Gammie and L. G. Perdue; Winona Lake, IN: Eisenbrauns, 1990).

female (1:8; 4:1), marriage limited to Jewish women (5:15–19), patrimony and heredity (5:10; 6:31); the claims of the "righteous" to the inheritance of the land over against those who dally with the "strange woman" (5:7–10); the support of the sacrificial system of the temple (3:9–10); the priestly language and practice of declaring something or some action is an "abomination or hateful to Yahweh" (ritual impurity, *tōʿēbâ* = Deut 7:25; 17:1; 18:12; 22:5; and unethical behavior = Prov 3:32, cf. *śānēʾ* in Prov 6:16–19; and a warning against joining brigands and revolutionaries (1:8–19; 3:31).

The theological and ethical materials found in Proverbs 1–9 probably derive from one or more school settings in the early half of the Persian period: temple school(s), family guilds, and/or civil academies.[23] More than likely a temple school emerged in the Persian period that educated scribes to assist the priests in interpreting the Torah written in Hebrew to a populace increasingly dependent on Aramaic (the lingua franca of the Persian period), in codifying and arguing case law for civil and religious regulations and disputes, in administrating and recording the temple's vast economic resources, and in shaping the major theological and political case for legitimating the claims to power and influence of the ruling class. Guilds (most likely centered in family households) continued to train scribes for service in the government or in the temple (1 Chr 2:55). Scribes also were needed by the Persian government at both the central (e.g., Ezra) and provincial levels to carry out administrative leadership and bureaucratic tasks, maintain records, and serve as notaries. These scribes perhaps were educated in civil academies supported by the central and provincial governments. Traditional sages sought through their writings and educational system to promote the interests of the prevailing social and religious order.[24]

---

[23] For more recent discussions of schools and wisdom, see J. L. Crenshaw, "The Sage in Proverbs," *The Sage in Israel and the Ancient Near East,* 208–10; G. I. Davies, "Were there schools in ancient Israel?" *Wisdom in ancient Israel* (ed. John Day et al.; Cambridge: Cambridge University, 1995) 199–211; D. W. Jamieson-Drake, *Scribes and Schools in Monarchic Judah: A Socio-Archaeological Approach* (Sheffield: JSOT, 1991); B. Lang, "Schule und Unterricht im alten Israel," *La sagesse de l'Ancien Israel* (ed. M. Gilbert; BETL 51; Gembloux: Duculot, 1979) 186–201; and A. Lemaire, *Les Ecoles et la formation de la Bible dans l'ancien Israël* (Göttingen: Vandenhoeck & Ruprecht, 1981); *idem,* "The Sage in School and Temple," *The Sage in Israel and the Ancient Near East,* 165–81. These authors generally affirm there is at the very least limited evidence for schools and that wisdom instruction and the education of sages and scribes occurred in them.

[24] See J. Blenkinsopp, "The Sage, the Scribe, and Scribalism in the Chronicler's Work," *The*

The critical wisdom tradition emerging in the Persian period is represented primarily by Job (the poetry), Agur (Proverbs 30), and Qoheleth. These texts also likely were produced by teachers as school literature. The sages who produced the critical wisdom literature were intellectuals who opposed traditional wisdom's social knowledge that was used to support the political power and economic advantages of the hierocratic movement. These teachers were critical of both earlier sapiential instruction and their traditional colleagues; questioned and at times even denied the justice of God; ranged from open criticism of to a deepening skepticism concerning the teaching that justice permeated the cosmic and social order and could be discovered by astute observation and then implemented in a life that would consequently experience success and well-being; held that God either remained hidden, was capricious and unjust, or was engaged in a struggle for justice that was never completely won; viewed both religious and civic leaders as corrupt; denied that the temple cult produced the dividends of blessing that the priests claimed; and witnessed a corrupt social order that oppressed not only the poor but even the righteous. Unlike their visionary contemporaries, these sages did not look to a future act of God that would transform heaven and earth and constitute a reality of justice in which they would participate as leaders among the redeemed. Instead, they either retreated into a deepening skepticism (Agur), avoided speculation about a hidden, capricious deity, taught their students to "seize the day" when joy in one's labor and family is experienced (Qoheleth), or concluded that moral living and resistance to the forces of chaos, while restrained and held in check by God, did not promise the exemption of the righteous from suffering or even final justification (the poetry of Job). However, while these critical sages questioned and thus would have undermined the epistemological and confessional assumptions undergirding and legitimating the current social world of Judah as a Persian colony, they do not construct for their students an alternative social reality. These teachers challenged the comfortable theological and ideological dogmas that promised advantages and privileges to students who persevered in their discipline of study and character formation. However, they offered no new constructive vision of social justice in their literature of dissent that would reshape the current political order of Persian rule.

Sage in Israel and the Ancient Near East, 307–15. While he deals with scribes in Chronicles, I suggest that the depiction of these officials, bureaucrats, and lawyers characterizes some of the social groups who wrote and redacted the wisdom literature of the post-exilic period.

Creation Theology as the Legitimation
of the Yehudite Social Order

P. Berger, among others, has taught us that religion, including at times even theology as ideology, may erect a "sacred canopy" that legitimates and maintains the existing social order.[25] Indeed, the religious teaching of Proverbs 1–9 may be seen as the "sacred canopy" developed by the class of traditional sages active in the schools and bureaucracies of the Persian colony of Yehud. This "sacred canopy," or world view, represented one of their literary attempts to support the existing social and religious order of the dominant hierocratic party that supported and in turn was supported by the Persian empire.

The literary positioning of the didactic poems in the first nine chapters underscores the centrality and essential role of (Woman) Wisdom in the origins of creation, in sustaining and enhancing the cosmos, society, and human life, in guiding or steering the moral behavior and skillful language that leads to the fullness of life for both the devotee of wisdom and the larger community, and in avoiding folly and evil that threaten life in all of its social and individual manifestations. In particular, Woman Wisdom, who embodies the tradition of the sages as divine instruction for both religious and social life, is counterpoised to Woman Folly, who represents not only the evil and frivolity of foolish life that strays towards destruction, but also both the allure of the "foreign woman" and her pagan religion and culture as well as the threat of the prostitute to the extended family.

Woman Wisdom in Proverbs 1–9 is the divine, creative force that originates and continues to permeate the cosmos, the social justice that shapes and provides a righteous character to human institutions, the alluring lover of the sage who seeks to find comfort and exhilaration in her charms and life-giving embrace, the darling daughter of God whose puerile endearment and her own delight in the world of human habitation form the affectionate bond between creator and the inhabited world, and the powerful queen of heaven who not only elects and enables to rule successfully and well the princes of the earth but also gives wealth and bestows honor to her royal lovers. But most of all Woman Wisdom, through the teachings of the wise whose tradition she embodies, is the voice of God whose invitations to come and learn of

---

[25] P. Berger, *The Sacred Canopy* (Garden City, NY: Doubleday, 1969); and P. Berger and T. Luckmann, *The Social Construction of Reality* (Garden City, NY: Doubleday, 1967).

her and whose instructions revealing divine knowledge and insight direct the simple on the path to the fullness of life.

Ultimately, the voices one hears in Proverbs 1–9 are not only those of the wise teachers of Israel or even of Wisdom herself who incorporates and articulates the sapiential tradition that is grounded in the order of creation. The audible undertone of the teachings and poems of the entire collection is sounded by the mouth of God who reveals to the simple and the wise the pathway to life.

The Superscription (1:1):
"The Sayings of Solomon, Son of David, King of Israel"

The superscription for both the first collection (chapters 1–9) and the entire Book reads: "The Sayings of Solomon, Son of David, King of Israel." The association of the Book of Proverbs and its first collection with Solomon is based on a long-standing tradition that depicts him as the wisest of the kings, the creator of wisdom texts, and the patron of the sages (1 Kgs 3–10). However, there may be another factor at play in the sages' staking their claim to Solomon in the opening superscription and in two later ones (10:1; 25:1). Sages in the Persian period sought to demonstrate that their teachings were a continuation of the tradition of the royal court given its most culturally developed expression by the renowned Solomon.[26] The temple, Jerusalem, the Torah, and the Zadokites had not yet achieved their positions of prominence in developing Judaism and would not do so until the fourth century B.C.E. and later, that is, in the latter part of the Persian period and the emergence of the empire of Alexander the Great and its rapid fracturing into Hellenistic states in the Near East. The final accommodation of wisdom to these hierocratic elements is well illustrated in the wisdom of Ben Sira (circa 190 B.C.E.). But the monarchy and creation were the two theological traditions the sages could exploit to legitimate their earlier work and its resumption in the first part of the Persian period. At a time when the fires of messianic expectation concerning the re-establishment of the dynasty of David were burning brightly, the sages of the period may have sought to lay claim to the dynasty's most famous ruler by associating their labors with him, thus expressing in a surreptitious way their support for the re-establishment of the house of David

---

[26] This tradition is carried forward by Qoheleth (1:1) and the Wisdom of Solomon.

that even suspicious Persian authorities would not recognize as threatening. The sages were seeking to show that their tradition was firmly in line with the institution of the house of David, and in particular its most esteemed representative. Thus, the sages not only lent their support, at least in this hidden fashion, to the re-establishment of the royal dynasty associated with Solomon, they also sought to legitimate the authority and authenticity of their own teachings and the prominent social position to which they aspired to a Jewish audience in the early part of the Persian period. This claim of royal association and continuity with the most famous king of Israel's past allowed the sages in the Persian period to align themselves with the developing hierocracy of the Zadokites without the risk of making any noticeable threat against the rule of Persia.

Purpose: Even though no serious scholar would suggest that the initial superscription reflects Solomonic authorship of Proverbs or even of the first collection, the language preserves some abiding memory of Solomon's association with the formation and patronage of court wisdom. This collective memory embedded in the sapiential tradition and the minds of its tradents continued to be reflected in the new literary creations of sages for a thousand years (1 Kings 1–11; Proverbs and three of its collections; Song of Songs; Qoheleth; Sir 47:12–22; and the Wisdom of Solomon).

When examining this steady stream of literary creations, it becomes clear that Solomon came to represent in ancient Israel and early Judaism a cultural symbol of a tradition that bore its own unique character and outlook. This does not mean incongruities were absent or that clashes in perspectives were avoided. Wisdom's openness to new understandings, reactions to changing historical fortunes of both the larger culture and its individuals, and tolerance of diversity precluded the formation of a unified tradition with singular and unchallenged views. But the symbolization of much of the wisdom tradition by reference to Solomon does mean that this continuing stream of literary works breathed its own creative spirit and articulated values that sought to claim the lives and devotion of students, some of whom would achieve for themselves positions of prominence in Israelite and Jewish society and would substantially shape its culture. The glories, achievements, intelligence, prosperity, success, and piety symbolized in the person of Israel's legendary king (1 Kgs 3–11) the major values of the wisdom tradition in a fashion not unlike the symbolization of the diversity of the faith and ethics of early Christianity in the person of Jesus in the canonical and non-canonical gospels.

Theology: If there is some historical kernel in the attribution of early sapiential literature to Solomon, as least as a royal patron, it may be found in the fact that new "forms of power" in the rule of a royal dynasty required "new modes of knowledge" that would express theoretically the political and religious legitimation of the newly formed monarchy and practically the administration of the new empire.[27] While perhaps not a Solomonic "enlightenment," the new political reality of the monarchy in the tenth century B.C.E. required fresh and invigorating modes of knowledge and cultural expression that went beyond the social customs and sacred stories of familial and clan religion and life. Canaanite religion provided the new capital Jerusalem and its royal house a sacred, mythological canopy that combined with the Israelite understandings of the divine election of the dynasty and God's perpetual covenant with David (2 Samuel 7; Psalm 89). Wisdom offered to this mix astute observation based on reason and tested in the arena of human experience. Wisdom's experiential, rational mode of understanding was needed both for administering and governing the empire, for developing a proto-scientific understanding and implementation of the rules of agriculture, economics, warfare, and architecture, and for planning future directions. The counsel of sages provided monarchs well planned strategies for the various facets of successful rule. The learning of the wise enabled kings to engage in international diplomacy and to shape a body of learning that legitimated their rule by reference to Yahweh who elected them and chose Zion/Jerusalem as the divine dwelling place. But even more the sages developed an ethos of behavior, grounded not in brute strength or unbridled passion, but in the sense of cosmic justice issuing from a class ethic of those of social prominence who nevertheless keenly felt a sense of obligation and loyalty to the community as a whole, including its poor. Finally, this intellectual tradition of the wise was open to and even encouraged careful scrutiny, welcoming new insights that challenged, transformed or even negated earlier teachings. It was this openness to new possibilities of understanding, regardless of their source, that allowed the indigenous traditions of Israel and Judah to be receptive, though critically so, to new learning that even derived from other cultures.

This symbolization of a new way of seeing the world in the person of Solomon may be one reason that the superscription associates the book and its first collection with Israel's wisest king. During monarchic times, the sages

---

[27] W. A. Brueggemann, "The Social Significance of Solomon as a Patron of Wisdom," *The Sage in Israel and the ancient Near East*, 117–32.

had been the "men of the king" (Prov 25:1) and perhaps sought to continue to be the adjutants of the royal house and its local governors later on in colonial times. Even the radical Book of Qoheleth, written at a time when apocalyptic fervor began to increase significantly (fourth century B.C.E.) with the impending demise of Persian tyranny and which intimates Solomon utters its narrative voice (Qoh 1:1), reminds its audience by this attribution that wisdom, symbolized in the person of its patron saint, continues to be receptive to new and even radical propositions. Even so, this sage's teachings imbues a spirit of cynicism that directly opposes the hopes and dreams of seers that point to an age of new Jewish freedom and dreams of nationalism's aspirations.

First Poem on Woman Wisdom (1:20–33):
Woman Wisdom's Invitation to the Simple

Introduction: Prov 1:20–33 is the first didactic poem in the initial collection and thus the entire book. Central to this poem, and the ones to follow in chapters 8 and 9, is the metaphor of wisdom as Woman Wisdom who is both an attribute of the divine character and a virtue to be sought, obtained, and embodied by students and sages.[28] Literary metaphors are common in biblical literature. These include Jerusalem/Zion as the daughter of Yahweh (Jer 6:26), Israel as the bride or wife of God (Jer 2:2; Hosea 2), and Jerusalem and Samaria as sisters who are married, yet unfaithful to God (Ezekiel 23; cf. chap. 16). However, the metaphor of wisdom, personified in a variety of female social roles (child, lover, teacher, and queen, and even figuratively at least a goddess) is limited to the literature of the sages: Job 28, Proverbs 8–9, Sirach 24, and Wisdom 10–19, and takes on great theological and social significance. In these texts, wisdom is the active means or design of God's creation, the daughter in whom he takes delight, the royal queen who chooses rulers and brings them wealth and success, the teacher who gives instructions of life to her students, the providential guide of Israel and the faithful through the course of salvation history, the creative mist and divine word that took up residence in Zion and the temple, and the voice of God who declares divine instruction to those who would find life and well-being. This metaphor, then, plays a key role in conveying both the theological and ethical content of wisdom as well as the quest to discover and embody its character. But the

---

[28] For a detailed study of metaphor and its use in biblical theology, see my book, *Wisdom in Revolt: Metaphorical Theology in the Book of Job* (JSOTSup 112; Sheffield: JSOT, 1991).

metaphor is also important in legitimating the existing social order in which traditional sages functioned in a variety of social roles.

Set in the first half of the Persian period, this poem embodies the invitation of the sages to the "simple" of Judah's more prominent families to take up wisdom's course of study in one of the post-exilic schools. What Woman Wisdom offers to these potential students is not simply the knowledge and skill of a profession, but a way of life that leads to well-being and secure dwelling in what was for the most part an unsettled and difficult time.

Literary Structure: This poem consists of four parts: a third-person introduction that portrays Woman Wisdom's issuing her invitation throughout the various parts of the city (vv 20–21), her first-person speech addressed to the simple who are exhorted to listen to her reproof (vv 22–23), her diatribe that warns of the disaster that engulfs those who do not heed her invitation to learn of and from her (vv 24–31), and her conclusion that contrasts the ease and secure dwelling of those who listen to her teaching with the death and destruction of complacent fools who despise knowledge and the simple who spurn the life obtained through discipline that she offers (vv 32–33).

Verses 20–21 depict Woman Wisdom as a peripatetic teacher, at least in her attempt to recruit the simple, for she goes to each of the major public arenas and thoroughfares of an ancient city in search of her students: the street, the market places, the top of the walls, and the entrances to the gates. This does not mean that these were the places where regular instruction occurred, but they are the contexts where teachers could come, issue their invitation (protrepsis) to passers-by, and attempt to persuade potential students to learn from them. Presumably the actual teaching and study would have occurred in schools located in public buildings or perhaps the courtyards of private houses.

The audience she primarily addresses are the "simple," i.e., those youth who are yet to take up the sages' course of study. Two other groups of people typically reject Wisdom's invitations: "scoffers" (*lēṣîm*), who are unteachable (Prov 13:1) because of their arrogance and contentiousness (Prov 21:24; 22:10) and "fools" (*kĕsîlîm*), who do not restrain either their emotions (Prov 12:16; 21:24; 29:8, 11) or their speech (Prov 10:18–21; 12:19; 14:7). Because they lack the discipline of wisdom, both of these latter groups create discord in that threatens and even disrupts a community's harmony and well-being (Prov 15:18).

These youth reside not only in the city (presumably Jerusalem), but also in the Jewish towns and villages economically, politically, and religiously connected to this urban center. These simple are not necessarily opposed to the teaching that the sages offer, but are young, lack the content of sapiential knowledge, and have not yet acquired the discipline of study, critical thinking, and proper behavior (Prov 1:22; 8:5; 9:4, 16). They are easily seduced by folly and led astray to experience disaster (Prov 14:18). More than likely, the simple comprised intelligent young men and likely women from well-to-do families (cf. Sir 38:24; Proverbs 31) in Judah who could provide their offspring the opportunities for advancement through education and did not need them to remain at home in order to survive economically as households.

Woman Wisdom's diatribe (vv 24–31) is a warning issued to the "simple" that the rejection of her invitation to come and learn of her will lead to their experiencing the same destruction that scoffers and fools are sure to encounter. Indeed, in times when fear and calamity engulf the simple, it will be too late to then seek the protection of life-giving counsel from Woman Wisdom and the school traditions she embodies. Wisdom who now calls and freely opens her teachings of life to the simple will in future times of calamity be called upon by the unlearned who failed to accept her invitation. But then it will be too late. Only those who, fearing God and thus who acknowledge Yahweh as the creator and providential sustainer of life, will undertake the intensive and dedicated study of wisdom and seek through discipline to incorporate its values to activate in everyday life and thus have the means by which to face the times of calamity and panic that threaten them and their community.

In striking irony, it will be Woman Wisdom who becomes the one who mocks and derides the simple when they in desperation seek too late the safety of her teachings. These times of panic and impending destruction could range from major disasters threatening the existence of the larger community of Jews (e.g., pestilence, crop failure, and military invasion; see Jer 18:17; Ezek 35:5; Obad 13) to individual calamities of various types (e.g., illness, poverty, robbery, war [2 Sam. 22:19 = Ps 18:19; Job 18:12; 21:17; 31:3, 23]). Without the guidance of counsel, i.e., careful planning that was designed to lead to success and to secure life,[29] both the community and individuals were vulnerable to

---

[29] P. A. H. de Boer, "The Counselor," *Wisdom in Israel and the Ancient Near East* (ed. Martin Noth and D. Winton Thomas; VTSup 3; Leiden: Brill, 1955) 42–71.

the impingements of disaster. This lack of preparation of the simple, who do not fear Yahweh and who, like the fools, hate knowledge (v 29; cf. v 22), is likely the "fruit of their way" they are to eat when calamity comes upon them. Thus in the words of retributive justice, the simple who reject Wisdom's invitation will suffer the results of their own folly.

In a fashion that is typical for instructions, the general conclusion (vv 32–33) contrasts the fate of the foolish and the wise. The simple turn away from Wisdom's invitation and thus miss their opportunity for life-preserving instruction. The complacency of fools, i.e., a careless sense of security that makes them unaware of danger, leaves them unprepared for the calamities of life. By contrast those who heed the call of Woman Wisdom will dwell securely and be at ease (cf. Deut 33:12, 28; Ps 102:29; Jer 23:6; 33:16). This promise to those who respond to Wisdom's invitation that draws on an image of dwelling at ease in the land is especially appealing in a period of insecurity. For a people whose land in an earlier time had been conquered by the Babylonians and whose leaders had been exiled, this promise of peaceful inhabitation would have been particularly compelling.

Purpose: The major purpose of this poem, in addition to the theological reasons given below, is that of the protrepsis or invitation of teachers to potential students to learn from them wisdom. Woman Wisdom, assuming the role of the teacher in search of students, issues the reasons why the simple should accept her call. Included in her protrepsis are not only the benefits that the study of wisdom offers but also the ravages of destruction that overtakes those who reject her invitation to take up her course of study. Socially, the sages are those who assume roles in the government, temple bureaucracy, and temple school. These sages are the mainstay of Jewish life during the first half of the Persian period. Because of their key roles and conservative politics, they most likely enjoyed not only the support of the presiding governor and the hierocracy of the Zadokite priesthood, but also that of the Persian authorities as well. Thus, they are assured by Woman Wisdom, who not only embody their tradition but also speaks the voice of Yahweh, that they will "dwell securely" and "be at ease" in their country and in their homes, even during times of political and economic upheaval, while "fools" and "scoffers" who have rejected wisdom's invitation will experience "calamity" and "panic" when disaster strikes.

Perhaps among these "fools" and "scoffers" are those who do not buy into the social world of Judah as a Persian colony that the traditional scribes in part construct and attempt to legitimate. It is doubtful that those who reject the teachings of the sages and their invitation to enter their temple school or guilds would be those who belonged to families of common laborers and the poor. However, it is more likely the "fools" and "scoffers" also belong to well-to-do class families. As youth they would have had the opportunity and means to take up the study of wisdom. Some may have bee those who were attracted to the alternative world view and life-style of the "visionaries," while others may have been those who preferred a life of leisure and frivolity to one of commitment an discipline leading to the formation of character. These groups would likely have been comprised mainly of the youth of aristocratic families who either sought a more radical life of commitment to significant change because of their attraction to the vision of marginal prophets, Levites, and other marginal groups or lacked the desire or the conviction of the reality of even traditional wisdom's cosmology to engage in the rigorous study of the wisdom curriculum of the temple and scribal schools.

Theology: First-person divine speeches, whether of Yahweh in the Hebrew Bible (e.g., Isa 42:8) or of gods and goddesses in other religions of the ancient world, were a common literary expression. C. Kayatz has drawn important parallels of the speeches of Woman Wisdom to those of Ma'at, the daughter of the sun god Re and the personification of the cosmic order of truth and justice that permeated reality.[30] In later texts, Isis, another Egyptian goddess, issues first person speeches that include an invitation, promises, and self-praise.[31] The sage or sages who composed this speech of Woman Wisdom may have drawn on the orations of deities from the ancient world to emphasize that the tradition of wisdom, embodied in this striking literary metaphor, is the embodiment of Yahweh's own knowledge and insight. This metaphor provides an engaging way of speaking of the divine authority of this voice of Yahweh who seeks out the simple to lead them to life. Yet the voice of Yahweh which Woman Wisdom utters offers not only salvation but also issues a dire warning: those who reject the teachings of wisdom will one day face disaster and panic that will engulf them and lead to their destruction. In a way, we have the "either/or" so typical of Deuteronomic preaching: obedience to the

---

[30] C. Kayatz, *Studien zu Proverbien 1–9: Eine form- und motivgeschichtliche Untersuchung unter Einbeziehung ägyptischen Vergleichsmaterials* (WMANT 22; Neukirchen-Vluyn: Neukirchener V., 1966), esp. 80–93.

[31] H. Conzelmann, "The Mother of Wisdom," *The Future of Our Religious Past* (ed. J. M. Robinson; New York: Harper & Row, 1971) 230–43.

teachings of the law lead to life, while disobedience results in death. Only now it is Wisdom who is the Deuteronomic preacher who offers the radical, life-claiming decision or "yes" or "no."

The metaphor of Woman Wisdom also serves to give a concrete, albeit literary form, to divine immanence in the world. The increasing transcendence of Yahweh in exilic and post-exilic literature raised the serious problem of how to depict God's divine presence in the world and among the chosen people. Woman Wisdom, who is God's virtue that leads to life, provides one of the more imaginative ways of addressing divine presence. Moving beyond the metaphor, the sages are saying that God through wisdom is not only the teacher of the divine tradition but is also present in its articulation in the proteptic invitation to take up the course of study, in the knowledge contained in sapiential teachings, sayings, and poems, in the actualization of what is learned in the formation of character, and in the behavior of the wise. Woman Wisdom and the tradition she embodies become the means by which the sages express the reality of divine presence in rather concrete ways. Divine immanence is given graphic, metaphorical expression in Woman Wisdom's assuming the role of the peripatetic teacher who goes throughout the areas of public gathering and discourse in the city (streets, market places, tops of walls, and entrances to city gates) in search of students, i.e., the "simple," who are offered the opportunity to say "yes" or "no" to her invitation of life.

Woman Wisdom also provides for the traditional sages a means of speaking about divine revelation and thus gives flesh to the abstract understanding of the life-creating, life-sustaining, and life-redeeming Word of God. The sages did not simply set forth their teachings on a take-it-or-leave-it basis, though they did encourage debate, examination, and testing to determine what was true. Even so, they argued that, to use their metaphor, Woman Wisdom was the voice of God who revealed the essential understanding for coming to a knowledge of the Holy, for conducting the moral life, and for forming the character that would lead to life. Wisdom permeated the cosmos, was present in the social order, mediated between God and the cosmos, and could take up her dwelling in the mind and moral life of the receptive sage. Through discipline that included the study of the tradition of the wise, the observation of the order present in the world, and the formation of human character students could come to understand the nature and will of God who creates and sustains all life, the elements of the moral life, and the order of justice that permeates the world.

Finally, in a time perhaps not too many years removed from exile, the promise that those who took up Wisdom's call would dwell securely and be at ease was an especially appealing one. This dwelling safely, presumably in the land of Judah, may at least suggest the promise that those who lived according to the dictates of wisdom would be confident of having a safe and appropriate place in Israelite society and would enjoy the protection and fruits of their household patrimony (cf. Ps 37:9–11).

Conclusion

The superscription (1:1), general introduction (1:2–7), and the first poem about Woman Wisdom (1:20–33) at least strongly suggest that the first collection of Proverbs 1–9 is not a bloodless, abstract teaching that is removed from the sociohistorical moorings that give life to its variety of poems, sayings, and instructions. Anchored in the early years of the Persian period, this "Solomonic" compilation of teachings was written and edited by traditional sages who sought to legitimize, maintain, and to control the emerging sociopolitical and religious order of the colony of Yehud in the late sixth and early fifth centuries B.C.E. To carve out a place for themselves and to align their social group with what would become the dominant ruling and religious party of the post-exilic period, i.e., the hierocracy of the Zadokite priesthood and centrist prophets who curried the favor of the Achaeminian rulers and who at least early in the period hoped for the restitution of the House of David even if only in a subservient role, the traditional sages brought together a collection of teachings that aligned their own social group with the traditional claims to rulership of the descendants of the house of David. And, perhaps even more daring, they placed their teachings within the order of divine creation and the providential guidance of the cosmos by seizing on the mythological metaphor of Woman Wisdom. In turn, they taught that the extended family, so central to early post-exilic life in its recreation on a social level, was to reflect this world order and its life-giving power.[32]

[32] H. H. Schmid, *Gerechtigkeit als Weltordnung* (BHT 40; Tübingen: Mohr [Paul Siebeck], 1968).

The Background to Proverbs 30:4aα

In a book filled with difficult patches, the Words of Agur (Prov 30:1–9) remain among the most difficult and contentious. Basic questions of genre, function, and the pericope's extent have not found a consensus.[1] This essay in honor of Roland Murphy seeks to make a contribution towards understanding the first cosmic question in v 4.

> Who has ascended the heavens and descended?
> Who has gathered the wind in his palm?
> Who has bagged the waters in (his) cloak?
> Who has set up all the ends of earth?

While the problems of verses 1–3 are notorious, these rhetorical questions seem straightforward, at least linguistically.[2] However, J. Crenshaw's recent emendation of "descended" (*wayyērad*) to "assumed dominion" (*wayyāred*) shows that even here nothing can be taken for granted. Crenshaw explains his

---

[1] For literature, see R. N. Whybray, *The Book of Proverbs: A Survey of Modern Study* (Leiden: Brill, 1995) 86–91. Roland E. Murphy (*The Tree of Life: An Exploration of Biblical Wisdom* [2d ed.; Grand Rapids, MI: Eerdmans, 1996] 25–26) follows P. Skehan in construing the questions of Prov 30:4 as a riddle concerning Yahweh and his son, Israel/Agur. See also, A. H. J. Gunneweg, "Weisheit, Prophetie und Kanonformel: Erwägungen zu Proverbia 30,1–9," *Altestamentlicher Glaube und biblische Theologie: Festschrift für Horst Dietrich Preuss zum 65. Geburtstag* (ed. Hausmann and H.-J. Zogbel; Stuttgart: Kohlhammer, 1992) 253–60.

[2] Apart from variant understandings of palm/cloak in line 2. See K. J. Cathcart, "Proverbs 30:4 and Ugaritic ḤPN, 'Garment'," *CBQ* 32 (1970) 418–20.

emendation in these terms: "This format appears vastly superior, inasmuch as the remaining interrogatives specify three acts by which the deity exercised sovereignty."[3]

Topos 1

Already in 1960, however, W. G. Lambert had shown that the motif of heavenly "ascent" was proverbial in Mesopotamia.[4] Lambert's comments occurred in response to two lines near the conclusion of the "Dialogue of Pessimism":

> 83   *a-a-ú ar-ku šá a-na šamê^e e-lu-ú*
> 84   *a-a-ú rap-šú šá erṣetim^{tim} ú-gam-me-ru*
> 83   Who is so tall as to ascend to the heavens?
> 84   Who is so broad as to compass the underworld [earth]?[5]

Lambert registered puzzlement regarding the meaning and translation of line 83:

> The general tenor of the saying is apparent, but the exact rendering is problematic. The first half might be an affirmation that men cannot get to heaven, but the Sumerian lá [of the original proverb] can hardly bear that sense. . . . The lines may refer to a somewhat incomprehensible concept found in other passages that certain things had their roots in the underworld, and reached to heaven with their uppermost limits.[6]

---

[3] J. L. Crenshaw, "Clanging Symbols," *Justice and the Holy: Essays in Honor of Walter Harrelson* (ed. D. A. Knight and P. J. Paris; Atlanta: Scholars, 1989) 51–64; reprinted in *Urgent Advice and Probing Questions: Collected Writings on Old Testament Wisdom* (Macon, GA: Mercer University, 1995) 375–76.

[4] W. G. Lambert, *Babylonian Wisdom Literature* (Oxford: Clarendon, 1960) 327. Lambert cites, inter alia, the Sumerian version in "Gilgameš and the Land of the Living," from S. N. Kramer, *JCS* 1 (1947) 10; cf. *ANET* 48, 28–29.

[5] *Babylonian Wisdom Literature,* 148–149. This proverb is also mentioned by W. W. Hallo, "Proverbs Quoted in Epic," *Lingering Over Words: Studies in Ancient Near Eastern Literature in Honor of William L. Moran* (ed. Tzvi Abusch et al.; HSS 37; Atlanta: Scholars, 1990) 216. Hallo provides a useful theoretical perspective on the intertextuality of proverbs in cuneiform literature. See also F. E. Greenspahn, "A Mesopotamian Proverb and its Biblical Reverberations," *JAOS* 114 (1994) 33–38.

[6] *Babylonian Wisdom Literature,* 327. For the Sumerian lá, see B. Alster, *Studies in Sumerian Proverbs* (Mesopotamia 3; Copenhagen: Akademisk Forlag, 1975) 88.

Lambert's observations and the texts he cites are a crucial starting point for our investigation. The cosmic merismus "heaven and earth" is of course extremely common in the ancient Near East and Egypt.[7] Yet, the various usages of this word-pair are not always adequately distinguished according to form and function. As we shall see, there are two different proverbial topoi combining *elû* ("ascend," cognate *ʿlh*) and *šamû* ("heaven"). The first topos (henceforth T1) is found in the Akkadian text quoted above. Here the collocation of *arku* ("tall") and *elû* shows that the usual sense of *elû* ("ascend") is inoperative. In this context, the verb *elû* conveys the sense "reach up."[8] If something is *tall* (*arku*), it does not *ascend* to heaven, but *reaches up* to it and, in some cases, extends down to *earth* (*erṣetu*, a term that ambiguously includes the netherworld).[9] The point of the proverb in this form (T1) is to present a picture of greatness through spatial *extension*, particularly with reference to the extremes of cosmic height and depth or breadth. Thus line 84 above contrasts horizontal extension to the vertical extension of line 83.

A poetic couplet praising the goddess Inanna makes the same vertical-horizontal contrast:

> You are as lofty as heaven
> You are as broad as earth.[10]

Lambert cites a Hymn to Papulegarra (Papnigingarra) which provides a good example of the cosmic merismus typical of T1. In this topos, some sacred entity or person stretches from the bottom to the top of the cosmos:

> The temple: let it bear (*na-ši*) its head high,
>   Below, let its roots grasp the netherworld.
> The Kesh temple: let its head be raised (*na-ši*) high,
>   Below, let its roots grasp the netherworld.
> Above, let its pinnacle rival heaven
>   Below, let its roots grasp the netherworld.[11]

---

[7] O. Keel, *The Symbolism of the Biblical World: Ancient Near Eastern Iconography and the Book of Psalms* (New York: Seabury, 1978) 16–60.

[8] Note B. R. Foster's rendering, "Who is so tall as to reach to heaven?" (*Before the Muses: An Anthology of Akkadian Literature* [Bethesda: CDL, 1993], 2. 817).

[9] See Foster, *Before the Muses*, 1. 18; 2. 646.

[10] Ibid.

[11] Foster, *Before the Muses*, 1. 73. See also the "Prescriptive Hymn to Ninurta," 2. 629 (see *Babylonian Wisdom Literature*, 120, for text).

The point is not travel to heaven or down to the (under)world, but the cosmic greatness of some sacred entity. The Kesh temple rivals the cosmic mountain, spanning heaven and earth.[12] It is an *axis mundi,* reaching up and down.[13] This topos, as Lambert noted, can also be applied to gods, who are often described as KUR/*šadû rabû,* "great mountain." The god IM.ḪUR.SAG is explicitly described as a cosmic mountain:

> *šá-du-ú rabû*[u] . . . *šá ri-šá-a-šú šá-ma-mi šá-an-na*
> *ap-su-u el-lim šur-šu-du uš-šú-šú.*[14]
> A great mountain . . . whose peak rivals the heavens,
> whose foundations are laid in the holy apsu.[15]

Another temple description affords an example of Tı that is closely parallel to the horizontal notion of "encompassing the earth":

> [Nippu]r, bond of heaven and earth,
>   li[nkage] of the four world regions . . .
> High indeed is [the temple's] head, it is the double of Ekur
>   Brilliant is its light, covering the whole inhabited world. . . .[16]

Lambert noted similar imagery in the Erra Poem in a description of a cosmic tree:

> Where is the wood . . .
> The sacred tree, splendid stripling, perfect for lordship,
> Whose roots thrust down an hundred leagues
>   through the waters of the vast ocean to the depths of hell,
> Whose crown brushed [Anu's] heaven on high?[17]

This tree has a parallel in the cosmic trees of Ezekiel 31 and of Dan 4:10–12 (Aramaic 7–9) with its echoes of Genesis 1. Lambert also saw the conceit in a description of a supernatural net:

---

[12] See R. J. Clifford, *The Cosmic Mountain in Canaan and the Old Testament* (HSM 4; Cambridge: Harvard University, 1972) 15–16, n. 12.

[13] See R. J. Clifford (*Creation Accounts in the Ancient Near East and in the Bible* [CBQMS 26; Washington: The Catholic Biblical Association of America, 1994] 31, n. 14) on the Duranki as the "pillar" or "axis" linking heaven and earth.

[14] *Babylonian Wisdom Literature,* 327.

[15] Translation from Greenspahn, "Mesopotamian Proverb," 34.

[16] Foster, *Before the Muses,* 2. 504, "Hymn to Ishtar"; cf. 629: "Eshumesha, the house which stretches to heaven and netherworld. . . ."

[17] Foster, *Before the Muses,* 2. 779 (see *Babylonian Wisdom Literature,* 327, for text).

a-mat-ka sa-pàr-ra ṣi-i-ru šá ana šamê u erṣetim tar-ṣa-at
Your word (is an) exalted, divine net which stretches to heaven
and earth.[18]

One may note that "the god's net" here is a metaphor for the cosmic scope of
the divine *word*. The personified divine word in Wisdom 18 provides a significant parallel to this topos (T1, collocated with T3, descent, see below):

> Your all-powerful word leaped from heaven, from the royal throne, into the
> midst of the land that was doomed, a stern warrior carrying the sharp sword
> of your authentic command, and stood and filled all things with death, *and
> touched heaven while standing on the earth* (Wis 18:15–16).

Lambert concludes his discussion of the Mesopotamian texts,

> These examples . . . show that the idea of greatness, whether applied to
> gods, temples, a god's net, or a mythical tree, is expressed in terms of filling
> the whole universe: based on the underworld and *reaching* to heaven. The
> proverb under discussion ["Dialogue," lines 83–84] affirms that man, unlike
> these other great things, does not *stretch* in this way.[19]

The "somewhat incomprehensible concept" of which Lambert spoke is well
known in studies of comparative religion, and cosmic mountains, temples,
trees, and their embodied superhuman analogues are widespread.[20] Of
course, both the commonalities and specific differences among examples of

---

[18] Text in *Babylonian Wisdom Literature,* 327, my translation. The same terms are used of
the Ešumeša temple in a hymn to Ninurta (ibid., 120, line 19). See also R. Borger, "Das dritte
'Haus' der Serie Bīt Rimki (VR 50–51, Schollmeyer HGŠ Nr. 1)," *JCS* 21 (1967) 8, 14, lines
67–68, "Gen Himmel hat er sein Netz ausgebreitet, die Vögel des Himmels hat er wie der Sturm
(gott) niedergeworfen." The net's spanning of heaven and *earth* is implicit in *niedergeworfen*
(*ir-ḫi-iṣ*).

[19] *Babylonian Wisdom Literature,* 327 (my emphases). See also Gilgamesh, IX, ii, 4–5
(*ANET,* 88) of Mashu, a mountain of supernatural awesomeness.

[20] M. Eliade, *Patterns in Comparative Religion* (New York: World Publishing [Meridian],
1963) 99–111, 265–267, 298–300, 374–380; *The Myth of the Eternal Return or Cosmos and
History* (Princeton: Princeton University, 1954) 12–17. In addition to Dan 4:10–15, 20–22 (with
a human homologue), the symbolism of the cosmic tree also appears in the Hodayot of
Qumran, in Ezekiel 31, and underlies Jesus' parable of the mustard seed becoming a tree (*den-
dron*) illustrating the cosmic scope of the kingdom. See 1QH 14:15–17 (E. Puech's numbering;
cf. F. G. Martínez, *The Dead Sea Scrolls Translated: The Qumran Texts in English* [Leiden:
Brill, 1994] 341) and Matt 13:31–32. For the cosmic stature of Mt. Atlas and its human homo-

such generalized concepts from comparative religion must be carefully delin-eated.[21]

Further instances of T1 may be adduced. Even where the T1 proverb does not itself appear, the idea of cosmos-spanning stature may be elaborated in other images and genres. A typical instance is the alternating description of the goddess Gula and her husband, whose divine greatness is portrayed in terms of physical, cosmic immensity. This passage collocates instances of T1 and T2:

> My towering husband . . . makes heaven and netherworld quake,
> lofty one among the Igigi-gods . . .
> *Who examines the heights of heaven,*
>   *who investigates the bottom of the netherworld.* . . .
> He is firm of foot in heaven, powerful in the depths,
> Great in the netherworld, sublime in Ekur. . . .
> Towering, with stately physique,
>   always ready to charge mountains . . .
> *He wears the heavens on his head, like a tiara,*
> *He is shod with the netherworld, as with [san]dals* . . .
> Foremost one, slayer, mountain. . . .[22]

Topos 2

The first pair of emphasized lines show that in this description of cosmic greatness yet another topos is embedded (T2). Its distinctive feature is to use the heaven-earth/underworld merismus to stress the cosmic scope of the god's *investigative knowledge,* in contrast to other gods or humans who lack

logue, see Hesiod, *Theogony,* lines 517–20; Herodotus, *Histories* IV, 184; Ovid, *Metamor-phoses* IV, 655–62. B. Lincoln, *Myth, Cosmos, and Society: Indoeuropean Themes of Creation and Destruction* (Cambridge: Harvard University, 1986) 10.

[21] Clifford, *Cosmic Mountain,* 7. Clifford's rejection of the term "cosmic mountain" with reference to Mesopotamia concerns an older view among Assyriologists, that the cosmos itself was a mountain. My use of the term "cosmic mountain" refers rather to a cosmic center in which a temple or mountain provides the linkage between heaven and earth/underworld. This view, I believe, comports with Clifford's, though his acceptance of the term "cosmic mountain" for Canaan and Israel is based on different grounds. See *Cosmic Mountain,* 21–25, 190–91. See fur-ther, A. Cooper, "Ps 24:7–10: Mythology and Exegesis," *JBL* 102 (1983) 37–60, esp. 44, n. 38.

[22] Foster, *Before the Muses,* 2. 493–97 (my emphases). Note also the immense size of Marduk, Enuma Elish I, 99–100.

such knowledge. This proverbial topos (T2) has its counterpart in a number of biblical texts:

> The height of heaven, the breadth of the earth,
> the abyss, and wisdom—who can find them out? . . .
> There is but one who is wise, greatly to be feared, seated
>   upon his throne—the Lord (Sir 1:3, 8).

Job 11:7–8 is similar:

> Can you find out the deep things of God?
> Can you find out the limit of the Almighty?
> It is higher than heaven—what can you do?
> Deeper than Sheol—what can you know? (cf. Prov 25:2–3;
>   Wis 9:16–18).

Typically, statements of the type T2 presuppose either T1 (cosmic stature spanning heaven and earth/netherworld, especially vertically but also horizontally) or T3 (the ability to ascend and descend between heaven and earth/underworld). Without cosmic size or mobility one's knowledge is obviously limited. The intent of the topoi is to exalt the greatness of a god and conversely to deny such greatness to others, especially humans. In Israel the images of Sir 1:3 and related texts express Yahweh's transcendent knowledge and mastery as creator and judge,[23] in contrast to humans for whom such things are *ʾyn ḥqr*, "inscrutable" (see Ps 145:3; Job 5:9; 9:10; Isa 40:28; cf. Job 36:26 [*lʾ ḥqr*]).

Topos 3

More recently, F. E. Greenspahn has discussed examples of T1 and T3 as an ancient Near Eastern proverbial motif with special reference to exemplars in the Hebrew Bible.[24] Greenspahn noted the texts cited by Lambert and added

---

[23] See Job 11:7–10; 28:3, 20–21, 27; Qoh 7:23–24; Wis 9:16. For the multifaceted continuation of this tradition in apocalyptic, see M. E. Stone's seminal article, "Lists of Revealed Things in the Apocalyptic Literature," *Magnalia Dei: The Mighty Acts of God: Essays on the Bible and Archaeology in Memory of G. Ernest Wright* (ed. F. M. Cross, et al.; Garden City, NY: Doubleday, 1976) 414–52; reprinted in M. E. Stone, *Selected Studies in Pseudepigrapha and Apocrypha* (SVTP 9; Leiden: Brill; 1991) 379–418.

[24] Greenspahn, "A Mesopotamian Proverb."

others. However, like Lambert and Hallo, he did not distinguish the separate traditions underlying T1 and T3. Consequently, to my knowledge, the specific character of the ancient tradition (T3) underlying Prov 30:4aα has remained unclarified.

As Hallo demonstrated, our proverb occurs in epic contexts. But Hallo did not note that the Sumerian version of Gilgamesh is an instance of T1, while the Old Babylonian version of Gilgamesh (Yale, iv, 5–8) is an instance of T3.[25] Though T1 and T3 are closely related and can occur together, their origins and specific functions are different. The Old Babylonian version of Gilgamesh makes explicit the point of ascending to heaven: only the immortal gods can do that; there is a great gulf between mortals and the gods:

> Who can go up to heaven (*e-lu-ú ša-m[a-i]*), my friend?
> Only the gods dwell (?) with Shamash forever.
> Mankind can number his days.
> Whatever he may achieve, it is only wind.[26]

Here the T3 proverb appears in its shortest form; only ascent to heaven is mentioned. Significantly, it occurs in the form of a rhetorical question, just as in Prov 30:4aα. While it is important to note occurrences of this topos, *as proverb*, in epic and other literary contexts,[27] it is significant that the topos of ascent to heaven occurs as an epic or heroic motif. Historical, legendary, or folk tale origins for proverbial sayings are well-known among paremiologists, and many examples exist, also in modern European languages.[28] A. Taylor's methodological principle concerning proverbs and fables may be applied, *mutatis mutandis,* to the ancient narrative forms considered here:

[25] See nn. 4, 5 for references to Sumerian "Gilgamesh and the Land of the Living" and to the Sumerian proverb collection edited by Alster.

[26] S. Dalley, *Myths From Mesopotamia: Creation, The Flood, Gilgamesh and Others* (Oxford: Oxford University, 1989) cited from paperback edition (1991) 144; Akkadian from J. Tigay, *The Evolution of the Gilgamesh Epic* (Philadelphia: University of Pennsylvania, 1982) 164.

[27] Paremiologists have established criteria for disembedding proverbs from literary contexts, and have been followed by ancient Near Eastern scholars. See Alster, *Studies in Sumerian Proverbs*; G. Beckman, "Proverbs and Proverbial Allusions in Hittite," *JNES* 45 (1986) 19–30; W. W. Hallo, "Proverbs"; C. R. Fontaine, *Traditional Sayings in the Old Testament: A Contextual Study* (Sheffield: Almond, 1982).

[28] L. Röhrich and W. Mieder, "Das Verhältnis des Sprichworts zu den anderen 'einfachen Formen,'" *Sprichwort* (Stuttgart: J. B. Metzlersche Verlagsbuchhandlung, 1977) 83–89.

The fable which can be positively recognized as the source of a proverb appears in its proverbial dress as an allusion, intelligible to those familiar with the story, and not as a summary.[29]

It is most likely that proverbs concerning heavenly ascent (T3) arose from more extended narrative treatments of the topos. Evidence supporting this view is found in recently published wisdom texts from Ugarit and Emar which supplement texts previously known texts from a variety of locations.[30] These recent texts (with Sumerian originals after 2000 and before 1660 B.C.E. and with Akkadian exemplars as late as Ashurbanipal's library) contemplate the futility of human existence. Each section of this wisdom poem begins with the same three lines:

> Rules were formulated by Enki,
> Regulations were laid down at the command of the gods.
> From days of old there has been vanity [lit., "wind"].

The thought here is not unlike that in the passage from the Old Babylonian Gilgamesh cited above: humanity is merely "wind." In the poem as preserved in Emar, a variant couplet combines T1 and T2:

> 7   Like the remote heavens, my hand has not reached (it).
> 8   Like the depths of hell, no one knows (it).

These lines exploit the idea of humanity's small stature vis-à-vis heaven and the netherworld (T1) to reveal the limitations of human knowledge (T2). But for insight into Prov 30:4, this poem's list of past kings and heroes from before and after the deluge is more important, for here the heavenly ascent topos (T3) appears with proverbial brevity, alluding to a well-known narrative. Like Ecclesiastes (a parallel Lambert explicitly makes), the Emar poem notes that the heroes and great ones of the past are dead:

> 19   The life of mankind does not [last] forever.
> 11   Where is Alulu, the king who reigned for 36,000 years?
> 12   *Where is Etana, the king who ascended to heaven?*

---

[29] A. Taylor, *The Proverb* (Cambridge, MA: Harvard University, 1931) 32.

[30] See W. G. Lambert, "Some New Babylonian Wisdom Literature," *Wisdom in Ancient Israel: Essays in honour of J. A. Emerton* (ed. J. Day, R. P. Gordon and H. G. M. Williamson; Cambridge: Cambridge University, 1995) 30–42, esp. 37–42; M. Dietrich, "'Ein Leben ohne Freude . . .'" *UF* 24 (1992) 9–29. I follow Lambert's translation.

13 Where is Gilgamesh, who sought life like Zi'usudra? . . .
17 Where are the great kings from days of yore to the present?

The hero-kings mentioned here (Huwawa and Enkidu also appear) are known from the famous Sumerian King List. There also, in a composition going back perhaps to Utu-hegal's liberation of Sumer from Gutian domination (about 2100 B.C.E.), we find Etana mentioned as king of Kish: "Etana, a shepherd, *he who ascended to heaven* (and) consolidated all countries . . ." (*ANET,* 265). Thus, one tradition of the heavenly ascent proverb begins in a legend concerning the remote historical figure Etana (early third millennium or "Early Dynastic I").[31] The narrative itself is extremely ancient and is unusual in that it is also represented graphically—as a sort of "visual proverb."[32] Cylinder seals from "about 2360–2180" represent Etana ascending heavenward on an eagle's back.[33] The story was evidently very well-known.

Three Akkadian versions of the Etana legend exist, in Old Babylonian, Middle Assyrian, and a Late Version.[34] In this story, Etana mounts an Eagle whom he has rescued, and ascends to heaven on its back. The Eagle is in some respects a foil to Etana. Earlier in the story, in sinful pride, the eagle verbally anticipates Etana's voyage heavenward. It plans to betray its friend, the snake, and eat the latter's children:

> "I will eat the serpent's children. . . .
> *"I will go up and d[well] in heaven,*
> *"If I descend* from the crown of the tree, . . . the king."[35]

---

[31] S. N. Kramer, *The Sumerians* (Chicago: University of Chicago, 1963) 43–44; cf. W. W. Hallo and W. K. Simpson, *The Ancient Near East: A History* (New York: Harcourt-Brace-Jovanovich, 1971) 40–42.

[32] Graphic representations of proverbs and narratives exist from the most ancient times to the present. Some, like Brueghel's "Netherlandish Proverbs," are famous; others appear in popular broadsheets and newspaper cartoons to the present day. For literature and orientation to one significant topos (also used by Brueghel), see my "Proverbs 30:21–23 and the Biblical World Upside Down," *JBL* 105 (1986) 599–610.

[33] *ANEP,* nos. 694, 695; pp. 221–22, 332–33.

[34] J. V. Kinnier Wilson, *The Legend of Etana: A New Edition* (Warminster: Aris & Phillips, 1985). See Foster, *Before the Muses,* 1. 437–60.

[35] Foster, *Before the Muses,* 1. 452. The latter line, about descent, is unfortunately not wholly clear. It is part, however, of a pattern of repetition in the story concerning various ascents and descents, besides Etana's famous trip to heaven. The "crown of the tree" seems suggestive of a *Weltbaum.*

Here Topos 3, in narrative form, represents the overweening pride of the eagle: it does not recognize its proper place or limits. The eagle's littlest fledging, however, is "exceedingly wise" (such stories all concern wisdom!) and tries to dissuade its errant parent:

> "Do not eat, my father!
>   The net of Shamash will hunt you down . . .
> Whoever transgresses the limits of Shamash,
>   Shamash [will deliver] him as an offender
>   into the hands of the [executioner]!"

The eagle's affront against the "limits of Shamash," the god of justice, is figuratively an ascent to heaven ("I will go up and dwell in heaven"), a taking to oneself the prerogatives of deity. The cosmic entailments of the eagle's descent from the tree to eat an ox (in which the snake is hiding) is made clear in another warning from the wise fledgling:

> "Do not *go down!*
>   No doubt [the serpent is lurking in the wild ox]!
> The netherworld will h[old you fast]."

This ironic opposition of heavenly ascent and underworldly descent anticipates Etana's own fate. In the Tablet IV/B of the Late Version, the first ascent of Etana to heaven is described. In the second flight (IV/C), the eagle and Etana ascend even beyond what is granted them; Etana panics and they fall to earth, barely surviving, their fall being cushioned by "a brushwood pile of poplar wood." Wilson rightly asks, "Was it the spirit of adventure that now takes command?"[36] Etana's experience of distance from the earth leads him declare,

> *ib-ri ul e-li a-na šamê*
> My friend, I cannot ascend to the heavens.[37]

---

[36] Wilson, *The Legend of Etana*, 11. For the parallel with the classical tale of Ganymede (Statius, *Thebais* I, 548–51), see C. J. Gadd, *The Cambridge Ancient History: Volume I: Part 2: Early History of the Middle East* (3d ed.; Cambridge: Cambridge University, 1971) 110. J. Aro ("Anzu and Simurgh," *Kramer Anniversary Volume: Cuneiform Studies in Honor of Samuel Noah Kramer* [AOAT 25; ed. B. L. Eichler et al.; Neukirchen-Vluyn: Neukirchener V., 1976] 25–28) traces further literary reflexes of this tale of a flight to heaven on an eagle's back.

[37] LV IV 43, Wilson, *The Legend of Etana*, 116.

According to Wilson, yet a third and fourth heavenly ascent takes place. The end of the story is lost, but it appears that "After they had ascended to the heaven of A[nu]" their sojourn was short and Etana returns to earth and dies. In the narrative logic common to many cultures and religions (think of Moses' repeated ascents and descents of Sinai), for humans, ascent (*anabasis*) entails descent (*katabasis*).[38] "What goes up must come down!" As S. N. Kramer sardonically remarked, "To be sure, Etana did not stay put in heaven, for . . . we find Etana residing in the netherworld whither all mortals, no matter how great their achievements—except, of course, the Flood-hero Ziusudra—must finally descend."[39] The point, once again, is human limitation in contrast to the gods.

Etana is not the only hero to ascend to the heavens. This topos attaches to several primordial characters. Notable among them is Adapa, the first and most famous of the seven predeluvian sages (*apkallu*)—quasi-human fishmen who bring the arts of civilization to humans.[40] In a fragmentary text, E. Reiner found a proverbial reference to Adapa's heavenly ascent which was virtually identical to the proverbial allusions to Etana's ascent cited above:

> [Adapa,] the purification priest of Eridu
> [. . .] who ascended to heaven.[41]

This text was later seen to be from Tablet III of the bilingual incantation series "Bīt Mēseri," and with fuller textual evidence, R. Borger translated the two lines in question as follows:

> An-Enlilda, der Beschwörer der Stadt Eridu,
> *Utuabzu, der zum Himmel emporgestiegen ist.*[42]

---

[38] See G. G. Stroumsa, *Hidden Wisdom: Esoteric Traditions and the Roots of Christian Mysticism* (Leiden: Brill, 1996) 169–83, with extensive bibliography.

[39] Kramer, *The Sumerians*, 44; see p. 214 for the "Pushkin Elegies," line 97. In the Elegies, Etana appears with Gilgamesh and Nedu as "gods of the netherworld." Cf. Gilgamesh VII, iv, 45–49.

[40] See J. Bottéro, *Mesopotamia: Writing, Reasoning, and the Gods* (Chicago: University of Chicago, 1992) 246–50.

[41] [. . .] *šá ana* AN-*e i-lu-*[*ú*] (line 4); E. Reiner, "The Etiological Myth of the Seven Sages," *Or* 30 (1961) 1–11; see 2 (text) and 4 (translation).

[42] R. Borger, "Die Beschwörungsserie *Bīt Mēseri* und die Himmelfahrt Henochs," *JNES* 33 (1974) 183–96, here 192; the emphases are Borger's.

This brief note of ascent finds its proverbial counterpart in an equally terse text which describes Utuaaba's (= Adapa's?) descent: "Utuaabba, der aus dem Himmel herabgestiegen ist."[43]

A difficulty in dealing with such fragmentary materials is that the sequence and names of the pre-deluvian sages vary considerably in the various lists of sages that have survived. Borger himself briefly treats three lists of sages, and argues that in certain traditions Utuabzu was the *seventh* primordial sage (not Adapa, the first), who thus corresponds to the biblical Enoch, "the seventh from Adam" (Jude 14). However, Utuaabba was identified with Adapa ("born of the sea") in scribal etymology.[44] In any case, the clear proverbial references to Etana and Adapa suggest that the topos of heavenly ascent (and descent) could attach to various figures.[45]

Be that as it may, the story of Adapa does shed clear light on T3. Adapa is exceedingly wise and beloved of Ea, the god of wisdom.

> He [the god] made him perfect in wisdom,
> revealing to him the designs of the land.
> To him he granted wisdom, eternal life he did not grant him.[46]

Because Adapa apparently abused the exceptional power of his wisdom (he had "broken the wing" of the South wind), Anu, god of heaven, summoned him into his presence to give an account. Ea, Adapa's divine "employer," counsels him on the heavenly protocol needed to appease Anu's anger, and tells him not to eat the heavenly food offered him, since it is "food of death." The messenger of Anu

---

[43] Borger, "Die Beschwörungsserie," 193.

[44] See Foster, "Wisdom and the Gods," 346, 347, n. 12. Borger ("Die Beschwörungsserie," 186) explains the identification of Adapa and Utuaabba as an instance of the (proverbial) use of "Adapa" to mean "wise" (cf. *CAD* A/1, s.v. *adapu*). Borger (p. 193) appeals to the late Uruk/ Warka text published by J. van Dijk in H. J. Lenzen, *XVIII. vorläufiges Bericht über die von dem Deutschen Archäologischen Institut und der Deutschen Orient-Gesellschaft aus Mitteln der Deutschen Forschungsgemeinschaft unternommen Ausgrabungen in Uruk-Warka: Winter 1959/60* (Deutsches Archäologisches Institut, Abteilung Baghdad; Berlin: Mann, 1962) 43–52, here 44–45. In this text, each Apkallu is paired with a king. Utuabzu's royal counterpart is Enmeduranki, whom a late Babylonian king (probably Nebuchadnezzer I) claimed as ancestor; see W. G. Lambert, "Enmeduranki and Related Matters," *JCS* 21 (1967) 126–33.

[45] See Eliade's important discussion (*Myth of the Eternal Return*, 37–46) of the mechanisms by which mythic or legendary patterns attach to historical figures in oral tradition.

[46] Foster, *Before the Muses*, 2. 430.

brought him along the [ro]ad to heaven,
He went up to heaven.
When he went up to heaven. . . .[47]

Anu is so taken with the clever Adapa that he offers him food of life and thus immortality. Unfortunately, Adapa obeys Ea's command, refuses the food, and forfeits his chance at immortality. He descends once again to the life of a mortal, to serve in Ea's realm below, much to the latter's delight. Though his heavenly journey enabled Adapa to survey reality "from the horizon to the heights of heaven,"[48] ensuring him unparalleled wisdom and fame, it did not gain him immortality. Once again, it appears that a story of heavenly ascent communicates mortality and limitation in contrast to the gods.[49]

The topos of heavenly ascent recurs in the late story of Erra (god of violence, plague, and the Underworld, also known as Nergal) and his companion Ishum (a counselor and god of fire). In this tale, Marduk's cult statue has grown shabby over time. Erra, who desires to create world-wide war and violence, entices Marduk to leave his throne to be refurbished. Yet, if Marduk goes in for repairs, the order of the universe will disintegrate, chaos will reign, as had happened once before (I 124–91). Marduk says,

> "When I rise [from] my dwelling,
>   the regulation [of heaven and earth] will disintegrate,
> "The [waters] will rise and sweep over the land,
> "Bright [day will turn] to dar[k]ness . . .[50]

Erra cleverly offers to take Marduk's place (for his own violent purposes) while the latter is being refurbished:

> "For that time I will govern and keep strong
>   the regulation of heaven and earth,
> "I will go up to heaven (*ana šamê elīma* . . .)
>   and issue instructions to the Igigi-gods,
> I will go down to the depths (*ur-rad ana apsî*)

---

[47] Ibid., 432.

[48] Ibid., 434. This line seems a variant of T2.

[49] On this story, see the incisive comments of B. Foster, "Wisdom and the Gods."

[50] Foster, *Before the Muses,* 2. 780. The passage is a typical instance of the "World Upside Down" topos. See my "Proverbs 30:21–23."

> and keep the Anunnu-gods in order.
> I will dispatch the wild demons to the netherworld. . . .[51]

Here the familiar language of heavenly ascent and subterranean descent are used to express Erra's assumption of the prerogatives of Marduk, the supreme god of the cosmos (cf. Enuma Elish), if only for a time. Erra's assumption of Marduk's place is, however, disastrous. The world descends into chaos. The heavenly and the netherworldly gods retreat to their respective places:

> The Igigi-gods were terrified and went up to h[eaven].
> The Anunna-gods were [fright]ened
> and [went down] to the pit [of hell].

According to P. Machinist, the poem of Erra

> appears to be a transparent "mythologization" of a specific historical event or period. This point is nowhere better illustrated than in Tablet IV:3, where, to describe how Erra caused a civil war and destruction in Babylon, the poet claims: *i-lu-ut-ka tu-šá-an-ni-ma tam-ta-šal a-me-liš*, "You changed out of your divinity and made yourself like a man."[52]

Part of Erra's man-like behavior is that, though he is a god, his pride leads him to leave his assigned place in the order of things. Even the gods are subject to cosmic order. Erra's proper function is to be a god of war; that is his proper activity or "noise."[53] Yet *excess* of action "loses all proportion . . . [and] breaks the established (Babylonian) world, both of gods and of men (IV 104–127; V 6–15). . . . [It] not only devastates human beings, but cracks the very boundaries of the cosmos."[54]

The topos of heavenly ascent to usurp the place of the most high god and consequent descent to the underworld appears also in the Bible, in the famous taunt song of Isaiah 14 (cf. 37:23–25). Here too, "mythologization" of history seems to take place. Indeed, one wonders if Isaiah 14 is in part a parody of the Erra poem. In the Isaian taunt song, the king of Babylon has

---

[51] Foster, *Before the Muses*, 2. 781. Text from *CAD* A/2, s.v. *arādu*.
[52] P. Machinist, "Rest and Violence in the Poem of Erra," *JAOS* 103 (1983) 221–26, here 221.
[53] Ibid., 224.
[54] Ibid., 225.

fallen from heaven and descended to the underworld: "Your pomp is brought down to Sheol" (*hwld š'wl g'wnk*, v. 11). Earlier he had made his proud boast:

I will ascend to heaven	*hšmym 'lh*
above the stars of El	*mm'l lkwkby-'l*
I will set my throne on high . . .	*'rym ks'y*
I will ascend (*'lh*) above the heights of the clouds,	
I will make myself like the Most High (*l'lywn* [vv 13–14]).	

Instead, like Etana and even the god Erra (sometimes assimilated to Gilgamesh, a figure associated with Etana in the underworld), the king of Babylon descends to Sheol (v 15):

But you are brought down to Sheol	*'k 'l-š'wl twrd*
to the recesses of the Pit.	*'l-yrkty-bwr*

Common to all these tales of heavenly ascent is the theme of failure to achieve what is not ordained for one. Mortals and lesser deities who attempt to attain the prerogatives of heaven find themselves returned to earth; often they descend to the netherworld.[55] Only (certain) divine beings can make such journeys with impunity.[56] Even the great gods can travel the vertical axis of the cosmos only with severe restraints, as is evident from the tale of Inanna's/Ishtar's Descent to the Underworld and the elaborate machinations required to get her out and up to resume her role as "queen of heaven." Central to the topos (T3) of ascent is the problem of limits: humans especially cannot gain the privileges and position of the immortal, heavenly gods. In the words of the Psalmist, "The heavens are the Lord's heavens, but the earth he has given to the sons of man" (Ps 115:16 [15]). The "moral" of such stories is well summed up by Gilgamesh in the words of our proverb:

---

[55] In Greek tradition, Bellerophon attempts an ascent to heaven on his horse, Pegasus, and dies. There is a lost play by Euripides on this hero, which was parodied in Aristophanes' *Peace*. The ironic hero of *Peace*, Trygaeus, ascends to heaven on the back of a giant dung beetle to confront the gods in his quest to free the goddess Peace. The legend of Icarus is a version of the myth in which *technology* is the instrument by which humans scale the heavens. There is nothing new under the sun. As the quintessential American proverb has it, "The sky's the limit!" which has come to mean for us that there are no limits. Surprisingly this proverb is not included among the 15,000 sayings in W. Mieder's monumental *Dictionary of American Proverbs* (New York: Oxford University, 1992).

[56] Cf. G. Sauer, *Die Sprüche Agurs* (Stuttgart: Kohlhammer, 1963) 99.

Who can go up to heaven, my friend?
Only the gods dwell with Shamash forever.
Mankind can number his days.
Whatever he may achieve, it is only wind.

In ancient Near Eastern cosmologies with their separation of heaven and earth, a fundamental religious problem is how humans can access the power and benefits of the gods above.[57] For this reason, cosmic mountains (with their heavenly reach up to heaven) find their homologue in cosmos-spanning temples which give humans access to the throne rooms of the gods.[58] The sacred mountain/temple is thus an institution that permits commerce between heaven and earth/underworld. This function appears clearly in the well-known Enuma Elish. After Marduk has created heaven and earth from the two halves of Tiamat's body, Babylon is created as a sort of celestial staircase that permits the gods to ascend and descend to assembly.[59] In this scenario, T1 (cosmic extension) provides the means for T2 (cosmic ascent and descent). This is apparent from Marduk's address to the other gods:

"A house I shall build . . .
When you go up from Apsu to assembly,
Let your stopping places be there to receive you.
When you come down from heaven to [assembly],
Let your stopping places be there to receive all of you.
I shall call [its] name [Babylon], Abode of the Great Gods."[60]

The cosmic expanse of the Babylonian temple-mountain is alluded to in the

[57] For Israel, see R. P. Knierim's important essay, "Cosmos and History," *The Task of Old Testament Theology: Substance, Method, and Cases* (ed. R. P. Knierim; Grand Rapids, MI: Eerdmans, 1995) 171–224. For Mesopotamia, W. G. Lambert, "The Cosmology of Sumer and Babylon," *Ancient Cosmologies* (ed. C. Blacker and M. Loewe; London: Allen & Unwin, 1975) 42–62, esp. 56–59, 61–62.

[58] On this general phenomenon, see Eliade, *Myth of the Eternal Return*. J. D. Levenson (*Sinai and Zion: An Entry into the Jewish Bible* [Minneapolis: Winston, 1985] 111–76) provides an extensive treatment of Mt. Zion as the cosmic mountain.

[59] Lambert ("Cosmology") shows that the author of Enuma Elish wrestled with the problem of combining traditions which variously pictured the cosmos as duple (heaven and earth) and triple (heaven, earth, and underworld or *apsu*). In the fullest elaboration of Babylonian cosmology, Lambert finds three levels of "heaven" and three levels of "earth."

[60] Enuma Elish V, 122–29; Foster, *Before the Muses*, 1. 382. Cf. Clifford, *Cosmic Mountain*, 19–20.

biblical "Tower of Babel" story with "its head in the heavens" (Gen 11:4; cf 28:12). But the story of Jacob's dream at Bethel provides the best parallel to the ascent and descent of divine beings on a "cosmic staircase" connecting heaven and earth (Gen 28:12).[61] That also this story alludes to Babylon's temple seems evident when Jacob calls the place, "a house of god/s" (*byt ʾlhym, not byt ʾl*) and "the gate of heaven" (Gen 28:17) an apparent play on the folk etymology, *Bāb-ilī,* "gate of the gods."

The Amarna tablets provide another instance of T3 (heavenly ascent) in proverbial form, within a letter. Here the complementary notion of descent, which is sometimes only implicit in the often fragmentary Mesopotamian narratives, appears explicitly. The passage in question provides a close parallel to the antithesis of *ʿlh smym* and *šʾwl/ʾrṣ yrd* in the Hebrew Bible. A Canaanite king argues his humble insignificance vis-à-vis the Pharaoh, "If we go up to the heavens or if we go down to the earth, our heads are still in your hands."[62] This text has well-known echoes in Psalm 139:8 and in Amos 9:2–4. In the Amarna letter, Psalm 139, and Amos 9, the conditional "if" in each case is unreal and hypothetical, its point being that no matter where the Canaanite kinglet, the Psalmist, or the wicked might go, they are in the hands of the divinity, Pharaoh or Yahweh respectively. The typical contrast of mortals and deities is again accentuated. In Amos 9 the topos makes a similar point: if humans could do the impossible, could dig down to Sheol or hide in the depths of the sea, they still could not escape Yahweh's judgment (cf. Jer 31:37). And even if they could scale heaven (*wʾm-yʿlw hšmym*) from there "I [Yahweh] would bring them down" (*mšm ʾwrydm*), thereby displaying who really has cosmic scope and power. Thus, our proverbial topos (T3) places us in the realm of *adynata:* things impossible for humans to do. As Greenspahn comments, the point of the biblical examples "is the same as that of the Mesopotamian proverb with which we began—that what distinguishes humanity from the gods is its lack of heavenly reach."[63]

Both Isa 40:12–14 and Job 38:4–6 provide rhetorical, cosmic questions similar to those of Prov 30:4, and with a similar function (cf. esp. Prov 30:4aγ and Isa 40:12aα). They distinguish almighty God from puny humans (Isa 40:15–17). In Proverbs 30 and Job 38, the issue in each case is knowledge frus-

---

[61] *Pace* V. P. Hamilton (*The Book of Genesis: Chapters 18–50* [Grand Rapids, MI: Eerdmans, 1995] 240), who follows H. Hoffner.

[62] Greenspahn, "Mesopotamian Proverb," 35 (Amarna letter #264, lines 15–19).

[63] "A Mesopotamian Proverb."

trated by human limitations, and expressed in identical, ironic language (*ky tdᶜ*). Such traditions, including Proverbs 30:1–9, have their counterpart in a vast post-biblical series of *adynata,* so ably surveyed in M. Stone's seminal article. "The point of such passages is to state the limitlessness and unknowability of the divine wonders."[64] The development, in the Second Temple period, of revelations and heavenly journeys were in various ways claims to special knowledge otherwise beyond human ken. Two of the topoi here surveyed (T2 and T3) could be used either positively, to arrogate to oneself special knowledge denied others, or negatively, to deny such knowledge to humans generally, including oneself. The latter posture seems to be that of Agur, Job, and Isaiah. The issue is not so much skepticism, as the severe epistemological limits to which humans are subject. To know "heavenly things" requires one who can descend and ascend. This capacity the Gospel of John ascribes to the Son of Man (John 3:12–13).

The opposition of ascending heaven and descending (to earth) also appears in Deut 30:11–12, which Greenspahn cites with some diffidence. It is, however, a good parallel to Prov 30:4a, since presumably the one who brought down the law to earth is Yahweh, via his servant Moses, with his many ascents and descents of the cosmic temple-mountain Sinai.[65] This is apparently the significance of the answer that *Midrash Mishle* gives to the first question in Prov 30:4, "Who has ascended heaven and come down?—

---

[64] "Lists of Revealed Things," 387 [422].

[65] *Pace* Levenson (*Sinai and Zion,* 40–41) who ascribes cosmic, mythic traditions to Zion and downplays cosmic in favor of historical significance for Sinai. But this contrast of cosmos and history is as anachronistic for ancient Israel as is that of law and grace, which Levenson rightly rejects. Moreover, it ignores the homology of Sinai and Tabernacle/Temple with their mutual cosmic symbolism. See M. Weinfeld, "Sabbath, Temple and the Enthronement of the Lord—The Problem of the Sitz im Leben of Genesis 1:1–2:3," *Mélanges bibliques et orientaux en l'honneur de M. Henri Cazelles* (ed. A. Caquot and M. Delcor; AOAT 212; Kevelaer: Butzon and Bercker, 1981) 501–12. In some respects, Levenson's view seems a corrective to the old Lutheran, tradition-historical efforts of von Rad and Noth to radically separate Sinai (as law and ritual) from its narrative context (as salvation history and grace). Sinai too is covenant, saving history. But it is also the cosmic mountain from which the creator-king of heaven and earth (Exod 15:18), who performed a "repetition" (Eliade) of creation in the separation of sea and dry land (cf. Josh 2:10–11), dispenses his covenant. The biblical narratives in which the Sinai pericopes appear are themselves is redolent with cosmic, "mythic" significance, without which Sinai and its "historical" covenant cannot be fully understood. See Knierim, "Cosmos and History," and T. E. Fretheim, *Exodus* (Interpretation; Louisville: Westminster/John Knox, 1991) passim.

Moses."[66] This view of Deut 30:11–12 comports well with the logic of Prov 30:1–9, which appears to reject apocalyptic heavenly journeys (30:2–4) and insist instead that humans find their religious truth in the written word of God (30:5–6), and in a humble piety that asks for an appropriate lot in life (30:7–9).[67]

Conclusion

This survey of the background to the first question in Prov 30:4 shows that it utilized a widespread and very ancient topos of heavenly ascent and descent, a sort of journey possible only for the gods and quasi-divine figures. This topos has near relatives in topoi concerning cosmic extension and knowledge, with which it is sometimes intertwined. In narrative accounts of heavenly ascents, the occasional humans who make the ascent do so only temporarily and with disastrous results, generally being returned to earth or the underworld. The main purpose of the topos is to reaffirm the great gulf that separates humans from the divine realm and the prerogatives of deity, such as immortality, superhuman knowledge, wisdom, and power.

[66] B. L. Visotzky, *The Midrash on Proverbs* (New Haven: Yale University, 1992) 117.

[67] See Gunneweg, "Weisheit, Prophetie und Kanonformel"; P. Franklyn, "The Sayings of Agur in Proverbs 30: Piety or Scepticism?" *ZAW* 95 (1983) 238–52; D. Moore, "A Home for the Alien: Worldly Wisdom and Covenantal Confession in Proverbs 30,1–9," *ZAW* 106 (1994) 96-107; and my forthcoming *Proverbs* (New Interpreter's Bible; Nashville: Abingdon, 1997).

PART THREE

Qoheleth

"Beyond Them, My Son, Be Warned": The Epilogue of Qohelet Revisited

It is for good reason that modern scholars almost universally consider Qoh 12:9–14 to be epilogic. The unit falls outside the thematic framework marked by the nearly identical statements in 1:2 and 12:8 that everything is absolute *hebel*. Moreover, these verses refer to Qohelet in the past tense and in the third person, whereas the first person style is used for the rest of the book—except for the superscription in 1:1, the thematic framework in 1:2 and 12:8, and a third-person reference to Qohelet in 7:27. Most importantly, this appendix appears to look back at the book and to reflect on the work of the sage in whose name the book is written; it talks *about* Qohelet.

Yet there is no consensus on the unity of these verses. A few scholars discern three different hands in these verses.[1] Some find two editions (usually vv 9–11, vv 12–14),[2] while others defend the unity of the entire piece as the work of a

---

[1] So, for example, H. W. Hertzberg identifies three portions: vv 9–11, v 12, vv 13–14 (*Der Prediger* [KAT 17/4; Gütersloh: Mohn, 1963] 217–21). F. Backhaus, however, sees the three units differently: vv 9–10, v 11, vv 12–14 ("Der Weisheit Letzter Schluß! Qoh. 12,4–14 im Kontext von Traditionsgeschichte und beginnender Kanonisierung," *BN* 72 [1994] 29–34). L. Di Fonzo also recognizes three differents hands, which he identifies as vv 9–10, vv 11–12, vv 13–14. See his *Ecclesiaste* (La Sacra Bibbia; Rome: Marietti, 1967) 329–38.

[2] So, for example, E. Podechard, *L'Ecclésiaste* (EBib; Paris: Gabalda, 1912) 472–85; K. Galling, "Der Prediger," *Die fünf Megilloth* (HAT 18; 2d ed.; Tübingen: Mohr, 1969) 124–25; W. Zimmerli, *Das Buch des Predigers Salomo* (ATD 16/1; Göttingen: Vandenhoeck & Ruprecht, 1962) 244–47; A. Lauha, *Kohelet* (BKAT 19; Neukirchen-Vluyn: Neukirchener V., 1978) 217–23; J. L. Crenshaw, *Ecclesiastes* (OTL; Philadelphia: Westminster, 1987) 189–92; J. Vilchez, *Eclesiastes o Qohelet* (Nueva Biblia Española; Navarra: Verbo Divino, 1994) 413–21.

single epilogist, who is said to have added these comments to the work of the author.[3] Those who take the view of multiple editions, whether two or three, see the first edition as more or less sympathetic toward Qohelet. In this view, the first version of the epilogue, namely, 12:9–11, is supposed to come from the hand either of the compiler or a disciple of Qohelet, perhaps after the death of the master.[4] The rest of the passage is thought to contain an implicit criticism of Qohelet (v 12) and an attempt to balance the presumably heterodox outlook of the rest of the book with a more orthodox voice (vv 13–14). Those who see a single epilogist at work generally also detect an apologetic undercurrent: Qohelet's point of view is defended (vv 9–11), but then, quickly placed within a more conservative theological stance (vv 13–14). In any case, the majority of scholars regard 12:9–14 as coming from some editor or editors, some person or persons other than the author of the book. Furthermore, it is commonly held that the second half of this passage (vv 12–14) manifests a certain "canon consciousness" (*Kanonbewußtsein*), in the sense of a recognition that Qohelet's supposedly radical teachings should somehow be brought into harmony with other more readily accepted writings.

M. V. Fox has argued, however, that neither the third-person reference nor the retrospective style of the epilogue is indicative of different origin.[5] In support of his thesis, he calls attention to a number of texts from Egypt and Mesopotamia—Instruction for Kagemeni, Instruction of Ptahhotep, Instruction of Dua-Khety, Prophecy of Neferti, Complaint of Ipuwer, Instruction of Onkhsheshonqy, Instruction of Shuruppak, Wisdom of Ahiqar—as well as the books of Deuteronomy and Tobit. Typically, according to Fox, the first person narrative of a story is framed by third-person retrospection, often evaluating and extolling the work of the principal figure in the main narrative. So he argues that all of 1:2–12:14 is in fact by the same hand—that of the epilogist, who is the real author of the book and who takes on the persona of the sage called Qohelet. It must be admitted, however, that these Egyptian parallels prove nothing about the provenance of the epilogue or its unity. One still

---

[3] So, for example, O. Loretz, *Qohelet and der alte Orient: Untersuchungen zu Stil und theologischer Thematik des Buches Qohelet* (Freiburg: Herder, 1964) 138–41, 290–97; G. Ravasi, *Qohelet* (Milan: Edizioni Paoline, 1988) 361–62; R. E. Murphy, *Ecclesiastes* (WBC 23A; Dallas: Word, 1992) 123–30.

[4] So S. Holms-Nielsen, "On the Interpretation of Qoheleth in Early Christianity," *VT* 24 (1974) 169.

[5] See his "Frame-Narrative and Composition in the Book of Qohelet," *HUCA* 48 (1977) 83–106; also *Qohelet and His Contradictions* (BLS 18; Sheffield: Almond, 1989) 311–29.

cannot be certain if the narrator of the epilogue is the very author of the book, as Fox would have it. It is also possible that an editor might have been responsible for compiling the words of the author Qohelet and for framing the composition. Nevertheless, it appears that Fox has successfully shown that the third-person retrospective style does not necessarily mean that there was a different epilogist or several different epilogists reacting to Qohelet's views and correcting them in some way. Indeed, the epilogue may contain the same views as the main body of the text, although those views are articulated in a different "voice."

A number of recent articles and commentaries have appeared since Fox first published his view in 1977. Even though there has been no systematic refutation of Fox's arguments, scholars have continued to discuss the epilogue as coming from a different hand or different hands, and the debate rages about "canon consciousness" within this text.[6] In this essay, therefore, I would like to revisit this passage and to reconsider the function of this epilogic portion of the book.

I. Qohelet Was a Sage (vv 9–11)

One's understanding of the function of the epilogue may have bearing on how one translates its very first words. The disjunctive accent (*zāqēp gādól*) on the first word (*wĕyōtēr*) suggests that the Masoretes took it to be syntactically separate from the rest of the sentence. Thus, the word is to be interpreted either as a noun meaning "an addition" or "an addendum," or a substantive used adverbially, meaning "additionally."[7] A number of scholars, however, prefer to disregard the punctuation and take *wĕyōtēr šehāyâ* as one accentual unit. Taking this approach, Robert Gordis cites two texts from the Talmud: *ywtr mmh šhʿgl rwṣh lynq hprh rwṣh lhynyq*, "more than (the fact that) the calf wishes to suck, the cow wishes to suckle" (*b. Pesaḥ*. 112a); and *ywtr mšhʾyš rwṣh lyśʾ hʾšh rwṣh lhnśʾ*, "more than (the fact that) a man wishes to marry, a woman wishes to be married" (*b. Yebam*. 113a).[8] On the basis of

---

[6] See, for example, C. Dohmen, "Der Weisheit letzter Schluß? Anmerkungen zur Übersetzung und Bedeutung von Koh 12,9–14," *BN* 63 (1992) 12–18; C. Dohmen and M. Oeming, *Biblischer Kanon, worum and wozu? Eine Kanontheologie* (Freiburg: Herder, 1992) 30–42; Backhaus, "Der Weisheit letzter Schluß!" 46–54.

[7] So LXX: *kai perisson*. See Lauha, *Kohelet*, 218; Hertzberg, *Der Prediger*, 216.

[8] R. Gordis, *Koheleth—the Man and His World* (3d ed.; New York: Schocken, 1968) 351.

these putative syntactical analogies, then, Gordis argues that "Koheleth was not merely a professional Wisdom teacher whose activity was limited to the scions of the rich; through his writings he taught Wisdom to the *people.*"[9] For Gordis, who has long held that the sages were from the elite of society, the instruction of the general public must have been regarded as something extraordinary for a sage, whose audience was generally upper-class youths.[10] Accordingly, *wĕyōtēr* is taken to indicate that Qohelet was "more than" a sage: Qohelet was not only a sage, he even taught the people knowledge (see the translations of *RSV, NRSV, NIV, JB*). Yet, the sages in Israel, whatever one may assume about their social location,[11] surely did not regard teaching of the public as something extraordinary. Public instruction was not what one did "besides being a sage" (so the translation in *JB*). One reads, for instance, of personified Wisdom teaching in the street-bazaars, the market-place, and at the city gates. Personified Wisdom calls out from the top of city walls and at the thoroughfares (Prov 1:20–21; 8:1–3). In Israel, public teaching was not contradictory to the task of the sages, but integral to it. In the words of personified Wisdom in Prov 8:4, "Unto you, O people (*ʾîšîm*) I call out, my cry is to humanity (*bĕnê ʾādām*)." The sages were supposed to teach the public, even humanity in general, and not just the elite (cf. Sir 37:25). Moreover, the idiom in the two Post-biblical Hebrew texts cited by Gordis is properly *yōtēr min*, not *yōtēr še-* as we have in our text, and it is the *min* that makes the expression comparative. And many other examples of this idiom may be cited: e.g., *ywtr mmny,* "more than me" (Esth 6:6); *ywtr mmny,* "greater than I" (*y. Ber.* IV.7d); *ywtr mdyʾ,* "more than enough"; and *ywtr mkšyʿwr,* "more than the proper amount" (*b. Moʿed Qat.* 27b). That very idiom (*yōtēr min*) is in fact found in Qoh 12:12, where *wĕyōtēr mēhēmmâ* means "beyond them." We should, therefore, take the particle *še-* in *šehāyâ* not as relative but probably as causal.[12] The point here is not that Qohelet taught the people con-

9 Ibid., 351–52; see also pp. 28–29, 76–77.

10 See R. Gordis, "The Social Background of Wisdom Literature," *HUCA* 18 (1943/1944) 77–118.

11 Sages were not necessarily of the upper-classes. As Qohelet himself tells us, "Bread does not belong to the wise, nor wealth to the intelligent, nor favor to the clever" (9:11). Indeed, there are sages even among the lower classes—people who are despised (9:13–16).

12 See the use of *še-* in Qoh 8:14; Cant 1:6; 5:2. Cf. also the use of *ʾăšer* in Qoh 4:9. On the uses of *še-* and *ʾăšer* in Qohelet, see B. Isaksson, *Studies in the Language of Qoheleth: With Special Emphasis on the Verbal System* (Studia Semitica Upsaliensia 10; Stockholm: Almqvist & Wiksell, 1987) 148–56.

stantly even though he was a sage, but that he taught the people precisely *because* he was a sage. This is, in other words, a testimony to his being a sage: "Because Qohelet was a sage, he constantly taught people knowledge."[13]

The text then proceeds to itemize some of Qohelet activities: "He listened and searched; he edited many proverbs."[14] These are all activities and traits of a sage, not something that Qohelet did "besides being a sage." The epilogue attests that Qohelet "listened" and "searched" probably because the wise were supposed to listen attentively and to investigate all matters carefully. In this regard, it is important to note the significance of the ear in the wisdom tradition and the frequent association of the wisdom with the willingness of the ear to hear (Prov 2:2; 4:20; 5:1, 13; 15:31; 18:15; 22:17; 25:12; Job 29: 11; 34:3; Sir 3:29; 6:33–35). In Akkadian, *uznu*, "ear," is a metaphor for wisdom and the expression *uznu rapaštu* (lit., "wide ear") means "intelligent."[15] Hence, it would appear that the epilogue is making the case that Qohelet was a *ḥākām* because he not only taught the general public constantly, he also listened and investigated. Furthermore, Qohelet worked with many proverbs.[16] The point

---

[13] For ʿôd, "constantly," see A. Schoors, *The Preacher Sought to Find Pleasing Words: A Study of the Language of Qoheleth* (Orientalia Lovaniensia Analecta; Louvain: Peeters, 1992) 116.

[14] The verb ʾizzēn is most readily identified as a denominative verb related to ʾōzen, "ear." All the ancient versions assume some association with ear, taking the word either as a noun or a verb. And the earliest interpreters all took the verb the same way, as did the medieval commentators, Rashbam and Rashi. A number of commentators, however, take the verb to mean "he weighed," assuming a denominative verb from mō(ʾ)zĕnayim, "scales." In modern Western cultures one speaks of "weighing" words in the sense of evaluating them or testing them, but it cannot be assumed that the idiom was also present in the ancient Near East. Such a usage of ʾzn is unattested anywhere else in classical Hebrew. The verb used for weighing something, even when used with the noun mō(ʾ)zĕnayim, "scales," is always šql (Jer 32:10; Ezek 5:1; Job 31:6), and the verb is never used with words or ideas as its object. Indeed, the noun mō(ʾ)zĕnayim is property related not to the root ʾzn but to yzn, Proto-Semitic *wzn (cf. Arabic wazana, "to weigh"). The noun is attested in Ugaritic, where it is spelled as mznm, presumably with the original *w contracted. This root is unrelated to the verb ʾizzēn, "to hear."

[15] See *AHW*, 1448.

[16] The usage of tiqqēn here is ambiguous. Elsewhere in the book (1:15; 7:13), the verb means "to straighten" that which is crooked. So this verb is sometimes taken to mean "to correct" (i.e., to "straighten out"). Yet, the verb need not mean that he only made corrections. In post-biblical Hebrew the verb has an interesting range of meanings besides "to straighten" or "to repair": "to fix in place, set in order, prepare, establish, introduce, improve." Creativity may be implied. This is the case in Sir 47:9, where tyqn may mean "he arranged" (music). In Akkadian, the verb tuqqunu means "to order, to bring to order" (see *AHW*, 1323), which also a possible nuance of the verb in Hebrew. Indeed, this meaning is conveyed by LXX, which has kosmion, "ordering. "

here can hardly be that Qohelet was responsible for a specific genre of wisdom literature or, even less, of the book of Proverbs, as is sometimes suggested.[17] Only a small amount of what Qohelet wrote or worked on falls in the category of proverbial sayings. Rather, the assertion is that his work, which deals with *mĕšālîm*, was typical of a sage (cf. 1 Kgs 5:12; Prov 1:6).

Then, in v 10, further proof is offered that the author was a sage: "Qohelet tried to find felicitous words and he wrote words of truth rightly."[18] Dohmen has argued that the term *ḥēpeṣ* should be understood as a technical expression for the instructions about life.[19] This is certainly an appropriate sense of the expression. Yet one must not separate the word *ḥēpeṣ* from its association with enjoyment, a connotation the word has elsewhere in the book (5:3; 8:6; 12:1).[20] At the same time, the word also occurs in 3:1, 17; 5:7; 8:6 in the sense of a timely or appropriate matter or activity. At Qumran, the word refers to specific assignments or tasks of individuals.[21] It is, in fact, likely that both nuances are intended here. Thus, *dibrê-ḥēpeṣ* refers to words that are both pleasing and appropriate. These words are felicitous in every sense of the term—both apt and aesthetically pleasing.

The meaning of the next phrase is disputed. There is a disjunctive accent on *yōšer*, but Fox prefers to take the word as a bound form in a construct

---

The Greek translators apparently understood Qohelet's work to be editorial: he collocated the proverbs—i.e., he gave them order (cf. *NAB*, "arranged many proverbs"). But this is true only in the sense that there are some proverbs that Qohelet placed within a new interpretive framework. He did not merely rearrange things; he placed them in their new contexts and gave them new meanings.

[17] So, for example, G. A. Barton, *A Critical and Exegetical Commentary on the Book of Ecclesiastes* (ICC; Edinburgh: T. & T. Clark, 1908) 197.

[18] MT has *wktwb* (*wĕkātûb*), which is also supported by LXX, *kai gegrammenon*, "and what is written." But five Hebrew MSS have *wktb*, interpreting the verb as active, "and he wrote." Aquila, Symmachus, Syriac, and Vulgate all translate the word as a finite verb in the past tense, "and he wrote." This does not necessarily mean, however, that their *Vorlage(n)* had the Qal perfect 3 ms form. Rather, they may be interpreting the form (*ktwb*) as an infinitive absolute used in place of a finite verb, as in 4:2; 8:9; 9:11. Thus we should not emend to read *wĕkātab*, as is commonly done. Rather, one should repoint the word to read *wĕkātôb*. Perhaps an early variant had the word spelled defectively (i.e., *wĕkātōb*) and, hence we find the translation in Aquila and other witnesses.

[19] "Der Weisheit letzter Schluß?" 14–15.

[20] The expression probably has reference to the elegance of language and literary forms. See G. C. Aalders, *Het Boek de Prediker* (Commentaar op het OudeTestament; Kampen: Kok, 1948) 254.

[21] See 1QS 3.17; CD 14.12.

chain, thus, *yōšer dibrê ʾĕmet*, "the most honest words of truth."[22] In support of this reading, he cites Prov 22:21, *qōšṭ ʾimrê ʾĕmet*, which he also takes to be a construct chain. The Proverbs text cited is notoriously problematic, however. The unique and morphologically strange form *qōšṭ* need not be interpreted as a construct noun and is not interpreted so by the Masoretes or the ancient versions.[23] We should probably retain the Masoretic punctuation and take *yōšer* as a noun used adverbially.

Most commentators detect a certain defensiveness in these words. Hence there is a tendency to interpret *yōšer* as "honesty," "sincerity," or the like.[24] The meaning of the entire verse, then, is supposed to be something like this: It is true that what Qohelet wrote is aesthetically pleasing (*dibrê ḥēpeṣ*), *but* what he wrote is honest. Indeed, in A. B. Ehrlich's rendering of this verse, one perceives a severe indictment of the sage's acomplishments: "Qohelet set out to make interesting observations, but what he should have rightly written are the important matters."[25] The translation of *NEB* assumes a more apologetic tone: "He chose his words to give pleasure, but what he wrote was the honest truth." In other words, as Barton puts it, Qohelet "never sacrificed matter to form."[26]

Underlying this interpretation is an assumption that the ancient readers were somehow suspicious of literary artistry, and so an apologist—presumably a friend or disciple of the sage—had to insist there is substance and sincerity behind the artistic forms. It is doubtful, however, if the ancients perceived a tension between artistry and truth. Certainly in the wisdom literature throughout the ancient Near East there is no such dichotomy. Truth was always expected to be conveyed eloquently.[27] Hence, proverbs were always formulated in pithy, memorable fashion. Indeed, it was the love of rhetorical artistry that has generated such a wide variety of texts in the wisdom corpus

---

[22] *Qohelet and His Contradictions,* 324; "Frame-Narrative," 97.

[23] The word is usually seen as a gloss. See O. Plöger, *Spüche Salomos* (BKAT 17; Neukirchen-Vluyn: Neukirchener V., 1984) 262–63.

[24] So, for example, R. N. Whybray, *Ecclesiastes* (NCBC; Grand Rapids, MI: Eerdmans, 1989) 171; Loretz, *Qohelet und der alte Orient,* 140 n. 32.

[25] A. B. Ehrlich, *Randglossen zur hebräischen Bibel* (Leipzig: Hinrich's, 1914) 107.

[26] Barton, *Ecclesiastes,* 197. Gordis sees a veiled criticism "that Koheleth had strained unduly after literary effect" (*Koheleth,* 352).

[27] This was the premise of The Tale of the Eloquent Peasant. See M. Lichtheim, *Ancient Egyptian Literature* (Berkeley: University of California, 1971), 1. 169–84. Hereafter this source will be cited as *AEL.*

worthy of the name "literature." And that love of eloquence is reflected in the longing of the sage for novel, subtle, and unique modes of expression.[28] Precision and elegance of speech are qualities valued in the wisdom tradition throughout the ancient Near East (see Prov 15:23; 16:21, 24). The sincerity of Qohelet is surely not in question in this passage, not even implicitly. It is preferable, therefore, to take *yōšer* to mean not "honesty" or "straightforwardness" (in contrast to the supposed crookedness of rhetorical artistry), but "correctness and legitimacy." One may compare the expression *ʾimrê yōšer*, "right words," in Job 6:25.[29] It is also not amiss to note that the noun *yšr*, "rightness," in Ugaritic may be a synonym of *ṣdq*, "legitimacy": *mtrḫt yšrh*, "his rightful bride" // *aṯt ṣdqh*, "his legitimate wife" (*KTU* 1.14.1.13). The parallelism is also found in a Phoenician inscription: *mlk ṣdq* // *mlk yšr*, "a legitimate king" // "a rightful king" (*KAI* 4. 6–7). Accordingly, we should probably take *yōšer* to be a noun ("rightness"/"rightfulness") used adverbially: "he wrote the words of truth rightly." The point, then, is the legitimacy and correctness of Qohelet's words. The entire verse is in fact an endorsement of Qohelet's aptitude as a sage. It claims that he was a bona fide sage precisely *because* he chose felicitous words and rightly (rightfully?) wrote them. Significantly, in the Book of Proverbs, Wisdom's teachings to all humanity are depicted in similar terms:

> Listen, for I speak noble things,
> Out of my lips (I speak) what is right (*mêšārîm*).[30]
> My mouth utters truth (*ʾĕmet*),
> Wickedness is an abhorrence to my lips.
> All the words of my mouth are right (*ṣedeq*);
> In them is nothing perverse or crooked.
> They are all straighforward to the perceptive,
> And right (*yĕšārîm*) to those who find knowledge. (Prov 8:6–9)

So the epilogue claims that Qohelet was a sage, not only because he constantly taught people knowledge, but also because he listen and searched, he dealt with many proverbs, and he tried to find "felicitous words" (*dibrê ḥēpeṣ*) and wrote "words of truth" (*dibrê ʾĕmet*) rightly.

---

[28] See, for example, The Complaint of Khakheperre-Seneb (*AEL* 1. 146).

[29] D. J. A. Clines (*Job 1–20* [WBC 17; Dallas: Word, 1989] 156, 161) renders the expression as "words of right judgment. "

[30] Cf. Prov 16:13, where we have *dōbēr yĕšārîm*, "one who speaks what is right."

It may be observed that similar commendations are found in the epilogue of the Egyptian text known as the Instruction of Anii. In that epilogue, the sage who wrote the instructions is said to be a learned or wise man (Egyptian *iw rḫ.tw*), "a man who is a master, whose strivings are exalted, whose every word is chosen" and whose "words please the heart."[31] Interestingly, the epilogue of this Egyptian wisdom text also shows an awareness that the words of the sage may be difficult to understand and to follow, as are the words of Qohelet. Thus, the epilogue in the Instruction of Anii, though in the form of a debate between father and son, serves as an apology for the efficacy and sufficiency of the sage's words. Therein the "son" is urged to take the words of the instructions of the book seriously, for they come from a true sage who chose his words carefully and presented them in a pleasing manner. By the same token, in the epilogue of the Instruction for Kagemeni, the words of the sage who wrote the book are said to be "more beautiful upon their hearts than anything that was in the entire land."[32] In the epilogue of Qohelet, the reader—who is addressed in v 12 as "my son"—is told that Qohelet was a knowledgeable sage whose words had been carefully crafted and correctly written.

From the words of a particular sage (vv 9–10), the text seems to turn to the words of sages in general (v 11). Yet, there is no doubt that the teachings of Qohelet are in view. The expression *dibrê ḥăkāmîm,* "the words of the sages," does not appear to be a technical term here. Rather, as in 9:17 (also Prov 1:6; 22:17), it refers simply to the advice of the wise. These teachings are said to be "like goads" (*dorbōnôt!*) and "like implanted pricks" (*maśmĕrôt nĕṭûᶜîm*). The term *dorbōnôt,* "goads," refers properly to the tip of an ox-goad.[33] As for the word *maśmĕrôt,* it may refer not only to a nails but to any

---

[31] *AEL,* 2. 144. For a discussion of these lines, A. Volten, *Studien zum Weisheitsbuch des Anii* (Danske videnskabemes selskab, historik-filolgiske meddelelser, xxiii, 3; Copenhagen: Levin & Munksgaard, 1937) 136–75.

[32] Egyptian *nfr st ḥr ib.sn r ḫt nbt nty m t3 pn r dr.f.* See Papyrus Prisse 11, lines 13–14.

[33] In Mishnaic Hebrew, the noun may refer to the iron tip of a *malmēd,* "goad" (*m. Kelim* 9:6; 25:2) and, by extension, to the goad itself (*b. Ḥag.* 3b). M. Dahood ("The Phoenician Background of Qoheleth," *Bib* 47 [1966] 282) cites Ugaritic *drb,* which occurs with "knives" and "spear" (*KTU* 4.385.8). C. F. Whitley (*Koheleth: His Language and Thought* [BZAW 148; Berlin/New York: De Gruyter, 1979] 102) accepts this cognate, citing Arabic *ḏariba,* "to be sharp." But, while Arabic *ḏrb* does correspond to Ugaritic *drb,* it should correspond to Hebrew **zrb,* not *drb,* unless the Hebrew is a loanword from Aramaic. But if the word is of Aramaic origin one should expect the *-ān* ending instead of *-ôn.* It is more likely that the proper Arabic cognate is not *ḏariba,* "to be sharp," but *dariba,* "to be(come) accustomed, habituated," a verb

kind of nail-like object.[34] We should think here of spikes or nails implanted at the end of sticks to be used as prods.[35]

The next expression, *baʿălê ʾăsuppôt,* literally, "masters/members of the assemblies" or "masters of the collections," is ambiguous. The expression is unique in the Bible, but it is attested in the Talmud, where it refers to the members of the Sanhedrin (*b. Sanh.* 12a; *y. Sanh.* X.28a; cf. *Num. Rabb.* 14). This is the interpretation of the Targum (*rbny-snhdryn,* "the masters of the Sanhedrin") and Vulgate (*magistrorum consilium,* "the council of masters"). If this interpretation is correct, one may assume from the parallelism with *dibrê ḥăkāmîm,* "words of the wise," that "(words of) the members of the assemblies" is meant.[36] We are not sure, however, if the term refers generally to the scholars of the community (i.e., the sages) or if formal assemblies/ councils are meant. Alternatively, *ʾăsuppôt* may be understood not as "assemblies" of people but as "collections" (of wisdom sayings). The word is apparently interpreted thus by the majority of the Greek translators.[37] If this is the meaning of *ʾăsuppôt,* then *baʿălê ʾăsuppôt* means "the masters of the collections."[38] In either case, *baʿălê ʾăsuppôt* is parallel to *dibrê ḥăkāmîm:* "The words of the sages are like goads; like implanted pricks are (the words of) the masters of the assemblies/the masters of the collections." It is the teachings of these sages and mentors, then, that are compared with goads and pricks. And they—these goads and pricks—are intentionally applied by a herder.[39] Clearly the herding imagery is still in effect, and so the herder must refer to

---

frequently associated with the training of animals. Thus, the word is related in meaning to *malmēd,* "prod" (i.e., a training tool), a word associated with the verb *lmd,* "to learn."

[34] See M. Jastrow, *A Dictionary of the Targumim, the Talmud Babli and Yerushalmi, and the Midrashic Literature* (Brooklyn, NY: Traditional Press, 1903) 809.

[35] K. Koenen points to the possibility of wordplay in this text: *drbnm,* "goads," is a play on *dbry,* "words of," and *mśmrwt* (with the *śin!*) may be intended as an allusion to the verb *šmr,* "observe, keep." See his "Zu den Epilogen des Buches Qohelet," *BN* 72 (1994) 25–26.

[36] So Ibn Ezra. See M. Gómez Aranda, *El Commentatio de Abraham Ibn Ezra al Libro del Eclesiastés* (Textos y Estudios 'Cardenal Cisneros' de la Biblia Poliglota Matritense 56; Madrid: Instituto de Filología del CSIC, 1994) 189.

[37] So LXX[SA] have *synagmatōn;* but LXX[B] and the recently published "Hamburg Bilingual Codex" have *synthematōn.* Aquila and LXX[S1], however, have *syntagmatōn,* which may either refer to "collections" or "assemblies" (cf. Job 15:8, where this word refers to the divine council).

[38] So one may compare the expressions like *baʿălê talmûd,* "masters of the Talmud," *bʿly mqrʾ,* "masters of the Bible," *bʿly ʾgdh,* "masters of the Aggadah." See Fox, *Qohelet and His Contradictions,* 324.

[39] As Fox has noted (*Qoheleth and His Contradictions,* 326–26), the word *ʾeḥād* is used

any teacher of wisdom—in this case, the sage himself, Qohelet. The point is that goads and pricks do not come upon one accidentally, without someone using these implements. Rather, one always knows that they are applied intentionally by some herder or another. The imagery of a herder using goads and pricks implies that there is some pain involved as one is prodded to go in the right direction.[40] The lesson may be difficult to learn, but the pain is necessary. This point of view is nothing new. The sages of the ancient Near East always assumed that good instructions may be painful for the learner, but some pain is necessary before one truly learns. The words of the wise may hurt; they are not what one may choose to hear. Yet, in the end, they are better for one's well-being (compare 7:5). Interestingly, the epilogue in the Instruction of Anii, which recognizes the difficulty of learning the sage's lessons, also uses the imagery of animals learning to behave: "Say: 'I shall do like all the beasts,' Listen and learn what they do."[41]

II. Do Not Go Beyond (v 12)

The second half of the epilogue begins with a warning: "Beyond these, my son, beware."[42] Commentators do not agree on what it is that one is asked not to exceed or why one must not do so. A number of scholars believe that the text evidences a certain "canon consciousness." According to this view,

---

here as the equivalent of an indefinite article, or it may even be used in the sense of "some" or "any" (see GKC §125.b). So too Aramaic *ḥd* may appear as an indefinite article. See B. Porten and A. Yardeni, *Textbook of Aramaic Documents from Egypt* (Jerusalem: Hebrew University, 1986–1993), 2. 1.52; 3. 1.1.38. *Any* herder would use whatever it takes to move the herd in the desired direction.

[40] Backhaus ("Der Weisheit letzter Schluß!" 40–41) is probably correct that the background of this saying is the schema of the two ways that one finds in the didactic wisdom texts. The sages prod their listeners—like animals—to go on the straight and safe tracks, rather than the crooked and dangerous ones. One notes in this connection that the "path" that one takes is often called *maʿgāl* (Prov 2:9, 15, 18; 4:11, 26; 5:6, 21) and *ʾōraḥ* (Prov 2:13, 15, 19, 20; 3:6; 4:14–18; 5:6), two terms that may originally have referred to paths for animals and animal-drawn wagons.

[41] *AEL*, 2. 144.

[42] Fox (*Qohelet and His Contradictions*, 326–27) maintains that a disjunctive accent should be placed on *wĕyōtēr*, as in v 9, and apparently takes the idiom to be *nizhar min*. But the idiom *yōtēr min* is well attested in classical Hebrew. Cf. *ywtr mmny*, "more than me" (Esth 6:6); *ywtr mmny*, "greater than I" (*y. Ber.* IV.7d); *ywtr mdʾy*, "more than enough"; and *ywtr mkšyʿwr*, "more than the proper amount" (*b. Moʿed Qat.* 27b). Cf. also Sir 8:13 ("beyond your means"). So Vulgate, Targum, Rashi, Rasbam, and many others. See Podechard, *L'Ecclésiaste*, 481.

the epilogist was reacting against the secular literature or various contemporaneous writings that are deemed to be substandard. As Crenshaw would have it, the epilogist is "warning against an open attitude toward the canon."[43] Fox, on the other hand, holds that it is the wisdom writings against which one is warned: "Writing is praiseworthy, but there is no point in overdoing it."[44] The warning is probably formulaic, however: it is intended to establish the authority of the text in question. In this case the warning is not to go beyond "the words of the wise" (the instructions of sages that are like goads and implanted pricks), although in context one understands that the words of Qohelet are meant. The "words of the wise" are as goads and implanted pricks applied by a herder—in this case, Qohelet. And the student (*bēn*), the reader, should stay on the course that this particular herder has directed with the goads of his words.

It is important to note a similar warning in the conclusion of the Instruction for Kagemeni—not only because of its third-person retrospective style, but also because it includes a comment on the reliability of the sage's teachings and a warning not to go beyond them:

> Then he said to them: "All that is written in this book, heed it as I have said it. Do not go beyond what has been set down." Then they placed themselves on their bellies. They recited it as it was written. It seemed good to them beyond anything in the whole land. They stood and sat accordingly.[45]

The epilogue in the Instruction for Kagemeni warns that one must not go beyond what is written ("all that is written in this book") and what is said ("as I have said it"). So, too, the epilogue of Ecclesiastes warns the reader, addressed as "my son" in v 12, not to go "beyond these"—presumably beyond the teachings of the wise, as written and spoken by Qohelet.[46] The text elab-

---

[43] *Ecclesiastes,* 191. So also Barton, *Ecclesiastes,* 198.

[44] *Qohelet and His Contradictions,* 327.

[45] *AEL,* 1. 60.

[46] As Fox ("Frame-Narrative," 99) has noted, by addressing the reader as *bĕnî*—lit., "my son"—the author calls to mind the narrative situation assumed in much of the wisdom literature of the ancient Near East. This form of address is, of course, a well-known wisdom topos. Thus, the Instruction of Anii is framed as a dialogue between a father and his son, where the son is exhorted to pay attention to the instructions of the sage, even though they are difficult to understand. The epilogue in the Instruction for Kagemeni also assumes this narrative situation. It depicts an old vizier calling his children together for instruction, and he warns them not to go beyond what has been set down.

orates on the matter: "There is no end to the excessive production of writings;[47] excessive talking wearies the body."[48] Everything intended by the author has already been said, it seems; there are no accidental omissions and no superfluous materials. So there is no need to go beyond the text (or to hold back its teachings)—either in writing or in speaking. The intent of the warning is the same as the so-called "canonical formula" found in Deut 4:2; 13: 1; cf. Jer 26:2; Prov 30:6; Sir 42:21; 43:27; Rev 22:18–19.[49] It serves to establish the completeness and reliability of the text in question.[50] In each case, the formula was intended only to assert the complete reliability of the respective text for its purpose and to ensure the integrity of the text in its preservation. The dogmatic usage of the formula (that is, as establishing a canonical corpus) was not attested for centuries. So, too, the epilogue in Ecclesiastes warns one not to go beyond the teachings of sages, meaning here the words of Qohelet, but the warning was not intended to be canon defining. There is no "canon consciousness" here.

[47] The Hebrew construction ʿăśôt sĕpārîm harbēh ʾên qēṣ (lit., "the making of writings excessively is without end") may be compared with lĕmarbēh hammiśrâ ûlĕšālôm ʾên-qēṣ ("the increase of authority and of peace there is no end") in Isa 9:6. In any case, harbēh is adverbial, as it is in the parallel line (lit., "talking excessively"). M. Fishbane makes the interesting observation that the verb ʿśh, lit., "to make," is similar to Akkadian uppušu (the D stem of epēšu, "to make"), a term used frequently in colophons together with other terms of scribal activities. See his *Biblical Interpretation in Ancient Israel* (Oxford: Clarendon, 1985) 31.

[48] MT wĕlahag is often explained on the basis of Arabic lahija, "to be devoted, dedicated." This Hebrew word is not attested in other contexts, however. The ancient versions all seem to assume some form of the root hgh (LXX: meletē, "practice"; Vulg: meditatio, "meditation"). This verse is quoted in the Talmud (b. Erub. 21b), where it is also explained in terms of hgh. Qoh. Rabb. also interprets the word to mean lahăgôt, "to talk about." A number of scholars, therefore, emend the text to lhg<wt>. It is difficult, however, to explain the loss of -wt. The infinitive absolute of hgh is attested as hāgōh and hāgô, but the infinitive construct is not attested anywhere. It is easier to assume a haplography of h and read lhg <h> and note that there are examples of infinitives of III-He verbs with final h instead of t: hĕyēh (Ezek 21:15); rĕʾōh (Gen 48:11); qĕnōh (Prov 16:16), etc. (see GKC §75. n). The word here means "talking" (so Pss 37:30; 38:13; 71:24; Isa 59:3; Prov 8:7). The parallelism of spr and hg in Ugaritic is also suggestive: dbl spr, "innumerable" (beyond recounting) // dbl hg, "unspeakable" (KTU 1. 14.II.37–38).

[49] The same formula is found in Qoh 3:14, where the author insists that what God wants to do will invariably be done, and no human being can hope to alter the course of things by sheer effort. Ben Sira too admits that God's decisions cannot be changed by mortals, for "one cannot substract from, or add to, or penetrate" the wonders of God (Sir 18:6; cf. 42:21).

[50] For the ancient Near Eastern background of the formula, see M. Fishbane, "Varia Deuteronomica," *ZAW* 84 (1972) 349–52.

III. End of the Matter (v 13a)

At the very end of the epilogue in the Instruction for Kagemeni, a colophon states: "It is finished." Similar notations are found at the end of other Egyptian wisdom texts.[51] So, too, v 13a probably marks the end of the book: "end of the matter;[52] everything has been heard."[53] The formula indicates the completeness of the book—beyond that one must not go. Barton makes the interesting suggestion that the book originally ended at just this point; what comes after that is an additional comment of a later editor.[54] This may be correct. Egyptian wisdom texts also end in such terse colophonic notations. It may be noticed, too, that there are no syntactical clues that link v 13b to 13a. There is nothing in the text that requires the subordination of this phrase to the preceding, as is implied in some translations (so *NJPS*: "When all is said and done: Revere God. . . ."). Rather, v 13a marks the end of the original epilogue; v 13b begins a gloss, a postscript of sorts.

IV. Postscript (vv 13b–14)

Apart from form-critical and syntactical considerations, the content of vv 13b–14 appears to be extraneous to the book. While the fear of God is a notion present in the teachings of Qohelet (3:14; 5:6; 8:12–13), the call to obey God's commandments is not. Qohelet does speak of one who keeps the commandment (*šômēr miṣwâ*) in 8:5, but there the command of a human despot seems to be at issue.[55] The charge to keep God's commandments in

---

[51] *AEL*, 1. 76, 144, 169, 182, 191; 2. 162; 3. 213.

[52] Barton (*Ecclesiastes*, 200–1) thinks the absence of the definite article on *dābār* indicates that this phrase is a technical expression—like the expression *sôp pāsûq*—marking the end of the editor's work. We may also compare the usage of *dābār* here with *dābār* in Deut 4:2, where the singular noun refers generally to Mosaic legislation: "You shall not add to the *dābār* which I am commanding you." By analogy, we understand *dābār* in this epilogue of Ecclesiates to refer generally to Qohelet's teachings. Cf. *qṣ dbr* in Sir 43:27.

[53] LXX (followed by Coptic) and Syriac assume an imperative ("hear!"), an easier reading that anticipates the two imperatives in the next line. The Vulgate takes the form to be the Qal imperfect: *audiamus*, "let us hear." In any case, this phrase is a variation of the closing formula. In fact, *sôp dābār*, "end of the matter," and *hakkōl nišmāʾ*, "all has been heard," are phrases in apposition to one another.

[54] See Barton, *Ecclesiastes*, 199. For Barton, vv 13b–14 are the words of a pious glossator, an additional corrective to a late epilogist's work (vv 12:9–13a).

[55] The *miṣwâ* in 8:5 refers to the same thing as *pî-melek* in 8:2 and *děbar-melek* in 8:3. Cf. also 1 Kgs 2:43; 2 Kgs 18:36; 2 Chron 8:15, where *miṣwâ* refers to royal commandment.

the epilogue, therefore, is an additional dimension to the teachings of Qohelet. Even Fox, who argues vigorously for the unity of the whole epilogue, concedes that "[t]he attitude expressed here is close to the traditional Wisdom epistemology, except insofar as it assumes a revelation of God's commandments."[56]

The perspective at the end of the epilogue is different from the rest of the book. It is true that Qohelet speaks of divine judgment in 3:17, but there he does not say how the deity will judge. The author is troubled by the injustice that prevails in the world, but he says simply "God will judge" (*yišpôṭ hā⁾ĕlōhîm*) in the same way that he affirms "God will seek the pursued" (*wĕhā⁾ĕlōhîm yĕbaqqēṣ ⁾et-nirdāp*, 3:15). For Qohelet, everything is in the hand of a mysterious God. He does not speak of God's judgment in the future in the sense of a judgment day, only of a deity who reserves the right to judge at any time and in any way. In 11:9, Qohelet says that God brings people into account, but there the context is a call to enjoy life while one is able. Enjoyment is a divine imperative for which one is accountable. Although the phraseology in 12:14 is partly similar to what we find in 11:9, the content is quite different. Here in 12:14 the accountability is specifically for keeping God's commandments. God will bring every deed into judgment (v 14). As Professor Murphy observes, it is ironic that the word used here is *ma⁽ăśeh*, "deed," since the word is used elsewhere in the book for God's inscrutable activities and for events that transpire in human life. But now, observes Murphy, "the 'work' or 'deed' (human) is here associated too easily to divine judgment."[57] It is probable that an eschatological judgment is meant in 12:14, for the text suggests that everything hidden will be revealed, whether good or bad.

It must be said that the perspective in vv 13b–14 is not contradictory to the rest of the book. Nowhere does Qohelet, or the writers of Proverbs for that matter, deny the importance of obedience to divine commandments. Nor is the possibility of an eschatological judgment explicitly rejected. Yet the final remark in the epilogue does puts a different spin on Qohelet's work by associating the fear of God with obedience to the commandments. G. T. Sheppard has called attention to a similar conjoining of the injunctions to fear God and to keep God's commandants throughout Ben Sira.[58] Sir 1:26–30 may be cited as an example of how the injunctions are combined:

---

[56] *Qohelet and His Contradictions*, 328.

[57] *Ecclesiastes*, 126.

[58] "The Epilogue to Qoheleth as Theological Commentary," *CBQ* 39 (1977) 182–89.

> If you desire wisdom, keep the commandments,
>> and God will supply it to you;
> For the fear of God is wisdom and learning,
>> and fidelity and humility are his delight.
> Do not be disobedient to the fear of God;
> Do not approach him with a duplicitous heart.
> Do not be a hypocrite before others,
>> keep watch over your lips.
> Do not exalt yourself lest you fall,
>> and bring dishonor upon yourself.
> God will reveal your secrets
>> and cast you down in public,
>> because you did not come in the fear of God
>> with your heart full of guile.

Since Ben Sira also manifests a conscious linking of the role of wisdom and the authority of the Torah (see Sir 2:16; 15:1; 19:20; 24:1–34), Sheppard argues that end of the epilogue in Ecclesiastes "represents a fairly sophisticated theological interpretation of sacred wisdom in relation to an authoritative Torah."[59] In a later essay, Sheppard proposed that "the final statements of the epilogue belong either to Ben Sira's period or later and may have played a constructive role in the canonization of the book."[60] But the link between Wisdom and the Torah is not all that clear in the epilogue of Ecclesiastes. The text does not explicitly link Wisdom and Torah. But even if the author of vv 13b–14 had intended to associate them, we cannot date that redaction to the time of Ben Sira. Already in the time of Ezra-Nehemiah, the expression "the wisdom of your God" appears to have been interchangeable with "the Torah of your God" (Ezra 7:14, 25). It is not only in the time of Ben Sira that such a linkage was possible. Indeed, the perspective of the redactor is not far different from Deuteronomy, where obedience to divine commandments is defined as wisdom: "Keep them and do them; for that will be your wisdom and your understanding" (Deut 4:6).

Without contradicting Qohelet, then, the redactor calls attention to an important dimension to be considered when all is said and done: that it is possible to hold the perspective of sages like Qohelet together with the cen-

[59] Ibid., 187.
[60] G. T. Sheppard, "Canonization: Hearing the Voice of the Same God Through Historically Dissimilar Traditions," *Ex Auditu* 1 (1985) 108.

tral tenets of Israelite faith.[61] Skeptical wisdom in the end need not be seen as contradictory to the call to obedience. And, indeed, it is the possibility of such a hermeneutical move that assured the acceptance of Ecclesiastes into the canon (see *b. Šabb.* 30b).

V. Conclusion

In general the epilogue in Qohelet functions in a similar manner to the epilogues in the Egyptian wisdom texts like the Instruction of Anii and the Instruction for Kagemeni. Written in a third-person retrospective style, it serves as an apology for the rest of the book, giving it a stamp of legitimacy. As in the Instruction of Anii, the epilogue of Qohelet praises its author as a sage. Like this Egyptian text, too, the epilogue of Qohelet implicitly recognizes that the teachings of the sage may be difficult to receive, and so it extolls the virtue of learning the lesson nonetheless. Like the ending in the Instruction for Kagemeni, the epilogue of Qohelet warns the reader not to go beyond what has been written and said. In effect it asserts that everything that the author meant to say and write has in fact been included. Finally, as frequently in the Egyptian wisdom text, the epilogue of Qohelet ends in a terse colophon in v 13a noting the very end of the whole text, including the epilogue. This was probably the original ending of the epilogue.

In sum, the original epilogue consists of Qoh 12:9–13a. This epilogue is in complete harmony with the rest of the book and was probably part of the original composition or compilation. Only vv 13b–14 may be regarded as secondary, but like vv 9–13a, the content of these verses is not contrary to the rest of the book.

---

[61] See the remarks of R. E. Murphy in "The Sage in Ecclesiastes and Qoheleth the Sage," *The Sage in Israel and the Ancient Near East* (ed. J. G. Gammie and L. G. Perdue; Winona Lake, IN: Eisenbrauns, 1990) 264–65.

ADDISON G. WRIGHT, S.S.

The Poor But Wise Youth and the Old But Foolish King (Qoh 4:13–16)

13 Better is a poor but wise youth than an old but foolish king who no longer knows caution, 14 even though (*kî*) from prison he came forth to rule, even though (*kî gam*) in his kingdom he had been born poor. 15 I saw all the living who move about under the sun with the youth the second (*hayyeled haššēnî*) who would stand in his place (*ya'ămōd taḥtāyw*). 16 There was no end to all the people, to all before whom he was (*lĕkōl 'ăšer-hāyāh lip-nêhem*), yet those who come later will not rejoice in him (*lō' yiśmĕḥû-bô*). Surely this also is vanity and a striving after wind.

The interpretation of this passage is a very tangled thing. The use of pronouns and the use of verbs with unidentified subjects as well as a very terse style combine to create a number of ambiguities internal to the story. Moreover the external context of the story (if any) is unclear. While the story does not relate to anything following it, the story can be understood as relating to a number of the ideas which precede it, and the meaning of the story keeps changing as one adjusts the context.

With so many internal and external options available, it is no surprise to find that the interpretation of the passage has gone in a number of different directions. The present study will explore those options and suggest that the number of viable options is fewer than might appear at first glance; it will also argue for an understanding of the passage which has hitherto been overlooked.

The Internal Ambiguities

a) The first ambiguity is the identity of the subject of the verbs in v 14. Is the one who knew prison and poverty a reference to the old king in v 13, as a few have maintained,[1] or to the youth, as the majority of commentators holds? If the subject of the verbs is the youth, the tenses would seem to indicate that he has already become king ("he came forth to rule").

b) The second and major ambiguity is the number of characters in the story. There is clearly the old king and the wise youth (youth A), but v 15 speaks of "the youth, the second" (*hayyeled haššēnî*). Is this the youth of v 13 (youth A) or yet another youth (youth B) to make a total of three characters? In other words, is it a story of a king and his youthful successor (youth A) or is it a story of a king and a youthful successor (youth A) who in turn has his own youthful successor (youth B)? Because of this ambiguity, the "his" at the end of v 15 (*taḥtāyw*) is also unclear; it may refer to the old king or to youth A.[2]

[1] G. Kuhn, *Erklärung des Buches Koheleth* (BZAW 43; Gressen: Töpelmann, 1926) 26; W. A. Irwin, "Eccles. 4:13–16," *JNES* 3 (1944) 256; O. Loretz, *Qohelet und der Alte Orient* (Freiburg: Herder, 1964) 71; R. B. Y. Scott, *Proverbs. Ecclesiastes* (AB 18; Garden City, NY: Doubleday, 1965) 224; D. Kidner, *A Time to Mourn, and a Time to Dance* (Downers Grove: InterVarsity, 1976) 51; J. J. Collins, *Proverbs, Ecclesiastes* (Knox Preaching Guides; Atlanta: John Knox, 1980) 87; L. D. Johnson, *Proverbs, Ecclesiastes, Song of Solomon* (Layman's Bible Book Commentary 9; Nashville: Broadman, 1982) 107. One can also refer the first half of v 14 to the youth and the second half to the old king (thus LXX, Vg, Tg; C. D. Ginsburg, *The Song of Songs and Coheleth* [London: 1857 and 1861; reprinted, New York: Ktav, 1970] 331–32). G. S. Ogden ("Historical Allusion in Qoheleth IV 13–16," *VT* 30 [1980] 310) understands the king as the subject of v 14 ("even if the king came to the throne after a period in prison or from poverty" like Joseph and David). However in his commentary (*Qoheleth* [Sheffield: JSOT, 1987] 72) it is the youth who is the subject of v 14 and who is like Joseph and David.

[2] The majority of commentators sees two characters (the king and youth A) but the following see a third character (youth B): A. H. McNeile, *An Introduction to Ecclesiastes* (Cambridge: Cambridge University, 1904) 67; G. A. Barton, *Commentary on the Book of Ecclesiastes* (ICC; Edinburgh: T. & T. Clark, 1908) 120; A. L. Williams, *Ecclesiastes* (Cambridge Bible for Schools and Colleges; Cambridge: Cambridge University, 1922) 54–55; H. Odeberg, *Qohaelaeth* (Uppsala: Almquist & Wiksella, 1929) 44; C. C. Torrey, "The Problem of Ecclesiastes IV 13–16," *VT* 2 (1952) 176; E. Jones, *Proverbs and Ecclesiastes* (Torch Bible Commentaries; London: SCM, 1961) 304; F. Ellermeier, *Qohelet I/1: Untersuchungen zum Buche Qohelet* (Herzberg: Jungfer, 1967) 222; K. Galling, "Der Prediger," *Die fünf Megilloth* (HAT 18; 2d ed.; Tübingen: Mohr/Siebeck, 1969) 100; W. J. Fuerst, *The Five Scrolls* (Cambridge Bible Commentary on the NEB; Cambridge: Cambridge University, 1975) 120; N. Lohfink, *Kohelet* (Die Neue Echter Bibel; Würzburg: Echter, 1980) 39; M. V. Fox, *Qohelet and His Contradictions* (Bible and Literature Series 18; Sheffield: Almond, 1989) 207–8; R. N. Whybray, *Ecclesiastes* (NCB; Grand

c) In v 16 there is a grammatical ambiguity as well as the continuing problem with the pronouns: *ʾên-qēṣ lĕkol-hāʿām lĕkōl ʾăšer-hāyâ lipnêhem*. Most see the "them" of *lipnêhem* as resuming the relative and referring to the people, and I have so rendered it in the translation of the passage given above ("There was no end to all the people, to all before whom he was"). In that case the "he" of *hāyâ* is either the king or youth A or youth B. But it is also possible to understand the subject of *hāyâ* as the people and the "them" of *lipnêhem* as referring to the rulers and to translate it, "There was no end to all the people, to all who lived prior to them" (temporal) or "there was no end to all the people, to all who were in front of them" (spatial).[3] Some do not see the second *lĕkōl* to be in apposition to the first but translate: "There was no end to all the people with each one who has become their ruler."[4]

d) At the end of v 16 who is the "him" of *bô*, the old king, or youth A or youth B or each one of them?[5]

If we leave aside the question of who came out of prison and poverty, a statement of the basic story line would be the following: surely the story tells of an old and foolish king who will be or has been succeeded by a wise youth, and those who come after will not take pleasure in the old king; the story may also say that the same thing will happen to the youth; the story may also say that the preceding generations take no pleasure in any characters in the story.

The Meaning of the Story as an Isolated Unit

Many commentators view the passage as an isolated unit with no connection to preceding ideas. They distill out the basic features as I have done above,

Rapids, MI: Eerdmans, 1989) 89–90; R. E. Murphy, *Ecclesiastes* (WBC 23A; Dallas: Word, 1992) 42–43; and the *REB*. G. S. Ogden (*Qoheleth*, 70–74) understands 4:13–16 as consisting of two separate sections. In vv 13–14 the thesis of v 13 is upheld by citing the two examples of Joseph and David in v 14 (see n. 1 above). However, he believes that *rāʾîtî* ("I saw") in v 15 begins a new section as in 3:10, 4:4, 6:1, etc. Thus vv 15–16 speak of an entirely different wise youth who stands under it (*yaʿămōd taḥtāyw*), i.e., under the sun, but never finds public acclaim, despite his wisdom.

[3] See, for example, the discussion in R. Gordis, *Koheleth—The Man and His World* (3d ed.; New York: Schocken, 1968) 245–46.

[4] Thus Ellermeier, *Qohelet*, 231–32; Galling, "Der Prediger," 99; Lohfink, *Kohelet*, 38; A. Lauha, *Kohelet* (BKAT 19; Neukirchen-Vluyn: Neukirchener V., 1978) 91; J. A. Loader, *Ecclesiastes: A Practical Commentary* (Grand Rapids, MI: Eerdmans, 1986) 56.

[5] Only a few understand the "him" as the old king: Irwin, "Eccles. 4:13–16," 257; Collins, *Ecclesiastes*, 87; Johnson, *Ecclesiastes*, 107.

and, focusing on the story line and its conclusion, see the narrative as illustrating the fleeting character of power and royal prestige, the short-lived popularity of the great, the transient nature of human achievement, the emptiness of hopes based on a change of ruler. The cause of this transience is seen either as the inevitable result of the passing of time, or more elaborately as the fickle and restless nature of subjects, the deterioration which comes with advancing years, the attractiveness of youth.

It is also possible to see this "succession-narrative" as having nothing to do with popularity at all, but as a story about a youth who lost his following because he became a fool too. The point then could be that power makes people foolish.[6]

Another way to view the narrative would be to focus on the opening words "wise" and "foolish" and to see the story as extolling the superiority of wisdom. Folly accompanied by wealth and power is set over against wisdom minus such assets; it is the latter which succeeds. In this understanding v 16, on the transitory nature of popularity, is only a sobering postscript and not the main point of the story.[7]

Conversely, the passage can be understood as a story on the frailty or worthlessness of wisdom. Wisdom is better than folly, for it can win the favor of the people and win the throne. But the mood of the people can change and reduce the value of wisdom to nothing. In this understanding v 16 is fully operative as the punch line.[8]

From the above interpretations it can be seen that yet another ambiguity exists within the passage in addition to those ambiguities created by the pronouns and by the unspecified subjects of the verbs, viz., which are the operative words in the narrative for the author?

---

[6] Thus H. Lamparter, *Das Buch der Weisheit: Prediger und Sprüche* (Stuttgart: Calwer, 1955) 73–75; R. Kroeber, *Der Prediger* (Berlin: Akademie, 1963) 138; Johnson, *Ecclesiastes*, 107.

[7] Thus E. T. Ryder, "Ecclesiastes," *Peake's Commentary on the Bible* (ed. M. Black and H. H. Rowley; New York: Nelson, 1962) 462. A variation on this is proposed by Irwin ("Eccles. 4:13–16," 255–57): youth A does not become king but "stood in his own place (*yaʿămōd taḥtāyw*)," i.e., continued in his own station in life. Nevertheless wisdom is superior.

[8] Thus F. Nötscher, *Kohelet* (Echter Bibel 4; Würzburg: Echter, 1954) 16; K. Galling, "Kohelet-Studien," *ZAW* 50 (1932) 286–87; Ellermeier, *Qohelet*, 232; Loader, *Ecclesiastes*, 56–57; Fox, *Qohelet*, 206–7; Whybray, *Ecclesiastes*, 91.

Is There a Wider Context?

In addition to the internal obscurities described above, there is also the problem of whether or not the passage is part of a wider context which controls its meaning and/or provides additional overtones for the story.

There has of course been the attempt to relate the passage to historical personages, and while such a relationship is thoroughly possible, the results of such attempts have been far from conclusive.[9] In any event, regardless of who the real personages might be, the point of telling the story at all is to be discovered from the way it is told and used in Qoheleth, and not in the historical events which might have inspired it. Moreover, the question of how many characters are in the story must be settled before any search for historical allusions is undertaken.

With regard to its setting in Qoheleth, all are agreed that the passage is not connected with anything which follows, but some commentators see a connection with what precedes and perceive additional dimensions to the story beyond those already mentioned.

1) Hertzberg sees the passage as belonging to a larger section consisting of 3:1–4:16 entitled "Everything Has Its Time." Our parable of the transitory nature of fame is one example among many of that larger theme.[10]

2) Lamparter sees the passage as belonging to 3:16–4:16, a section which he entitles "Riddle Upon Riddle." The story of the king and the youth, understood as an illustration of the point that power makes people foolish, is one of those riddles of life.[11]

3) Some view this story as part of a grouping of units consisting of 3:16–4:16 or 4:1–16 and entitled "Social Problems," "Emptiness," "The Wrongs and Miseries of the World," "Our Inhumanity to One Another." The story speaks of the transitory nature of popularity, but picks up additional overtones from the surrounding material.[12]

---

[9] For the attempts at identifying possible historical allusions see Barton, *Ecclesiastes*, 119–20; Williams, *Ecclesiastes*, 56–57; Gordis, *Koheleth*, 243–44; H. Hertzberg, *Der Prediger* (KAT 17/4; (Gütersloh: Mohn, 1963) 116–18; K. D. Schunck, "Drei Seleukiden im Buche Kohelet?" *VT* 9 (1959) 192–201; Ogden, "Historical Allusion," 309–15.

[10] Hertzberg, *Der Prediger*, 96–99, 115–18.

[11] Lamparter, *Prediger*, 59–61, 73–75.

[12] E. H. Plumptre, *Ecclesiastes* (Cambridge Bible for Schools and Colleges; Cambridge: Cambridge University, 1881) 99; Williams, *Ecclesiastes*, 49; A. Strobel, *Das Buch Prediger (Kohelet)* (Düsseldorf: Patmos, 1967) 69, 77–79; F. Buck, "Ecclesiastes," *A New Catholic Com-*

4) Gordis and Scott see the larger section as 4:4–16 and understand it as a development on the theme of the folly of hard work. Our story on the transitory nature of fame is therefore a warning about the vanity of ambition.[13]

5) Glasser understands the story as a complementary reflection on 3:16–4:3. In that passage the wickedness of courts and the oppressions of the powerful are described. Picking up on that picture, the story of the king and the youth states that now and again a good king does come along, and his contemporaries can rejoice in him. It is too late, however, for preceding generations who have had to suffer bad government. Also since the good king is not immortal, generations to come will not benefit from him either. Hence the story is entitled "An Exception Which Proves the Rule." In this understanding the story recognizes the transitory nature of power, but it is really saying that bad government is the rule.[14]

6) Others see the section to which our story belongs as consisting of 4:7–16. In this case the section begins with a picture of the solitary life (7–8), followed by a series of examples which extol companionship (two are better than one; 9–12). Our story concludes the section. It is understood as presenting a king "who will no longer take advice" (a frequent alternate translation for "no longer knows caution" in v 13). The king is in a state of pathetic isolation and the story shows the dire consequences of that attitude (he is replaced and forgotten), and shows the benefits of being wise and being able to take advice (the success of the youth). In this understanding the operative words are "will not take advice." In v 16 the conclusion that "those who come after will not rejoice in him" is referred either to the old king as the final evil consequence of his folly, or else to the youth as a sober postscript (wise and successful as he was, he is not, however, exempt from the common fate of all; he too will lose his popularity).[15]

As with any such story or parable so with this one, the meaning varies as the context changes, and varies as one changes the operative words ("wise/fool-

---

mentary on Holy Scripture (ed. R. C. Fuller et al.; London: Nelson, 1969) 516; Fuerst, *The Five Scrolls*, 118–20; Lohfink, *Kohelet*, 33–38.

[13] Gordis, *Koheleth*, 160–61; Scott, *Ecclesiastes*, 224–25.

[14] E. Glasser, *Le procès du bonheur par Qohelet* (LD 61; Paris: Cerf, 1970) 79–82.

[15] D. Bergant, *Job, Ecclesiastes* (OTM 18; Wilmington: Glazier, 1982); Ginsburg, *Coheleth*, 326–30. Similarly, but with different section limits, Collins, *Ecclesiastes*, 86–88; M. A. Eaton, *Ecclesiastes* (Tyndale OT Commentaries; Downers Grove: InterVarsity, 1983) 95. Murphy (*Ecclesiastes*, 41–43) understands the section as 4:7–16, but sees vv 13–16 as dealing with human fickleness and as only loosely connected with vv 7–12.

ish"; "will not take advice"; v 16), or as one supplies something and emphasizes it (the youth becomes foolish).

A Narrowing of the Options

I have published elsewhere a structural analysis of Qoheleth on the basis of patterns of recurring refrains, and also subsequently published descriptions of the two independent sets of numerical patterns which that structure was discovered to possess.[16] I believe that the numerical patterns sufficiently prove that the structure recovered in the initial literary analysis is indeed Qoheleth's concept of the structure of the book, and that the results of the entire analysis can confidently be brought to bear upon the assorted problems of the book. This study therefore presumes the argumentation contained in that analysis with regard to the limits of sections.

The analysis indicates that our story is indeed part of a larger section and that the limits of that section are 4:7–16. Consequently position #6 above is the direction in which a solution is to be sought. That narrows down the external contextual options considerably. However, there is still the problem of which are the operative words in the story as well as the problem of the other internal ambiguities. Let us examine the whole section and see how it is developed.

> 7 Again I saw vanity under the sun: 8 there is a person and he has no second (*yēš ʾeḥād wěʾên šēnî*), neither son nor brother, and there is no end to all his toil, and riches do not satisfy his greed. For whom do I toil and deprive myself of good things? This also is vanity and an unhappy business.

Whether his avarice is the cause of his solitary situation, or whether his miserly habits were contracted because he was single is not stated. Not clear either is the significance of the words, "neither son nor brother." Do these words primarily suggest that the solitary man has no heir, or do the words "neither son nor brother" serve to underline how truly and unusually alone he is? It may mean both. In any event it is quite clear that the vanity consists in the

---

[16] A. G. Wright, "The Riddle of the Sphinx: The Structure of the Book of Qoheleth," *CBQ* 30 (1968) 313–34; "The Riddle of the Sphinx Revisited: Numerical Patterns in the Book of Qoheleth," *CBQ* 42 (1980) 38–51; "Additional Numerical Patterns in Qoheleth," *CBQ* 45 (1983) 32–43.

fact that he has "no second"—no one with whom to share the fruits of his labor in any manner; his toil benefits no one else.

The examples that follow in vv 9–12 extol the value of companionship:

> 9 Two (*haššěnayim*) are better than one; they have a good reward for their toil. 10 For if they fall, the one will lift up his companion, but woe to one who falls and there is no second (*wě'ên šēnî*) to help him up. 11 Also if two (*šěnayim*) lie together they are warm, but for one alone there is no warmth. 12 If one may be overpowered, two (*haššěnayim*) together can resist. A three-ply cord is not quickly broken.

Clearly companions are an advantage.

With the constant repetition of the words "second" and "two" in vv 8, 9, 10, and 12 (*šēnî . . . haššěnayim . . . šēnî . . . šěnayim . . . haššěnayim*), when the reader gets to the concluding story of the king and the youth, it is the word "the second" in v 15 (*hayyeled haššēnî;* "the youth the second") which stands out as the operative word if one is reading the text in Hebrew. And evidently the word "the second" was designed to stand out as the operative word, for, as has often been noted, the expression is awkward here and peculiar in usage, something that serves only to give it further emphasis. Far from being a word to delete (as some have suggested[17]) or to treat as a mere *Stichwort,* and far from being a word to obscure with some translation other than "second" (as *NRSV, NJB, NAB, REB,* and *TEV* have managed to do for all three occurrences in vv 8, 10 and 15), the word "the second" in v 15 provides the key to the story of the king and the youth in its present context—*and this would be the case even if this section of the book were understood as having its beginning prior to 4:7.* In fact an awareness of the repetition of the words "two" and "second" is essential to an understanding of the whole section (vv 7–16) and it is hard to see how the words "two" and "second" could have been made more prominent.

The meaning of the word "the second" in v 15 is determined by its use in vv 8 and 10 where it was last employed:

> There is a person and he has no second, neither
> son nor brother (8).

---

[17] E. Podechard, *L'Ecclésiaste* (EBib; Paris: Gabalda, 1912) 332–33; M. Jastrow, *A Gentle Cynic* (Philadelphia: Lippincott, 1919) 215. Galling ("Der Prediger," 99–100) deletes the word "the youth."

Woe to one who falls and there is no second to help
him up (10).

It means "companion" or "associate" as all translators recognize. There is no
youth B in the story, because the word "second" is not used in an enumerative
sense (i.e., second, third, fourth) but in the sense of "companion/associate."
The youth described as "the second" is not a second to the youth mentioned
in v 13, i.e., a second youth in the story. He is a second to the king, i.e., an
associate or in this case a future successor. The word "the second" is a substantive in apposition and is not an attributive adjective.

In whatever way one reads the rest of the story (and we will examine it
below) everyone agrees that it turns out badly for the king if not also for the
youth. Since the word "the second" is the operative word, the story tells of an
old king who has grown foolish and who will lose his popularity to a
"second," his young and wise successor. In this case a "second" is of no help or
advantage at all. In fact he becomes a catalyst for the change in attitude of the
people. The availability of the second serves only to aggravate the situation,
and the "second" is really a liability.

The function of the story, then, is to qualify the examples in vv 9–12. While
Qoheleth has emphasized that there is an advantage to a "second" in vv 9–12,
he feels obliged in vv 13–16 to point out also that that maxim is not always
true. Sometimes a "second" is a disadvantage. Perhaps Qoheleth means
specifically that a "second" is an advantage with regard to companions but a
liability with regard to successors, but that may be a precision which goes
beyond his intent. The story may simply be a warning that "two are better
than one" is not always true. Hence I have in previous writings entitled vv
7–16 "The Problem of the Second."

To reflect further on the story: if there were two youths in the narrative,
then the narrative would be about the liability of youth A having a successor
(youth B) and the old king would cease to be at the core of the story—a result
which would run counter to the opening line (v 13) where the youth and the
king are contrasted and share the spotlight. Rather the narrative continues to
focus on the two and is simply saying: "Better is a wise youth than an old and
foolish king and that is why a second is not always an advantage." With only
one youth in the story the narrative is quite coherent, and the motivation of
the people and their shift of attitude is completely explained by the description of the youth and the king. If, however, there were two youths in the story,
the qualities of the second youth which caused his success and the reasons for

the loss of favor for the first youth would be left unexplained—a peculiar outcome given the author's initial care to delineate the qualities of the youth and the king in vv 13–14.

But let us look at the rest of the story. If we continue to pursue this understanding of the story with the youth of v 15 being seen as the same youth as in v 13, then the "his" of *taḥtāyw* in v 15 is a reference to the old king and not to the youth.[18]

In v 16 it is best to view the suffix of *lipnêhem* as resuming the relative pronoun and as referring to the people (with the majority of the commentators). If it were to refer to the rulers in a temporal sense ("the people who lived prior to them"), it would produce an irrelevancy (it is irrelevant how many persons lived before these events), and if it were to refer to rulers in a spatial sense ("the people who were before them") it would produce an unusual idiom because, as Gordis points out, the king is usually described as being "before his people" (cf. 1 Sam 18:16; Ps 68:8; 2 Chr 1:10), not the people before the king.[19]

If *lipnêhem,* then, refers to the people, there are two possibilities for the subject of *hāyâ* ("he was"): the king or the youth, and the identity of the "him" (*bô*) at the end of the sentence is of necessity going to be the same person as the subject of *hāyâ* because it is generally agreed that the antecedent of *bô* does not go back beyond *hāyâ.* That leaves us with two options for a closure to the story:

> Better is a wise youth than an old, foolish king.
> I saw all the living with the youth who was to stand in the king's place.

X	Y
There was no end to all the people over whom the king	There was no end to all the people over whom the youth

---

[18] Irwin ("Eccles. 4:13–16," 255–57) understands *taḥtāyw* as referring to the youth, the last mentioned person: "He stayed in his own place," i.e., his own station in life. The reflexive use is grammatically possible, but Irwin refuses to deal with the word "the second," dismissing it with "whatever it may mean," and he assumes that the story is primarily about the supremacy of wisdom. However, the meaning of "the second" leads the story in another direction, and the reflexive use is thereby excluded. The youth must become king for the story to work and cohere.

In v 15 the *ʿim* can be understood as "with/as well as" or as "on the side of" (i.e., flocking to the banner of), depending on how the reader fills in the gaps of the story.

[19] Gordis, *Koheleth,* 245–46.

| ruled but those later will | ruled but those later will |
| not rejoice in the king. | not rejoice in the youth. |

In Y we have a conclusion for which no foundation has been laid in the story. If v 15 spoke of a second youth who would stand in the first youth's place, then the first youth's loss of favor would be explained. But there is only one youth, and Y is a gratuitous ending. X is a superior form of the story since the conclusion has prior foundation in the narrative. Moreover, if the story is about a king who has a "second" and shows how the "second" is a disadvantage to the king, then X is the stronger version since it concludes by describing what the effect of the "second" was on the old king. Y is hardly likely since it concludes with a description of what will happen to the "second" and ignores what will happen to the old king—an odd ending indeed.[20]

Not only is X a superior form of the story with regard to content, but X is a superior form of the story grammatically in that there is a consistent interpretation of the third person pronoun in vv 15–16: "in his place ... he was ... in him"—it is consistently seen as the old king, and each pronoun leads into the next, and that is the natural reading of the sentences. The "he" of *hāyâ* should be the same person as the "his" of *taḥtāyw* in v 15 because that is the last person mentioned and there is no indication of a change of antecedent.

Furthermore, if we return to v 14 at the beginning and make the king the subject of the two verbs there so that the king is the one who emerged from poverty and prison to rule, and if we do that on the grounds that no change of subject from the preceding clause is indicated, then there is a completely consistent use of the third-person pronoun throughout the whole story. He (the king) came forth from prison and poverty; the youth would stand in his (the king's) place; he (the king) was over all of them; those later will not rejoice in him (the king).

---

[20] For these same reasons the proposal described in n. 4 above is not likely (i.e., "There was no end to all the people with each one who became their ruler, but those who come later will not rejoice in either of them"). The reason for the dissatisfaction with the youth is not explained. *Mutatis mutandis* the same must be said of Ogden's proposal described in n. 2 above. Ogden believes that *rā'îtî* ("I saw") begins a new section just as he believes it does in 3:10; 4:4; 6:1, etc. But *rā'îtî* does not begin a new section in 1:14; 2:13; 2:24; 3:22; 8:9; 8:17 and 10:7 and consequently is not to be mechanically interpreted as an introductory formula in this book. Moreover, the neglect of the second youth in Ogden's reading remains unexplained and unmotivated in the wording of the text. That is a substantial defect in the interpretation and prevents it from being taken seriously. Rather vv 13–16 are bound together into a unit by the meaning of "the second" as demonstrated above.

It is no wonder that the author saw no ambiguity in the story and let it stand as it is; he had used the pronouns consistently.

In fact, if one reads the story "by the book," i.e., by the basic grammar book, without invoking peculiar usage, all the problems vanish. The king is the subject of v 14 since there is no indication of a change of subject. The meaning of "second" is determined, as it should be, by its twice repeated immediately previous use in vv 8 and 10. The "them" of *lipnêhem* resumes the relative as it very frequently does. The "his" in v 15 refers to the old king and therefore so also does the "he" and the "him" in v 16 because there is no indication of a change of antecedent. And the whole story so understood fits the context of the previous verses about the "second" perfectly.

Aside from the meaning of *haššēnî* ("the second"), the problems in the story arise when readers understand in v 14 that it is the youth who "has come forth to rule" and that he is therefore already king, and when readers then go on to understand v 16 as describing the youth ruling and later losing popularity. Those two judgments are the two crucial stages in the interpretation of the narrative, and in both cases a change of subject from the last mentioned person (the king) is not at all warranted. In fact the youth only becomes king in a time frame subsequent to this narrative for in this reading of the story the *yiqtōl* form *yaʿămōd* in v 16 must be taken as a future and is the first indication in the story that the youth will become king.

Some have suggested that there is no point in describing the previous history of the king and that v 14 must be describing the youth. But there is every reason to narrate the king's fabulous past to explain the similarity of his origins to those of the youth, his phenomenal rise and worth, and the tragedy of it all. Without those details the story would have no poignancy.[21]

A quite separate matter which is in no way a part of the above proposal and which in no way affects it is the question of a textual emendation. One is reluctant to tinker with the text of such a passage as this, but a suggestion of Allgeier and Buzy[22] merits consideration. It is an idea that has not been men-

---

[21] Whybray (*Ecclesiastes,* 88–89) states that the youth is clearly the one in v 13 who is singled out for attention and is therefore the subject of 14, and that the repetition of poverty in v 14 indicates the same. But at the end of v 13 it remains to be seen who will become the central figure. In v 13 there is also a contrast between the king and the youth and that could be the development in v 14. Which way it goes cannot be prejudged. A decision on v 14 should be left to the end, and the matter should be decided on the basis of grammar and the meaning of "the second," and when it is, the king emerges as the central figure in the story, not the youth.

[22] A. Allgeier, *Das Buch des Predigers oder Koheleth* (Die Heilige Schrift des Alten Testa-

tioned for some time and it ought not be lost to future scholarship. With a simple redividing of the consonants *lkl hʿm lkl* in v 16 to read *lkl hʿml kl,* the sentence "There was no end to all the people, to all before whom he was, etc." becomes "There was no end to all the toil; all before whom he (the king) was and those who would come after would not rejoice in him." In the interpretation of the story being proposed in this paper the toil would be the toil of the king expended in his rise from prison and poverty to the throne. This reading has the merit of eliminating the awkward and curious expression "There was no end to all the people." It brings in the present unhappy subjects as one might expect. It also provides us with a picture of great toil with no one enjoying to match the initial picture of great toil with no one enjoying in v 8. It furthermore provides a stronger inclusion for the whole section; "There is no end to all the/his toil" in 8 and 16 becomes the inclusion instead of simply "There is no end to all."

Conclusion

The story in its present context is not primarily about the advantage of wisdom or its vulnerability, or about the transient nature of human achievement and popularity, or about the fact that power makes people foolish, nor does the story primarily illustrate v 13, although all of those ideas remain in the background for readers rightly to supply as they may wish on a secondary level to explain the causality of the story. But the primary point of the narrative in its present context is that a "second" is not always an advantage.

---

ments; Bonn: Hanstein, 1925) 34; D. Buzy, "L'Ecclésiaste," *La Sainte Bible* (ed. L. Pirot and A. Clamer; Paris: Letouzey et Ané, 1946), 6. 230.

PART FOUR

Sirach

Honor, Shame, and the Hermeneutics of Ben Sira's MS C

The concepts of honor and shame constitute an essential part of Ben Sira's ideological matrix. In earlier papers, I have used contemporary Mediterraneanists' analysis of the so-called "honor-shame complex"[1] to analyze the particular form of patriarchy one encounters in this book[2] and the effect of this gendered cultural code on Ben Sira's theology of wisdom, Torah and cult.[3] Such an approach seemed validated by Ben Sira's reliance on the vocabulary of honor and glory to designate essential attributes of both God and man, combined with a two-fold concept of shame.

Nominal and verbal forms of the Greek δόξα occur no fewer than 85 times, along with τιμή (14×) and ἔντιμος (3×). In the Hebrew manuscripts, these three words translate a variety of roots, most often כבד (21×) and הדר (7×). The honor concept itself can refer to the Lord, the stars, wisdom, and one

---

[1] For an excellent introduction to the anthropological discussion, see D. D. Gilmore, ed., *Honor and Shame and the Unity of the Mediterranean* (Washington: American Anthropological Association, 1987).

[2] C. Camp, "Understanding a Patriarchy: Women in Second Century Jerusalem Through the Eyes of Ben Sira," *"Women Like This": New Perspectives on Jewish Women in the Greco-Roman World* (ed. A.-J. Levine; SBL Early Judaism and Its Literature 1; Atlanta: Scholars, 1991) 3–39.

[3] C. Camp, "Honor and Shame in Ben Sira: Anthropological and Theological Reflections," paper presented at the First International Conference on Ben Sira, Soesterberg, the Netherlands, 1996.

who fears the Lord . . . ; it can also refer to a human status, recognized by other humans . . . . Δόξα is, then, a quintessential ideological term serving not only as a religious symbol valorizing the worshipper and the object of worship in the cultic context, but also as a cultural symbol defining the worshiper's status goals within society.[4]

Shame-vocabulary also appears in heavy measure: nominal and verbal forms of αἰσχύνω (23×), ἀτιμάζω (16×), and ἐντρέπομαι (3×); verbal forms of καταισχύνω (7×); and the noun ἀσχημοσύνη (3×). Hebrew roots include *bwš, qlh, bwz, ʾwl,* and *knʿ.* J. Sanders has made the case for the importance of shame in what he calls Ben Sira's ethics of caution, in particular the necessary ability of the sage to distinguish between a proper shame (that is, an appropriate modesty) and improper shame in decisions about when and when not to speak (Sir 4:20-28).[5] This two-fold sense of shame is, however, a classic example of a way of thinking that is repeated constantly in anthropological analysis of the contemporary Mediterranean, where its topoi more usually match those of Sirach's other major shame discourse in 41:16-42:8: control of women and control of resources.[6]

The anthropological honor-shame framework, moreover, highlights the fact that shame does not appear in isolation in this work, but as part of a concept pair. One acquires the essential social and theological good of honor by practicing proper shame and guarding oneself against improper shame. Honor and shame are, then, controlling ideological categories, manifesting specifically in the sage's relationship to women, wealth, friends or associates, and language.

Further consideration of Sirach through the lens of honor and shame leads me to suggest here that the perspective might also lead to some interesting observations about the textual history of the book. Indeed, had I attended more carefully to the differences in the manuscript traditions in my previous work, I may have found my belabored argument for the relevance of this anthropological approach unnecessary—unneces-

---

[4] Camp, "Understanding," 6.

[5] J. T. Sanders, "Ben Sira's Ethics of Caution," *HUCA* 50 (1979) 84.

[6] Gilmore, for example, describes as "an almost universal thread in the [anthropological] literature" the "organic connection between sexuality and economic criteria in the evaluation of moral character ("Introduction," *Honor and Shame and the Unity of the Mediterranean* [see n. 1], 6). See Camp, "Understanding," for a detailed discussion of these issues in Ben Sira.

sary because, as I shall argue here, the editor of MS C had already done my work for me.

MS C, part of a significant collection of fragments of Sirach in Hebrew from the Cairo Genizah, is generally recognized as an anthology of selections from the book. In his 1988 article on hermeneutics in the book of Ben Sira, however, P. Beentjes goes beyond this simple observation to argue for what he terms "creative anthologizing" in MS C, involving not only the selection but also the re-arrangement of texts to emphasize certain themes.[7] Beentjes points out that in MS C, after a number of lines in the expected order on Leaf I (recto [3:14-18, 21-22]), the reverse side surprises us with the sudden addition of 41:16 after 3:22b, followed by 4:21, then 20:22-23, then back to 4:22-23. This re-ordering can only be explained by the editor's interest in highlighting the two kinds of shame a man might experience, that "laden with guilt" and that which "merits honor and respect" (4:21).[8] Thus, Beentjes adduces, shame is one of at least three important themes in MS C, the other two being the wise man (especially in Leaf IV)[9] and the wife (Leaves V and VI).[10] These three themes are, in their MS C rendition, remarkably open to analysis in terms of the honor-shame complex. The remainder of this paper will build upon Beentjes' work by offering some further suggestions and conjectures along these lines.

1. The anthropological perspective would recommend seeing shame not simply as one item on the hermeneutical agenda of MS C, but as the the hermeneutical key to the rest. I propose, that is, that in gathering and thus highlighting otherwise scattered references to the two-fold nature of shame from the original text, the anthologizer acknowledged, long before contemporary biblical social scientists started going on about it, the ideological weight of these concepts in his own context.

2. Though the extant MS C fragments begin with 3:14-16, a focus on honor and shame allows an educated guess at what preceded this material in the anthology. If shame marks the conglomerate sequence of 41:16;

---

7 P. Beentjes, "Hermeneutics in the Book of Ben Sira: Some Observations on the Hebrew Ms. C," *EstBib* 46 (1988) 46–47.

8 Ibid., 47–49.

9 Ibid., 51–54, 57.

10 Ibid., 54–57.

4:21; 20:22-23; 4:22, we would expect honor in the near vicinity, and both reasonably close to the beginning of the anthologizer's work. 3:1-16 is unquestionably a unit in the full-length version of the book; however, lacking the first thirteen of these verses in MS C, we might miss the fact that references to honor dominate the passage, though they do not appear in vv 14-16. Thematically, the passage calls "children" to listen to their "father" (3:1), and then proceeds to an inordinately repetitive instruction on honoring father and mother. The Greek of 3:1-13 contains seven nominal and verbal variants of δοξάζω (1× in the negative, ἀδοξία) and eight variants of τιμάω (3× in the negative). This is an extraordinary density of honor/glory vocabulary, giving preference to the δόξα/τιμή lexicon, even when expressing its opposite.[11] Similarly, the extant Hebrew (3:3[?], 8-13) uses *kbd* seven times in seven verses. Is it possible, then, that MS C originally began at 3:1, thereby introducing (with a heavy hand, one might add) the subject of its entire lesson?

3. Beentjes expresses some surprise at the fact that the two leaves devoted to the wife-topos constitute fully a third of the extant MS C[12] (25:8, 13, 17–24; 26:1–3, 13, 15–17; 36:22–26).[13] This section would certainly represent a smaller percentage of the entire anthology, but relatively a lot of space nonetheless. If the editor's overarching theme is honor and shame, however, this is no surprise at all. For the Mediterranean anthropologist knows well that, whatever other considerations may enter in, it is above all the shame of women that determines the honor of men.[14] Acquiring the right kind of woman and not the wrong kind is of paramount importance and thus deserving of more than its share of attention.

4. Beentjes offers a reasonable conjecture about the content of a leaf he believes is missing from between our current Leaves II (which ends with

[11] This as opposed to more typical vocabulary for shame. Ἀδοξ- occurs in only one other place in Ben Sira (10:31). Ἀτιμ- occurs more frequently (16×, including the 3 in this passage), but is not as common as variants of κατα/αισχύνω (33×). I suggest, in other words, that the Greek translator of 3:1–16 sought to keep the focus on honor, even when mentioning shame.

[12] Ibid., 54.

[13] If the first verse is seen as an introduction to the unit and the last two verses a conclusion, the rest is constituted by an even balance of ten bicola on the good wife and ten on the bad.

[14] See Gilmore, *Honor and Shame,* for analyses that demonstrate the various components of the honor-shame system, e.g., physical prowess, family autonomy, hospitality, integrity and generosity. No matter the complexity of the issue, however, the shame of women is never missing from the picture.

36:19a) and III (which begins with 6:18).[15] Based on the unusual word *ḥyk* ("palate") that appears both in 36:19a and in 6:5, he argues that we might expect the next leaf to take up the topic of friendship in 6:5–17. His proposal can be reinforced by anthropological logic. One's dealings with one's compatriots is an important part of the honor-shame matrix. Honor is only honor when a person's claim to it is socially recognized; it is an agonistic game played out by means of challenge and response.[16] Friends, then, present a particular problem: one must rely on them while remaining always in some degree of competition with them; friendships are often relationships of convenience (6:8). It is no accident, therefore, that Ben Sira's comments on friendship, like those on wives, stress the need to discern between two kinds of friends, the good and the bad. A faithful friend is "a sturdy shelter," "beyond price," "a life-saving remedy" (6:14–16); yet only "one in a thousand" should be trusted for counsel (6:6). Friends must be tested[17] and, tragically, many will fail in time of trouble (6:7–13). If what MS C offers is a lesson on honor and shame, this section on friends proposed by Beentjes fits well indeed.[18]

5. Leaf IV contains a unit designated by Beentjes as a "tract on the crucial theme of the 'wise man'" (20:5–7; 37:19, 22, 24, 26; 20:13).[19] The overall section is compact, yet dense with information for the aspiring sage. The following discussion will not only call attention to the one obvious references to honor in this unit, but will also suggest how a reading of it through the lens of honor and shame might nuance certain questions in translation and interpretation.

(a) The first three verses of the tract on the wise man (20:5–7) form its introduction. They reflect on wisdom and silence, as Beentjes notes.

---

[15] Beentjes, "Hermeneutics," 49–51.

[16] B. Malina, *The New Testament World: Insights from Cultural Anthropology* (Atlanta: John Knox, 1981) 30–33.

[17] The motif of testing was examined in a paper by N. Calduch-Benages, "The Trial Motive in Ben Sira," for the First International Conference on Ben Sira, Soesterberg, the Netherlands, 1996.

[18] See further Camp, "Understanding," 16, 20; and, for a fuller and recent discussion of friendship in Sirach, J. Corley, *Ben Sira's Teaching on Friendship* (Ph.D. dissertation, Catholic University of America; Washington, 1996).

[19] Beentjes, "Hermeneutics," 52.

> One person is silent and is thought wise;
> another, for being talkative, is disliked. (20:5)

Beyond this obvious distinction between the silent wise man and the talkative fool, however, lies a finer distinction: the tension between two kinds of silence.

> One person is silent because he has nothing to say;
> another is silent, biding his time. (20:6)

The last of these introductory verses then returns to the first distinction of silence and verbosity, while linking this to two kinds of time, the right time at which the sage does his talking and the any-old-time of the fool's boasting.

> The wise is silent till the right time comes,
> but a boasting fool ignores the proper time. (20:7)

Beentjes observes, furthermore, that 20:7, the last verse of the introduction, is linked to the final extant verse of the whole unit (20:13) by means of the double inclusion of the wise (*ḥkm*) and the fool (*ksyl*). This word-pair is, of course, a favorite pedagogical antithesis of the wisdom tradition, constituting an assertion, in effect, that there are two kinds of men. In this context, however, Ben Sira ties discernment between the two kinds of men to observations about two kinds of silence and two kinds of wisdom, verses relating to the first issue (20:5–7 and 20:13[20]) forming an inclusio around verses relating to the second (37:19, 22, 24, 26).

The reason why the compiler of Ms C has inserted a number of lines from Sir 37:19–26 between the חכם maxims of Sir 20:7 and Sir 20:13 must be explained by the coherence of that pericope in chapter 37. Since all other maxims on the subject "wise man" have been dispersed all over the Book of Ben Sira, in Sir 37:19–26 we find the only passage with a concentration of maxims on חכם. By putting this thematic block within a firm *inclusio* of two חכם lines (Sir 20:7 and 20:13), the compiler has created a kind of tract on the crucial theme of the "wise man."[21]

---

[20] The translation of 20:13 is subject to debate. I shall return to this issue below.
[21] Beentjes, "Hermeneutics," 52.

Important for our purposes is the fact that both the inclusion and the center are tied to honor and shame. In stressing the topic of silence, the introductory and concluding verses call to mind an earlier passage in the anthology, the verses excerpted from 4:23–5:13 on Leaves I–II (4:23, 30–31; 5:4–7, 9–13), where the focus is on speaking at the right time so as not to hide one's wisdom (4:23).[22] Here too the sage acknowledges the risk involved in speech and, in the concluding verse of the section, connects it to honor and shame:

> Honor (*kbwd*, δόξα) and dishonor (*qlwn*, ἀτιμία) are in the hand
>   of the babbler,
> and the tongue of a man is his downfall/deliverance. (5:13)[23]

In the middle section, reference to honor (*kbwd*, τιμή) appears directly, here in parallel with another important component of the honor-shame system, regard for one's name.[24]

> One wise for his people wins a heritage of glory,
> and his name lives on and on. (37:26)

Looking back for a moment, let us recall: two kinds of shame, two kinds of wives, two kinds of friends, two kinds of speech, two kinds of silence, two kinds of time. We will return to this point below.

---

[22] Note that the opening verse, 4:23, and the closing section, 5:9–13, create an inclusio with the theme of speech around several verses with other content. The hermeneutics of this arrangement deserves attention.

[23] My translation, based on MS C, though with evidence of the ambiguity in the final word. Ms C reads *mpltw*, from *plt*, "to escape." Ms B reads *mplytw*, perhaps just a variant spelling or perhaps, as the Greek translator apparently thought, some form of *npl*, though it is not clear which form. I doubt the ambiguity is accidental! This proverb sounds echoes of Prov 18:21, "Death and life are in the hand of the tongue / and those who love her will eat her fruits." The tongue, in other words, can lead in either of two directions! Ben Sira's substitution of honor/dishonor for death/life is not unpredictable, from the perspective of his particular appropriation of honor/shame ideology. Loss of honor, and thus of name, is the social and theological equivalent of death. See Camp, "Understanding," 35–37.

[24] On the connection of name and shame in Ben Sira, see Sanders, "Ethics," 82–84. For analysis of these topoi in relation to Mediterranean anthropology, see Malina, *New Testament World*, 33–34; and Camp, "Understanding," 35–37.

(b) The last extant verse of the tract on the wise man, 20:13, is not only linked to 20:7, as mentioned above, but also, in several ways, with the quartet of verses inserted from chapter 37 (19, 22, 24, 26), whose theme is that of the benefits of two kinds of wisdom, namely, wisdom for oneself and wisdom for many. Though the exact sense of 20:13a is debatable, two links are obvious: (1) *npšw* ("himself" or "his life") appears in 37:19, 22, and 24, as well as in 20:13, bonding these verses. (2) A second link is formed by the antithetical parallelism of *rbym* ("many") in 37:19 with *mʿṭ* ("make few") in 20:13.

I would like to explore here the possibility that there may be a third (missing) link between 37:19b and 20:13a, that is important to the passage's instructional point. Both verses are marked by translational difficulties. With respect to 37:19, the sense of the Greek is quite different from that of the Hebrew. The Hebrew reads:

> *yš ḥkm lrbym nḥkm*
> *wlnpšw huʾ gwʾl*
> There is a wise man who is wise on behalf of many
> and for himself, he is redeemer.

The Greek, rather ironically, reads:

> Ἔστιν ἀνὴρ πανοῦργος πολλῶν παιδευτής,
> καὶ τῇ ἰδίᾳ ψυχῇ ἐστιν ἄχρηστος.
> There is a villainous man who is instructor of many,
> and for his own self he is unprofitable.

English translations tend toward an inexplicably odd mix of these variants. Skehan and Di Lella, for example, read:

> A person may be wise and benefit many
> yet appear to himself to be foolish.[25]

I find no English translation that reads the last word of the Hebrew (*gwʾl*) at all, much less in its most obvious sense of "kinsman-redeemer."[26] Let us assume for a moment, however, that the sense of 37:19 is that the

---

[25] P. W. Skehan and A. A. Di Lella, *The Wisdom of Ben Sira* (AB 39; New York: Doubleday, 1987) 434.

[26] D. Barthélemy and O. Rickenbacher classify 37:19's *gwʾl* as a pual, intending perhaps a reading of *gʾl* (II), "desecrated" (*Konkordanz zum hebräischen Sirach* [Göttingen: Vandenhoeck & Ruprecht, 1973] 68), but such a cultic connotation does not make a lot of sense in this context.

wise man whose wisdom benefits many will also be able to "act as kins-man" for himself, that is, be sufficiently prosperous that he needs no one else to do it for him. This reading may provide a clue, in the form of a miss-ing link, to the problematic Hebrew text of 20:13a: *ḥkm bmʿṭ dbr npšw*. This simply doesn't make a lot of sense as is: "A man wise in few words himself"(?) or, pointed otherwise, "A man wise in small things speaks him-self"(?). The Greek supplies more sense with a verb phrase, ἑαυτὸν προσ-φιλῆ ποιήσει ("makes himself beloved"), but is complicated by debate about the reading of another phrase. Rüger reads ἐν λόγῳ, while Ziegler and Vattioni read GII's ἐν ὀλίγοις.[27] Thus, one might have

ὁ σοφὸς ἐν λόγῳ ἑαυτὸν προσφιλῆ ποιήσει
The man wise in words makes himself beloved.

or

ὁ σοφὸς ἐν ὀλίγοις ἑαυτὸν προσφιλῆ ποιήσει
The man wise in little things makes himself beloved.

It is possible that, as in 32:8 (35:12), ἐν ὀλίγοις functions ellipti-cally, under the assumption that the reader will supply the missing term—"a few [words]"—from context. The immediate context in the full-length Sirach (20:9–17) is not, however, concerned with speech but rather with finances, especially discernment between gifts that benefit from gifts of fools, and ὀλίγου/ὀλίγα, with the sense of "small quantities of material goods," appears in vv 12 and 15. Although this unit is surrounded by units on speech (20:1–8; 18–20), the nearer context suggests that an economic allusion to "wisdom in small things" would not have been inappropriate. Although one would hardly dare propose an "original" Hebrew for a text as problematic as 20:13a, such a concern for the sage's economic life in relationship to his honor is a dominant concern of the full text of Sirach.[28] It should not surprise us if this were the import of this verse as well.

---

[27] H. P. Rüger, *Text und Textform im hebräischer Sirach: Untersuchungen zur Textgeschichte und Textkritik der hebräischen Sirachfragmente aus der Kairoer Geniza* (BZAW 112; Berlin: De Gruyter, 1970) 2–3; J. Ziegler, *Sapientia Iesu Filii Sirach* (Septuaginta 12/2; Göttingen: Vandenhoeck & Ruprecht, 1965) 217; F. Vattioni, *Ecclesiastico. Testo ebraico con apparato critico e versioni greca, latina e siriaca* (Naples: Istituto Orientale di Napoli, 1968) 102.

[28] Camp, "Understanding," 7–18, 23–34.

In our only extant Hebrew—that is to say, MS C—the appearance of both *bmʿt* and *dbr* may suggest that this editor was retroverting from the Greek and either became confused (aurally?) by the similarity between ἐν λόγῳ/ and ἐν ὀλίγοις or, alternatively, intentionally tried to reproduce what he perceived as a double entendre that suited well his purpose, that is, to tie together in his conclusion the topos of wisdom and silence/speech from the introduction of his unit with that of wisdom and economic advantage from the middle section.

One way or the other, however, he seems to have lost his verb. How, then—whatever we might conjecture about the "original Hebrew" of 20:13a—might we make sense of this verse within the hermeneutics of MS C? One might appeal to the only other verse, 4:7, in which the Greek phrase "make [one]self beloved" appears. Here the Hebrew is *hʾhb lnpšk*, which could be supplied in 20:13 as well. One might better consider, however, 20:27, where the Greek tells us that "one wise ἐν ὀλίγοις advances (προάξει) himself." The concern for honor and its material gains fits our context, but the verb προάγω does not appear elsewhere in Sirach, leaving us to guess what it might have translated. It strikes me that, given the other connections between 20:13 and 37:19, a likely candidate would be the much ignored *gwʾl* from 37:19.[29] With this addition, 20:13 now forms the eminently sensible:

> A man wise in making words few [will be redeemer] for
>   himself,
> but the prosperity of fools is poured out.

Wisdom in speaking is thereby explicitly tied in v 13a to wisdom in economic matters, a reading that has led me to use an alternative translation for *twbt* in 13b. Most English translations follow the Greek χάριτες, "courtesies." The Hebrew word has, however, a much more material sense, thus my "prosperity." The verse is, in other words, as much about the material success and social honor attached to wisdom as it is to wise words themselves.

---

[29] Adding *gʾl* to the present text would make the stich too long, but that problem exists for any inserted verb. If we assume intentionality rather than mere blunder here, we will also have to assume that the anthologizer was either willing to live with a over-weighted colon or that he simply expected the reader to carry the thought along from the earlier verse. It is of course possible that the original text of Sirach already contained an "extra" word, though this is not thought likely by recent translators and commentators (see n. 27).

(c) This reading of 20:13 links this final extant verse of the "tract on the wise man" not only with the teaching about the silence of sages and fools in its opening verses but also with the further teaching of the inserted verses from chapter 37, which deal with "benefit," "advantage," "inheritance," and "honor"—that is, with matters economic. Unfortunately, Leaf IV breaks off at just about this point, offering us but one additional word to suggest what follows. Beentjes has argued, however, that this word, *ḥkmh* ("wisdom"), is a telling one.[30] Appearing, otherwise inexplicably, at the end of 20:13 in MS C, it must begin the next verse. Of the two verses that begin with *ḥkmh* (20:30 and 24:1), context makes 20:30, which continues reflection on the wise man, the more logical choice.

> Hidden wisdom and unseen treasure—
> of what value is either?

Based on the preceding argument, I would add support to this reconstruction with the observation that 20:30 continues the anthologizer's weaving of motifs in his patchwork unit: wisdom, silence/speech and treasure are drawn together once again with proverbial pith. We might further speculate that our anthologizer would have concluded his "tract on the wise man" with 20:31 (also the concluding verse of Ben Sira's unit in the full-length version), thus creating a three-verse conclusion (20:13, 30, 31) to balance its three-verse introduction. Even with only the hard evidence of 20:13, we can see that the larger topical structure of this three-part unit in MS C—speaking, economics, economic speaking—reproduces that of the macro-unit (20:1–20) in the original.[31]

(d) The middle section of MS C's wise man discourse (37:19, 22, 24, 26), has to do, however, not only with the prosperity that comes through wisdom but also, more subtly, with the two kinds of relationships a sage must conduct, the two kinds of wisdom involved in these relationships, and, ultimately, with two kinds of "prosperity" one might achieve thereby.

The subsection begins with relationships: the sage must be both wise for himself and wise for many (37:19a). The fruits of self-wisdom are seen

---

[30] "Beentjes, "Hermeneutics," 53–54.

[31] The fact that 20:30 repeats the allusion to hidden wisdom found earlier in 4:23 (Leaf II) raises the possibility that there is a larger structure to the anthologizer's work. Whether this can be tested with the extant fragments is beyond my scope here.

in his material prosperity (his ability to redeem himself, 37:19b), in his physical person (37:22b), and in his public recognition (he will be "called happy," 37:24b). The last phrase is virtually synonymous with the public ascription of honor desired by the traditional Mediterranean man.[32] As good as these results may be, being wise for others is better yet.

This preference is already adumbrated in the use of *gwytw* ("his body") in 37:22b:

> *yš ḥkm lnpšw nḥkm*
> *pry dᶜtw ᶜl gwytw*
> When one is wise for himself,
> the fruits of his knowledge are seen in his body.

In four of the five occurrences of this noun outside chap. 37 (10:9; 41:11; 44:14; 49:15), it connotes physicality as related to mortality.[33] Twice the term stands in direct antithetical relationship to one's name (41:11; 44:14),[34] an antithesis perhaps implied but distinctly softened in MS C's selection and arrangement of verses. Prosperity of the body and immediate social approbation derived from self-wisdom constitute a good, but a temporary one at best, the intertexts suggest. The enduring name and glory that come from being wise for (the?) people are the real prize.

> One wise for people[35] inherits honor
> and his name stands in life forever (37:26).

There are, then, two kinds of reward, two levels of honor, attached to the two practices of wisdom. Both are good, but one is preferable.

---

[32] See Camp, "Understanding," 24–25, on the public as opposed to private force of "happiness" for Ben Sira.

[33] In terms of the ideology of honor and shame, the one apparent exception is the one that proves the rule. In 47:19, Solomon is accused of bringing his body into subjection by laying his loins beside women and thereby putting a stain on his honor (on his *kbwd*) and defiling his posterity (47:20; contrast 44:13–15). The linkages of honor, posterity, name, death, wisdom, and the body deserve further discussion; for now we simply note the (at least secondary) connection between one's body and death, in the form of defiled posterity.

[34] Though the body of one with an honorable name will receive its ultimate rest in proper form (44:14; cf. 49:15–16).

[35] Not atypically, the definite article is missing. Here, however, in omitting v 25, with its explicit reference to "Israel," the anthologizer leaves some doubt as to whether to read this verse covenantally or universalistically.

But this apparently optimistic logic of the two honors, one building on the other, may be deceptive. In the full text of Ben Sira, the dual source and context of honor—societal and eternal—are closely connected to a deep ambivalence about wealth: wealth is something that should be connected both to social honor and to wisdom, but is not always (11:11–14 and *passim*).[36] Thus, the sage must sometimes depend on the ultimately enduring, but proximately less tangible, honor of his name as compensation for lack of social recognition. The logic of the two honors, that is, is a slippery logic that provides an ideological cover for the contradiction between the ideal and the real in a world marked by honor and shame. Based on the admittedly incomplete data of our present MS C, however, it would appear that the anthologizer rejects or, at least resists acknowledgment of this contradiction. Not only do the selected verses from chap. 37 emphasize the purportedly obvious harmony between social and eternal honor, but, if Beentjes' conjecture is correct, the next verse in this so-called tract on the wise man continues its naive assurances:

> Hidden wisdom and unseen treasure—
> of what value is either? (20:30)

Wisdom displayed, treasure at hand. Our anthologizer seems to have little sense of the shifting lines of expectation regarding wisdom and prosperity that the sage of Ben Sira's own day had to negotiate.

6. Given this softening in MS C of a much more conflictive point in the larger book, it may not be surprising that, in his excerpt from the wisdom poem of 6:18–31 at the beginning of Leaf III, the anthologizer chooses only the verses that promise Woman Wisdom's availability, comfort, and delight (vv 18, 19, 28), omitting observations about the harsh testing and burdensome bondage one must endure to attain the desired ends.

In summary, I have attempted to work dialogically between the text of MS C and the theoretical perspective of honor-shame anthropology. As a result, I think that Beentjes' literary observations about the hermeneutics of MS C have been both confirmed and also sociologically complemented. If I have correctly understood MS C's hermeneutics, we find here an early interpreter of Ben Sira's full text who has carved open a fatted calf and

---

[36] Camp, "Understanding," 7–18.

laid bare its ideological bones of honor and shame.[37] Indeed, one might suggest that, in specifying these commonly-held anthropological categories with reflections on two kinds of wisdom and two kinds of silence, the anthologizer has tailored a version of honor-shame thinking to the ethos of the sage.

In particular, by limning the idea of "two kinds,"[38] the anthology highlights the public and contentious quality of this social discourse by which this sage has defined his understanding of the path of wisdom. Choices must be constantly made, and pitfalls are many. On the other hand, whereas a sense of risk if not outright danger marks the full text of Ben Sira, MS C significantly reduces the level of anxiety by failing to include questions about the wise man who does not receive his full share of honor and prosperity, and by omitting reference to the harshness of Woman Wisdom's discipline. The few theological reflections included in the extant MS C contain neither the questions of theodicy nor the accompanying hymnic bombast so evident in the original.[39] The reader is assured simply that God will favor the humble (3:18) and attend to the wicked (5:6). The sage will take this advice:

> What is too sublime for you, seek not;
>   into things beyond your strength, search not.
> What is committed to you, attend to;
>   what is hidden is not your concern (3:17–18).

---

[37] It would be my contention at this stage in our research that any reading of this book must be done in cognizance of this fundamental matrix at its heart. In making such a statement, I do not mean that all interpreters must woodenly apply the honor-shame framework to whatever topic they discuss. What I do mean is that this conceptual field cannot be ignored in any effort to understand the book as part of its ancient context.

[38] The only extant portions of MS C that do not obviously fit the "two kinds" paradigm are the section after the wisdom poem on Leaf III, excerpted from 6:35–8:7a (it is tempting to assume that this section once closed with 8:8, a nice inclusio to 6:35) and that at the beginning of Leaf IV, 18:31–19:2a, 3b. The first of these is something of a potpourri, though it introduces or echoes motifs that appear elsewhere in the anthology: honor, relative to humility and death (7:4, 6, 17; 8:7; cf. 37:19, 22, 24, 26); the faithful, wise servant (7:20–21; cf. 4:30–31). Control of one's household, especially daughters (7:20–25), and control of one's own desires (18:31–19:3) are, however, fundamental issues in establishing honor and avoiding shame (Camp, "Understanding," 19–37). These sections are thus fitting to the anthologizer's overall theme.

[39] See J. Crenshaw, "The Problem of Theodicy in Sirach: On Human Bondage," *JBL* 94 (1975) 47–64, for a discussion of Ben Sira's multifold attempt to deal with this theological concern. Interestingly, Crenshaw notes that the idea of "complementary pairs" within the structure

This theological advice to confine one's search to one's strength is repeated at the social level as well.

> Seek not from God authority,
> nor like a king a place of honor (7:4).

In conclusion, then, one might suggest a change in social location from the context of the original text to the anthology. Whereas the MS C editor can direct reflection to the moral life of the wise on its own terms, Ben Sira assumed his pupils would be required to use this knowledge in the midst of a life marked by doubt and tension about its value and results, consorting with the powerful on earth and asking questions of the powerful in heaven, dangerous though that may have been.

---

of the divinely-created universe is one of Ben Sira's original contributions to the issue. It is possible that Ms C's emphasis on "two kinds" contains echoes of this idea but, if so, the force of the motivating question has apparently been lost.

JAMES L. CRENSHAW

The Primacy of Listening
in Ben Sira's Pedagogy

The last three decades have brought remarkable progress in clarifying the text of Sirach, the historical background for the author, his central concerns and means of presenting them, and the place of the book in the development of Israelite wisdom.[1] Scholars have also addressed special issues with considerable vigor: was Ben Sira a priest?[2] why did he omit Ezra in his catalogue of national heroes?[3] what canon of scripture did he use?[4] how did he view women?[5] Nevertheless, a notable gap in the discussion exists, particularly

---

[1] Two examinations of research on Sirach indicate the scope of scholarly interest in the second half of the twentieth century: J. Marböck, "Sirachliteratur seit 1966: Ein Überblick," *TRev* 71 (1975) 177–84, and D. J. Harrington, "Sirach Research Since 1965: Progress and Questions," *Pursuing the Text: Studies in Honor of Ben Zion Wacholder on the Occasion of his Seventieth Birthday* (ed. J. C. Reeves and J. Kampen; JSOTSup 184; Sheffield: Sheffield Academic Press, 1994) 164–76. An assessment of the evidence can also be found in the introduction to the forthcoming commentary on Sirach by J. L. Crenshaw in the *New Interpreters Bible*.

[2] J. D. Sawyer, "Was Jeshua ben Sira a Priest?" *Proceedings of the Eighth World Congress of Jewish Studies* (Jerusalem: World Union of Jewish Studies, 1982) 65–71, answers the question affirmatively, pointing to (1) the author's positive attitude to the priesthood, (2) the large number of later *ḥăkāmîm* who were priests, and (3) his Zadokite name. S. M. Olyan, "Ben Sira's Relationship to the Priesthood," *JTR* 80 (1987) 261–86, reaches the same conclusion, as does H. Stadelmann, *Ben Sira als Schriftgelehrter* (WUNT 6; Tübingen: Mohr-Siebeck, 1980). J. G. Snaith, "Ben Sira's Supposed Love of Liturgy," *VT* 25 (1975) 167–74, finds no evidence in Sirach for enthusiastic support of the priesthood.

[3] P. Höffken, "Warum schwieg Jesus Sirach über Esra?" *ZAW* 87 (1975) 184–202, explains the silence about Ezra in terms of Ben Sira's ideological difference with levitical priests, whereas C. Begg, "Ben Sira's Non-mention of Ezra," *BN* 42 (1988) 14–18, thinks Ben Sira concentrates on those persons involved in building projects involving the city and temple.

[4] J. L. Koole, "Die Bibel des Ben-Sira," *OTS* 14 (1965) 374–96.

with regard to Ben Sira's pedagogy.[6] Did he understand education primarily as a matter of listening to intelligent people talk or did he assume that students read literary texts? That is the subject of this investigation, one that explores the extent of literacy in second century Yehud.[7]

Recent Research on Sirach

Establishing the text of Sirach is notoriously difficult, but that task has become less daunting as a result of discoveries of more than two thirds of the Hebrew text (four manuscripts from the Geniza in Cairo, a manuscript from Masada, and a portion of one from Qumran),[8] as well as the publication of the Greek text in the Göttingen Septuagint project.[9] Two concordances,[10] text critical studies on specific chapters[11] and on the Syriac text,[12] and the text

---

[5] According to W. C. Trenchard, *Ben Sira's View of Women: A Literary Analysis* (Brown Judaic Studies 38; Chico, CA: Scholars, 1982), misogynism correctly describes Ben Sira's attitude to women. A much more nuanced interpretation appears in C. V. Camp, "Understanding a Patriarchy: Women in Second Century Judaism through the Eyes of Ben Sira," *"Women Like This": New Perspectives on Jewish Women in the Greco-Roman World* (ed. A.-J. Levine; Atlanta: Scholars, 1991) 1–39.

[6] The single exception of interpretation dealing with the philosophy of education is "Erziehung und Bildung," chap. 10 in O. Wischmeyer, *Die Kultur des Buches Jesus Sirach* (BZNW 77; Berlin/New York: De Gruyter, 1995) 174–200.

[7] My fuller analysis of education, literacy, and epistemology in ancient Israel, tentatively entitled *Across the Deadening Silence: Education in Ancient Israel*, is scheduled to be published in 1998 in the Anchor Bible Reference Library.

[8] On the history and scope of the discoveries of Hebrew manuscripts, see the discussion in P. Skehan and A. A. Di Lella, *The Wisdom of Ben Sira* (AB 39; New York: Doubleday, 1987) 51–62.

[9] J. Ziegler, *Sapientia Iesu Filii Sirach* (Septuaginta 12/2; Göttingen: Vandenhoeck & Ruprecht, 1965).

[10] D. Barthélemy and O. Rickenbacher, *Konkordanz zum hebräischen Sirach mit syrisch-hebräischen Index* (Göttingen: Vandenhoeck & Ruprecht, 1973) and *The Book of Ben Sira: Text, Concordance and an Analysis of the Vocabulary* (Jerusalem: Academy of the Hebrew Language and the Shrine of the Book, 1973).

[11] H. P. Rüger, *Text und Textform in hebräischen Sirach: Untersuchungen zu Textgeschichte und Textkritik der hebräischen Sirachfragmente aus der Kairoer Geniza* (BZAW 112; Berlin: De Gruyter, 1970); T. Penar, *Northwest Semitic Philology and the Hebrew Fragments of Ben Sira* (BibOr 28; Rome: Biblical Institute, 1975), and F. V. Reiterer, *"Urtext" und Übersetzungen: Sprachstudie über Sir 44:16–45:26 als Beitrag zur Siraforschung* (Arbeiten zu Text und Sprache im Alten Testament 12; St. Ottilien: EOS, 1980).

[12] M. D. Nelson, *The Syriac Version of the Wisdom of Ben Sira Compared to the Greek and Hebrew Materials* (SBLDS 107; Atlanta: Scholars, 1988).

in various languages, set out in parallel columns,[13] have greatly assisted those students who wish to learn more about Sirach.

Examinations of the context of Ben Sira have oscillated between wholesale endorsement of Hellenism as the prevailing spirit in his teachings[14] and insistence that Jewish thought adequately explains his vocabulary and interests.[15] The older claim that he declared war against Hellenism[16] has been nuanced further by awareness of the extent of Greek influence on Judaism as a whole.[17] Ben Sira's affinities with Demotic wisdom, especially Papyrus Insinger, and his apparent acquaintance with the older Egyptian Instruction for Duauf, commonly known as The Satire of the Trades, indicate that he truly was cosmopolitan in spirit.[18] That recognition has not carried over into a conviction that he subscribed to Stoic philosophy,[19] despite some linguistic similarities with this system of thought.

The structure of the book has eluded detection, although several attempts to solve this enigma have been made. These vary from an effort to view Sirach in terms of a textbook of increasing difficulty[20] to a more plausible under-

[13] F. Vattioni, *Ecclesiastico: Testo ebraico con apparato critico e versioni greca, latina e siriaca* (Testi 1; Naples: Istituto Orientale di Napoli, 1968).

[14] T. Middendorp, *Die Stellung Jesu Ben Siras zwischen Judentum und Hellenismus* (Leiden: Brill, 1973) thinks Ben Sira drew extensively from anthologies of Greek texts while also relying heavily on canonical Jewish literature.

[15] V. Kieweler, *Ben Sira zwischen Judentum und Hellenismus. Eine Auseinandersetzung mit Th. Middendorp* (Frankfurt am Main: Peter Lang, 1992), recognizes the considerable variety within both Hellenism and Judaism at the time of Ben Sira and understands his response as one brought on by an aggressive Greek culture.

[16] R. Smend, *Die Weisheit des Jesus Sirach* (Berlin: Georg Reimer, 1906) xxiii, declares that in selecting the earlier motto, "the fear or the Lord is the beginning [= inner essence] of wisdom," "formuluiert er die Kriegserklärung des Judentums gegen den Hellenismus."

[17] M. Hengel, *Judaism and Hellenism: Studies in their Encounter in Palestine during the Early Hellenistic Period* (2 vols.; Philadelphia: Fortress, 1974), especially 131–53 for Ben Sira.

[18] J. T. Sanders, *Ben Sira and Demotic Wisdom* (SBLMS 28; Chico, CA: Scholars, 1983).

[19] D. Winston, "Theodicy in Ben Sira and Stoic Philosophy," *Of Scholars, Savants, and their Texts: Studies in Philosophy and Religious Thought, Essays in Honor of Arthur Hyman* (ed. R. Link-Salinger et al.; New York: Peter Lang, 1989) 239–49; but see R. Pautrel, "Ben Sira et le Stoicisme," *RSR* 51 (1963) 535–49.

[20] W. Roth, "Sirach: The First Graded Curriculum," *TBT* 29 (1991) 298–302, and "On the Gnomic-Discursive Wisdom of Jesus Ben Sirach," *Semeia* 7 (1980) 59–79. Roth thinks Ben Sira began with elementary ethical considerations, then moved to advanced theological issues, finally to his own creative reflections that go beyond the tradition he inherited. The work resulted from several stages, according to Roth. An original book (1:1–23:27; 51:1–30) in four

standing of it in the light of separate units introduced by hokhmatic or doxological reflections.[21] The concluding praise of men of worth has evoked a theory about the epic as a charter ideology for the temple[22] and has prompted the suggestion that two encomia conclude the book, the first in praise of wisdom, the second lauding the creator and honoring heroes of the past, as an appropriate way of paying homage to Simeon, the high priest in Ben Sira's time.[23] The correctness of the Greek genre, encomium, has elicited criticism,[24] and the mixture of genres within the entire book contributes in large measure to the difficulty of breaking it down into convenient sections that cohere from the modern standpoint. In this respect, Sirach resembles earlier biblical wisdom,[25] but in significant ways it marks a decisive transition to a new kind of piety.[26] That has been labeled priestly instruction in written form, although precious little in the book pertains to exclusive concerns of the priestly profession.

Perhaps the most extensive discussions have focused on themes within the book. Does Ben Sira think first and foremost in terms of religious piety,[27] the fear of God, or does he draw more heavily from sapiential categories? Does

---

sections was thematically arranged on the basis of words beginning with the letters of the alphabet in sequence, and three times Ben Sira felt compelled to add further reflections to this original book.

[21] Skehan and Di Lella, *The Wisdom of Ben Sira,* adopt such a reading, emphasizing the introductory praise of wisdom in several units.

[22] B. Mack, *Wisdom and the Hebrew Epic: Ben Sira's Hymn in Praise of the Fathers* (Chicago/London: University of Chicago, 1985) emphasizes the historical understanding of Ben Sira in forging national consciousness and thinks the priestly scribe is transformed via Hellenism into the office of teacher-sage, "a *novum* indeed" (107).

[23] T. Lee, *Studies in the Form of Sirach 44–50* (SBLDS 75; Atlanta: Scholars, 1986).

[24] C. A. Rollston, *The Non-Encomiastic Features of Ben Sira 44–50* (M.A. Thesis; Emmanuel School of Religion, 1992). Rollston's critique reveals the considerable freedom with which Ben Sira treated Greek encomia, if he actually adapted them for rhetorical use.

[25] On genres in biblical wisdom, see J. L. Crenshaw, "Wisdom," *Old Testament Form Criticism* (ed. J. Hayes; Trinity University Monograph 2; San Antonio: Trinity University, 1974) 225–64; reprinted in J. L. Crenshaw, *Urgent Advice and Probing Questions: Collected Writings on Old Testament Wisdom* [Macon, GA: Mercer University, 1996] 45–77) and R. E. Murphy, *Wisdom Literature* (FOTL 13; Grand Rapids, MI: Eerdmans, 1981).

[26] J. Marböck, *Weisheit im Wandel: Untersuchungen zur Weisheits-theologie bei Ben Sira* (BBB 37; Bonn: Peter Hanstein, 1971) teems with valuable insights into the literary and theological significance of Sirach.

[27] J. Haspecker, *Gottesfurcht bei Jesus Sirach: Ihre religiöse Struktur und ihre literarische und doctrinäre Bedeutung* (AnBib 30; Rome: Biblical Institute, 1967).

he accept the concept of free will,[28] or does he subscribe to a theory of two inclinations, the good and the evil, as later developed in rabbinic literature? What function does theodicy play in his thinking,[29] particularly in light of his rhetorical flourishes that seem directed at persons who questioned divine goodness and justice? Was Ben Sira actually a misogynist, or does he cite prevalent views regarding women, from which he separates himself? What does Ben Sira think about the ancient commandment to honor one's parents?[30] What principle of selection operates in the praise of famous men? What role does prayer play in Ben Sira's piety?[31] How do suffering and death affect his pedagogy and theology?[32] Does he believe in a messiah[33] and in the resurrection of the dead?[34]

In the realm of commentaries, progress has been extremely slow, perhaps owing to Sirach's dubious canonical connection and textual uncertainty, but students need not despair. They will find reliable translations and notes,[35] exhaustive treatments of linguistic features, and literary/theological

[28] J. Hadot, *Penchant mauvais et volonté libre dans la Sagesse de Ben Sira (L'Ecclesiastique)* (Brussels: Presses Universitaires de Bruxelles, 1970), answers the question in the affirmative.

[29] G. L. Prato, *Il problema della teodicea in Ben Sira* (AnBib 65; Rome: Biblical Institute, 1975) and J. L. Crenshaw, "The Problem of Theodicy in Sirach: On Human Bondage," *JBL* 94 (1975) 49–64; reprinted in *Urgent Advice and Probing Questions*, 155–74.

[30] R. Bohlen, *Die Ehrung der Eltern bei Ben Sira: Studien zur Motivation und Interpretation eines familienethischen Grundwertes in frühhellenistischer Zeit* (Trier Theologische Studien 51; Trier: Paulinus V., 1991).

[31] J. L. Crenshaw, "The Restraint of Reason, the Humility of Prayer," *Urgent Advice and Probing Questions*, 206–21; J. Marböck, "Das Gebet um die Rettung Zions Sir 36, 1–22 (G:33, 1–13a; 36:16b–22) im Zusammenhang der Geschichtsschau Ben Siras," *Memoria Jerusalem* (ed. J. B. Bauer; Jerusalem/Graz: Akademische Druck und Verlagsanstalt, 1977) 93–116; and P. C. Beentjes, "Sirach 22:27–23:6 in zijn Context," *Bijdragen* 39 (1978) 144–51.

[32] L. Schrader, *Leiden und Gerechtigkeit: Studien zu Theologie und Textgeschichte des Sirachbuches* (BBEuT 27; Frankfurt am Main: Peter Lang, 1994).

[33] . D. Martin, "Ben Sira's Hymn to the Fathers: A Messianic Perspective," *Crises and Perspectives: Studies in Ancient Near Eastern Polytheism, Biblical Theology, Palestinian Archaeology and Intertestamental Literature* (Leiden: Brill, 1986) 107–23.

[34] E. Puech, "Ben Sira 48:11 et la resurrection," *Of Scribes and Scrolls: Studies on the Hebrew Bible, Intertestamental Judaism, and Christian Origins Presented to John Strugnell on the Occasion of his Sixtieth Birthday* (ed. H. W. Attridge et al.; Lanham, MD: University Press of America, 1990).

[35] L. Alonso-Schökel, *Proverbios y Eclesiastico: Los libros sagrados* (Madrid: Christiandad, 1968), and Skehan and Di Lella, *The Wisdom of Ben Sira*.

analyses[36] that should stimulate interest and encourage them to examine the wide range of secondary literature on the book.

Orality versus Literacy

The virtual silence of commentators on the subject of education in Ben Sira's environment matches that on ancient education generally, one that has resulted from the dearth of direct evidence in the Hebrew canon. Recent epigraphic finds have prompted a more venturesome approach to the problem,[37] particularly when parallels with ancient Near Eastern cultural centers are taken into account. Still, methodological difficulties abound,[38] and renewed interests in the oral register have raised the issue of the extent of literacy in ancient Israel.[39] Where does Ben Sira fit in this oral/literary continuum? Is he closer to parental instruction implied by earlier proverbs or to the explosive literary activity indicated by the remarkable texts at Qumran?[40]

None would question the presence of a core elite group of scribes in the great city states of Mesopotamia from ca. 3100 B.C.E. and from Egypt a century or so later, but this specialized education was directed inwards and was

---

[36] Crenshaw, *Sirach* (forthcoming).

[37] A. Lemaire, *Les Ecoles et la formation de la Bible dans l'ancien Israël* (OBO 39; Fribourg: Editions Universitaires/Göttingen: Vandenhoeck & Ruprecht, 1981). Lemaire speculates on the basis of epigraphic evidence that schools dotted the landscape, marking the whole spectrum of education from elementary to advanced professional training. He also understands the canonical process as the direct result of these educational institutions.

[38] J. L. Crenshaw, "Education in Ancient Israel," *JBL* 104 (1985) 601–15 = *Urgent Advice and Probing Questions*, 235–49; S. Weeks, *Early Israelite Wisdom* (Oxford: Clarendon, 1994) 132–56; G. I. Davies, "Were There Schools in Ancient Israel?" *Wisdom in Ancient Israel* (ed. J. Day et al.; Cambridge: Cambridge University, 1995) 199–211; and F. Golka, "Die israelitische Weisheitsschule oder 'des Kaisers neue Kleider'," *VT* 33 (1983) 257–70.

[39] S. Niditch, *Oral World and Written Word: Ancient Israelite Literature* (Louisville: Westminster/John Knox, 1996). The difficulty of finding the right criteria by which to determine oral tradition remains, despite Niditch's powerful defense of the persistence of orality in Israel until quite late. Her comparison of creation myths in Genesis 1 and 2 with Ezekiel 28 graphically illustrates the problem, for precisely those characteristics in the latter text that she takes to be literary strike me as signs of orality—"its erudite use of synonyms for sin and its list of gem-quality materials" (38).

[40] N. Lohfink ("Gab es eine deuteronomistische Bewegung?," *Jeremia und die "deuteronomistische Bewegung"* [ed. W. Gross; BBB 98; Athenaum: Beltz, 1995] 313–83, esp. 341–42) mentions over one thousand exemplars, including 33 from the Psalter, 27 from Deuteronomy, 20 from Isaiah, 16 from Jubilees, and many others, in addition to sectarian writings.

characterized by manipulation of scarcity.[41] For the most part, education
served the wishes of royal administrators, eventually filtering down to benefit
wealthy entrepreneurs and commerce of all kinds. Much of the literary activity was highly technical: religious texts of various types (omens, execration
texts, myths and epics, hymns, prayers), royal propaganda, inventories and
archives, mathematical texts, and grammatical aids (word lists, bilingual
vocabularies, scribal exercises, school texts). Because of the difficult character of the cuneiform script and Egyptian hieroglyphs, literacy was restricted
to a tiny percentage of the population, perhaps one to two percent. Schools
certainly existed, but admission into the ranks of scribes was severely limited.

The development of a phonetic alphabet in fourteenth-century Syria-Palestine and its eventual adoption throughout the Ancient Near East—an interesting case of a vanquished culture exercising linguistic dominance over its
victors—introduced a different situation into the entire Fertile Crescent.[42]
Still, an Aramaic lingua franca did not usher in mass education and literacy,
for no positive correlation between simplicity of an alphabet and literacy
exists—witness the illiteracy in Medieval Europe and the exceptional literacy
in China. An agrarian Israelite society lacked an incentive to introduce widespread literacy, although from the eighth century on certain features of society begin to elevate writing as something of value.

To what extent did the Israelite monarchy employ professional scribes?
The answer to this important question is highly controversial, and even a
maximalist response does not settle the matter of educational opportunity in
the land. Even if, as is likely, the royal administrations in Israel and Judah
employed trained scribes like their counterparts elsewhere, this does not necessarily suggest that such training proliferated among rank and file Israelites.
Vested interests undoubtedly kept the number of professional scribes sufficiently low to guarantee employment. The customary guilds among artisans
and craftsmen functioned as a protective measure for the family, and scribes,
who experienced a comparable vulnerability, must have guarded their ranks
both to enhance their prestige and to increase their earnings.

[41] The term is used by J. Bains, "Literacy and Ancient Egyptian Society," *Man* 18 (1983) 577.

[42] A. Demsky, "Literacy," *The Oxford Encyclopedia of Archaeology in the New East* (ed. E.
Meyers; 5 vols.; New York/Oxford: Oxford University, 1996), 1. 367: "It [Aramaic] became the
Reichsprach, a most unusual example of a conquered people's language becoming an instru-
ment of the conqueror in empire building."

Any learning acquired by ordinary citizens would probably have been minimal—perhaps an ability to read and write their names, to recognize various items from inventories, and the like. An actual verse in the book of Isaiah (29:11–12) posits a situation in which wholly different responses occur: one person lacks the ability to read whereas another possesses that skill. Ancient Hebrew texts were not "reader friendly," for they lacked the several aids to understanding contributed by later guardians of sacred literature, Sopherim and Massoretes. Small wonder a coterie of trained interpreters of the torah in Ezra's day engaged in the task of assisting the populace to become familiar with the written word imposed on the people who returned from exile in Babylon.

Composers and guardians of canonical wisdom fall into an exceptional category where education is concerned—at least, one would think. After all, these individuals valued learning and devoted their waking hours to transmitting their teachings to youth, or so it seems. Nevertheless, they rarely use the verb *kātab,* and, unlike Egyptian Instructions such as Merikare, Amenemopet, Anii and Anksheshanky, Israelite sages never instruct students to read a text or to write anything as an exercise in learning.[43] The text in Prov 22:17–24:22 that shows affinities with the Instruction of Amenemopet opens with a question about the author's having written thirty sayings; an epilogist to Qoheleth observes that the teacher wrote reliable words (12:9–10); and a distraught Job imagines a written testimonial to his integrity (19:23–24). In two instances the teacher in the initial collection of sayings within Proverbs urges the son to write his, or divine, teachings on the tablet of the heart (3:3 and 7:3), but the language is necessarily symbolic—unlike comparable instructions in Deuteronomy, which enjoin hearers to write the divine commandments on doorposts and to wear them on the body.

A similar situation exists in the Sayings of Ahiqar, where one finds a single instance of the verb *qārāʾ,* but with the sense of naming rather than reading, and not one occurrence of *kātab.*[44] Given the ostensible setting of this work

---

[43] Merikare mentions written texts which the student is told to copy, advises against killing "one with whom you have recited the writings," and refers to reading in the Sipu-book. Anii reminds his son of his mother's support of his education, for she enrolled him in school where he was taught to write. The much later Ankhsheshonky urges readers to teach sons to write—along with plowing, fowling, and hunting.

[44] This conclusion is based on the glossary in J. M. Lindenberger, *The Aramaic Proverbs of Ahiqar* (Baltimore/London: Johns Hopkins, 1983).

in the royal court, although removed by circumstances to a place of incarceration, the absence of direct allusions to reading and writing stands out. Necessity forces Ahiqar to adopt a literary medium until his reinstatement as the king's counsellor takes place. Ben Sira's restricted use of the verb *kātab* to his own literary endeavor, with rare exceptions, accords with longstanding reluctance among Israelite sages to employ verbs of writing and reading. For him, the verb *kātab* applies to sacred texts (a prediction about Elijah's role in eschatological times, 48:10), musical compositions (44:5), engraving (45:11), and his own teachings (39:32).

Education in Canonical Wisdom

In the canonical book of Proverbs emphasis falls on hearing as the medium of learning. The ears play the decisive role in the acquisition of knowledge, and whenever the eyes come into play they observe human behavior rather than pore over written texts. According to Prov 18:15, the ear of the wise actively seeks knowledge, just as an intelligent mind (*lēb*) acquires it. Culpability comes from failing to listen to instruction, not from refusing to read assigned texts (5:13–14). This extraordinary concession on the part of a teacher, like that of the pharaoh Merikare who admitted to having committed an act of wrongdoing, removes the gulf between student and teacher that Anii's son, Khonshotep, felt so keenly.[45] The biblical sage confesses that he did not obey his teachers or incline his ears to his instructors, thereby jeopardizing his place among the assembled people. His offense concerned listening, not refusal to do what he had read.

The collection in Proverbs that incorporates several sayings that also appear in the Instruction of Amenemopet begins with explicit reference to inclining the ear (22:17) and proceeds to mention, in interrogative form, written sayings (22:20), but the emphasis within this section reverts to hearing as the means of acquiring knowledge. Thus one reads in 23:12, "Apply your mind to discipline and your ears to knowledgeable sayings." In 23:26 the teacher invites the student (*běnî,* "my son") to observe him and to delight in his conduct. Personal example, rather than written texts, however lofty, serves here as inspiration to the object of instruction.

---

[45] Khonshotep found himself in a moral dilemma; while approving the teachings of his father and admiring him for embodying them, the son believed himself unable to live up to such noble deeds.

Not all instruction derived from words. A particularly informative narrative in 24:30–34 describes the process of acquiring knowledge through keen
observation of circumstances, in this instance a neglected vineyard coming to
ruin. The combination of laziness and time's passage gradually brought dev-
astation, leading the observer to conclude that even a little indolence will
open the gate for poverty to enter like a robber.

Nevertheless, the parental warning in 19:27 best exemplifies the importance of hearing to biblical sages: "My son, stop hearing instruction only to
depart from words of knowledge." This silence about written instruction per-
sists in the two collections of foreign wisdom, the sayings of Agur in Prov
30:1–14 and the Instruction to Lemuel by his mother in Prov 31:1–9. Furthermore, the late acrostic in Prov 31:10–31 has nothing to say about written
instruction, all the more noteworthy if the word *ṣôpiyyâ* in 31:27 contains an
aural pun on the Greek word for wisdom, *sophia*.[46] This remarkable wife
opens her mouth with wisdom, and gracious teaching adorns her tongue
(31:26).

The choice of the verb *wĕʾizzēn* in Qoh 12:9 may owe something to an
auditory pun, connoting both listening and assessing.[47] In preparing to teach
the people knowledge, he listened and weighed the significance of what he
heard, probing deeply and arranging numerous aphorisms. Then he endeav-
ored to discover pleasing expressions, which he subsequently recorded in
writing. The following caveat against the intellectual enterprise, its endless
preoccupation with producing more written texts, evokes a different environment from that reflected in the book of Proverbs, justifying the placing of
the epilogues of Qoheleth toward the literacy end of the oral/literacy continuum.[48] Whether or not that judgment applies to the rest of the book is
unclear, but the poem in 3:2–8 does not include the polarities "reading and
writing." Evidently the author did not consider it necessary to isolate times
for normal scribal activity. The epilogist did not hesitate to identify Qoheleth
as a professional sage, a *ḥākām* (12:9), and to associate him with literary activity, but Qoheleth himself seems to have lived up to his name, the assembler,

---

[46] A. Wolters, "Ṣôpiyyâ (Prov 31:27) as Hymnic Participle and Play on *Sophia*," *JBL* 104
(1985) 577–87.

[47] C. F. Whitley, *Koheleth: His Language and Thought* (BZAW 148; Berlin/New York: De
Gruyter, 1979) 102, translates as follows: "And he listened and considered the arrangement of
many proverbs."

[48] Niditch, *Oral World and Written Word*, 117–29, offers four different models in evaluating
the degrees of orality and literacy in a given text.

and to have addressed hearers with his oral teachings, which he later wrote for posterity.

A similar ambiguity prevails in the book of Job. On the one hand, the instruction within the book always belongs to the oral register. The three friends verbally harangue Job, as do Elihu and the deity. In return, Job tries to set the friends right by word of mouth; he says nothing to Elihu and only slightly more to the deity. On the other hand, this "slightly more" consists of a surprising rejection of what he had heard at some time in the past in favor of immediate sight (42:5). Still, the preference for sight over hearsay, or the potent combination of hearing divine speeches with the accompanying insight, has absolutely nothing to do with reading and writing. The unreliable and therefore dismissable hearing constituted second-hand reports about divine mystery, now seen for what they were. This means little more than that all teaching has to be evaluated in the light of one's own experience.

To sum up, canonical wisdom literature presupposes a predominantly oral culture.[49] That is true not only of older proverbial sayings, most of which probably arose among the populace and were transmitted orally from parents to children, but also of later instructions, domestic and foreign.[50] Similarly, the books of Job and Qoheleth imply that teaching came primarily, if not exclusively, in the form of oral sayings. The occasional references to writing fall into the category of a testimonial for the benefit of deity and posterity, or they represent a sort of colophon inscribed by another hand than the speaker of the original work.

An Oral Culture?

The question arises, however, whether or not such concentration on hearing can exist in a literate sub-culture. In ancient Sumerian educational circles an emphasis fell on hearing, leading to a bizarre description of the learned Marduk as possessor of four ears. Similarly, Egyptian scribes identify a sage as

---

[49] This assessment of the matter comes closer to the view represented by C. Westermann, *Wurzeln der Weisheit: Die ältesten Sprüche Israels und anderer Völker* (Göttingen: Vandenhoeck & Ruprecht, 1990) than to that of M. V. Fox, "The Social Location of the Book of Proverbs," *Texts, Temples, and Traditions: A Tribute to Menahem Haran* (ed. M. V. Fox et al.; Winona Lake, IN: Eisenbrauns, 1996) 227–39.

[50] On foreign wisdom in the book of Proverbs, see J. L. Crenshaw, *Urgent Advice and Probing Questions*, 371–95.

"one who hears,"[51] and the Instruction of Ptahhotep has a long conclusion that makes this point most tellingly. The true scribe is the one who hears, which means that his actions embody the teachings. Such remarks about the importance of hearing may have originated in earlier times when instruction was oral, but they persisted in later times when scribes practiced the art of reading and writing. Writing certainly existed, as demonstrated by copious inscriptions and letters that have survived in Syria-Palestine,[52] but such evidence does not erase the overwhelming impression within canonical wisdom that instruction took the form of oral delivery.

Ben Sira as Scribe

Did that situation continue into the first three decades of the second century when Ben Sira took on the role of teacher? On the basis of his own advice to the youth of his day, the answer is "yes." Presumably, Ben Sira resided in Jerusalem, although most of Yehud was rural. He refers to a hierarchy in society, with the ruler at the top, followed by the High Priest, judges, physicians, sages, artisans and craftsmen, merchants, ordinary citizens.[53] The cult at the temple exercised a significant influence on Ben Sira, at least aesthetically, but he seems to have remained on the periphery insofar as strict dietary laws were concerned, and indeed, he ignores the ritual features of priestly legislation. For this reason, the claim that he belonged to the priesthood lacks cogency; moreover, his silence in this regard makes no sense if he actually could have made such a boast. Nevertheless, he was definitely moved by pomp and circumstance associated with special religious days, as his ebullient description of Simeon demonstrates.

Ben Sira really understood himself as a sage, a teacher who continued in the tradition of earlier *ḥăkāmîm,* with one decisive difference. He resisted

---

[51] N. Shupak, *Where Can Wisdom Be Found: The Sage's Language in the Bible and in Ancient Egyptian Literature* (OBO 130; Fribourg: University Press/Göttingen: Vandenhoeck & Ruprecht, 1993) provides an exhaustive comparison between the vocabularies of wisdom in the Bible and in Egypt.

[52] A. Millard, "An Assessment of the Evidence for Writing in Ancient Israel," *Biblical Archaeology Today: Proceedings of the International Congress of Biblical Archaeology, Jerusalem, 1984* (Jerusalem: Israel Exploration Society, 1985), as well as forthcoming articles on "The Knowledge of Writing in Late Bronze Age Palestine" and "The Knowledge of Writing in Iron Age Palestine."

[53] Wischmeyer, *Die Kultur des Buches Jesus Sirach.*

the earlier isolation of Israelite sages, their self-conscious universalism. Instead, he joined together the national heritage in religion and the Jewish legacy of international wisdom. Viewing his own contribution to the latter as inspired and therefore worthy of inclusion in a treasury of sacred literature, he sought eagerly to instruct disciples who would transmit that legacy to the next generation. To that end he boldly issued an invitation to students, urging them to seek instruction in his *bêt hammidrāš* or his *yĕšîbâ*. Such language has nothing to do with institutional schools, whether one thinks in terms of Greek schools or later Jewish instruction in synagogues.[54] It rather implies private instruction in a teacher's home, a type of training akin in some ways to peripatetic instruction by Greek philosophers. The emphasis in Ben Sira's teaching fell on moral formation, an ethics firmly grounded in theology. This approach to learning was both elitist and practical. Ben Sira considered most people ineducable, a judgment based on their indifference to morals.

The goal of education, in his view, was to demonstrate the reality that righteous actions issue from religious allegiance. The fear of God, the ancient sages' term for religion, manifested itself in compassionate deeds. This conviction explains a curious feature of Ben Sira's teachings—the manner in which the concept "fear of God" rivals the notion of wisdom. Subscribing to the introductory motto in the initial collection within the Book of Proverbs, 1:1–9:18, which asserts that wisdom begins in and achieves its highest expression in religious devotion, Ben Sira tries to spell out the implications of this insight. Nevertheless, he does not teach torah, for all his insistence that students meditate on it. The subject matter of his teaching always belongs to the category of wisdom, even when he enters the realm of doxology.

Despite the lofty enterprise to which he subscribed, Ben Sira remained very much a child of his times.[55] In at least two areas his views raise modern eyebrows: his attitude to women and slavery. In the latter area, the author of Deuteronomy moved from theological perceptions about the people of

---

54 The understanding of these references to a place of instruction as symbolizing the book of Sirach loses force because of the verb "lodge" rather than "meditate."

55 J. D. Martin, "Ben Sira—A Child of His Time," *A Word in Season: Essays in Honor of William McKane* (ed. J. D. Martin and P. R. Davies; JSOTSup 42; Sheffield: JSOT, 1986) 141–61, and B. L. Mack, "Wisdom Makes a Difference: Alternatives to 'Messianic' Configurations," *Judaisms and their Messiahs at the Turn of the Christian Era* (ed. J. Neusner et al.; Cambridge: Cambridge University, 1987).

Yahweh in Egyptian bondage to humane treatment of slaves,[56] but Ben Sira's compassion for the poor did not extend to slaves. Nor did his frequently-expressed admiration for good wives prevent him from obscene remarks about daughters.

In retrospect, it appears that Ben Sira pitched his camp with representatives of the past rather than the future. His deep respect for the priestly class and temple cult, his refusal to endorse radically new views such as life beyond the grave, his elitism—these attitudes placed him nearer the later Sadducees than the Pharisees, whose openness to popular ideas and deep piety appealed to the masses.

A Test Case, Sirach 6:18–37

We return to the question posed earlier, "Did an oral culture persist as late as the first quarter of the second century B.C.E.?" The preliminary answer is "yes." To test that response, we turn to the discussion of educational training in 6:32–37. The larger context, 6:18–37, consists of twenty-two bicola, suggesting comprehensiveness like the complete alphabet. Its topic appeared obvious to the person who added a title in the Vulgate (*De Doctrina Sapientia*). An inclusio built on the Hebrew noun *ḥokmâ* links the first and last verses of the unit, 18 and 37, and a direct address, *bĕnî*, sets the three sub-sections apart from the whole. The imagery of farming and hunting dominate the first two smaller units, whereas the third graduates to a picture of vigorous conversation and deep thought.

Although Ben Sira thinks of education as especially applicable to the young, he recognizes its lifelong appeal. His language concedes the harsh nature of ancient education, about which scribes in Mesopotamia and Egypt had much to say.[57] Ben Sira urges the youth to approach their education eagerly, like farmers who plow the ground and sow seed, anticipating a bountiful harvest. A short-sighted person stoops to pick up a heavy rock but quickly drops it, rather than relocating it to help control the rapid runoff of heavy rains. Like the discarded stone, wisdom conceals its real use. Here Ben Sira

[56] N. Lohfink, "Poverty in the Laws of the Ancient Near East and of the Bible," *TS* 52 (1991) 34–50.

[57] Even the Egyptian hieroglyph for instruction (*sb3*) reinforces this cruel reality; it depicts an arm raised in a threatening manner, poised to whip errant boys (Shupak, *Where Can Wisdom Be Found,* 31).

probably plays on the words *mûsār* ("instruction") and *sûr* ("to turn away," in its passive form), the former root returning in v 33 (*tiwwāsēr*). With its allusion to *hoi polloi*, the Greek rendering of this complex pun sounds elitist (*kai ou pollais estin phanera*).

The second sub-section continues the idea of wisdom's seeming harsh ways but quickly transforms the images. Students are likened to oxen and urged to submit willingly to the yoke. Then the image changes to hunting, with the hint that wisdom wishes to be found so as to grant rest to the weary hunter. Ben Sira's love of lavish apparel manifests itself in an extended description of conversion: fetters become protection, a collar turns into a splendid robe, the yoke changes to a golden ornament, and bonds are transformed into a purple cord. Work clothes have been cast off in favor of royal attire, a purple robe and a crown. With this bold description of transformation through education, Ben Sira gives his personal view about the social ramifications of an education. These words are not just anybody's opinion, but that of an authoritative teacher. Verse 23 stresses Ben Sira's authority through the threefold repetition of the possessive pronoun "my," at least in the Hebrew; the Greek translator drops one of them but makes up for the difference by an intensive form, *mē apanainou*. The notion of receiving the torah like a yoke struck a responsive chord in later Christian and rabbinic literature (Matt 11:29; *Pirqe Aboth* 3:6; *ʿErub.* 54a).

Not every image in this section is transparent, giving rise to suggestions that the idea is that of nets, and to weights used by athletes in training, or blocks placed on slaves' ankles. Ben Sira employs three imperatives to describe the hunt. Besides the verbs *dĕraš* and *biqqēš,* which refer to careful searching, the imperative *ḥăqar* implies that one traces out a route. Combined, the three imperatives suggest thorough research leading naturally to discovery, *wĕtimṣāʾ.* An adverb of time ("at last") and a personal pronoun ("for you") express the decisive nature of this turnaround (*nehpāk*), as does the word "joy."

The third sub-section stresses the importance of motivation, the firm resolve to acquire an education at any cost, indicates the diverse character of learning, and gives it a theological complexion. Ben Sira advises young people to keep their ears open in the assembly of elders, listening for intelligent speech. Then they are told to take advantage of every opportunity to learn from perceptive individuals—even to the point of making themselves a nuisance. Moreover, Ben Sira alerts his hearers to two different kinds of intelligence, one that expresses itself in witty sayings, another that takes the form of exposition. Here he characterizes wisdom as preserved in the canon: aphorisms and reflective, or theoretical, discourse. Finally, he insists that those who want to learn should meditate on torah, confident that God will reward them with wisdom. Here Ben Sira uses a rare word *śîḥâ* which occurs only three times in the Hebrew Bible (Job 15:4; Ps 119:97, 99). An educated mind achieves its loftiest expression in a divine gift of insight.

Conclusion

Nowhere in this unit does Ben Sira mention the reading of texts or exercises in writing. His students learn by listening to intelligent conversation; Ben Sira still lives in a predominantly oral culture. He himself reads torah and writes what he hopes will be viewed as inspired teaching, yet he transmits his instructions to students orally, and he expects them to learn by astute listening.[58]

[58] As occupant of the office that Roland Murphy graced during his years at Duke University, I cannot escape his spirit in life and in work—nor do I wish to do so. I shall always cherish his friendship.

ALEXANDER A. DI LELLA, O.F.M.

Fear of the Lord and Belief and Hope in the Lord amid Trials: Sirach 2:1–18

Introduction

Scholars generally agree on the importance of fear of the Lord in the thought and teaching of Ben Sira. In fact, right after the poem that serves as an introduction to his book (1:1–4, 6, 8–10ab[1]), Ben Sira devotes an elegantly crafted 22-line poem (1:11–30) to the fear of the Lord as the essence of wisdom.[2] In the entire book the expression "the fear of the Lord" or its equivalent occurs some 55 to 60 times.[3] In the poem 2:1–18, following immediately after 1:11–30, Ben Sira introduces a new idea: the close connection between fear of the Lord on the one hand and on the other hand belief as well as hope in the Lord when one is put to the test. In 2:1–18 the expression φοβεῖσθαι with (τὸν) κύριον as object, "to fear the Lord," occurs six times,[4] and the phrase τῷ φόβῳ αὐτοῦ, "the fear of him [i.e., the Lord]," occurs once (2:10c); thus, the root φοβ- occurs seven times, a significant number.[5] This poem, like many

---

[1] The GII additions in 1:5,7, and 10cd are glosses, and not original Ben Sira material.

[2] See A. A. Di Lella, "Fear of the Lord as Wisdom: Ben Sira 1:11–30," in the forthcoming proceedings of the First International Ben Sira Conference (28–31 July 1996) held at the conference center Kontakt der Kontinenten in Soesterberg, The Netherlands.

[3] So J. Haspecker, *Gottesfurcht bei Jesus Sirach: Ihre religiöse Struktur und ihre literarische und doktrinäre Bedeutung* (AnBib 30; Rome: Biblical Institute, 1967) 82.

[4] This verb occurs more than any other verb in the poem.

[5] See M. H. Pope, "Number, Numbering, Numbers," *IDB* (4 vols.; Nashville: Abingdon, 1962), 3. 561–67; and "Seven, Seventh, Seventy," ibid., 4. 294–95.

of the others in the Wisdom of Ben Sira, employs typical Deuteronomic phrases to make its point; these will be pointed out in the commentary.

Text and Structure of Sir 2:1–18

Since the Hebrew text of this poem is not extant, I have employed and analyzed a critically established text of the grandson's Greek, consulting as well the Syriac and Latin versions and the patristic quotations and then giving the major variants found in these sources.[6] To avoid as much as possible any subjectivity I make no attempt at retroversion of the Greek into an assumed original Hebrew.[7] In only one case (2:18d) did I engage in any form of

---

[6] Throughout this article I cite the chapter- and verse-numbers in Ben Sira as given in their proper order in J. Ziegler, *Sapientia Jesu Filii Sirach* (Septuaginta 12/2; Göttingen: Vandenhoeck & Ruprecht, 1966), which I used for the Greek textual criticism of the poem. For the Syriac, I used the facsimile of A. M. Ceriani, ed., *Translatio Syra Pescitto Veteris Testamenti ex codice Ambrosiano sec. fere VI photolithographice edita* (2 vols.; Milan: Pogliani, 1876–83) (= Ambrosian); P. A. de Lagarde, *Libri Veteris Testamenti apocryphi Syriace* (Leipzig-London: F. A. Brockhaus-Williams & Norgate, 1861), an important diplomatic edition of a sixth-century codex, British Library 12142 (= Lagarde); *Biblia sacra juxta versionem simplicem quae dicitur Pschitta* (Beirut: Imprimerie Catholique, 1951) (= Mosul); and B. Walton, *Biblia sacra polyglotta,* 4 (London: Thomas Roycroft, 1657) (= Walton). For the Latin, I used *Biblia sacra iuxta Latinam vulgatam versionem,* 12: *Sapientia Salomonis, Liber Hiesu filii Sirach* (Rome: Typis Polyglottis Vaticanis, 1964), and W. Thiele, ed., *Vetus Latina: Die Reste der altlateinischen Bibel nach Petrus Sabatier neu gesammelt und in Verbindung mit der Heidelberger Akademie der Wissenschaften hg.v. der Erzabtei Beuron* (Band 11/2: *Sirach* [*Ecclesiasticus*], fasc. 3: Prologue and Sir 1:1–3:31; Freiburg: Herder, 1989). For the concordance work of the MT, I used the elegant and powerful Macintosh computer program called acCordance/GRAMCORD MT Research Module (Version 1.1.1; Vancouver, WA, 1994); and for the LXX (Rahlfs' text forms the data base, which gives GI but not GII of Sirach) I used acCordance/GRAMCORD Septuagint Research Module (Version 1.1.1; Vancouver, WA, 1995). For the Hebrew of Ben Sira, I consulted D. Barthélemy and O. Rickenbacher, eds., *Konkordanz zum hebräischen Sirach mit syrisch-hebräischem Index* (Göttingen: Vandenhoeck & Ruprecht, 1973). All translations of Ben Sira and other biblical texts are my own.

[7] One can see evidence of subjectivity in the attempts various scholars have made to retrovert chap. 2 into the assumed Hebrew original of Ben Sira; no two attempts fully agree. See, e.g., N. Calduch-Benages (*En el crisol de la prueba: Estudio exegético de Sir 2* [Extract of an S.S.D. Dissertation; Rome: Pontifical Biblical Institute, 1995] 23–57), who gives a verse-by-verse textual criticism of 2:1–18 along with the views of scholars who retroverted the text into Hebrew and then provides her own opinion regarding the original Hebrew; she concludes the abstract with her reconstructed text of HI (p. 56) as well as HII (p. 57).

retroversion; I retroverted that colon from Syriac into Greek, as explained in the critical note. The poem has seven strophes: 3 + 3 + 3 + 3 + 3 + 3 + 2 bicola, for a total of 20, the structure of which I will explain below. In my critical text given below, the poem has 253 words.

I

2:1   ⁸τέκνον εἰ προσέρχῃ δουλεύειν κυρίῳ,⁹

       ἑτοίμασον τὴν ψυχήν σου εἰς πειρασμόν· ¹⁰

2:2   εὔθυνον τὴν καρδίαν σου καὶ καρτέρησον¹¹

       καὶ μὴ σπεύσῃς ἐν καιρῷ ἐπαγωγῆς.

2:3   κολλήθητι αὐτῷ καὶ μὴ ἀποστῇς,

       ἵνα αὐξηθῇς ἐπ᾽ ἐσχάτων σου.¹²

II

2:4   πᾶν ὃ ἐὰν ἐπαχθῇ σοι δέξαι¹³

       καὶ ἐν ἀλλάγμασιν ταπεινώσεώς σου μακροθύμησον· ¹⁴

2:5   ὅτι ἐν πυρὶ δοκιμάζεται χρυσὸς

---

⁸ Before v 1 Codex 248 alone has a title for the poem: περὶ ὑπομονῆς, "Concerning Patience/Endurance/Steadfastness," a noun used in 2:14a.

⁹ Latin adds after v 1a: (fili accedens servituti Dei) sta in iustitia et timore, "remain in righteousness and fear," an addition probably influenced by LXX Ps 2:11: δουλεύσατε τῷ κυρίῳ ἐν φόβῳ, "Serve the Lord in fear."

¹⁰ For v 1 Syr reads: "My son, when you come to the fear of God, devote yourself to all trials/testings." R. Smend (Die Weisheit des Jesus Sirach erklärt [Berlin: Reimer, 1906] 18); H. Duesberg and I. Fransen (Ecclesiastico [La Sacra Bibbia . . . di S. Garofalo: Antico Testamento, ed. G. Rinaldi; Turin: Marietti, 1966] 98); and Haspecker (Gottesfurcht, 56) believe that in v 1a Syr has the better reading.

¹¹ After 2:2a Lat adds a colon: declina aurem [other MSS, + tuam] et excipe verba intellectus, "Incline the [your] ear and accept words of understanding." This addition echoes Sir 51:16a. Syr omits v 2.

¹² For v 3 Lat reads: Sustine sustentationes Dei [= Antonius Melissa (PG 136. 1216), μεῖνον τὴν ἀναμονήν κυρίου] coniungere Deo et sustine ut crescat in novissimo vita tua, "Endure the endurances of God; be united with God and endure, so that your life may grow at the end." Syr reads: "Cling to it [f. pronoun referring to 'fear' in v 1] and do not let go of it, so that you may be wise in your ways." The purpose clause derives from the Syr of Prov 19:20b.

¹³ The Oʹ MSS add ἀσμένως, "gladly." Lat adds: et in dolore sustine, "and in suffering endure," the same verb used in v 3.

¹⁴ For v 4b Syr reads: "and in sickness and poverty be patient," a reading that is similar to the GII addition to v 5; see below.

καὶ ἄνθρωποι δεκτοὶ¹⁵ ἐν καμίνῳ¹⁶ ταπεινώσεως.¹⁷

2:6 πίστευσον αὐτῷ¹⁸ καὶ ἀντιλήμψεταί σου·
καὶ εὔθυνον τὰς ὁδούς σου καὶ ἔλπισον ἐπ᾿ αὐτόν.¹⁹

III

2:7 οἱ φοβούμενοι ²⁰κύριον, ἀναμείνατε τὸ ἔλεος αὐτοῦ²¹
καὶ μὴ ἐκκλίνητε²² ἵνα μὴ πέσητε.

2:8 οἱ φοβούμενοι κύριον, πιστεύσατε αὐτῷ,
καὶ οὐ μὴ πταίσῃ²³ ὁ μισθὸς ὑμῶν.²⁴

2:9 οἱ φοβούμενοι κύριον, ἐλπίσατε εἰς ἀγαθὰ
καὶ εἰς εὐφροσύνην αἰῶνος καὶ ἔλεος.²⁵

IV

2:10 ἐμβλέψατε εἰς ἀρχαίας γενεὰς καὶ ἴδετε

---

¹⁵ Instead of this expression, Syr has simply *barnāšā᾿*, "a human being."

¹⁶ Ms 421 reads καμάτῳ, "toil, trouble," an interesting variant.

¹⁷ Mss 493–694 add σωθήσονται, "will be saved." GII adds v 5c: ἐν νόσοις καὶ πενίᾳ ἐπ᾿ αὐτῷ πεποιθὼς γίνου, "In sicknesses and poverty be confident in him." Syr (Lagarde, Ambrosianus, and Walton) places v 6 before v 5; Mosul omits v 6.

¹⁸ The O Mss and other witnesses read κυρίῳ; Antonius Melissa (PG 136. 768) has τῷ θεῷ, as also Lat and Syr.

¹⁹ As v 6b the O Mss read: καὶ ἔλπισε ἐπ᾿ αὐτόν, καὶ εὐθύνει τὰς ὁδούς σου, "and hope in him, and he will make straight your paths," a reading found also in Syr (Lagarde, Ambrosianus, and Walton) except for the first "and." The second half of this reading is a quotation of Prov 3:6b in the MT and Syr. Lat adds after v 6b: *serva timorem illius et in illo veteresce*, "keep the fear of him and in it grow old."

²⁰ Many Mss add τόν as also in 2:8a, 9a, 15a, 16a, and 17a.

²¹ As v 7a Syr reads: "You that fear the Lord hope for good things," which simply is a repetition of v 9a.

²² Syr reads, "and do not delay in following him."

²³ A large number of cursives read πέσῃ, "fall."

²⁴ For v 8b Syr reads, "and he will not keep through the night your [Lagarde, Walton, Mosul; Ambrosianus: their] wages," a reading that reflects Lev 19:13 and Tob 4:14.

²⁵ The reading ἔλεος, also preferred by Rahlfs and Ziegler, is found only in a few witnesses; the rest read ἐλέους. Instead of "mercy," Syr reads *pūrqānā᾿*, "redemption, salvation." GII adds v 9c, ὅτι δόσις αἰωνία μετὰ χαρᾶς τὸ ἀνταπόδομα αὐτοῦ, "for his recompense is an eternal gift with joy," a Christian gloss alluding to the afterlife. For v 9 Lat has a couplet: *qui timetis Deum sperate in illum et in oblectatione veniet vobis misericordia; qui timetis Deum diligite illum et inluminabuntur corda vestra*, "You that fear God hope in him and in joy mercy will come to you; you that fear God love him and your hearts will be illumined."

τίς ἐνεπίστευσεν κυρίῳ²⁶ καὶ κατῃσχύνθη;
ἢ τίς ἐνέμεινεν τῷ φόβῳ αὐτοῦ²⁷ καὶ ἐγκατελείφθη;
ἢ τίς ἐπεκαλέσατο αὐτόν καὶ ὑπερεῖδεν αὐτόν;²⁸

2:11 διότι οἰκτίρμων καὶ ἐλεήμων ὁ κύριος²⁹
καὶ ἀφίησιν ἁμαρτίας καὶ σῴζει ἐν καιρῷ θλίψεως.³⁰

V

2:12 οὐαὶ καρδίαις δειλαῖς³¹ καὶ χερσὶν παρειμέναις³²
καὶ ἁμαρτωλῷ ἐπιβαίνοντι ἐπὶ δύο τρίβους.³³

2:13 οὐαὶ καρδίᾳ παρειμένῃ ὅτι οὐ πιστεύει·
διὰ τοῦτο οὐ σκεπασθήσεται.³⁴

2:14 οὐαὶ ὑμῖν τοῖς ἀπολωλεκόσιν τὴν ὑπομονήν·
καὶ τί ποιήσετε³⁵ ὅταν ἐπισκέπτηται ὁ κύριος;³⁶

---

²⁶ Chrysostom (PG 55. 129, 144, 331, 452; 56.161; 62.199), Maximus Confessor (PG 91.908), Antiochus Monachus (PG 89. 1437), and Antonius Melissa (PG 136. 788) read: ἤλπισεν ἐπὶ κύριον, "(who) has hoped in the Lord," also found in Lat.

²⁷ Lat reads *in mandatis eius,* "in his commandments," a reading found also in Sahidic and in Chrysostom (PG 56. 161), ἐν ἐντολαῖς αὐτοῦ.

²⁸ Syr gives an expanded form of v 10: "Know what has happened before, and understand and see what is from the generations of the ages: who has believed in him, and he abandoned him; or who has trusted in him, and he cast him down; or who has called him, and he did not answer?"

²⁹ Several GII MSS, and Bohairic, add: μακρόθυμος καὶ πολυέλεος, "patient and most merciful."

³⁰ Syr gives an expanded form of v 11b: "and he hears and saves in every time of adversity, and he hears the voice of those who do his will." For v 11b Lat reads: *et remittit in tempore tribulationis peccata omnibus exquirentibus se in veritate,* "and he remits in time of tribulation sins for all who seek him in truth."

³¹ Syh and three cursives read δισσαῖς that is reflected in Lat and Ethiopic; cf. 1:28b.

³² For v 12a Lat reads: *vae duplici corde et labiis scelestis et manibus malefacientibus et peccatori terram ingredienti duabus viis,* "Woe to the double heart and wicked lips and hands that do evil and to the sinner walking in the land on two ways."

³³ For v 12 Syr reads: "A cowardly heart and enfeebled hands is the one who treads on many paths."

³⁴ For v 13 Syr reads: "Woe to the heart that does not believe! It will not even abide." Lat reads: *vae dissolutis corde qui non credunt Deo; ideo non protegentur ab eo,* "Woe to the dissolute in heart who do not believe in God! Therefore, they will not be protected by him."

³⁵ Mss S A C V *l* read ποιήται and *L*·²⁴⁸ ποιήσηται, "(and what) is to be done."

³⁶ For v 14 Syr reads: "Woe to you, men of trust [or, steadfast heroes]! What shall you do when the Lord judges?" Lat reads: *vae his qui perdiderunt sustinentiam, qui dereliquerunt*

VI

2:15 οἱ φοβούμενοι κύριον οὐκ ἀπειθήσουσιν ῥημάτων αὐτοῦ,[37]
  καὶ οἱ ἀγαπῶντες αὐτὸν συντηρήσουσιν τὰς ὁδοὺς αὐτοῦ.

2:16 οἱ φοβούμενοι κύριον ζητήσουσιν εὐδοκίαν αὐτοῦ,
  καὶ οἱ ἀγαπῶντες αὐτὸν ἐμπλησθήσονται τοῦ νόμου.[38]

2:17 οἱ φοβούμενοι κύριον ἑτοιμάσουσιν καρδίας αὐτῶν
  καὶ ἐνώπιον αὐτοῦ ταπεινώσουσιν[39] τὰς ψυχὰς αὐτῶν.[40]

VII

2:18 ἐμπεσούμεθα[41] εἰς χεῖρας κυρίου
  καὶ οὐκ εἰς χεῖρας ἀνθρώπων·[42]
  ὡς γὰρ ἡ μεγαλωσύνη αὐτοῦ, οὕτως καὶ τὸ ἔλεος αὐτοῦ·
  καὶ ὡς τὸ ὄνομα αὐτοῦ, οὕτως καὶ τὰ ἔργα αὐτοῦ.[43]

---

vias rectas et devertunt in vias pravas et quid facietis cum inspicere coeperit Deus, "Woe to those who have lost perseverance, who have departed from right ways and turned toward wicked ways! And what will you do when God begins his visitation?"

[37] Syr reads: ". . . do not hate his word."

[38] For v 16 Syr reads: "Those who fear the Lord agree with his will, and those who love him learn his law." Then Syr (Mosul and Walton) add: "The one who fears God increases his possessions, and his seed will be blessed after him," a bicolon that is found in Lagarde after Syr v 18ab (= my v 18cd). Curiously, Ambrosianus does not have the addition at all.

[39] For this verb Lat reads *sanctificabunt,* "they will sanctify."

[40] For v 17 Syr reads: "The one who fears God, his heart is steady; but the one who abandons him destroys his spirit." After v 17 Lat adds: *qui timent Dominum custodiunt mandata illius et patientiam habebunt usque ad inspectionem illius,* "Those who fear the Lord will keep his commandments *and they will have patience till the time of his visitation.*" The italicized part of this addition is found also in Antonius Melissa (PG 136. 1216), καὶ μακροθυμήσουσιν ἕως ἐπισκοπῆς αὐτοῦ.

[41] Instead of a future indicative, *L*ʹ⁻²⁴⁸ has the optative ἐμπεσοίμεθα, and 307 the subjunctive ἐμπεσώμεθα. I have translated the verb as a volitive, as in the variants and as the underlying Hebrew would allow. See 2 Sam 24:14 in MT and LXX, the background of this text.

[42] Syr omits 18ab. As a continuation of its addition to v 17 Lat reads: *dicentes* [λέγοντες as in O and Armenian] *si paenitentiam non egerimus incidemus in Dei manus et non in manus hominum,* "saying, If we do not do penance, we will fall into the hands of God and not into the hands of human beings."

[43] Verse 18d is my retroversion into Greek on the basis of Syr which has this reading; this colon is found also in Geniza MS A, but in the wrong place, after 6:17b: וכשמו כן מעשיו. The colon is necessary here to complete the balanced structure of the couplet, or as R. Smend (*Weisheit,* 22) puts it: "Die Worte sind rhythmisch unentbehrlich."

In the somewhat literal translation below I have followed the Greek word order whenever English idiom would allow. Also I have translated the few Greek words that are repeated more than once by the same English expression.

I

2:1 My son, when you come to serve the Lord,
      prepare yourself for testing.
2:2 Make straight your heart and be steadfast,
      and do not become troubled in time of distress.
2:3 Cling to him and do not fall away,
      so that you may increase at your latter end.

II

2:4 Everything that befalls you accept,
      and in periods of your humiliation be patient.
2:5 For in fire gold is tested,
      and acceptable people in the furnace of humiliation.
2:6 Believe in him, and he will help you,
      and make straight your ways and hope in him.

III

2:7 You that fear the Lord, wait for his mercy,
      and do not turn away lest you fall.
2:8 You that fear the Lord, believe in him,
      and your reward will not fail.
2:9 You that fear the Lord, hope for good things
      and for lasting joy and mercy.

IV

2:10 Look at the ancient generations and see:
      has anyone trusted in the Lord and been put to shame?
   Or has anyone remained in his fear and been forsaken?
      or has anyone called upon him, and he overlooked him?
2:11 For compassionate and merciful is the Lord;
      and he forgives sins and saves in time of trouble.

V

2:12 Woe to cowardly hearts and drooping hands,
      and to the sinner who walks on two paths!

2:13 Woe to the drooping heart, for it does not believe!
          on account of this it will have no shelter.
2:14 Woe to you that have lost your steadfastness!
          and what will you do when the Lord makes his visitation?

VI

2:15 Those that fear the Lord do not disobey his words,
          and those that love him keep his ways.
2:16 Those that fear the Lord seek his good will,
          and those that love him are filled with the law.
2:17 Those that fear the Lord prepare their hearts,
          and before him they humble themselves.

VII

2:18 Let us fall into the hands of the Lord
          and not into the hands of humans;
      For like his majesty, so also is his mercy;
          and like his name, so also are his works.

The use of τέκνον, "My son," as the first word, marks the beginning of a new poem, as often in Ben Sira; see, e.g., 3:17–24; 4:20–31; 6:18–37; 18:15–19:17. As regards the structure proposed above, the most obvious discrete units are strophe III (2:7–9), which has οἱ φοβούμενοι (τὸν) κύριον, "(you) that fear the Lord," followed by an imperative, at the beginning of each bicolon; strophe V (2:12–14), which has οὐαί, "Woe," at the beginning of each bicolon; and strophe VI (2:15–17), which again has οἱ φοβούμενοι (τὸν) κύριον at the beginning of each bicolon. Strophe I (2:1–3) has a more subtle unity: a series of four imperative verbs, at least one in each bicolon (2:1b; 2:2a [*bis*]; 2:3a). The use of asyndetic πᾶν, "everything," at the beginning of 2:4a signals the start of strophe II, which also has four imperative verbs: 2:4a; 2:6a; and 2:6b [*bis*]. Strophes I and II also have a thematic unity: the Lord uses adversity to test the sincerity of one's fear of the Lord. Strophe IV begins with an asyndetic imperative ἐμβλέψατε, "Look at," and has a coordinating imperative καὶ ἴδετε, "and see," at the end of 2:10a. Then follow three rhetorical questions (2:10bcd). The strophe closes with a causal clause extolling the compassion and mercy of the Lord (2:11). Strophe VII serves as an epilogue; it is a couplet that begins with an asyndetic cohortative (2:18ab) followed by an extended causal clause extolling the majesty and mercy of the Lord as well as his name and his works, all of which allude back to Strophe I that urges the student to prepare for testing by a merciful God.

Commentary and Intertexual Analysis

Strophe I (2:1–3)

Ben Sira begins his poem with the verb προσέρχεσθαι, "to come, approach," a *mot crochet* with 1:30e in the final bicolon of the preceding poem, 1:11–30. Then he continues by using a typical Deuteronomistic phrase, "to serve the Lord" (2:1a); see, e.g., Judg 2:7; 1 Sam 7:4; 12:14, 20, 24. There is an inclusio between 2:1, the opening bicolon of strophe I, and 2:17, the closing bicolon of strophe VI. Note in both verses the use of the verb ἑτοιμάζειν and the noun ψυχή; both the verb and the noun occur only twice in the poem. For the wording of 2:1 and 2:17, the grandson employs some of the vocabulary of LXX 1 Sam 7:3: ἑτοιμάσατε τὰς καρδίας ὑμῶν πρὸς κύριον καὶ δουλεύσατε αὐτῷ μόνῳ, "Prepare your hearts for the Lord and serve him alone." The ideas in 2:1 and 2:17 call to mind what I call "the Deuteronomic equation" found in such texts as Deut 4:5–6; 6:1–5, 24; 8:6; 10:12, 20; 13:5; 17:19; 31:12–13: to fear the Lord = to love the Lord = to serve the Lord = to obey his words = to walk in his ways = to keep the commandments/Law = to worship the Lord = to be wise. Elements of this equation appear in many passages of Ben Sira: 2:7–10, 15–17; 4:11–16; 15:1, 13; 19:20; 21:11; 23:27; 25:6, 10–11; 27:3; 32:14, 16; 33:1; 34:14–18; 40:26–27.

Even though one makes the free choice "to serve the Lord," one must nevertheless prepare oneself for testing. The reason is that testing (presumably by God or by divine permission, as in the case of Job 1–2) can serve, even for the virtuous, as a means of purification or probation; see Gen 22:1; Judg 2:22–3:6. This notion of testing (2:1b) appears also in Sir 4:17b and 44:20d and throughout the rest of the Bible; see, e.g., Exod 15:25; 16:4; 20:20; Deut 8:2, 16; 13:3; Tob 12:14; Jdt 8:26; Wis 3:5; 11:10; Matt 6:13; Luke 11:4; Jas 1:2–4. Apparently, this notion made a profound impact on early Church writers many of whom quote or allude to 2:1.[44]

The first words of 2:2a, εὔθυνον τὴν καρδίαν σου, derive from Josh 24:23, which in the LXX reads, εὐθύνατε τὴν καρδίαν ὑμῶν πρὸς κύριον θεὸν Ισραηλ, "make straight your heart toward the Lord God of Israel":

---

[44] For the extensive quotations see the second apparatus in Thiele, *Vetus Latina*, 202–4.

these are the only two places in the LXX where the expression εὐθύνειν τὴν καρδίαν occur. The verb καρτερεῖν, "to be steadfast, patient," though common enough in classical Greek, occurs only ten times in the entire LXX, including five times in 4 Maccabees, and only once in the NT (Heb 11:27). Ben Sira employs the verb σπεύδειν (2:2b), "to hurry, hasten; be zealous; become troubled in mind," two other times: 11:11a and 36:7a where it means "to hurry, hasten." Here the verb means "to become troubled in mind," as in LXX Exod 15:15. The phrase καιρὸς ἐπαγωγῆς, "time of distress, or misery," a *hapax legomenon* in the entire LXX, simply means troublesome or difficult periods in one's life. The grandson apparently liked the noun ἐπαγωγή, for he uses it eight other times in his translation: 3:28a; 5:8b; 10:13c; 23:11f; 25:14a [*bis*]; 38:19a; 40:9b. Ben Sira uses a synonymous phrase, καιρὸς θλίψεως, "time of tribulation, or affliction," in 2:11b.

In time of testing (2:1) Ben Sira urges his readers to remain single-hearted (= single-minded) in their determination to serve the Lord and not to become troubled when adversity strikes (2:2), as it inevitably will. Every Jew familiar with the heroes of faith whose stories are told in the earlier books of the OT would acknowledge, without discussion, that principle. The vocabulary of 2:3 echoes LXX 2 Kgs 18:6 that describes the fidelity of good King Hezekiah: καὶ ἐκολλήθη τῷ κυρίῳ οὐκ ἀπέστη ὄπισθεν αὐτοῦ, "and he clung to the Lord and did not fall away from following him." This description harks back to Deut 10:20: "You shall fear Yahweh your God; him alone shall you worship; to him shall you cling [LXX: πρὸς αὐτὸν κολληθήσῃ], and by his name shall you swear." See also LXX Ps 62:9 (63:8). The result of steadfastly clinging to the Lord will be a prosperous future (2:3b)—long life; vigorous health; fertility of the womb, land, and flocks; and descendants to keep alive one's good name; see, e.g., Lev 26:3–13; Deut 28:1–14; Sir 30:4–5; 41:11–13. The promise of a blessed future recurs also in 1:13a: τῷ φοβουμένῳ τὸν κύριον εὖ ἔσται ἐπ' ἐσχάτων, "For the one who fears the Lord it will be well at the end." The phrase "at the end" appears in a negative context in 3:26, καρδία σκληρὰ κακωθήσεται ἐπ' ἐσχάτων καὶ ὁ ἀγαπῶν κίνδυνον ἐν αὐτῷ ἀπολεῖται, "A hard heart will fare badly at the end [Geniza MS A: *ʾḥrytw*, 'its end,' as also Syr], and the one that loves danger will perish in it."

Strophe II (2:4–6)

This strophe expands on the implications of 2:1–3, offering encouragement in time of trial. Ben Sira begins with an aphorism: you should accept everything that comes your way (as did Job) and be patient "in periods [ἀλλάγ-μασιν, lit., "changes, vicissitudes"] of your humiliation" (2:4).[45] In 2:4b Syriac, as indicated in the critical notes, is more specific: "and in sickness and poverty be patient." Ben Sira then explains why, using the proverbial imagery of fire testing gold (see Prov 27:21; Zech 13:9; 1 Pet 1:7; Rev 3:18) as a symbol of humiliation to test whether or not people are "acceptable," δεκτοί, presumably to the Lord (2:5). The thought of 2:5 derives from Prov 3:11–12. An *a:b::b´:a´* chiasm adds emphasis: ἐν πυρί:χρυσός::ἄνθρωποι δεκτοί:ἐν καμίνῳ ταπεινώσεως. For the cultic associations of the adjective δεκτός see Lev 22:19, 21, which stipulate that for the sacrificial animal to be acceptable [LXX: δεκτά] it must be a male without blemish. In Prov 11:1 an accurate weight is judged "acceptable," LXX δεκτόν, to the Lord. In Isa 48:10 the prophet speaks of the Lord testing people "in the furnace of affliction," the probable source of Ben Sira's language in 2:5b; for similar ideas see Prov 17:3; Ps 66:10; Wis 3:6. In his speech to the household of Cornelius, Peter says: "In every nation anyone who fears him [God] and does what is upright is acceptable [δεκτός] to him" (Acts 10:35).

Now comes the main point of the strophe: you must believe in the Lord if you want him to help you, and to believe involves to "make straight your ways and hope in the Lord" (2:6b); see the textual note. Authentic faith in God involves trusting in him and doing what is right, as Ps 37:3 makes clear: "Trust [LXX Ps 36:3: ἔλπισον, "hope," as in Sir 2:6b] in Yahweh and do good, so that you may live in the land, and enjoy security." See also Pss 37:5; 71:5–6; and especially Ps 56:3–4, 11 (LXX Ps 55:4–5, 12 in each of which verses the verb ἐλπίζειν occurs). For the imagery of "your ways" to describe a person's manner of life, see Gen 6:12. Leading an upright life involves following "the Lord's ways" (see, e.g., Deut 8:6; 10:12; 11:22; 19:9). The verb πιστεύειν[46] (2:6a) recurs in 2:8a and 2:13a and a compound form, ἐμπιστεύειν, in 2:10b, thus connecting strophe II with strophes III, IV, and V; and ἐλπίζειν (2:6b) recurs in 2:9a, offering another tie between strophes II and III. Believing and hoping in the Lord constitute essential elements in one's life with God.

---

[45] See the critical notes above on 2:4 and 2:5.

[46] See D. R. Lindsay, "*Pistis* and *pisteuein* in Jesus Ben Sirach," in his *Josephus and Faith: pistis and pisteuein as Faith Terminology in the Writings of Flavius Josephus and in the New Testament* (AGJU 19; Leiden: Brill, 1993) 39–51.

Strophe III (2:7–9)

Now Ben Sira makes a threefold appeal to "you that fear the Lord" (2:7a, 8a, 9a). We see in these verses how the fear of the Lord is at the heart of OT faith and hope for mercy and salvation. As I noted above, Ben Sira describes at length in 1:11–30 how the fear of the Lord is essential if one wishes to possess true wisdom. The Lord's mercy (2:7a) is a given in the OT, as Ben Sira states explicitly in 2:11a, at the end of strophe IV. He implies that only those who fear the Lord can expect his mercy for which they should wait in patience (2:7a); see Jdt 8:17. The noun ἔλεος, "mercy," appears in the opening and closing cola of the strophe, thus forming an inclusio; the noun recurs for the third and most emphatic time in 2:18c, connecting strophes III and VII. The root of the verb ἀναμένειν (2:7a) recurs in ἐμμένειν (2:10c), thus suggesting a connection between "waiting for the Lord's mercy" (2:7a) and "remaining in the fear of the Lord" (2:10c) as a link between strophes III and IV. The injunction "do not turn away," μὴ ἐκκλίνητε, from the fear of the Lord (2:7b) echoes the warning in Deut 5:32: in doing all that the Lord has commanded you to do, "you shall not turn [LXX οὐκ ἐκκλινεῖτε] to the right or to the left." The expression to turn away also alludes back to the image of "ways" in 2:6b, the point being that if one turned away from the ways of the Lord, one would fall into sin.

In 2:8a Ben Sira implies that "fearing the Lord" and "believing in him" go hand in hand. Or put differently, you cannot fear the Lord without first believing in him. Belief is so important that πιστεύειν appears, as I indicated above, three times; and a compound form of the verb is used in 2:10b. No other verb in the poem appears more than twice except, of course, for φοβεῖσθαι (six times). The verbs πιστεύειν (2:8a) and ἐλπίζειν (2:9a) serve as *mots crochets* with 2:6 where the two verbs recur, thus connecting this strophe with the preceding. In 2:8b Ben Sira gives a creative exegesis of Lev 19:13: "your reward will not fail," implying that the Lord will not hold your wages overnight, as the Syriac renders the colon (see the critical note). Those who fear the Lord can indeed hope for "good things and for lasting joy and mercy" (2:9b) because the reward for fidelity takes place in the present life, according to the Deuteronomic doctrine of retribution to which Ben Sira subscribed. [47]

---

[47] See A. A. Di Lella, "Conservative and Progressive Theology: Sirach and Wisdom," *CBQ* 28 (1966) 143–46.

The expression εὐφροσύνη αἰῶνος (2:9b) derives from εὐφροσύνη αἰώνιος in LXX Isa 35:10 and 61:7; see also Isa 51:11 and Sir 1:11–12; 15:6.

Strophe IV (2:10–11)

Now Ben Sira pulls out all the stops, appealing to the past in order to corroborate his argument regarding the fear of the Lord and trust in him. He begins with a twofold imperative to "look at the ancient generations" and "see." The expression ἀρχαίας γενεάς (2:10a) appears nowhere else in the Greek OT, but it does recur, but with the words reversed, in the pseudepigraphical Psalms of Solomon 18:12, γενεῶν ἀρχαίων. In typical homiletic fashion Ben Sira employs three rhetorical questions (2:10bcd) to dramatize his point. Though the expected answer to these questions is an emphatic "No," faithful Jews knew from bitter experience as well as the history of their people that quite often those who "trusted in the Lord" or "remained in his fear" or "called upon him"—note the progressive parallelism in these verbal phrases —were often "put to shame," and "been forsaken," or "overlooked" by the Lord. But Ben Sira's main point remains valid: in the long run the faithful will prevail; see Job 41:7–17. An a:b::b´:a´ verb root chiasm links this strophe with the preceding: ἀναμείνατε (2:7a):πιστεύσατε (2:8a)::ἐνεπίστευσεν (2:10b):ἐνέμεινεν (2:10c).

The grandson may have derived the combination of ἐνεπίστευσεν and κατῃσχύνθη (2:10b) from LXX Isa 28:16: ὁ πιστεύων ἐπ᾽ αὐτῷ οὐ μὴ καταισχυνθῇ, "the one who believes in it [the foundation stone in Zion] will not be put to shame." For the notion that the one who hopes and trusts in the Lord would not be put to shame, see Pss 22:5–6 and 37:25. The faithful also prayed never to be put to shame; see, e.g., Pss 25:2, 3, 20; 31:2. The reason is that life without honor was a life not worth living; see Prov 21:21; 22:4; 2 Macc 6:25.

The important motive clauses in 2:11 explain why the faithful can rest assured of ultimate vindication despite occasional setbacks: The Lord is "compassionate and merciful," οἰκτίρμων καὶ ἐλεήμων, MT *rḥwm wḥnwn*, a stereotyped expression found many other times in the OT; see, e.g., Exod 34:6; Pss 86:15; 103:8; 111:4; 112:4; Joel 2:13; Jonah 4:2; 2 Chr 30:9; Neh 9:17, 31. Moreover, the Lord "forgives sins and saves in time of trouble" (2:11b), a comforting truth found also in Isa 63:9; Pss 34:7; 37:39–40; 138:7; 145:18–19; 2 Chr 20:9; Neh 9:27.[48] The phrase ἐν καιρῷ θλίψεως recurs also in Sir

---

48. For the interesting expanded form of 2:11b, see the critical note above.

22:23; 35:26; 37:4; 40:24; and often elsewhere in the LXX; see, e.g., Judg 10:14; Isa 33:2; Jer 15:11; Ps 36:39; Neh 9:27; 1 Macc 13:5.

Strophe V (2:12–14)

Having exhorted and encouraged the faithful to remain ever constant in the fear of the Lord in spite of trials, Ben Sira in this strophe employs the three-fold, hence emphatic, prophetic "Woe," οὐαί, MT *ʾwy* or *hwy*, to excoriate those Jews who have compromised their faith. Instead of "cowardly (or fearful) hearts," καρδίαις δειλαῖς (2:12a), some witnesses, as noted above, read καρδίαις δισσαῖς, "double hearts," a reading perhaps influenced by "two paths" in 2:12b; see also 1:28b. The grandson uses the phrase καρδία δειλή also in 22:18. For the imagery and vocabulary of καρδία δειλή see LXX Deut 20:8; Judg 7:3; and 2 Chr 13:7; and for χερσὶν παρειμέναις, "drooping hands," see LXX Zech 3:16.[49] Since the heart according to Hebrew thought is the seat of intelligence and will, the phrase "cowardly hearts" is hard hitting. Such caustic expressions at the beginning of the strophe convey Ben Sira's utter disgust for those Jews who have lost their confidence in the great promises made to Israel. In semantic parallelism with the moral weakling of 2:12a is the one "who walks on two paths," ἐπιβαίνοντι ἐπὶ δύο τρίβους (2:12b). Such a person attempts the impossible: you simply cannot walk the wrong path of Hellenism and at the same time walk the right path of Judaism. Ben Sira may have had in mind Jer 18:15: "But my people have forgotten me . . . ; they have stumbled in their ways, the paths of old, to walk on bypaths, not the highway." "Sinner," ἁμαρτωλός, is the only word to describe such a person. In 41:8 Ben Sira uses "Woe" for the fourth and final time to condemn once again sinners of this kind: οὐαὶ ὑμῖν ἄνδρες ἀσεβεῖς οἵτινες ἐγκατελίπετε νόμον ὑψίστου, "Woe to you, O wicked people, who forsake the Law of the Most High!"

The second "Woe" expands on the imagery of the first. Ben Sira now calls the sinner's heart (intelligence, will) "drooping" (2:13a), the same adjective used in 2:12a to describe their hands, because it does not "believe," πιστεύει, the verb found also in 2:6a, 8a, and a biform in 10b, thus connecting this strophe with strophes II, III, and IV. Faith, the basis of any meaningful rela-

---

[49] In Sir 25:23 the grandson uses the same expression as well as "quaking knees" to describe the husband of a wife who brings him no happiness.

tionship with the Lord (see, e.g., Gen 15:1–6), is precisely what the Jewish compromisers lack. For that reason such people "will have no shelter," οὐ σκεπασθήσεται (2:13b), the idea being that the Lord, who holds them accountable for their life-style, will provide no cover or salvation for them; see Pss 17(LXX 16):8; 27(26):5; 31(30):21; 64(63):3; Wis 5:16; 19:8; Zeph 2:3 in the LXX of all of which texts the verb σκεπάζειν recurs.

The third and most emphatic "Woe" condemns those "who have lost," ἀπολωλεκόσιν, their ὑπομονήν, "steadfastness, perseverance, fortitude, patience" (2:14a), the noun Codex 248, as noted above, has in the title of the poem.[50] The probable source of this colon is Isa 46:12 in the LXX of which appears the expression οἱ ἀπολωλεκότες τὴν καρδίαν, "those who have lost heart." The virtue of ὑπομονή is, in a nutshell, precisely what the Jewish compromisers lack; see strophes II and III. To conclude this "Woe" strophe Ben Sira asks an attention-grabbing question, meant to stir up the conscience of the back-sliders: What will you do when the Lord "makes his visitation," ἐπισκέπτηται (2:14b)? Usually, the verb ἐπισκέπτεσθαι, like the underlying Hebrew *pqd* with its wide semantic range, takes a direct object (as in 46:14b, the only other occurrence of the verb in the grandson's translation); see, e.g., Gen 50:24, 25; Ruth 1:6; 1 Sam 2:21; Zeph 2:7. Elsewhere in the OT *pqd* with God or the Lord as subject often implies a friendly visit or divine saving activity. But here the verb is used intransitively, with the implied sense, "to make a visitation to punish."

Strophe VI (2:15–17)

In sharp contrast to the waffling Jews Ben Sira has just denounced are "those that fear the Lord," οἱ φοβούμενοι κύριον, the expression at the beginning of the strophe's three bicola, as also in strophe III. These stalwart souls never "disobey," ἀπειθήσουσιν, the words of the Lord (2:15a); the same verb is used also 1:28a: "Do not disobey the fear of the Lord." Those who fear the Lord remain as steadfast and reliable as the ordered universe each creature of which "never crowds its neighbor, nor do they ever *disobey his word*," οὐκ ἀπειθήσουσιν τοῦ ῥήματος αὐτοῦ (Sir 16:28), the identical vocabulary as here; see also LXX Deut 1:26; 9:23; and 32:51. Regarding the blessings for such obedience see Deut 28:13; 30:16; Prov 1:33; 8:33. Those those "that fear

---

[50] The same verb and noun recur in the Greek of 41:2 to describe the weak person at the point of death.

the Lord" are at the same time those "that love him" (2:15, 16), the two verbs being in synonymous parallelism; see 1:25–27. They keep his "ways," ὁδούς (2:15b), the noun used also in 2:6b in the command to "make straight your ways," thus connecting this strophe with strophe II. The implication is that "the ways" of loyal Jews correspond to "the ways" of the Lord. Thus, unlike "the sinner who walks on two paths" (2:12b), the upright walk only in the ways of the Lord; see Pss 18:22 and 25:4. In 6:26 Ben Sira urges his students to pursue wisdom vigorously: ἐν πάσῃ ψυχῇ σου[51] πρόσελθε αὐτῇ καὶ ἐν ὅλῃ δυνάμει σου συντήρησον τὰς ὁδοὺς αὐτῆς, "With all your soul come to her [wisdom], and with all your might keep her ways." Note the two Deuteronomic prepositional phrases. Wisdom's ways coincide with the ways of the Lord since the essence of wisdom is the fear of the Lord (1:11–30), as noted above.

In synonymous parallelism with to "keep his ways" (2:15b) is the expression, to "seek his good will," ζητήσουσιν εὐδοκίαν αὐτοῦ (2:16a), which occurs only one other time in the LXX (1 Chr 16:10). Those who love the Lord also "are filled with his law," ἐμπλησθήσονται τοῦ νόμου (2:16b). The only other occurrence in the LXX of a similar expression appears in Sir 32:15: ὁ ζητῶν νόμον ἐμπλησθήσεται αὐτοῦ, "the one who seeks the law is filled with it." Finally, those who fear the Lord "prepare (ἑτοιμάσουσιν, the same verb as in 2:1b) their hearts" (2:17a; see LXX 1 Sam 7:3), i.e., their mind and will, for the service of the Lord. This involves humbling oneself before the Lord (2:17b), thus acknowledging his sovereignty and mystery; see also 2:1b, 4b, 5b. Ben Sira often stresses the need for humility (3:17–18, 20–24; 7:17; 18:21). In a word, those who fear and love the Lord observe all the elements of "the Deuteronomic equation" I mentioned above, and they remain steadfast even in times of testing and distress; see Job 1:20–21 and 2:10; and Jas 1:12.

Strophe VII (2:18)

Having developed his theme that amid trials the faithful can feel secure because of their fear of the Lord as well as their belief and hope in him, Ben Sira concludes his poem with an exhortatory couplet to encourage the faithful in time of distress. The thought and vocabulary of 2:18ab derive from LXX

---

[51] Syr "your heart." The basis of both expressions is of course Deut 6:5. Geniza MS A has extant only the final ה of this verse.

2 Sam 24:14 (parallel 1 Chr 21:13)—the words of David, who is in dire straits, before choosing pestilence as punishment for his sin: ἐμπεσοῦμαι δὴ ἐν χειρὶ κυρίου ὅτι πολλοὶ οἱ οἰκτιρμοὶ αὐτοῦ σφόδρα εἰς δὲ χεῖρας ἀνθρώπου οὐ μὴ ἐμπέσω, "Let me fall [MT: let us fall] into the hand of the Lord, for very many are his mercies, but into the hands of a human may I never fall." Ben Sira supports this principle by two motive clauses (2:18cd) some of the vocabulary of which recurs in 18:4–6 that also extols the Lord's "majesty," μεγαλωσύνη, "his works," τὰ ἔργα αὐτοῦ, and "his mercies," τὰ ἐλέη αὐτοῦ. See also Wis 11:23 and 12:16. As regards "his name" (2:18d), Ben Sira alludes perhaps to the name of God he uses in 50:19b, "the Merciful One," *rḥwm* in Geniza MS B, ἐλεήμονος in the grandson's translation. If so, we can then see an *a:b::b´:a´* chiastic parallelism in the nouns of 2:18cd: ἡ μεγαλωσύνη αὐτου:τὸ ἔλεος αὐτοῦ::τὸ ὄνομα αὐτοῦ:τὰ ἔργα αὐτοῦ.

Ben Sira's point is clear: those who fear the Lord can trust in the Lord's mercy and in his works just as surely as they acknowledge his majesty and his holy name. A fitting conclusion to the poem.

PART FIVE

Other Studies

MICHAEL L. BARRÉ, S.S.

"Terminative" Terms in Hebrew Acrostics

The third section of the Hebrew Bible (the "Writings") contains two short editorial notices announcing the conclusion of a series of poetic utterances attributed to two major biblical figures. At the end of Book II of the Psalter, after the conclusion of Psalm 72 (v 20), appear the words: *kālû tĕpillôt dāwīd ben-yīšāy*, "The prayers of David, son of Jesse, are ended." Similarly, at the end of Job 31 (v 40b), after the conclusion of Job's last discourse, comes the notice: *tammû dibrê ʾiyyôb*, "The words of Job are ended." In the course of reviewing recently the various ancient Hebrew acrostics known to scholarship to date I began to notice the occurrence of these two verbs—*k-l-y*, "to run out, finish, reach an end," and (less frequently) the synonymous *t-m-m*— in a fair number of these poems. In acrostics, of course, the *kaph* verse normally marks the end of the first half of the poem and the *taw* verse the end of the second half. What struck me as noteworthy in my survey of acrostic poems was the appearance of *k-l-y* in the *kaph* verse and of *t-m-m* in the *taw* verse of a number of them. Could this be ascribed to mere coincidence? In such passages the subjects of these verbs are not "prayers" or "words" as in Ps 72:20 or Job 31:40. Rather it seems that the authors were using these roots here to signal to the reader by way of double entendre that the first part of the acrostic (in the case of *kaph*) or the entire poem (in the case of *taw*) had "reached an end." Further investigation suggests that other, more or less synonymous roots turn up with some regularity at junctural points in Hebrew acrostics, where they arguably serve the same function.

We consider first the root *k-l-y* in the *kaph* verse of several acrostics. In Psalm 37 (v 20b) the last word is *kālû*.[1] In this case the subject is *ʾôyĕbê yhwh*, "Yahweh's enemies." Its presence here—especially as the *last* word in this verse—announces the end of the first half of the psalm. The conclusion that the *kaph* verse marks the limit of a section of the poem finds support in the fact that some commentators see the next verse, v 21, as beginning a new subtheme and therefore a new subsection.[2]

The same phenomenon occurs, albeit on a much larger scale, in Psalm 119. The eight-line *kaph* section contains a cluster of occurrences of the root *k-l-y* distributed over three lines in this section: the first, second, and seventh:

81	*kālĕtâ litšûʿātĕkā napšî*	My soul languishes for your salvation
82	*kālû ʿênay lĕʾimrātekā*	I have cried my eyes out for your promise[3]
87	*kimʿat killûnî bāʾāreṣ*	They almost annihilated me on the earth.[4]

The threefold occurrence of this term at this juncture in the poem can hardly be ascribed to coincidence.[5] Other considerations show that the poet intended a clear division between the *kaph* lines and the *lamed* lines—in other words, making the former a conclusion of sorts. W. Soll, for example, has pointed out that content-wise the *kaph* lines (vv 81–88) mark the nadir of the psalm, after which there is an abrupt upswing in mood.[6]

---

[1] Another *kālû* appears two words before this. This may indicate the presence of some textual corruption but does not affect the point I am making here—namely that a derivative of the root *k-l-y* occurs in the *kaph* bicolon of Psalm 37 (specifically, in the final colon).

[2] So, e.g., G. Ravasi, *Il Libro dei Salmi: Volume Iᵒ (1–50)* (Bologna: Edizione Dehoniane, 1988) 674.

[3] For this meaning of the idiom *k-l-y ʿênayim*, see M. I. Gruber, *Aspects of Non-Verbal Communication in the Ancient Near East* (Studia Pohl 12/1; Rome: Biblical Institute, 1980), 1. 390–400, esp. 398.

[4] The root occurs elsewhere in the psalm only once, viz., in v 123.

[5] Moreover, *killûnî* may have a special terminative significance insofar as it is the third occurrence of the root in this section, appears in the seventh line, and is the fortieth word in the *kaph* verses. All three of these numbers (3, 7, 40) can denote completeness or finality in Hebrew literature.

[6] W. Soll, *Psalm 119: Matrix, Form, and Setting* (CBQMS 23; Washington: The Catholic Biblical Association of America, 1991) 30–31: "In Psalm 119, where the *Kaph* strophe represents the nadir of the psalm in its expression of grief and sorrow, the *Lamed* strophe provides a decisive shift in mood, passing directly to the heavens ...."

Nah 1:2–9 is a unique example in the MT of a semi-acrostic, i.e., the first half of the alphabet, *aleph* through *kaph*. Some have tried to find the allegedly "missing" second half in the subsequent verses, but the general agreement at this point is that this is in fact a partial acrostic.[7] In any case, this unit concludes with a double *kaph* section, opening with the noun *kālâ*, "termination" > "annihilation": *kālâ yaʿăśeh mĕqûmāh* [MT: *mĕqômāh*], "He shall wreak annihilation on the opposition" (v 8b),[8] the beginning of a tricolon. A similar expression, in which *kālâ* again figures as the first word, appears in the next bicolon, v 9b: *kālâ hûʾ ʿōśeh*, "He is going to wreak annihilation."

The root *k-l-y* also appears in the *kaph* verses of two acrostic chapters of Lamentations. Lam 2:11a reads: *kālû baddĕmāʿôt ʿênay*, "My eyes have run out of tears."[9] Lam 4:11a begins: *killâ yhwh ʾet-ḥămātô*, "Yahweh has given full vent to his wrath."

In the texts considered thus far *k-l-y* appears, as might be expected, in the *kaph* section of the acrostic. But in Lamentations 2 it turns up in the final or *taw* verse, creating an inclusion with *kālû* in the *kaph* verse and appearing as the last word in the poem: *ʾōyĕbî killām*, "My enemy has annihilated [lit., "terminated"!] them."

A possible variation on the terminative use of this root may be *kôl/kōl*, "all." This word derives from *k-l-l*, which is related to the root *k-l-y* and has a similar meaning: "to be complete." Further, in many verbal and nominal realizations of these roots only the first two radicals are evident—*k* and *l*. There is some evidence that *kôl/kōl* in biblical Hebrew could denote the completion or end of a composition, like *k-l-y* and *t-m-m*. Compare the use of *k-l-y* in Ps 72:20 with that of *kôl/kōl* at the conclusion of Qoheleth (12:13): *sôp dābār hakkōl nišmāʿ*, "(Here is) the end of the matter, *all* has been heard."[10] The problem here is that *kōl* is an extremely common word in Hebrew, far more so than *k-l-y*. Nonetheless it is possible that as the lead-

---

[7] So Soll, ibid., 20 n. 56; J. J. M. Roberts, *Nahum, Habakkuk, and Zephaniah: A Commentary* (OTL; Louisville: Westminster/John Knox, 1991) 45.

[8] For this reading and translation, see Roberts, *Nahum, Habakkuk, and Zephaniah*, 48–49.

[9] See Gruber, *Aspects of Non-Verbal Communication in the Ancient Near East*, 1. 390–400, esp. 399.

[10] This is admittedly a post-classical text. On the dating of Qoheleth, see recently C. L. Seow, "Linguistic Evidence and the Dating of Qoheleth" (*JBL* 115 [1996] 643–66), who makes a convincing case for dating Qoheleth "between the second half of the fifth century and the first half of the fourth" (ibid., 666).

word in the *kaph* verse of some acrostics this word also may allude to termination through double entendre, as if to say, "That is all (of this section of the poem)."

In Psalm 119 *kōl* is the lead-word in the sixth *kaph* line (v 86). Thus as this unit is introduced by forms of *k-l-y* beginning its first and second lines (vv 81–82), the collocation of *kol-* (lead-word in 86) and *killûnî* (second word in 87) in the sixth and seventh lines respectively may be seen to form a sort of penultimate inclusion to the *kaph* section.

In Lamentations 1 too *kol-* introduces the *kaph* unit (v 11)[11] and appears only here in this section. The fact that there is a switch from third to second person in the immediately following *lamed* unit ("O all you who pass by, look and see . . .") further indicates that the *kaph* unit signals the conclusion of a subsection of this chapter.

It has been frequently noted that Psalm 1, though not an acrostic in the strict sense, has a number of acrostic features. It begins with an *aleph* word, *ʾašrê* (v 1), and ends with a *taw* word, *tōʾbēd* (v 6), the former connoting well-being, the latter woe. It also contains a *kaph* and a *lamed* line (vv 3c, 4a). The *kaph* line begins with *kōl*: *kōl ʾăšer yaʿăśeh yaṣlîaḥ*, "All that he does prospers."[12] This is immediately followed by a *lamed* line: *lōʾ-kēn hārĕšārîm*, "Not so the wicked." The latter marks the major thematic juncture in the poem: the righteous (vv 1–3) and the wicked (vv 4–6).

A more difficult case is Psalm 25. This is an atypical acrostic in the sense that it lacks a *waw* verse (and may never have had one) and ends with a (second) *pe* verse. It is thus a twenty-two line poem in which the eleventh line is the *lamed* verse and the twenty-second is the second *pe* verse. In this arrangement the *kaph* and *taw* verses are penultimate, not final, in their respective sections. *Kol* appears as the lead-word in its *kaph* line: *kol-ʾorḥôt yhwh ḥesed weʾĕmet*, "All the ways of Yahweh are steadfast love and fidelity" (v 10). But how could the *kol* signal finality if in fact it is not the final verse of the first half of the acrostic? If Psalm 25 in its present form is reworked from an earlier psalm with the standard acrostic pattern (which, it seems to me, cannot be entirely excluded from the realm of possibility), then the *kaph* and *taw* lines would have been final within their respective sections (first half and second

---

[11] It also occurs immediately after the *taw* word at the end of the poem (v 22).

[12] Omitting the initial *w-* here, which frequently appears as a secondary addition to the beginning of cola in Hebrew poetry.

half) in this earlier version.[13] The possibility that the *kaph* and *lamed* verses played their normal, terminative roles within an earlier form of the acrostic is corroborated by the presence of several literary devices which suggest the author intended to establish a connection between these two verses. (1) Both lead-words are monosyllabic nominal forms with the phonic pattern /c_1oc_2/ (*kol/kōl, tōm*). (2) The verb *n-ṣ-r* appears in both bicola, and only here in the entire psalm.[14]

We now turn to a consideration of the second root mentioned at the beginning of this essay, namely *t-m-m*. It appears in the *taw* section of several acrostics. As we have just seen, in Psalm 25 the *taw* verse is penultimate within the present structure of the poem but may have been the final verse in its original form, before the addition of the second *pe* verse. The *taw* line begins: *tōm wāyōšer yiṣṣĕrûnî*, "May integrity and uprightness preserve me" (v 21).

In Lamentations 4 the *taw* section begins: *tam-ᶜăwōnēk bat-ṣiyyôn*, "The punishment for your iniquity has come to an end, O Daughter Zion" (v 22a). In this case *tam* is not a subtle allusion to the root meaning of *t-m-m* but plainly translates, "It has come to an end." Note also the synonymous *lōʾ yôsîp*, "no more," in the next colon.

Finally, as *k-l-y* is found mainly in the *kaph* section of acrostics but in the *taw* section in at least one instance (Lamentations 2), so *t-m-m* appears in

---

[13] D. N. Freedman in "Patterns in Psalms 25 and 34," *Priests, Prophets and Scribes: Essays on the Formation and Heritage of Second Temple Judaism in Honour of Joseph Blenkinsopp* (ed. E. Ulrich et al.; JSOTSup 149; Sheffield: Sheffield Academic Press, 1992) 127 favors the position that in Psalm 25 one (original) line has been omitted (the *waw*-verse) and another added (the second *pe*-verese) in order to create a 22-line acrostic: "Alternatively and better, we could say that one of the internal lines of the poem *has been omitted* in order to allow for or to accommodate *the addition of* a final closing line" (emphasis mine). These remarks support the view that the author of the canonical form of Psalm 25 has reworked an *earlier* poem with the "normal" acrostic form of the 22-letter alphabet.

Another consideration that may be relevant here has to do with word-count. The *aleph* through *kaph* lines of Psalm 25 contain *seventy-eight words,* and the *aleph* verse originally no doubt contained one or two more. (Verse 2 begins with *ʾĕlōhay*, which almost certainly began a second colon, forming a bicolon with *ʾēlêkā yhwh napšî ʾeśśāʾ*. This second colon must have consisted at least one or two words following *ʾĕlōhay*.) The *lamed* through (second) *pe* verses contain *eighty words.* This means that as to actual length (in terms of word-count) the *kaph* verse does mark the end of the first *half* of the poem in its canonical form.

[14] Recall the connection forged between the *kaph* and *taw* verses of Lamentations 2 by means of verbs formed from the root *k-l-y* (vv 11, 22).

one *kaph* verse. In the acrostic poem "Apostrophe to Zion" known from Qumran Cave XI (11QPsᵃ 22:1–15) the *kaph* verse runs:

kmh qww lyšuᶜtk
wytᵓblw ᶜlyk tmyk
How they have hoped for your salvation,
(how) your blameless ones have mourned over you![15]

Note that the *t-m-m* derivative is the *last* word in the *kaph* line and therefore in the first half of the poem.

Thus far we have seen three roots used in acrostics to suggest the idea of termination of the first and/or second part of the poem: *k-l-y*, *k-l-l*, and *t-m-m*. Other roots with similar meanings may also function in this way.

Unlike *k-l-y* and *t-m-m*, *ᵓ-b-d* (Qal) cannot be used with words, psalms, or the like as subject. On the other hand, its basic sense of "perish, vanish" is related to the idea of termination. What perishes or vanishes has ceased to be, has come to an end. Hence a poet might use this root to allude subtly to a literary termination—the end of the first or second half of an alphabetic poem.

In the imperfectly preserved acrostic Psalms 9–10 *ᵓ-b-d* occurs toward the end of the *kaph* line (9:19):

kî lōᵓ lāneṣaḥ yiššākaḥ ᵓebyôn
tiqwat ᶜăniyyîm [Qere] *tōᵓbēd lāᶜād*
For the needy will not always be forgotten,
nor shall the hope of the afflicted forever perish/vanish.

The content of this psalm supports the terminative role of the *kaph* section: *lamed* marks a transition from thanksgiving to lament.

We have already seen that termination is hinted at in the *kaph* section of Psalm 37 by means of the final word, *kālû*, the last word in the second bicolon of this section. But in this case another terminative signal is given by the last word of the first bicolon, *yōᵓbēdû: kî rěšāᶜîm yōᵓbēdû*, "But the wicked (will) perish." Although the *taw* word in Psalm 112 is *taᵓăwat*, the *taw* line (v 10c) and indeed the entire poem ends with *tōᵓbēd: taᵓăwat rěšāᶜîm tōᵓbēd*,[16] "The hope of the wicked will perish/vanish." In the eight-line *taw*

---

[15] J. A. Sanders, *The Dead Sea Psalms Scroll* (Ithaca, NY: Cornell University, 1967) 124–25.

[16] This is the only occurrence of the root *ᵓ-b-d* in this psalm.

section of Psalm 119, the last line of the poem contains the root ²-b-d: tāʿîtî kĕśeh ʾōbēd, "I have gone astray like a lost sheep." It is significant that this is matched by two other occurrences of this root in vv 92 and 95, which fall within the *lamed* section. Thus ²-b-d creates both a conclusion and an inclusion, connecting the *lamed* and *taw* sections, i.e., the beginning and ending strophes of the second half of this psalm. Finally, as mentioned above, note that Psalm 1 ends with the same word Psalm 112 ends with, namely tōʾbēd[17] (both also begin with the same *aleph*-word, ʾašrê).

Two other roots should be mentioned in this connection. The basic sense of the root *š-l-m* is completion, like some of the other verbs we have been considering. In the apocryphal Psalm 155 from Qumran Cave XI (11QPs^a 24:3–17) this root forms the last word in the *kaph* line and may also cue the listener to the end of the unit:[18]

> kbwd ʾth yhwh
> ʿl kn šʾlty mlpnykh šlmh[19]
>
> You are glorious, O Yahweh,
>
> therefore my request is fulfilled by you.

The *taw* line of Psalm 34 (v 22) begins with a verb from the root *m-w-t*, "to die," which is surely a terminative term if any word may be so called: tĕmôtēt rāšāʿ rāʿâ, "Evil will bring death to the wicked." In this case the poet may have been playfully alluding to the root *t-m-m* by means of the homophonous *tm-* at the beginning of this word.

Although acrostics are sometimes disparaged as mechanistic compositions, they do display a fair amount of ingenuity. It would be presumptuous of modern scholarship to proclaim that it has uncovered all their subtleties.[20]

---

[17] This is the only occurrence of the root ²-b-d in this psalm.

[18] Note the appearance of the root *š-l-m* in the *last* verse of a number of psalms: 4:9; 29:11; 61:9; 62:13; 120:7; 125:5; 128:6.

[19] Sanders, *The Dead Sea Psalms Scroll*, 110–11.

[20] Some as yet unnoticed subtleties of acrostics would include examples of what A. R. Ceresko has referred to as "alphabetic thinking" ("The ABCs of Wisdom in Psalm xxxiv," *VT* 25 [1985] 99), among which I would list the following. (1) In the acrostic Psalms 9–10 the first and last words of each colon of the *kaph* bicolon (v 19) clearly allude to the first and last halves of the alphabet. In the first part of this *kaph* bicolon the first word begins with *kaph* and the last with *aleph* (the beginning and end of the first half of the alphabet in reverse) and in the second colon

One such subtlety may be the use of certain terms to announce to the listener/reader through a kind of double entendre that a major section of the acrostic has reached its end. The foregoing study reveals that these terminative terms may occur frequently enough to be considered a common feature in ancient Hebrew acrostics. If the hypothesis presented here is on the mark, they occur in almost three-quarters (i.e., 72%) of the eighteen poems that make up the corpus of acrostics or partial acrostics in ancient Hebrew literature known to us at the present time, which consists of the following poems: Psalms 1,[21] 9–10, 25, 34, 37, 111, 112, 119, 145; Prov 31:10–31; Lamentations 1, 2, 3, 4; Nah 1:2–9; Sir 51:13–30; Apostrophe to Zion (11QPs[a] 22:1–15); Psalm 155 (11QPs[a] 24:3–17).[22] Even if one disallows the examples in which *kôl/kōl* occurs as a terminative term the number of examples of this phenomenon still remains impressive.

It is frequently observed that acrostics appear to have some relation to wisdom in Israel. A. Ceresko is no doubt correct when he asserts that the very fact the acrostic "can be appreciated only in the written form" testifies to its origin within a literate (i.e., scribal) milieu and that this in turn points to its

---

the first word begins with *taw* and the last with *lamed* (the beginning and end of the second half of the alphabet in reverse): *k-* ... *ɔ-* // *t-* ... *l-*. (2) Something similar appears in Lamentations 4, in the *kaph* and *lamed* bicola (vv 11a and 12a):

> *killâ yhwh ʾet-ḥămātô*
> *šāpak ḥărôn ʾappô*
> *lōʾ heʾĕmînû malkê-ʾereṣ*
> *wĕkōl yōšĕbê tēbēl*
> Yahweh has vented his wrath,
> he has poured out his anger.
> The kings of the earth did not believe,
> nor any of those who dwell in the world.

Note that the *kaph* bicolon ends with *ʾappô*—thus the bicolon begins with a *kaph* word and ends with an *aleph* word; the *lamed* bicolon begins with a *lamed* word and ends with a *taw* word. This also yields the two halves of the alphabet, but in chiastic order: *k-* ... *ɔ-* : *l-* ... *t-*. (3) The last colon in Lamentations 2 reads: *ʾōyĕbî killām*, "My enemy has annihilated them." Not only does this contain the "terminative" root *k-l-y* (as noted above), but here too the two final words allude to the first half of the alphabet (*ɔ-* ... *k-*). Note further the alphabetic run formed by the last four letters of these words: *y, k, l, m*.

[21] I include Psalm 1 in this computation since although it is not acrostic or even semi-acrostic in the usual sense, it has too many acrostic features to be excluded from this category.

[22] The acrostics that do not contain any of the terminative terms discussed here are Psalms 111; 145; Prov 31:10–31; Lamentations 3; Sir 51:13–30.

connection with "wisdom" circles.[23] In other words, while not every acrostic must be classified as wisdom literature, the acrostic form itself appears to be intimately connected to wisdom and the scribal profession. Hence refinements of the acrostic pattern, such as the phenomenon described in this paper, may also have their origins in a sapiential milieu or at least reflect a "wisdom" mindset.

---

[23] Ceresko, "The ABCs of Wisdom in Psalm xxxiv," 99. Note also the comment of P. A. Munch, "Die alphabetische Akrostichie in der jüdischen Psalmendichtung," *ZDMG* 15 (1936) 708–9: "Jetzt soll daran erinnert werden, dass die 'Weisheit' im Altertum überall mit der Schreibkunst in allerengster Verbingdung steht. Der Grund und Boden aller Weisheit ist die Schreibfertigkeit" (cited by Ceresko, ibid., 103 n. 4).

CAROLE R. FONTAINE

More Queenly Proverb Performance: The Queen of Sheba in Targum Esther Sheni

It is a commonplace in folklore studies to note that nowhere may a culture's world view be more readily seen in its aspects of both theory and practice than in the composition and social use of folk genres. This is especially true for those genres which represent "common wisdom" and folk use as opposed to those which require specialized performance training and execution. In the composition and use of folk genres, then, we may expect to find ideas about gender explicitly and implicitly encoded not only in the genre items themselves, but also in the use to which they are put. Dynamics of performance, then, must be included along with the collection of any genre items like proverbs, riddles, jokes, legends, proverbial phrases, and so on. Collection of this kind of data has not always been the norm in the field of folklore, so that early works in the field often lack the very sorts of demographic and performance information needed to make a critical analysis of the gendered use of genre.[1] While this lacuna has now been corrected in modern scholarship, those of us who labor in the study of folk genres of the past are still faced with methodological handicaps when we begin our inquiries into the role of gender and genre.

Consider, for example, the plight of the biblical folklorist in wisdom. Our proverbs from different times and places have been assembled into one book where they now exist only in the literary context of a collection. Biblical

---

[1] See the present writer's *Traditional Sayings in the Old Testament: A Contextual Study* (Bible and Literature 5; Sheffield: Almond, 1982) for a fuller discussion, along with S. Niditch, *Folklore and the Hebrew Bible* (Minneapolis: Fortress, 1993) 24–31.

riddles, where they have survived, have usually fared no better (riddle contests in Judges 14 and 1 Esdras 3 are exceptions). Further, it may be a matter of some debate as to how much the item finding its home in a collection formed by elite bureaucrats can actually be said to reflect folk composition, as the two-line wisdom saying in the Book of Proverbs shows far more signs of "literary shaping" by a self-conscious author than one typically sees in the one-line traditional sayings found embedded in narrative outside the wisdom writings proper.[2] In earlier studies of the contextual use of such folk genres as traditional sayings and riddles in Israel and the Ancient Near East, it has been demonstrated that gender is *indeed* a critical factor in composition, the selection of the folk item used and the dynamics of that performance itself.[3] That being the case, it is a continued frustration that so few examples of contextual use—whether we imagine such performance to be a literary fabrication or a mirror of actual folk practices—have survived. Examples of proverbs and riddles about women, used by women, or directed to women are few and far between, and never come to us in the form of a pristine folklore case study collected under stringent methodological controls. Hence, we are destined to cross boundaries of time, space and discipline to round out our perceptions of the role that gender plays in the shaping and use of these typical wisdom forms. To this end, we must consider the case of the Queen of Sheba, a wisdom genre "performer" on a par with Samson and other riddlers in the biblical text. Although no riddles or proverbs appear in her brief story in the Hebrew Bible, if we examine her appearance in midrash, we find her there arrayed with the splendor of her own wisdom put to pointed diplomatic ends.

Sheba's story, recorded in 1 Kgs 10:1–10, 13 (2 Chr 9:1–9, 12; Josephus, *Antiquities*, VIII, 6, 5–6), is tucked in amongst the other international ventures and accomplishments of Solomon:

---

[2] Compare, for example, the views of "literariness" versus "orality" of the proverb collections held by H.-J. Hermisson, *Studien zur israelitischen Spruchweisheit* (WMANT 28; Neukirchen-Vluyn: Neukirchener V., 1968) with those of C. Westermann, *Wurzeln der Weisheit: Die ältesten Sprüche Israels und anderer Völker* (Göttingen: Vandenhoeck & Ruprecht, 1990) 9–13 and passim.

[3] See the present writer's "Queenly Proverb Performance: The Prayer of Puduhepa (KUB XXI, 27)," *The Listening Heart: Essays in Wisdom and the Psalms in Honor of Roland E. Murphy, O. Carm.* (ed. K. G. Hoglund et al.; JSOTSup 58; Sheffield: Almond, 1987) 95–126, and C. R. Fontaine and C. V. Camp, "The Words of the Wise and Their Riddles," *Text and Tradition: The Hebrew Bible and Folklore* (ed. S. Niditch; Semeia Studies; Atlanta: Scholars, 1990) 127–52.

Now when the queen of Sheba heard of the fame of Solomon concerning the name of the LORD, she came to test him with hard questions. 2 She came to Jerusalem with a very great retinue, with camels bearing spices, and very much gold, and precious stones; and when she came to Solomon, she told him all that was on her mind. 3 And Solomon answered all her questions; there was nothing hidden from the king which he could not explain to her. 4 And when the queen of Sheba had seen all the wisdom of Solomon, the house that he had built, 5 the food of his table, the seating of his officials, and the attendance of his servants, their clothing, his cupbearers, and his burnt offerings which he offered at the house of the LORD, there was no more spirit in her. 6 And she said to the king, "The report was true which I heard in my own land of your affairs and of your wisdom, 7 but I did not believe the reports until I came and my own eyes had seen it; and, behold, the half was not told me; your wisdom and prosperity surpass the report which I heard. 8 Happy are your wives! Happy are these your servants, who continually stand before you and hear your wisdom! 9 Blessed be the LORD your God, who has delighted in you and set you on the throne of Israel! Because the LORD loved Israel for ever, he has made you king, that you may execute justice and righteousness." 10 Then she gave the king a hundred and twenty talents of gold, and a very great quantity of spices, and precious stones; never again came such an abundance of spices as these which the queen of Sheba gave to King Solomon. 11 Moreover the fleet of Hiram, which brought gold from Ophir, brought from Ophir a very great amount of almug wood and precious stones. 12 And the king made of the almug wood supports for the house of the LORD, and for the king's house, lyres also and harps for the singers; no such almug wood has come or been seen, to this day. 13 And King Solomon gave to the queen of Sheba all that she desired, whatever she asked besides what was given her by the bounty of King Solomon. So she turned and went back to her own land, with her servants (1 Kg 10:1–13 [RSV]).

The account is tantalizingly brief, and genre critics usually consider it a legend, interrupted by a historical report or notice of Hiram's fleet which has been interpolated in vv 11–12.[4] Interspersed with a eulogy (vv. 6–7, 9b), and

---

[4] B. O. Long, *1 Kings, with an Introduction to Historical Literature* (FOTL 9; Grand Rapids, MI: Eerdmans, 1984) 115–20; J. A. Montgomery, *A Critical and Exegetical Commentary on the Book of Kings* (ed. H. S. Gehman; New York: Charles Scribner's, 1951) 212–19, and so with other commentators. It is probable that the insertion of Hiram's fleet here occurs because it is yoked to folk traditions of Hiram and Solomon holding riddle contests (see the account by Josephus), for which the loser must pay a monetary fine.

two wisdom forms (a praise speech including a blessing formula [v 9a], and a beatitude or *ʾašrê*-saying [v. 8]), the legend here is "a story which has rather more concern for the stupendous characteristics of its character than in developing the dramatic possibilities inherent in the plot," according to B. O. Long.[5] For him, it is precisely this legendary character which causes the story to live on in popular storytelling traditions and to be lovingly embellished by Jewish, Islamic, Ethiopian and African-American audiences of later times.

Two elements of the biblical text may have operated to authorize the later retellings of Sheba's encounter with Solomon: in v 2, the verb *bwʾ*, "to come," is used to describe Sheba's visit, and is a well-established euphemism for sexual intercourse. In v 13 we read: "And King Solomon gave to the queen of Sheba all that she desired, whatever she asked . . . ,"[6] phrases which stirred the imagination of those who read sexual overtones in v 2. We will find that in the versions of this meeting from late antiquity and the medieval period, a sexual encounter is more or less assumed, and Sheba is said to have borne a son to Solomon: in the Alphabet of Ben Sira (eleventh century C.E., provenance in the Jewish Diaspora), the son is Nebuchadnezzar, as is also the case in the *Maʿaseh Malkath Sheba* of Saadiah ben-Yosef, a Yemenite version from Jewish and Islamic sources (text dated to 1702 C.E., but with much earlier oral elements).

The story of Sheba's visit is also found in the Quran in Sura XXVII, "The Ant." In the eleventh century Islamic version of al-Kasāʿī, the son is Rehoboam and he is born after Sheba has converted to Islam, having been urged by Allah's great prophet, Sulayman. In the Ethiopian tradition of the *Kebra Nagast* (Ethiopic version, fourteenth century), Sheba, after being tricked and seduced by Solomon, gives birth to Menelik, who becomes the founder of the royal dynasty of that region. Later, after Menelik visits his father, he bears the Ark of the Covenant away to Africa where legend has it that it remains until this very day.[7] In one way or another, the union of

[5] Long, *1 Kings*, 19.

[6] *wĕhammelek šĕlōmōh nātan lĕmalkat-šĕbāʾ ʾet-kol-ḥepsāh ʾăšer šāʾalâ* . . . .

[7] E. Ulendorff, "The Queen of Sheba," *BJRL* 45 (1963)496–98; for translations of variant texts, see J. Lassner, *Demonizing the Queen of Sheba: Boundaries of Gender and Culture in Postbiblical Judaism and Medieval Islam* (Chicago: University of Chicago, 1993). See also W. Montgomery Watt, "The Queen of Sheba in Islamic Tradition" and "The Queen of Sheba in Judaic Tradition," pp. 85–103 and 65–84 respectively in *Solomon and Sheba* (ed. J. B. Prichard; London: Phaidon, 1974).

Solomon and Sheba is thought to have brought misery to Israel, by means of the actions of the son they produced.

But what of Sheba's motivations in her visit?[8] The Hebrew Bible says only that she comes to test Solomon—but why? Islamic and Jewish versions, which show a mutual sharing of motifs not appearing in the biblical text, agree that the initiative was actually Solomon's. Having learned through a fabulous bird-servant, the hoopoe, that an independent queen is ruling in faraway Arabia Felix, Solomon commands that she come to him to submit to his imperial kingship (or Allah's true religion, Islam). Sheba consults her courtiers and they tell her they have no fear of any distant king. Sheba, however, is not so sure—how is one to hold off invasion from a monarch whom even the birds hail as king? When a discreet gift to Solomon does not abate his wish that she appear before him, she undertakes the tedious journey, along with what must be assumed to be a substantial retinue and many fabulous gifts. It seems likely, given the other riddle contests reported in the Hebrew Bible (Samson and the Philistines in Judges 14 and the noble Jew Zerubbabel in 1 Esdras 3–5) where an "outsider" attempts to gain glory and win membership within the dominant group, that Sheba's riddles to Solomon fill some similar diplomatic need.[9] Perhaps if she can win out against Solomon in all his glory, she may find a way to maintain her independence and that of her country.

The variant retellings all suggest that Sheba's rise to power was perhaps unconventional, if not contested outright. She is supposedly the daughter of a jinn in the versions of ben-Yosef, al-Kasāʿī aṭ Ṭālabî's "Stories of the Prophets," and in the mystical Zohar, she is the demon Lilith outright. Her behavior is certainly demonic in some of the Islamic texts: al-Kasāʿī and aṭ Ṭālabî report that she comes to the throne after cutting of the head—in the name of Allah, of course—of her husband, the wicked young man whom her nobles had chosen to rule instead of her at the death of the previous king (who is either conceived of as her father, or her husband). Sheba has good reason, then, to think that her throne may not be secure, given her lack of a husband in a male-dominated society, and the manner in which she attained

---

[8] See the present writer's "Wily Queens and Uppity Slaves: Women as Ritual Experts in Wisdom Performance," *Smooth Words: Studies on Women, Proverbs, and Performance* (Sheffield: Sheffield Academic Press [forthcoming]) for a complete discussion of Sheba's identity and variant texts about her visit to Solomon.

[9] See C. R. Fontaine and C. V. Camp, "The Words of the Wise and Their Riddles," 127–52, for a discussion of the dynamics of biblical riddle performances.

rulership in the first place. Perhaps her nobles ignore Solomon's first command to Sheba, thinking that a male invader may be more to their taste than their current queen, with her bloodthirsty methods of dealing with male usurpers. Even the jinn, Sheba's kin who acknowledge her as their queen also, fail to act in solidarity with their kinswoman: in the Quran they aid Solomon in transporting her throne to Jerusalem so that the one who supposedly came to test the king with riddles is herself tested by the riddle of her throne presented to her in the midst of a foreign court.[10]

So Sheba's power struggles are two-fold: on the one hand, she must be ever watchful of her own nobles and the kinfolk jinn (who are bound in service to the magician Solomon), and on the other she must deflect the various hidden and overt threats posed by Solomon. To this end, she masterfully uses both proverbs and riddles to attempt to achieve her goals of carving out a relatively secure space for herself in a world ruled by men. Though all the texts portray her as the loser in the riddle contest with Solomon, whose wisdom is the stuff of legend, in the Targum Esther Sheni (fifth–tenth century C.E., with a provenance in the southern Levant), we see her make deft use of a proverb to handle both her retinue and the Israelites she has come to visit.

As has been discussed in previous studies, "proverb performance" is a social use of metaphor. It figures primarily in situations where the one who quotes a proverb or saying hopes to establish an interpretation of a situation using the shield of "traditional wisdom" to mask his or her own agenda in putting forth an interpretation. Supposedly, every member of a folk group among whom the cited proverb is current will be familiar with the categories it sets up for analyzing new situations, and will accede to the relationships between those terms as *true*. Using folklorist Peter Seitel's model of proverb performance in African society, a model which has been successfully applied to ancient Near Eastern contexts, three sets of contexts emerge in the social citation of such genres (see Figure 1)[11].

The first context is the Interaction Situation; it is defined by the actual social exchange in which the proverb is cited. The Proverb User (in our case, Sheba) is seldom of the same status as the Proverb Receiver (her retinue); this discrepancy in status relationship is marked in Seitel's diagram by the sign ≠. Although elite females may be perceived as having higher status than the men who serve them, in fact, the construction of gender made by patriarchal soci-

---

[10] A. J. Arberry, *The Koran Interpreted* (New York: MacMillan, 1955) 76–85.
[11] For full discussion, see *Traditional Sayings*, 57–63.

eties counteracts and in great part negates the status advantages Sheba holds as queen. As woman, she will always be at a disadvantage in dealings with men, but her use of wisdom works in her favor to help her "hold her own." That Sheba recognizes her disadvantage as female is found in the humility formula attributed to her in Sura XXVII of the Quran, v 31, where she tells her male council: "I am not used to decide an affair until you bear me witness." Sheba knows her place in our Interaction Context, and it is a slippery one, for all its elevation.

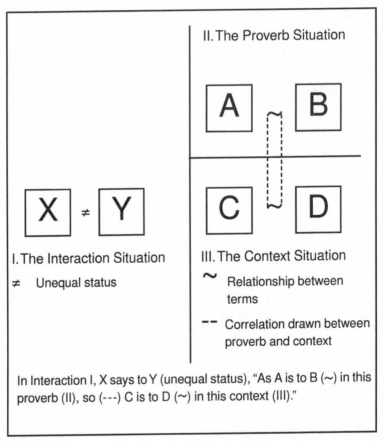

Figure 1: Proverb Performance. After P. Seitel, "Proverbs: A Social Use Metaphor," *Folk Genres,* 129.

The second context appearing in any event of proverb performance is that of the "Proverb Situation": the topic (A) and the comment (B) of the proverb bear some meaningful relationship to each other, whether it be one of identity, causation, negation, better-than evaluations, etc. (marked in our diagram by ~). The presumption in the citation of a proverb is that the audience hearing the citation already accedes to the basic appraisal of the connection between terms A and B. One can imagine bystanders nodding their heads in agreement with the proverb as an affirmation of the traditional wisdom of the group. Studies have shown that this sort of citation of authorizing genres is a feature of the speech of those groups who are (or perceive themselves to be) less powerful than those they are trying to convince.

The final context which figures in proverb performance events is that of the Context Situation, where the Proverb User correlates (----) the terms of the Proverb topic and comment and the relation between them (A ~ B) with the topic and comment elements in the Context (C ~ D). At this point, the Proverb User may suggest that there is an exact identity between the Proverb Situation and the Context Situation (cf. Judg 8:2, 21; 1 Sam 16:7; 1 Kgs 20:11, Ezek 16:43–47), and this is often the most typical form of correlation found in Ancient Near Eastern proverb performance. However, Proverb Users may also choose to surprise their audiences by suggesting that the Context Situation *does not match* the Proverb Situation, i.e., that something new or unexpected has happened and must be properly charted before the situation can be understood (1 Sam 24:14; Jer 31:29). This latter set of negative correlations drawn between the wisdom of former generations and the current situation is a favorite of exilic and post-exilic prophets, in fact, since they are faced with the proclamation of a new way of viewing community guilt and divine potentials as they effect the individual's ability to hope in the future.[12] In other words, in times of social upheaval, conventional wisdom which seems so tried and true, so *safe,* may not actually express the new movements of the Hebrew God's love for the community which is in special relationship to that deity. It has been demonstrated that during times of entrenchment of "status quo theology," Israel's god often acts in the role of a "trickster"[13]; this observation itself has been given proverbial form lest wisdom tradents tend to

---

[12] Ibid., 242–52.

[13] N. R. Bowen, "Can God Be Trusted? Confronting the Deceptive God," *A Feminist Companion to the Latter Prophets* (ed. A. Brenner; Sheffield: Sheffield Academic Press, 1995) 354–65.

think that they have *all* the answers: "No wisdom, no understanding, no counsel, can avail against the Lord!" (Prov 21:30).

Turning to the second Targum to Esther, we find considerable embellishment of themes which seem to stray far and wide from the Persian court of Ahasuerus and his Jewish bride, who is, not coincidentally, an Out-group female of high status. Sheba's story is told, and the encounter which concerns us occurs just before her riddle contest with the great Israelite king.[14] After dispatching a great armada of presents to the king (some of which would figure as living riddles in her later contest), she sets out from her capital of Kitor, making the seven-year journey in only three. The Targum continues:

> And so, after three years the Queen of Sheba came to King Solomon. When he heard of her arrival, he sent Benaiah son of Jehoiada to meet her. He was as handsome as the morning star shining nightly in the firmament and as elegant as the lily that graces the pond's edge. When she saw Benaiah son of Jehoiada, the queen dismounted and so he asked, "Why do you dismount?" "Are you not King Solomon?" she asked. "I am not King Solomon," he replied, "only one of those who serve him." At once, she turned to her notables and offered the following based on a (well-known) proverb: "If you do not see the lion, you see his lair. So, if you do not see Solomon, then see the handsomeness of the man that stands before him." Benaiah son of Jehoiada then escorted her to the king.[15]

This episode is constructed with both wisdom vocabulary, in the forms of proverbial phrases ("handsome as the morning star . . . ," "elegant as the lily . . . ,") and a proverb, as well as "wisdom performance" when the narrator tells us specifically that Sheba quotes a well-known proverb. The Queen might also be viewed as a "wisdom figure," since the connection of queen mothers with the giving of instructions is explicitly made within the Book of Proverbs (and some tellings of Sheba's visit end with her motherhood).[16] In terms of evaluating this text for the much sought-after, but hard to define "wisdom influence," we might note that the presence of wisdom items

---

[14] For a full discussion of Sheba's riddles, see "Wily Queens and Uppity Slaves: Women as Ritual Experts in Wisdom Performance."

[15] Lassner, 166–67. See also B. Grossfeld, *The Two Targums of Esther: Translated, with Apparatus and Notes* (The Aramaic Bible 18; Collegeville, MN: Liturgical Press, 1986) 116.

[16] C. R. Fontaine, "The Social Roles of Women in the World of Wisdom," *A Feminist Companion to Wisdom Literature* (ed. A. Brenner; Sheffield: Sheffield Academic Press, 1995) 38–40.

(vocabulary and forms), wisdom functions (performances such as citing a proverb, giving counsel or instruction), and a wisdom character (a royal personage in a diplomatic context) allows us to rate this text fairly high on the scale of elements required to posit such influence (see Figure 2).[17]

It is easy to see why Sheba quotes a well-known proverb in this Interaction Situation. Commanded by visit Solomon to visit him, but with little support from her "notables" for such an action, the queen nevertheless set forth on her own terms to make the journey in record time. Now, as her travel nears its conclusion, she commits a dreadful *faux pas,* one which causes her to look more like a "country bumpkin" than a sophisticated queen: she mistakes the man of service for his master! Anxious to make the best impression on Solomon (who does not deign to meet her himself, but rather sends Benaiah), she has even gone so far as to dismount to offer her greeting, thinking that the brilliantly handsome male before her *must* be the great king of legendary fame. The context of the interaction suggests her natural chagrin when Benaiah corrects her misapprehension. Although she has high status with respect to both Solomon's servant and her own retinue, her lack of perspicuity in this case of mistaken identity must surely lower her in their eyes, shaming her and those who accompany her. One can imagine the smug, sidelong glances of those who accompany her catching her attention, and in a bid to save face—at least with her own people!—her strategy is to move into the embarrassed silence following her mistake with a proverb to which all standing must surely assent.

Here we see the negation of a familiar motif found in both in the Bible and subsequent literature interpreting it: a woman of one's own group, either by her native insight or her knowledge of divine plans or requirements entrusted to her group, manages to outwit or "show up" a male outsider (Jael versus Sisera; Judith versus Holofernes; the "Virgin Israel" versus Sennacherib [2 Kgs 19:21b], etc.).[18] We might characterize this performance motif as "In-group Female shown superior to Out-group Male" ("own ♀" > "other ♂ ").

---

[17] C. R. Fontaine, "A Response to the Bearing of Wisdom," *A Feminist Companion to Samuel-Kings* (ed. A. Brenner; Sheffield: Sheffield Academic Press, 1994) 166.

[18] For women as keepers and teachers of Torah knowledge, see A. Goldfeld, "Women as Sources of Torah in the Rabbinic Tradition," *The Jewish Woman: New Perspectives* (ed. E. Koltun; New York: Schoken, 1976) 257–71 and J. Z. Abrams, *The Women of the Talmud* (Northvale, NJ: Jason Aronson, 1996). In fact, women's merit acquired in study of the Torah may protect them during the magical "trial" of the Sotah (Numbers 5); J. Nadich, *The Legends of the Rabbis* (2 vols.; Northvale, NJ: Jason Aronson, 1994), 2. 160, n. 113.

Figure 2
Categories of Wisdom Motifs Contributing to Wisdom Influence

Wisdom Items	Wisdom Characters	Wisdom Functions*
Vocabulary:	Sage/Fool	Teaching
wise/foolish	Righteous/Wicked	Counselling
righteous/wicked	Rich/Poor	Governing
wisdom/folly	Woman Wisdom	Conducting diplomacy
rich/poor	Goddess figures	Managing
counsel/teaching	Wife/Mother figures	Judging
"blessed—"	Prophetic figures	Nurturing
tree of life	Strange Woman	Healing
etc.	Foreign Woman	Conflict Resolution
Forms:	Prostitute	Writing
proverbs	Adulteress	Collecting
admonitions	King/Commoner	Editing
prohibitions	Queen (Mother)	
instructions	Foreign Ruler	Proverb Performance**
wisdom poems	Scribe	Riddle Performance**
parables	Court Counsellor	
numerical sayings	Courtiers	
riddles	Wise Woman	
better/than sayings	Author/Redactor	
"blessed/happy" sayings	Teacher/Student	
proverbial phrases	Economic Manager	
example story	Tree of Life*	
Themes:		
Duality of all kinds:		
good/evil		
wise/foolish,etc.		

*We note here only
socially "positive" func-
tions; each might be bal-
anced with foolish,
"negative" functions, such
as wastefulness, seduc-
tion, failure to judge, etc.

Wise King
Woman Who Brings
  Death
Wisdom Who Brings
  Life
importance of:
  choice, counsel,
  teaching
deft use of language
etc.

*Because of Tree of Life's
close association with
Woman Wisdom in her
goddess aspect, I view
her as a character and not
an inanimate object.

**May occur as an
embedded feature within
other functions.

Revised from C. R. Fontaine, "A Response to the Bearing of Wisdom," *A Feminist Companion to Samuel-Kings* (ed. A. Brenner; Sheffield: Sheffield Academic Press, 1994) 166.

There are several variants possible for this action motif: an Out-group Female may be used to shame an In-Group Male. This is the New Testament's use of Sheba in Matt 12:42 (Luke 11:31): Sheba, the female outsider "Queen of the South," who came to hear Solomon, had more sense than the males of Jesus' generation, who have been presented with something greater even than Solomon. This same impulse is continued in the medieval legends of the True Cross (*Legenda Aurea,* of Dominican Jacobus de Voragine, thirteenth century): Solomon has had cut down a tree grown from a branch of the Tree of the Knowledge of Good and Evil, hoping to use it in construction of the Temple. When it is found unsuitable for that purpose, it is made into a bridge. On Sheba's visit to Solomon, she perceives "in spirit" that this very bridge will one day hold the Savior of the world, and refuses to set foot on it, kneeling to adore the wood instead.[19] Once again, an outsider, and a mere woman at that, has seen something which the insider king and his servants could not perceive.

Our episode in Targum Esther Sheni negates this motif, by locating both negatives (female, out-group) in the same figure, Sheba. By having a mere servant (the Hebrew Bible tell us that Benaiah, for all his accomplishments, is not numbered among the highest of the elite), but an insider and a male nevertheless, shown in such magnificence that an elite outsider female loses all sense of proportion when she looks at him, the foreign woman is humiliated by embarrassing herself, and by implication, the men who accompany her are also shamed.[20] But just at the moment when Sheba's wisdom is cast in doubt by her social gaffe, she takes refuge in the covering wisdom of a known saying to redirect the interpretation of her courtiers. We are now able to "fill in" the final parameters of Sheba's proverb performance (see Figure 3).

Both the proverbial phrases and the proverb used provide the reader with a dramatic example of the exquisite "intertextuality" displayed by the author of this Targum. Intertextuality differs from allegory in that the "co-texts" cited by the author are related together as Signifiers, each retaining its own referent. Rather than being Signifiers whose Signifieds have been exchanged or displaced on the paradigmatic axis of language (metaphorical/associative mean-

[19] P. F. Watson, "The Queen of Sheba in Christian Tradition," *Solomon and Sheba,* 121–23. Naturally, this event must precede her meeting with Solomon, since afterwards, the Hebrew Bible says she had "no spirit" left in her.

[20] For the role of honor and shame in maintaining order in the definition of in-group/out-group boundaries, see B. J. Malina, "Mediterranean Sacrifice: Dimensions of Domestic and Political Religion," *BTB* 26 (1996) 37–26.

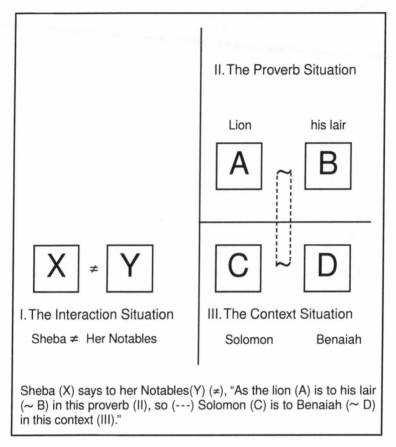

Figure 3: Proverb Performance in Targum Esther Sheni

ings) for other (more significant or acceptable) Signifieds, which is what occurs in the process of allegorization, these co-texts make new or enhanced meaning by their relationship *to each other* (at the syntagmatic (combinative/metonymic) level of language).[21] Here, the "morning star" shining brightly in the firmament, like the "lily gracing the pond's edge" continues

---

21. See D. Boyarin's excellent study, *Intertextuality and the Reading of Midrash* (Bloomington: Indiana University, 1990) 1–38. For discussion of the two axes of language acts, see T. Hawkes, *Structuralism and Semiotics* (Berkeley: University of California, 1977) 76–82.

to stand for and signify Benaiah, but at the same moment, the Song of Songs is evoked and yoked to our episode of proverb performance by Sheba in this Targum. There, of course, the lily is equated with the figure of the female Beloved; her lover pastures his flock among the lilies (Cant 2:1–2; 6:2–3; 7:2). Elsewhere, the Lover, like Benaiah the (white?) lily gracing the pond, is "like a dove beside springs of water, bathed in milk, fitly set" (Cant 5:12 [*RSV*]).[22] One other intertextual connection which may be drawn for the lily in Sheba's story is its prominent use as a motif in the splendid architecture of Solomon's temple, which Sheba will later tour (1 Kgs 7:19, 22, 26; 2 Chr 4:5 cf. 1 Kgs 10:4–5). Elsewhere, scholars have commented upon the striking correspondence between the description of the Lover of the Song in 5:10–16 and the architectural elements of the Jerusalem Temple.[23]

Likewise, the description of Benaiah, "handsome as the morning star shining nightly in the firmament" is suggestive of the celestial (and frightening) beauty of of the Beloved in the enigmatic verse of Cant 6:10: "'Who is this that looks forth like the dawn, fair as the moon, bright as the sun, terrible as an army with banners?'" Beyond this, we may also be led to ponder the identity of the woman and her retinue coming up from the desert (Cant 3:6; 8:5), and whether, like her, Sheba is not also considered darkly lovely as the tents of Salmah (Cant 1:5).[24] In our passage, all the beauty belongs to the In-group male, and yet we are left with the anticipation of Sheba's meeting with Solomon. The phrases selected not only confer proverbial beauty upon Benaiah, but also suggest the erotic interlude to come between his master and the foreign queen.

But Benaiah son of Jehoida is known in the biblical text for other things than his beauty: as Solomon's henchman, he is in part responsible for the establishment of Solomon as king instead of Adonijah (1 Kgs 1:8–44). He was also the executioner of Joab, at Solomon's behest (1 Kgs 2:25–46). In 2 Sam 23:20–23, we find a notice of his earlier exploits:

---

[22] This verse is notoriously difficult; see Roland Murphy's translation, "His eyes, like doves by the water streams./[His teeth,] washed in milk, set in place" and notes (*The Song of Songs* [Hermeneia; Minneapolis: Fortress, 1990] 164, 166 n. 12.

[23] M. H. Pope, *Song of Songs* (AB 7C; Garden City, NY: Doubleday, 1977) 538–48.

[24] Most post-biblical retellings speak of Sheba's great beauty, as well as her strange physical characteristics; for discussion, see "Wily Queens."

And Benaiah the son of Jehoiada was a valiant man of Kabzeel, a doer of great deeds; he smote two ariels[25] of Moab. He also went down and slew a lion in a pit on a day when snow had fallen. And he slew an Egyptian, a handsome man. The Egyptian had a spear in his hand; but Benaiah went down to him with a staff, and snatched the spear out of the Egyptian's hand and slew him with his own spear. These things did Benaiah the son of Jehoida, and won a name beside the three mighty men. He was renowned among the thirty, but he did not attain to the three. And David set him over his bodyguard. (*RSV*)

This mighty warrior then is known for several things relating to his service to his king: he is willing to do the "dirty work" associated with an irregular succession (perhaps Solomon and Sheba are not so unalike in regard to their respective rises to power). He is a known expert at disarming a threat in the shape of a foreigner, no matter how handsome; he can even kill a lion in the snow. Solomon could have chosen no better, nor more intimidating, envoy to greet the wealthy queen in his stead.

When the author of our Targum attributes a lion/lair proverb to Sheba in this Interaction Situation designed to interpret Benaiah's beauty and Sheba's mistake, a variety of connections are being made. The lion is, first of all, a stock "character" in proverbial lore and poetic metaphor. It occurs frequently as a word pair with "lioness,"[26] "young lion,"[27] "bear,"[28] "eagle,"[29] "leopard,"[30] "oxen,"[31] and less frequently, with "wolf" (Jer 5:6; Zeph 3:3), "cherubim" (1 Kgs 7:29, 36; Ezek 10:14), "gazelle" (1 Chr 12:8), and "dog" (Qoh 9:4). The subspecies *Pantherea leo persica* was found in the southern Levant until the fourteenth century C.E., with some survivors living in the marshes of Syria and Mesopotamia until as late as the nineteenth century. The animal was the favorite target of sport-hunting by elites, as art from Egypt and Mesopotamia demonstrates.[32]

[25] Lions? Champions?

[26] Gen 49:9; Num 23:24; 24:9; Job 4:11; Isa 30:6 (also with viper); Ezek 19:2; Joel 1:6; Nah 2:12.

[27] Job 4:10; 38:39; Pss 17:12; 91:13 (also with adder); Isa 5:29; Jer 51: 38; Ezek 19:2, 6; Hos 5:14; Amos 3:4; Mic 5:8; Nah 2:11.

[28] 1 Sam 17:34, 36, 37; Prov 28:15; Isa 11:7; Lam 3:10; Hos 13:8; Amos 5:19; Rev 13:2.

[29] 2 Sam 1:23; Ezek 1:10; 10:14; Dan 7:4, Rev 4:7.

[30] Cant 4:8; Isa 11:6; Hos 13:7; Rev 13:2.

[31] Ps 22:21; Isa 11:7; 65:25; Ezek 1:10; Rev 4:7.

[32] "Lion," *Harper's Bible Dictionary* (ed. P. J. Achtemeier; San Francisco: Harper & Row, 1985) 563–64.

The salient features of the animal which form its biblical portrait belong to its head: mouth, tongue, fangs and teeth which roar, growl, seize, rend, tear, break bones, and devour the prey it hunts and carries off. The "lair," "den," "covert," "jungle" and "thicket" where the lion lurks and performs these fierce, life-threatening activities also receive frequent mention in our texts (Cant 4:8, Jer 4:7, 5:6, 12:8, 25:38, 49:19, 50:44; Dan 6:7, 12, 16, 19, 20, 24; Nah 2:11, 12; Zech 11:3). Lions are known for their pride (Prov 30:30; Job 28:8), strength (2 Sam 1:23), and their fierceness, properties associated with their "heart" (2 Sam 17:10). Their presence may be viewed as an index of divine displeasure and punishment (1 Kgs 13:24–28; 20:36; 2 Kgs 17:25–26; Hos 11:10; 13:7; Isa 15:9; 31:4; etc.); when lions behave peaceably, it is a sign of God's peace and the presence of the Messiah (Isa 11:6–7; 35:9; 65:25). Lions frequently appear as metaphorical designations of evil-doers and other human predators (Prov 28:15; Isa 5:29; Pss 7:2; 10:9; 22:13, 21; 35:17; 57:4; 58:6; Isa 38:13; Ezek 22:25; etc.). When humans contend with God, both parties accuse the other of lion-hood (Job 10:16; Jer 12:8; Lam 3:10). Because of their various associations, lions also form a significant decorative motif in Solomon's temple (1 Kgs 7:29, 36; 10:19–20; 2 Chr 9:18–19).

In the world of wisdom writings, lions have other significant associations which are elicited by Sheba's proverb. In Samson's riddle contest with the Philistines, a contest involving the motifs of love, foreignness and conflict as we have in our text, the lion figures as the referent Signified of an idiosyncratic "neck" riddle.[33] Lions also have a specific association with royals beyond being hunted by them:

> A king's wrath is like the growling of a lion,
>> but his favor is like dew upon the grass (Prov 19:12).
> Like a roaring lion or a charging bear
>> is a wicked ruler over a poor people (Prov 28:15).
> The dread wrath of a king is like the growling of a lion;
>> he who provokes him to anger forfeits his life (Prov 20:2).

We must also mention here, given our context of Sheba's visit to Solomon, that the Lover in the Song of Songs issues the following invitation to his bride:

> " . . . Depart from the peak of Amana,
> from the peak of Senir and Hermon.

---

[33] A "neck" riddle is one told to save the Riddler's neck; see Camp and Fontaine, "The Words of the Wise and their Riddles," for discussion.

from the dens of lions,
from the mountains of leopards"(Cant 4:8b).

It might be argued that Sheba's citation of her proverb, "You have not seen
the lion, but you have seen his lair," does not actually "fit" the Context Situation as well as it might: Benaiah, after all, does not "contain" or "house"
Solomon his king, as the "lair" contains the "lion" and its dreadful activities.
Further, the feature of Benaiah to which Sheba is supposedly calling her notables' attention is his "beauty" and magnificence, which would hardly be an
accurate description of the relationship of a lion to its lair. Clearly, Sheba is
relating the terms of her Proverb and Context Situations metonymically: the
part stands for the whole, and features of the whole (lion/Solomon) may be
deduced from observing the part (lair/Benaiah), just as in modern American
usage the "White House" stands for the President who resides in it.[34]

However, to end our analysis with noting the somewhat skewed metaphorical "fit" of Sheba's proverb to her context in this interaction is to underesti-
mate the surplus of meaning woven into the episode. On the surface, the use
of a figure of a proud, kingly, fierce, noble, powerful animal may seem to flatter both Solomon and his envoy, but, in fact, Sheba's proverb brings other
possibilities to mind for the point she is trying to convey to her retinue. Above
all, the citation of a proverbial lion at this point reminds us of the dangerous
king, lurking in his covert/court, waiting to devour Sheba, personally and
politically—Solomon is, after all, a Lion of Judah (Gen 49:9), son of a shepherd who even as a boy could hunt and kill lions as well as any Assyrian king
(1 Sam 17:34–37). Further, Solomon is served by a courtier who will commit
any violent act for his king, and who is associated with killing a lion in the
close confines of its pit. Not without reason does Sheba think of lions and
their dens at this moment, however much she may seem bedazzled by the
handsome head of the king's servant who is to take her to his master's lair!
She knows full well the heritage of Judah and its king, the damage that proud,
beastly head can do, and what is likely to befall her in the den to which she is
being carried away. She cites a proverb which only loosely fits her context, but
which nicely sums up her knowledge of the foreign king, his family traditions,[35] his servants, the lore of his people, and her own intimations of her

---

[34] By implication, the president's administration is also indicated by this term.

[35] The content of Sheba's riddles makes the same point, since they draw heavily on the
deceptive nature of appearances, as well as her knowledge of biblical traditions about the rather
dubious origins of the tribe of Judah (see "Wily Queens and Uppity Slaves").

future encounter. This diplomatic maneuver is a skillful deployment of the language of wisdom. It may even be that Sheba sees more positive possibilities for herself: perhaps, like the Bride of the Song of Songs, she too may come forth from the den of lions as a lover with a devoted partner, rather than as a meal for a devouring predator. This alien woman proves her worthiness to craft her own fate through her astute knowledge and the quick wit which allows her to apply it in diplomatic interactions. However much Sheba may have been an object of distrust to her own notables and some later tellers of her story, for the author of Targum Esther Sheni who has placed this proverb in her mouth at a crucial moment, this foreign queen is truly "fit for a king," just like the noble Out-group Queen, Esther, who is the author's real concern.[36]

[36] It is with great affection that I dedicate this article to my dear friend, sage, and mentor, Fr. Roland Murphy, on the occasion of his 80th birthday. O King, live forever!

Die Beobachtungsgedichte
im Alten Testament

Meinem Kollegen und Freund Roland Murphy in Dankbarkeit und mit dem Wunsch um Gottes Segen für seine Gesundheit und sein weiteres Wirken.

I. Die Zahlensprüche in Proverbia 30:15–30[1]

Es ist eine Gruppe von Gedichten (nicht eigentlich Sprüchen), die die Sprüche der frühen Weisheit voraussetzen. Die Zahlensprüche sind eine gemeinorientalische Form (sie begegnet besonders oft in Ugarit), die von einem Dichter dazu benutzt wird, einzelne Beobachtungen weiterzudenken über diese hinaus; sie werden in einen weiteren Horizont gestellt, einer Beobachtung werden weitere zugefügt, die etwas mit ihr gemeinsam haben, womit eine Beobachtungsreihe entsteht. Die Zahlen zwei, drei, vier sind keine Festlegung; sie meinen nur, der einen Beobachtung lassen sich mehrere zufügen. Soll der einzelne Spruch ein treffendes Wort in eine bestimmte Situation sein, so wird hier ein weiterer Schritt getan; es ist ein Weiterdenken, das einen weiteren Horizont eröffnet.

Es sind einzelne Beobachtungen—wie bei den Beobachtungssprüchen—die keine Beziehungen zueinander haben; auch der weitere Horizont, den die Zufügungen bilden, ist jeweils ein ganz verschiedener, er ist eine jeweils eigene Entdeckung.

[1] Zusätze sind Verse 17, 20, 32, 33.

A. *30:15–16: Die Unersättlichen*

Der Blutegel hat zwei Töchter: Gib her! gib her!
Drei sind es, die nicht satt werden;
   vier sprechen: nie genug!
Die Scheol und der unfruchtbare Mutterschoss,
Die Erde, die des Wassers nicht satt wird
und das Feuer, das nie spricht: genug!

Das Gemeinsame ist jedesmal etwas Staunenswertes, Wunderbares, so R. E. Murphy: "the marvel admired by the sage."[2] Darin stimmen die Gedichte mit den Sprüchen der Beobachtung überein. Beobachtet ist hier die Unersättlichkeit, die beim Blutegel sprichwörtlich ist (15a bestand wahrscheinlich als selbständiger Spruch). Der Dichter weitet diese Eigenschaft in einer erstaunlichen Weise aus; sie findet sich in der Weite des Kosmos, bei der Unterwelt (die Toten), bei der Erde (Regen) und bei den Elementen Wasser und Feuer. Dazu aber auch bei Tieren und beim Menschen.

Es zeigt sich überraschend ein weiträumiges, weit umgreifendes Denken; an der Eigenschaft des Unersättlichen haben so weit voneinander entfernte Phänomene wie ein kleines Tier, ein Mensch und kosmische Elemente teil.

Es ist nun eine Eigenart aller dieser Gedichte, dass sie in ihrer äusserst sparsamen Kürze zum Nachdenken anregen wollen. Die Frage drängt sich auf: Worin gehören die hier aufgezählten Phänomene zusammen? Es kann nur gemeint sein: sie alle sind Geschöpfe Gottes. Das weit umgreifende Denken meint die grosse Weite der Schöpfung, zu der sie alle gehören. So kann einer nur denken, wenn er vom Ganzen her denkt. Vielleicht mag auch angedeutet sein: Die Unersättlichkeit bei den Menschen sollte nicht schnell verurteilt werden, wenn man ihre kosmische Weite bedenkt.

B. *30:18–19: Das Unbegreifliche*

Drei sind es, die mir zu wunderbar sind
   und vier, die begreife ich nicht:
Des Adlers Weg am Himmel,
   der Schlange Weg auf einem Felsen,

---

[2] R. E. Murphy, *The Tree of Life: An Exploration of Biblical Wisdom Literature* (Anchor Bible Reference Library; New York: Doubleday, 1990) 26.

des Schiffes Weg inmitten des Meeres,
und der Weg des Mannes beim Weibe.

Beherrschend in diesem Gedicht ist die Erkenntnis: Es gibt das Unbegreifliche. Das sagt einer, der selbst auf der Suche nach Erkenntnis ist. Er weiss, dass er bei seinem Suchen an Grenzen kommt und er bejaht die Grenzen seines Erkennens. Sie gehört zu seiner Geschöpflichkeit. Aber im Wissen um diese Grenzen sucht er weiter. Als der Suchende bleibt er der Staunende. Sein Staunen mag beim Blick auf "des Adlers Weg am Himmel" eingesetzt haben. Wo andere gar nichts Wunderbares daran finden, sagt er: "Ich kann es mir nicht erklären," und als unerklärtes fasziniert es ihn. Eben darin ist er ein Weiser: seine Blicke gehen zu weiteren unbegreiflichen Wegen. Wieder ist es ein weiter Horizont, in dem seine Blicke schweifen; so entdeckt er ganz verschiedene "Wege." Wieder sind dabei Menschen, Tiere der Luft und der Erde mit ihren Kontrasten nahe beieinander und das Schiff sieht er auch als ein Lebendiges.

Das Gedicht ist bestimmt von der Ehrfurcht vor dem Schöpfer, der in seinem Wirken so unerschöpflich reich ist.

Er sinnt diesem Reichtum nach: es sind so viele und so verschiedene Wege, die man nicht verstehen kann; was alles können Wege sein!

So entsteht aus dem Nachsinnen der Begriff Bewegung (R. E. Murphy: "the mystery of movement"[3]). So entsteht der Begriff "Bewegung," den der Dichter hier noch nicht gebraucht, es gibt im Hebräischen noch keine Vokabel dafür; aber er hat den Begriff in seinem Denken schon konzipiert. Es ist ein für die Spruchweisheit bezeichnender Vorgang, wie hier über dem staunenden Beobachten ein Begriff entsteht.

C. 30:21–23: Die Unerträglichen

Unter dreien erbebt die Erde
und unter vieren kann sie es nicht aushalten:
Unter einem Sklaven, wenn er König wird,
und einem Niederträchtigen, der Brot die Fülle hat,
Unter einer Verschmähten, wenn sie zur Ehe kommt,
unter einer Magd, wenn sie die Herrin verdrangt.

[3] Ebd.

Hier liegen die Beobachtungen in einem anderen, kleineren Kreis und zur Beobachtung tritt die Erfahrung. Es sind soziale Mißstände und Einbrüche in der ständischen Ordnung, die das Land erschüttern. Sie bewirken einen Zustand, unter dem die Betroffenen unerträglich leiden. Die Vorgänge sind einander ähnlich (zwei unter Männern, zwei unter Frauen), obwohl es verschiedene Gruppen von Menschen sind. Hinter allen steht ein plötzlicher, unnatürlicher Aufstieg. In allen vier Vorgängen wäre der zusammenfassende Begriff: "Revolution"; zwar unter anderen Umständen als denen der Neuzeit, aber ihnen entsprechend. Es ist auch die gleiche Wirkung: das ganze Land wird davon erschüttert in einer Zeit, in der noch eine ständische Ordnung herrschte.

Es ist dem Dichter gelungen, zwar von vier einzelnen, voneinander verschiedenen Vorgängen zu reden, dabei aber doch den Eindruck eines umgreifenden Geschehens, eben einer umfassenden Umwälzung zu bewirken, auch hier auf dem Gebiet des Sozialen; er denkt auch hier vom Ganzen her. Auch wenn es sich in den letzten beiden "Revolutionen" um ein familiäres Ereignis handelt, sieht er, dass beides nicht zu trennen ist.

Wenn die vier Vorgänge eine schwere Erschütterung zur Folge haben ("Unter dreien erbebt die Erde . . ."), so redet der Dichter von etwas Bedrohendem, was in jedem der Vorgänge liegt. So will er davor warnen und zugleich darauf aufmerksam machen, dass jede Gemeinschaft von solcher Umwälzung betroffen werden kann und der weise Vorausblickende nur mahnen kann, den Anfängen zu wehren.

D. 30:24–26: Die Kleinen und doch Weisen

Vier sind die Kleinsten auf Erden
    und sind doch unter den Weisen:
Die Ameisen sind ein Volk ohne Kraft
    und bereiten doch im Sommer ihre Nahrung.
Die Klippdachse sind ein Volk ohne Stärke
    und bauen doch an den Felsen ihre Behausung.
Einen König haben die Heuschrecken nicht,
    und ziehen doch wohlgeordnet aus.
Die Eidechse kann man mit Händen greifen
    und sie hält sich doch auf in Königspalästen.

Vier Beobachtungen werden aneinandergereiht; dabei wird in ihnen etwas Gemeinsames entdeckt, das auch hier etwas Erstaunliches, Bewundernswertes ist: so klein sind sie, und so Grosses bringen sie zustande! Die kleinsten Lebewesen auf der Erde sollen nicht unterschätzt werden! Das Bewundernswerte wird in einem Kontrast dargestellt: Sie sind ein "Volk ohne Kraft," "ein Volk ohne Stärke," und doch bringen sie solche Leistungen zustande! In diesem Kontrast ist es begründet, dass der Dichter diese kleinen Kreaturen unter die Weisen rechnet. Sie verfügen über Fähigkeiten ganz ohne physische, körperliche Kraft. Ähnliches kann von Weisen gesagt werden (21:28): "Ein Weiser ersteigt die Stadt des Starken und stürzt die Wehr, auf die er vertraut."

Dass die kleinen, winzig kleinen Lebewesen im Haushalt der Natur ebenso wichtig sind wie die grossen Tiere ist in der Naturwissenschaft schon sehr früh gefunden worden und heute ist es allbekannt. Aber die Menschheit hat einen langen Weg gebraucht, um zu dieser Erkenntnis zu kommen. Nur hat es damals beigetragen zur Ehrfurcht vor dem Leben, und die ist heute selten geworden.

Sieht man mit diesem Gedicht in Zusammenhang, dass die Tiere im Alten Testament, vor allem in den vielen Vergleichen in den Sprüchen, den Psalmen den Prophetenbüchern eine sehr wichtige und sehr geistvolle Rolle spielen, ist das eines der vielen Beispiele dafür, dass die modernen Ausleger des Alten Testaments nur in ihm sehen, was ihnen selbst wichtig ist; das andere lassen sie einfach beiseite.

E. 30:29–31: Die stattlich Schreitenden

Drei sind es, die da stattlich schreiten
und vier, die feierlich einhergehen:
der Löwe, der König unter den Tieren,
der vor niemanden kehrtmacht;
der Hahn, der unter den Hennen stolziert,
der Bock, der die Herde leitet,
der König, der vor sein Volk tritt.

Hier ist es eine Verhaltensweise, die den vieren gemeinsam ist: ein betont würdiges Schreiten in bestimmten Situationen, die es erfordert. Dieses würdige Schreiten hebt sich ab vom gewöhnlichen Gehen; es will in einer Körperhaltung, einer Gebärde oder Geste dieser Würde Ausdruck geben.

Das Aneinanderreihen von vieren, die die Geste des feierlichen Augenblickes vollziehen, will nur eines sagen: diese Geste ist Menschen und Tieren gemeinsam. Er bringt es mit einem leisen Humor zum Ausdruck, wenn auf den Löwen der Hahn folgt und auf den Bock der König.

Aber es liegt mehr darin: Die Betonung des Kontrastes birgt einen verdeckten Parallelismus: Wie die Geste des stattlichen Schreitens kleinen wie grossen Tieren eignet, so verbindet sie auch die Menschen mit den Tieren. Eine Geste des natürlichen Adels gibt es hier und dort. Es gehört eine grosse Gabe der Beobachtung dazu, diese Gemeinsamkeit der Geste zu entdecken und dann in den Kontrasten so überzeugend auszudrücken. Nur angedeutet ist dabei, dass die Würde, die die Geste ausdrückt, nicht nur den Grossen eignet.

Bei diesem Gedicht wird besonders deutlich, dass das Gedicht zum Nachdenken anregen will. Man fragt unwillkürlich: zu welchen Situationen gehört das würdige Schreiten? Ist es wirklich Menschen und Tieren gemeinsam? Gibt es in unserem mechanisierten Leben überhaupt noch ein stattliches Schreiten? Vielleicht noch in einigen Riten, die aus ferner Vergangenheit übrig geblieben sind? Sind wir auf dem Weg, es ganz zu verlieren und haben wir dann etwas Wichtiges verloren? Daran mögen sich weitere Fragen schliessen. Es ist jedenfalls eine fruchtbare Frage, die weiterzudenken lohnend ist.

F. Zusammenfassung und Weiterdenken

Die Zahlensprüche sind eine Weiterführung der Beobachtungssprüche. Man kann sie nur verstehen als solche. Wie bei diesen jede einzelne Beobachtung für sich bleibt, so ist es auch bei den Gedichten. Jedes steht für sich, damit für jedes Raum zum Nachdenken gegeben sei.

Auch das ist gemeinsam: beobachtet wird bei allen das Erstaunliche, Wunderbare, auch das Furchtbare.

Dass das Teilhaben an der Weisheit die Tiere mit den Menschen verbindet, ist nur unter dem Gesichtspunkt der Gemeinsamkeit der Geschöpfe und des Schöpferwirkens sinnvoll. Wie wichtig dem Dichter diese Gemeinsamkeit von Mensch und Tier ist zeigt er auch in A (15–16), B (18–19), E (29–31).

Ebenso ist es eine Entfaltung des Schöpferwirkens, wenn beides im Zusammenhang gesehen wird: die Beobachtung setzt beim Kleinen, Unscheinbaren ein (A, D, E), und dann umspannt sie weite Räume, einmal den ganzen Kosmos (A). Seine Beobachtungen gehen vom Kleinsten zum

Grössten, denn er denkt von der Schöpfung her, die das Ganze umspannt.[4] Es braucht dabei nicht ausdrücklich vom Schöpfer und der Schöpfung geredet zu werden.

Wird so das einzelne Geschaffene in einen weiten Horizont gestellt, gerade dann rührt das Beobachten an seine Grenzen, das Beobachten geht über in die Ehrfurcht vor dem Schöpfer.

Das Nachdenken, zu dem der Dichter der Zahlensprüche anregt, kann in verschiedene Richtung gehen.

Zu D (30:24–26): Hier zeigt der Dichter, was für ihn Weisheit ist. Wenn er auch die kleinen Tiere mit ihren grossen Leistungen zu den Weisen rechnet, dann ist ihm das Wesentliche an der Weisheit nicht Wissen und nicht Bildung, sie ist die vom Schöpfer verliehene Möglichkeit und Fähigkeit weisen Denkens und weisen Handelns, die sich bei Tieren und bei Menschen findet; es gibt dafür eine Fülle von Beispielen.

Zu B (30:18–19): Die Zahlensprüche sind eines der deutlichsten Zeugnisse dafür, dass es nicht richtig ist, wenn die traditionelle Theologie des Alten Testaments das Geschichtshandeln Gottes so sehr betont und in die Mitte stellt als sei Gottes Gottsein beinahe ganz auf die Geschichte bezogen. In diesen Gedichten kreist das Beobachten und Nachdenken ganz ausschliesslich um die Schöpfung und das Wirken des Schöpfers. Und in den Gedichten führt gerade dieses zur Ehrfurcht vor dem Schöpfer und der Ehrfurcht vor dem Leben.

Schon dass der Dichter diese Fragen stellte, darüber nachdachte, zeigt, wie er das Menschsein als fragendes, als auf der Suche versteht, der nicht über ein fertiges Wissen, auch nicht ein Wissen über Gott verfügt, sondern offen ist für die Welt, in die ihn Gott gestellt hat, offen für das, was um ihn geschieht, ein Mensch, der nachdenkt.

Zu A, B, E: Wenn mehrfach das Tier und Mensch gemeinsam betont wird, hat das gewiss auch den Sinn, dass der Mensch sich ernsthafter als Geschöpf verstehen würde, nähme er wahr, dass die Kreatürlichkeit beide umfasst. Wenn er Tiere sinnlos leiden lässt, leidet darunter immer auch die Menschlichkeit.

In anderen Teilen des Alten Testaments hat das Zusammengehören der Kreaturen, Mensch und Tier, Mensch und die sonstigen Geschöpfe, auch eine hohe Bedeutung, im Gotteslob, in den Psalmen, den Gottesreden im

---

4 "Vom kleinsten bis zum grössten Stern"—Goethe.

Hiobbuch und der Verkündigung Deuterojesajas. Das ist bekannter und offenkundiger. Aber zu der Verbundenheit der Kreaturen im Gotteslob tritt in den Gedichten der Zahlensprüche die andere Möglichkeit des Nachdenkens, der Reflexion, die in der stillen Ehrfurcht vor dem Schöpfer zu ihrem Ziel kommt. Meist wird dieses nicht in Worten sich äussernde Nachdenken wenig beachtet, achtet man aber darauf, dann spürt man schon, wie es zur Gottesbeziehung gehört: "Maria aber . . . behielt alle diese Worte und bewegte sie in ihrem Herzen." In besonderer Weise gehört es zur Weisheit; mehrere Sprüche drücken das auf verschiedene Weise aus. In den Zahlensprüchen ist es das vom Beobachten ausgehende Nachdenken, das zur Ehrfurcht vor dem Wirken des Schöpfers führt, der Ehrfurcht vor dem Leben.

Im Unterschied zu den Anfängen der griechischen Philosophie ist das Nachdenken in diesen Gedichten kein abstraktes, auf das Sein gerichtetes, es geht vielmehr aus vom Beobachten der Wirklichkeit; das zeigt eine so feine Beobachtung wie die, dass die Geste des würdigen Schreitens Mensch und Tier gemeinsam ist. Es zeigt sich auch darin, dass zur Beobachtung der Schöpfung die aus der Geschichte gewonnene Erfahrung tritt (auch bei den Sprüchen gehören Beobachtung und Erfahrung zusammen): denn aus der Erfahrung sind die Gedichte A (15b–16) und C (21–23) gewonnen. Beobachtung und Erfahrung sind auf die Wirklichkeit gerichtet.

II. Schilderungsgedichte im Alten Testament

A. Schilderungen von Tieren

Im ersten Teil wurden die Tiere in den Zahlensprüchen behandelt. Im übrigen Alten Testament begegnen Schilderungen von Tieren vor allem in den Gottesreden des Hiobbuches, Kap. 38–42. Nicht das Tier als Gestalt, sondern das sich bewegende, lebendige Tier in seinen Tätigkeiten, nahe dem Erzählen.

1) Die freien Tiere: am Himmel: der Falke und der Adler; auf der Erde: die Steinziegen, die Wildesel, der Wildochs, der Strauss, das Streitross, alle als wilde, die Freiheit liebende Geschöpfe.
   —der Wildochs (Hiob 39:9–12):
   "Wird dir der Wildochs dienen wollen,
      wird er des Nachts an deiner Krippe liegen?"
   —der Falke und der Adler (Hiob 39:26–30):

"Hebt durch deine Weisheit der Falke die Schwingen,
breitet seine Flügel aus nach Süden?"

2)   Mythische Tiere: das Flusspferd, das Krokodil.

Hiob hat Gott herausgefordert, Gott antwortet: Wie kannst du mich herausfordern! Bist du denn der Schöpfer? Dann aber geht die Frage des Streitgesprächs in Schilderung über:

"Auf Felsen wohnt und hortet er . . .
von dort erspäht er sich die Beute. . ." (39:12–13)

Der Dichter verstärkt durch die Schilderung die Frage des Schöpfers: sind denn diese wunderbaren, herrlichen Geschöpfe dein Werk?

So erwächst eine erzählende Schilderung, ein Gedicht, aus der Frage nach Schöpfer und Geschöpf; dabei gewinnt es eine gewisse Selbständigkeit ohne den Zusammenhang mit dem Vorgang zu verlieren.

Der Vorgang, Gottes Frage an Hiob, bleibt in der ganzen Rede Gottes bestehen; aber bei jedem der Geschöpfe geht er in Schilderung über. Bei der Schilderung des Streitrosses (39:19–25) ist es von der Situation so abgelöst, dass es ganz wie ein selbstandiges Gedicht wirkt.

Zu den mythischen Tieren: Sie sind ganz anders geschildert, in grossen, ausführlichen Gedichten. Der Dichter will mit den gewaltigen Tieren an die Mythen und Drachen der Vorzeit erinnern, die auch zur Schöpfung, zu den Geschöpfen Gottes gehören.

B. *Schilderung von Landschaften*

Landschaftsschilderungen als Kunstwerke um ihrer selbst willen, ob in Prosa oder als Gedicht, kennt das Alte Testament nicht. Beides hatte seinen Höhepunkt in den Gedichten und Novellen der Romantiker; im Vergleich mit ihnen sieht man, worin die Eigenart der Landschaftsschilderung im Alten Testament liegt. Wie die Schilderungen der Tiere, stehen sie in einem Zusammenhang, aus dem sie erwachsen. Bei ihnen sind es drei. In den Stammessprüchen (Gen 49 und Dtn 33), in Sehersprüchen (Num 22–24), in der Segensschilderung vor allem im Buch Deuteronomium. Diese drei gehören dem weiteren Zusammenhang des Überganges aus der Wanderung durch die Wüste in das gelobte Land an. In den Stammessprüchen sind es noch die Stämme, die allmählich Schritt für Schritt im Land Fuss fassen; in den Sehersprüchen ist es das Volk dem das gelobte Land verheissen wird, in den Segenssprüchen sprechen schon die Erfahrungen des Volkes beim Sesshaftwerden mit.

1) Die Stammessprüche (Gen 49):
Den Führern der Stämme wird verheissen, dass sie ihren Stamm in ein fruchtbares Land führen werden. Von Juda wird gesagt (Gen 49:11):

> "Er bindet seinen Esel an den Weinstock,
>> und an die Rebe das Füllen seiner Eselin.
> Er wäscht sein Gewand in Wein
>> und in Traubenblut seinen Mantel."

In überschwenglicher Weise wird die Fruchtbarkeit des Landes gerühmt. Oder der Führer wird mit einem Fruchtbaum verglichen (Gen 49:22):

> "Ein junger Fruchtbaum ist Joseph,
>> ein junger Fruchtbaum am Quell;
>> seine Schosse ranken über die Mauer."

2) Die Schau des Sehers (Num 24:5–7):

> So spricht Bileam, der Sohn Beors:
> "Wie schön sind deine Zelte, Jakob,
>> deine Wohnungen, Israel!
> Wie Täler, die sich ausbreiten,
>> wie Gärten am Strom.
> Wasser rinnt aus seinen Eimern,
>> reichlich Wasser hat seine Saat!"

3) Segensschilderung (Dtn 7:13–15):

> "Er wird dich lieben und dich segnen und mehren.
> Er wird segnen die Frucht deines Leibes,
>> die Frucht deines Landes,
> Dein Korn, deinen Wein und dein Öl,
>> den Wurf deiner Kühe
>> und die Zucht deiner Schafe."

Es sind keine Gedichte in unserem Sinn, weil sie eine Erweiterung der Segensverheissung zur Schilderung sind; dennoch klingen manche dieser Sätze, die eine schöne Landschaft schildern, an Gedichte an. Das Schöne ist eine Gabe des Segens und das Schöne ist hier zugleich das Gute. Das Schönsein einer Landschaft ist zugleich das Gutsein für das Leben darin durch den vielfältigen Ertrag der Felder und der Bäume.

Die Schilderung der Fruchtbarkeit geht über in die Schilderung des schönen Landes. Beides wird erst gesondert im Begriff des Ästhetischen, der einen absolute Selbstwert des Schönen bezeichnet. Damit, dass der Segen seine Bedeutung verlor, hörte auch die Einheit von gut und schön auf. Für die Maler des Mittelalters scheint jedoch die Verbindung zwischen beidem noch bestanden zu haben, wenn sie vor allem in den Bildern von der Geburt Christi die schöne Landschaft in ihre Bilder einbezog ebenso wie die Beteiligung der Tiere an dem heiligen Ereignis.

C. Schilderung des Menschen

1) Gedichte, die die Schönheit eines Menschen schildern, füllen im Alten Testament ein ganzes Buch, das Hohe Lied Salomos,[5] ein ganzer Band von Liebesgedichten. Z.B. 3 ff:

> "Auf meinem Lager nächtlicherweile suche ich ihn,
>   den meine Seele liebt.
>   Ich suche ihn, doch ich fand ihn nicht.
> So will ich mich aufmachen,
>   die Stadt durchwandern, die Strassen und Plätze,
>   will ihn suchen, den meine Seele liebt."

2) Der König. Der Preis des Königs Psalm 45 ist auch der Preis eines schönen Mannes. Es ist kein Psalm, sondern ein Gedicht, zum Vortrag bestimmt. In den Kanon ist es gekommen, weil man es auf den Heilskönig der Zukunft deutete, gedichtet wurde es auf einen lebenden König zum Vortrag bei einem Hoffest, wahrscheinlich der Feier seiner Thronbesteigung:

> "Du bist der Schönste unter den Menschen,
>   Anmut ist ausgegossen über deinen Lippen.

5. R. E. Murphy, *The Song of Songs: A Commentary on the Book of Canticles or Song of Songs* (Hermeneia; Minneapolis: Fortress, 1990).

Denn Gott hat dich auf ewig gesegnet.
Gurte dem Schwert an die Hüfte, du Held!
In Pracht und Prunk fahre hin mit Glück!"

Sowohl die Liebesgedichte wie auch das Gedicht auf den König sind eindeutig Gedichte. Beides sind Beispiele hoher Wortkunst.

Der Ort, an dem sonst von schönen Menschen gesprochen wird, ist die Erzählung, von der Erschaffung des Menschen an (Gen 2:18–23) über die Vätergeschichten und die Erzählungen von David. Statt der bildenden Kunst ist es die Kunst der Erzählung, die vom schönen Menschen redet.

D. Einzelne Gedichte

Während es sich bisher um Gruppen von Gedichten handelte (auch Preislieder auf den König gab es gewiss mehr), begegnen auch einzelne in ganz verschiedenen Zusammenhängen, die nur aus diesen erklärt werden können, es sind Schilderungen menschlicher Tätigkeit.

1) Die Schilderung eines Bergwerkes (Hiob 28:1–21)
Es ist ein Gedicht von besonderer Schönheit:

". . . man holt heraus das Eisen aus der Erde,
und das Gestein schmilzt man zu Kupfer um.
Der Finsternis bereitet man ein Ende
und man durchwühlt das Feldgestein . . ." (2–3)

Hiob 28 ist die Erweiterung eines Weisheitsspruches in der Form von Frage und Antwort (die Verse 12 und 23). Es ist ein Gleichnis, aber ein Gegenbild-Gleichnis: den Zugang zu der Tiefe des Berges hat der Mensch durch die Kunst des Bergbaus erreicht; den Zugang zur Weisheit kann er nicht erzwingen. Aber der Bergbau als solcher ist achtungsvoll und bewundernd geschildert. Es sind zwar noch viele andere menschliche Tätigkeiten im Alten Testament erwähnt; zu der Schilderung in einem Gedicht ist es hier nur gekommen, weil sie als ein Gleichnis dienen sollte.

2) Die Herstellung eines Gottesbildes
Auch sie ist in Jes 44:9–20 nicht um ihrer selbst willen geschildert, es ist vielmehr ein Spottgedicht, es ist ein polemisches Eintreten für das zweite Gebot: du sollst dir kein Bild machen! Die Schilderung ist lebendig und instruktiv; der Handwerker, der nur im Auftrag handelt, wird dabei nicht heruntergemacht.

3) Fragment einer Ballade (Richter 5:28–30)

> Durch's Fenster späht
> und schaute aus die Mutter Siseras durch das Gitter:
> "Warum verzieht sein Wagen, zu kommen?"

Es ist der Abschluss des Deboraliedes; die Mutter Siseras erwartet die Rückkehr ihres Sohnes, ihr antwortet eine ihrer Frauen und vertröstet sie. Eine kleine äussert lebendig geschilderte Szene, die ebenso die Szene in einer Ballade sein könnte.

III. Lehrgedichte

Die späte Weisheit besteht zumeist aus Lehrgedichten (Prov 1–9, dazu 22–24 zum Teil), Gedichten, die den Lehrvorgang unterstützen und erleichtern sollten, denn gedichtete Sprache behält sich leichter. Im Unterschied zu allen anderen sind es Zweckgedichte.

Die Lehre setzt ein mit der Aufforderung zum Hören (22:17–21):

> "Neige dein Ohr und höre meine Worte,
> sei bedacht, zu erkennen, wie lieblich sie sind!
> Wenn du sie in deinem Innern verwahrst,
> werden sie stets auf deinen Lippen bereit sein,
> dass du dem der dich fragt,
> richtig antworten kannst."

Dazu kommen Gedichte zum Lob der Weisheit und eine lange Reihe von Mahnungen und Warnungen in Gedichtform. Besonders betont sind dabei Warnungen vor der Trunkenheit und vor der fremden Frau. Die Weisheit als eine Frau lädt ein zu einem Festmahl; die Weislieit wird hoch gerühmt; sie sei schon bei der Schöpfung dabeigewesen.

Daneben stehen Gedichte, die Erweiterungen eines Einzelspruches sind, das schönste und längste das Lob der tüchtigen Hausfrau Prov 31:10–31 und humorvolle Gedichte wie 24:30–34: "Ich ging am Acker des Faulen vorüber...," oder die Verlockung des Weines 23:31–35: "Schau nicht auf den Wein, wie er rot funkelt!"

IV. Zum Abschluss

Es gibt im Alten Testament die Sprachform Gedicht. Es sind im Verhältnis wenige Gedichte, die sich in ihm finden. Das ist verständlich, da die spätere

Literaturform Gedicht noch nicht entwickelt ist. Umso interessanter ist, an den wenigen Texten eine Entwicklung wahrzunehmen, die einiges über das Entstehen des Gedichtes erkennen lässt. Ein Motiv des Entstehens ist die Freude am Schildern, die sich besonders auf Tiere und Landschaften, zum Teil auch auf Menschen richtet.

Am deutlichsten ist es bei den Tierschilderungen in den Gottesreden des Hiobbuches, in dem sich aus der Antwort Gottes auf Hiobs Herausforderung die Form der Anrede an Hiob in die Schilderung der einzelnen Tiere übergeht. Hier ist es ganz offenkundig die Freude des Dichters an der Schilderung der Geschöpfe Gottes, die auf die Form des Gedichtes zuführt. Dabei bleiben die Schilderungen noch in dem Zusammenhang, dem sie angehören. Deutlich ist auch der Übergang der Verheissung des schönen Landes, die ja zugleich Ausdruck der Sehnsucht nach einem schönen Land ist (wie in so vielen Gedichten) in eine Schilderung des schönen Landes.

Diese Ansätze zur Literaturform des Gedichtes, die sich im Alten Testament an mehreren Stellen finden, sollten einmal in einer literaturgeschichtlichen Untersuchung weitergeführt werden. Das gilt auch für die weiteren Ansätze, die ich genannt habe.

BIBLIOGRAPHY

Roland E. Murphy, O.Carm.

Roland E. Murphy
Bibliography

(Bibliography does not include book reviews)

1943

The Life of Marie de Sacre Coeur by Mère Agnes de Jésus (trans. R. E. Murphy and J. Smet, O.Carm.; Englewood Cliffs, NJ: Carmelite).

1948

"A Study of Psalm 72(71)," *Studies in Sacred Theology* (Series 2, 12; Washington: The Catholic University of America).

1949

"An Allusion to Mary in the Apocalypse," *TS* 10:565–73.
"The Epistle for All Saints," *AER* 121:203–9.
"The Structure of the Canticle of Canticles." *CBQ* 11:381–91.

1952

"A Fragment of an Early Moabite Inscription from Dibon," *BASOR* 125:20–23.

1953

"Israel and Moab in the Ninth Century B.C.," *CBQ* 15:409–17.

1954

"The All Beautiful One," *Mary* 15:7–11.

"The Canticle of Canticles and the Virgin Mary," *Carmelus* 1:18–28.
"Recent Literature on the Canticle of Canticles," *CBQ* 16:1–11.

1955
"The Canticle of Canticles in the Confraternity Version," *AER* 133:87–98.
"*Job* in the New Confraternity Version," *AER* 133:16–29.
"The Pensées of Coheleth," *CBQ* 17:304–14 (= pp. 184–94: paginated separately as FS E. O'Hara)

1956
"The Dead Sea Scrolls and New Testament Comparisons," *CBQ* 18:263–72.
The Dead Sea Scrolls and the Bible (Westminster: Newman) = *Le couvent de la Mer Morte et la Bible* (Maredsous, 1957).
"Insights into the New Testament from the Dead Sea Scrolls," *AER* 135:9–22.
"Those Dead Sea Scrolls . . . ," *AER* 134:361–73.

1957
"The Dead Sea Scrolls—Ten Years After," *Extension* 52/2:12–13, 46–47.
"Notes on Old Testament Messianism and Apologetics," *CBQ* 19:5–15.

1958
"*Šaḥat* in the Qumran Literature," *Bib* 39:61–66.
"*Yēṣer* in the Qumran Literature," *Bib* 39:334–44.

1959
"BŚR in the Qumrân Literature and Sarks in the Epistle to the Romans," *SP* (ed. J. Coppens et al.; BETL 12–13; 2:60–75. Paris: Lecoffre/Gembloux: Ducolot).
"A New Classification of Literary Forms In the Psalms," *CBQ* 21:83–87.
"Sharing the Same Book," *Worship* 34:53–54.

1960
The Book of Exodus (Paulist Pamphlet Bible Series 4–5; New York: Paulist).
"Élie (le prophète)," *DS* 4:564–67.
"The Old Testament for Seminarians: The Purpose of the Course," *National Catholic Education Association Bulletin* 57/1:89–93.
Seven Books of Wisdom (Milwaukee: Bruce).

1961

The Book of Ecclesiastes and the Canticle of Canticles (Paulist Pamphlet Bible Series 38; New York: Paulist).

"GBR and GBWRH in the Qumran Writings," *Lex Tua Veritas: Festschrift für Herbert Junker zu Vollendung des siebzigsten Lebenjahres am 8. August 1961* (FS H. J. Junker; ed. H. Gross and F. Mussner; Trier: Paulinus V.) 137–43.

"A New Theology of the Old Testament," *CBQ* 23:217–23.

1962

"A Consideration of the Classification 'Wisdom Psalms'," VTSup 9:156–67. Reprinted in *Studies in Ancient Israelite Wisdom* (Library of Biblical Studies; ed. J. L. Crenshaw; New York: Ktav, 1976) 456–67.

"The Concept of Wisdom Literature," *The Bible in Current Catholic Thought* (ed. J. L. McKenzie; FS M. J. Gruenthaner; New York: Herder and Herder) 46–54.

"The Old Testament: The Unfolding of Salvation History," *Ascent* 67–72.

"Promise and Preparation," *The Gospel of Jesus the Christ: A Symposium by Roland E. Murphy* (ed. J. Oesterreicher and D. Stanley; Seton Hall, NJ: Seton Hall University) 11–19.

"Where is the Wise Man?" *TBT* 1:30–37.

1963

"Divino Afflante Spiritu—Twenty Years After," *Chicago Studies* 2:16–28.

"The Incarnational Aspects of Old Testament Wisdom," *TBT* 9:560–66. Reprinted in *Contemporary New Testament Studies* (ed. M. R. Ryan; Collegeville, MN: Liturgical Press, 1965) 77–83.

"The Problem of Authority: A Roman Catholic View," *Christianity and Crisis* 23:98–99.

"Eclesiástico," *Enciclopedia de la Biblia* (6 vols.; Barcelona: Garriga, 1963), 2. 1056–58.

"Elias," *Enciclopedia de la Biblia*, 2. 1210–13.

"Libro de los Proverbios," *Enciclopedia de la Biblia*, 5. 1318–20.

"Libro de la Sabiduría," *Enciclopedia de la Biblia*, 6. 301–7.

"Salvation History and the Bible," *Marian Forum* 3:74–79.

"To Know Your Might is the Root of Immortality (Wis 15,3)," *CBQ* 25:88–93.

1964

"The Biblical Instruction," *Commonweal* 80:418–20.

"The Old Testament Wisdom Literature and the Problem of Retribution," *The Scotist* 20:5–18.

"The Relationship Between the Testaments," *CBQ* 26:349–59.

"The Significance of the Bible in the Life of the Church," *Marian Forum* 4:23–33.

1965

The Human Reality of Sacred Scripture = *Concilium* 10 (ed. P. Benoit, B. van Iersel, and R. E. Murphy; New York: Paulist).

"The Wisdom Literature of the Old Testament," *The Human Reality of Sacred Scripture* = *Concilium* 10 (ed. P. Benoit, B. van Iersel, and R. E. Murphy; New York: Paulist) 126–40.

Introduction to the Wisdom Literature of the Old Testament (Old Testament Reading Guide 22; Collegeville, MN: Liturgical Press).

"Old Testament Studies," *Theology in Transition* (ed. E. O'Brien; New York: Herder and Herder) 41–77.

"The Relevance of Old Testament Studies for Ecumenism," *Scripture and Ecumenism* (ed. L. J. Swidler; Duquesne Studies, Theological Series 3; Pittsburgh: Duquesne University) 95–109.

"The Dead Sea Scrolls," *Catholic Youth Encyclopedia*.

1966

The Dynamism of Biblical Tradition = *Concilium* 20 (ed. P. Benoit and R. E. Murphy; New York: Paulist).

Foreword to *Man Before God: Toward a Theology of Man* (ed. D. Burkhard and W. T. Merten; New York: P. J. Kenedy) vii–ix.

"The Kerygma of the Book of Proverbs," *Int* 20:3–14.

"The Old Testament Canon in the Catholic Church," *CBQ* 28:189–93. Reprinted in *A Symposium on the Canon of Scripture* (1969) 247–52. Correction in *CBQ* 28:484–85.

"Praying the Psalms," *Ascent* 14–18.

"Present Biblical Scholarship as a Bond of Understanding," *Torah and Gospel: Jewish and Catholic Theology in Dialogue* (ed. P. Scharper; New York: Sheed and Ward) 81–96.

1967

"Alphabetic Psalms," *New Catholic Encyclopedia* (15 vols.; New York: McGraw–Hill), 1. 336.

"Assumptions and Problems in Old Testament Wisdom Research," *CBQ* 29:407–18. Published separately in FS L. F. Hartman, 101–12.

"Canticle of Canticles," *New Catholic Encyclopedia* (15 vols.; New York: McGraw–Hill), 3. 68–69.

"A Catholic Foreword," W. D. Wagoner, *The Seminary: Protestant and Catholic* (New York: Sheed and Ward) ix–xiv.

How Does the Christian Confront the Old Testament? = Concilium 30 (ed. P. Benoit, B. van Iersel and R. E. Murphy; New York: Paulist).

"Penitential Psalms," *New Catholic Encyclopedia*, 11. 85–86.

"Psalm," *New Catholic Encyclopedia*, 11. 935.

"Book of Psalms," *New Catholic Encyclopedia*, 11. 935–39.

"Sapiential Books," *New Catholic Encyclopedia*, 12. 1081.

"Wisdom (in the Bible)," *New Catholic Encyclopedia*, 14. 971–74.

1968

The Jerome Biblical Commentary (ed. R. E. Brown, J. A. Fitzmyer and R. E. Murphy; Englewood Cliffs, NJ: Prentice-Hall) = *Comentario Biblico "San Jerónimo"* (Madrid: Ediciónes cristiandad, 1971); *Grande Commentario Biblico* (Brescia: Queriniana, 1973).

"Canticle of Canticles," *The Jerome Biblical Commentary*, 1:506–10.

"Ecclesiastes (Qoheleth)," *The Jerome Biblical Commentary* 1:534–540.

"A History of Israel" (with A. G. Wright and J. A. Fitzmyer), *The Jerome Biblical Commentary*, 1:671–702.

"Introduction to the Wisdom Literature," *The Jerome Biblical Commentary*, 1:487–94.

"Psalms," *The Jerome Biblical Commentary*, 1:569–602.

"The Figure of Elias in the Old Testament," *Carmelus* 15:230–38. Reprinted as "The Figure of Elijah in the OT," *Ascent* (1969) 8–15.

"Salvation in History," *CBQ* 30:86–87.

1969

The Breaking of Bread = Concilium 40 (ed. P. Benoit, B. van Iersel and R. E. Murphy, eds.; New York: Paulist Press).

"Form Criticism and Wisdom Literature" (Presidential Address), *CBQ* 31:475–83.

"The Interpretation of Old Testament Wisdom Literature," *Int* 23:289–301.
The Presence of God = *Concilium* 50 (ed. P. Benoit, B. van Iersel and R. E. Murphy; New York: Paulist).

1970

"Christian Understanding of the Old Testament," *TD* 18:321–32.
"The Hebrew Sage and Openness to the World," *Christian Action and Openness to the World* (ed. J. Papin; The Villanova University Symposia; Villanova, PA: Villanova University) 219–44. Reprinted in *Theological Folia of Villanova University: Biblical Studies* (ed. J. Papin; Villanova, PA: Villanova University, 1975) 11–36.
"History, Eschatology and the Old Testament," *Continuum* 7:583–93. Reprinted as "Geschichte, Eschatologie und das Alte Testament," *Eschatologie im Alten Testament* (ed. H. D. Preuss; Darmstadt: Wissenschaftliche Buchgesellschaft, 1978) 325–41.
Immortality and Resurrection = *Concilium* 60 (ed. P. Benoit and R. E. Murphy; New York: Herder and Herder).
"Reading II: The Church's Attitude Toward the Old Testament" (Alternate Reading No. 8; p. 346 of *Christian Readings VI*, Year 2 [Second Nocturn, Second Sunday of the Year]).
"The Relevance of the Old Testament for Preaching in the '70's," *Preaching Today* 5:1–12.

1971

"The Book of Joel," *The Interpreter's One-Volume Commentary on the Bible* (ed. C. M. Laymon; Nashville: Abingdon) 461–64.
"The Book of Jonah," *The Interpreter's One-Volume Commentary on the Bible* 480–82.
"The Book of Obadiah," *The Interpreter's One-Volume Commentary on the Bible* 477–479.
"The Role of the Bible in Roman Catholic Theology, Part 1," *Int* 25:78–86.
Theology, Exegesis, and Proclamation = *Concilium* 70 (ed. R. E. Murphy; New York: Herder and Herder).

1972

"Biblical Theology (Bibliography)," *Duke Divinity School Review* 37:74–75.
Office and Ministry in the Church = *Concilium* 80 (ed. B. van Iersel and R. E. Murphy; New York: Herder and Herder).

1973

"Deuteronomy—A Document of Revival," *Spiritual Revivals = Concilium* 89 (ed. C. Duquoc and C. Flortstan; New York: Herder and Herder) 26–36 = "Das Deuteronomium als Dokument einer Erweckung," *Theologisches Jahrbuch* (ed. W. Ernst et al.; Leipzig, 1975) 150–55.

"Form-Critical Studies in the Song of Songs," *Int* 27:413–22.

"Modern Approaches to Biblical Study," *The New Oxford Annotated Bible* (Oxford: Oxford University) 1519–22.

1974

"The Authority of the Scriptures," *Seminar on Authority* (ed. J. W. Angell; Winston-Salem, NC: Wake Forest University) 31–39.

"Focus on Faculty," *Duke Divinity School Review* 38:181–83.

"A Form-Critical Consideration of Ecclesiastes 7," SBLASP, 1. 77–85.

"The Old Testament as Word of God," *A Light unto My Path* (FS J. M. Myers; ed H. N. Bream et al.; Philadelphia: Temple University) 363–74.

"Mowinckel, Sigmund," *New Catholic Encyclopedia*, Supplementary Volume 16 (Washington: Publishers Guild) 304–5.

"Rowley, Harold Henry," *New Catholic Encyclopedia*, Supplementary Volume 16, 392–93.

1975

"Israel's Psalms: Contribution to Today's Prayer Style," *Review for Religious* 34:113–20. Reprinted in *Scripture in Church* 7 (1976) 98–108.

"Wisdom and Yahwism," *No Famine in the Land* (FS J. L. McKenzie; ed. J. W. Flanagan and A. W. Robinson; Missoula, MT: Scholars) 117–26.

"The Theology of Hope: The Cardinal Cook Lecture," *The Camillan* (Houston: National Association of Catholic Chaplains, 11th Annual Convention Proceedings).

"Qohelet der Skeptiker," *Concilium* (German edition) 12:567–70.

"Song of Songs," *IDBSup* 836–38.

"Wisdom Theses," *Wisdom and Knowledge* (FS J. Papin; ed. J. Armenti; Villanova, PA: Villanova University), 2:187–200.

1977

"Biblical Wisdom and Christian Ministry," *Duke Divinity School Review* 42:175–77.

"'Nation' in the Old Testament" *Ethnicity = Concilium* 101 (ed. A. Greeley and G. Baum; New York: Seabury) 71–77.

The Psalms, Job (Proclamation Commentaries; Philadelphia: Fortress) = *Giobbe, Salmi* (Leggere oggi la Bibbia; Brescia: Queriniana, 1977).

"Symposium on Biblical Criticism," *TToday* 33:364–65.

"Towards a Commentary on the Song of Songs," *CBQ* 39:482–96.

"What and Where Is Wisdom?" *CurTM* 4:283–87.

1978

"Moral Formation,"*Moral Formation and Christianity* = *Concilium* 110 (ed. F. Böckle and J.-M. Pohier; NewYork: Seabury) 29–36.

"The Understanding of Revelation in Prophecy and Wisdom," *Chicago Studies* 17:45–57 = "Concetti di rivelazione nei libri profetici e sapientiale," *Catechismo Biblico* (ed. G. Dyer; Brescia: Queriniana, 1979).

"Vatican III—Problems and Opportunities of the Future: The Bible," *Toward Vatican III: The Work that Needs to Be Done* (ed. D. Tracy; Colloquium at the University of Notre Dame, 1977; New York: Seabury) 21–26.

"Wisdom—Theses and Hypotheses," *Israelite Wisdom: Theological and Literary Essays in Honor of Samuel Terrien* (ed. J. G. Gammie et al.; Missoula, MT: Scholars) 35–42.

1979

"A Biblical Model of Human Intimacy: The Song of Songs," *The Family in Crisis or in Transition: A Sociological and Theological Perspective* = *Concilium* 121 (ed. A. Greeley; New York: Seabury) 61–66.

"Interpreting the Song of Songs," *BTB* 9:99–105.

"Qohelet's 'Quarrel' with the Fathers," *From Faith to Faith* (FS D. G. Miller; ed. D. Y. Hadidian; PTMS 31; Pittsburgh: Pickwick) 235–45.

"The Unity of the Song of Songs," *VT* 29:436–43.

"Wisdom and Salvation," *Sin, Salvation, and the Spirit* (ed. D. Durken; Collegeville, MN: Liturgical Press) 177–83.

1980

"The Faith of the Psalmist," *Int* 34:229–39.

"The Old Testament as Scripture," *JSOT* 16:40–44.

1981

"Biblical Insights into Suffering: Pathos and Compassion," *Whither Creativity, Freedom, Suffering? Humanity, Cosmos, God* (ed. F. A. Eigo; Proceedings of the Theology Institute of Villanova University; Villanova, PA: Villanova University) 53–75.

"The Faces of Wisdom in the Book of Proverbs," *Mélanges bibliques et orientaux en l'honneur de M. Henri Cazelles* (ed. A. Caquot and M. Delcor; AOAT 212; Neukirchen-Vluyn: Neukirkener V.) 337–45.

"Hebrew Wisdom," *JAOS* 101:21–34.

"Israel's Wisdom: A Biblical Model of Salvation," *Studia Missionalia* 30:1–43.

"Patristic and Medieval Exegesis–Help or Hindrance?" *CBQ* 43:505–16.

Wisdom Literature: Job, Proverbs, Ruth, Canticles, Ecclesiastes, and Esther (FOTL 13; Grand Rapids, MI: Eerdmans).

1982

"Prophets and Wise Men as Provokers of Dissent," *The Right to Dissent* = *Concilium* 158 (ed. H. Küng and J. Moltmann; New York: Seabury) 61–66.

"Qohelet Interpreted: The Bearing of the Past on the Present," *VT* 32:331–37.

1983

Wisdom Literature & Psalms (Interpreting Biblical Texts; Nashville: Abingdon).

1984

"A Response to 'The Task of Old Testament Theology'," *Horizons in Biblical Theology* 6:65–71.

"The Theological Contributions of Israel's Wisdom Literature," *Listening* 19:30–40. Reprinted in *A Companion to the Bible* (ed. M. Ward; New York: Alba, 1985) 269–83.

1985

"Cant 2:8–17–A Unified Poem?" *Mélanges bibliques et orientaux en l'honneur de M. Mathias Delcor* (ed. A. Caquot et al.; AOAT 215; Neukirchen-Vluyn: Neukirchener V.) 305–10.

"The Proverbs," *HBD* 831–32.

"Reflections on the History of the Exposition of Scripture," *Studies in Catholic History in Honor of John Tracy Ellis* (ed. N. Minnich et al.; Wilmington: Glazier) 489–99.

"Two Dangerous Books?" *Duke University Letters* 69:1–4.

"The Song of Solomon," *HBD* 978–79.

"Wisdom," *HBD* 1135–36.

"Wisdom and Creation" (Presidential Address), *JBL* 104:3–11.

1986

"Wisdom's Song: Proverbs 1:20–33," *CBQ* 48:456–60.

(With Burton Mack) "Wisdom Literature," *Early Judaism and Its Modern Interpreters* (ed. R. A. Kraft and G. W. Nickelsburg; The Bible and Its Modern Interpreters 2; Atlanta: Scholars) 371–410.

"The Song of Songs: Critical Scholarship vis-à-vis Exegetical Traditions," *Understanding the Word: Essays in Honour of Bernhard W. Anderson* (ed. J. T. Butler et al.; JSOTSup 37; Sheffield: JSOT, 1985) 63–69.

"Proverbs and Theological Exegesis," *The Hermeneutical Quest: Essays in Honor of James Luther Mays on His Sixty-Fifth Birthday* (ed. D. G. Miller; Princeton Theological Monographs 4; Allison Park, PA: Pickwick) 87–95.

"History of Exegesis as a Hermeneutical Tool: The Song of Songs," *BTB* 16:87–91.

"The Writings," *The Biblical Heritage in Modern Catholic Scholarship* (ed. J. J. Collins and J. D. Crossan; Wilmington: Glazier) 85–105.

1987

Preface to *Medieval Exegesis of Wisdom Literature: Essays by Beryl Smalley* (ed. R. E. Murphy; Reprints and Translation Series; Atlanta: Scholars).

"Dance and Death in the Song of Songs," *Love and Death in the Ancient Near East: Essays in Honor of Marvin H. Pope* (ed. J. Marks and R. Good; Guilford, CT: Four Quarters) 117–19.

"Update on Scripture Studies," *Religious Education* 82:624–36.

"The Faith of Qoheleth," *Word and World* 7:253–60.

"Proverbs 22:1–9," *Int* 41:398–402.

"Scripture and Church History," *Exodus–A Lasting Paradigm* (ed. B. van Iersel and A. Weiler; Edinburgh: T. & T. Clark) 3–8.

"Religious Dimensions of Israelite Wisdom," *Ancient Israelite Wisdom: Essays in Honor of Frank Moore Cross* (ed. P. D. Miller, P. D. Hanson and S. D. McBride; Philadelphia:Fortress, 1987) 449–58.

1988

"Wisdom and Eros in Proverbs 1–9," *CBQ* 50: 600–3.

"The Riddle of Love and Death," *Mysteries of the Bible* (Pleasantville, NY/Montreal: The Reader's Digest Association) 229–30.

"The Symbolism of the Song of Songs," *The Incarnate Imagination: Essays in Theology* (FS A. Greeley; ed. I. H. Shafer; Bowling Green, OH: Popular Press) 229–34.

"The Listening Heart," *Biblical People as Models for Campus Ministry* (ed. M. Galligan-Stierle et al.; Dayton, OH: Catholic Campus Ministry Association, 1988) 47–56.

"In Our Image," *Biblical People as Models for Campus Ministry,* 201–10.

"The Psalms in Modern Life," *TBT* 25:231–39.

1989

"Song of Solomon," *The Books of the Bible* (2 vols.; ed. B. W. Anderson; New York: Scribner's), 1. 241–46.

Foreword to G. P. Fogarty, *American Catholic Biblical Scholarship: A History from the Early Republic to Vatican II* (San Francisco: Harper & Row, 1989) xii–xiv. (See the references to Roland E. Murphy in the index.)

1990

The New Jerome Biblical Commentary (ed. R. E. Brown, J. A. Fitzmyer, R. E. Murphy; Englewood Cliffs, NJ: Prentice Hall).

"Introduction to the Pentateuch," *The New Jerome Biblical Commentary* 3–7.

(With R. J. Clifford) "Genesis," *The New Jerome Biblical Commentary* 8–43.

"Introduction to Wisdom Literature," *The New Jerome Biblical Commentary* 447–52.

"Canticle of Canticles," *The New Jerome Biblical Commentary* 462–465.

(With R. A. F. MacKenzie) "Job," *The New Jerome Biblical Commentary* 466–88.

(With A. G. Wright and J. A. Fitzmyer) "A History of Israel," *The New Jerome Biblical Commentary* 1219–52.

The Tree of Life: An Exploration of Biblical Wisdom (Anchor Bible Reference Library; New York: Doubleday).

The Song of Songs (Hermenia; Minneapolis: Augsburg/Fortress).

"The Old Testament/Tanakh—Canon and Interpretation," *The Hebrew Bible or Old Testament? Studying the Bible in Judaism and Christianity* (ed. R. Brooks and J. J. Collins; Christianity and Judaism in Antiquity 9: Notre Dame, IN: University of Notre Dame) 11–29.

"The Song of Songs and St Thérèse," *Experiencing St Thérèse Today* (ed. J. Sullivan; *Carmelite Studies* V: Washington: Institute of Carmelite Studies) 1–9, 191–92.

"The Sage in Ecclesiastes and Qoheleth the Sage," *The Sage in Israel and the*

Ancient Near East (ed. J. G. Gammie and L. Perdue; Winona Lake, IN: Eisenbrauns) 263–71.

1991

(With Bruce M. Metzger) R. E. Murphy, ed., *The New Oxford Annotated Bible/New Revised Standard Version, with the Apocryphal/Deuterocanonical Books* (Oxford/New York/Toronto: Oxford University) (R. E. Murphy's contributions: "Introduction to the OT," "Introduction to the Poetical Books or 'Writings'," "Modern Approaches to Biblical Study." Introductions and Annotations to Job, Proverbs, Ecclesiastes, Song of Songs, Lamentations, Wisdom of Solomon, Ecclesiasticus [Sirach].)

The Revised Psalms of the New American Bible (New York: Catholic Book Publishing) (one of six editors).

"Old Testament and Christian Unity," *Dictionary of the Ecumenical Movement* (ed. N. Lossky et al.; Geneva: World Council of Churches: Grand Rapids, MI: Eerdmans) 745–46.

"On Translating Ecclesiastes," *CBQ* 53:571–79.

"Qoheleth and Theology," *BTB* 21:30–33.

"The Biblical Elijah: A Holistic Perspective," *A Journey with Elijah* (ed. P. Chandler, O. Carm.; Carisma e Spiritualità 2; Rome: Institutum Carmelitanum) 21–27.

"Proverbs in Genesis 2?" *Text and Tradition: The Hebrew Bible and Folklore* (ed. S. Niditch; SBL Semeia Studies; Atlanta: Scholars) 121–25.

"Reflections upon Historical Methodology in Biblical Study," *The Land of Carmel* (ed. P. Chandler and K. J. Egan; Rome: Institutum Carmelitanum) 19–25.

1992

"The Psalms: Tune into the Original Soul Music," *U.S. Catholic*, February 1992, 57:20–27. Edited and reprinted in *God's Word Today*, May 1993, 39–44.

"Book of Song of Songs," *The Anchor Bible Dictionary* (6 vols.; ed. D. N. Freedman; New York: Doubleday), 6. 150–55.

"Wisdom in the OT," *The Anchor Bible Dictionary*, 6. 920–31.

"Images of Yahweh: God in the Writings," *Studies in Old Testament Theology* (FS David Hubbard; ed. R. L. Hubbard et al.; Dallas: Word) 189–204.

Ecclesiastes (WBC 23A; Waco, TX: Word).
"The Psalms and Worship," *Ex Auditu* 8:23–31.
"The Fear of the Lord: The Fear to End All Fears," *Overcoming Fear Between Jews and Christians* (ed. J. H. Charlesworth; Shared Ground Among Jews and Christians: A Series of Explorations 3; New York/Philadelphia: Crossroad/American Interfaith Institute, 1992–1993) 172–80.
The New Jerome Bible Handbook (ed. R. E. Brown, J. A. Fitzmyer, R. E. Murphy; London: Chapman/Collegeville, MN: Liturgical Press).

1993

"Reflections on Contextual Interpretation of the Psalms," *The Shape and Shaping of the Psalter* (ed. J. Clinton McCann; JSOTSup 159; Sheffield: JSOT) 21–28.
"The Book of Psalms," *The Oxford Companion to the Bible* (ed. B. M. Metzger and M. D. Coogan; New York/Oxford: Oxford University) 626–29.
"Solomon," *The Oxford Companion to the Bible* 707–8.
"Recent Research on Proverbs and Qoheleth," *Currents in Research: Biblical Studies* 1:118–40.
The Psalms are Yours (New York: Paulist).
L'albero delta vita: una esplorazione delta letteratura sapienziale biblica (Brescia: Queriniana). Translation of *The Tree of Life* (1990).
"Fireside Chat II," Cassette Recording, Annual Meeting of the AAR/SBL (November 1993).

1994

"Watch Your Language: Why We Should Mind our Hes and Shes . . . ," *U.S. Catholic*, February 1994, 32–35.
"Wisdom Literature and Biblical Theology," *BTB* 24:4–7.
"The Psalms: Prayer of Israel and the Church," *TBT* 32:133–37.
Responses to 101 Questions on the Psalms and Other Writings (New York: Paulist).
"Israelite Wisdom and the Home," *"Où demeures–tu?" (Jn 1,38): La maison depuis le monde bibllique* (FS Guy Couturier; ed. J.-C. Petit; Montreal: Fides (= *Journal for the Study of Judaism in the Persian, Hellenistic and Roman Period* 25 [1995]) 199–212.
"Worship, Officials, Wealth and its Uncertainties: Ecclesiastes 5:1–6:9,"

Reflecting with Solomon: Selected Studies on the Book of Ecclesiastes (ed. R. B. Zuck; Grand Rapids, MI: Baker, 1994 [reprinted from R. E. Murphy's *Ecclesiastes*, 1992]) 281–90.

1995

"The Personification of Wisdom," *Wisdom In Ancient Israel: Essays in Honor of J. A. Emerton* (ed. J. Day et al.; Cambridge: Cambridge University) 222–32.

1996

Responses to 101 Questions on the Biblical Torah: Reflections on the Pentateuch (New York: Paulist).

The Tree of Life: An Exploration of Biblical Wisdom Literature (2d ed.; Grand Rapids, MI: Eerdmans).

"The Old Testament and the New Catechism," *TBT* 34:253–59.

"Reflections on 'Actualization' of the Bible," *BTB* 26:79–81.

"Job," *The Collegeville Pastoral Dictionary of Biblical Theology* (ed. C. Stuhlmueller et al.; Collegeville: Liturgical Press) 492–93.

"Proverbs," *The Collegeville Pastoral Dictionary of Biblical Theology* 796–98.

"Wisdom," *The Collegeville Pastoral Dictionary of Biblical Theology* 1081–85.

Index of Ancient Sources

Index of Authors

Contributors

Michael L. Barré, S.S.
St. Mary's Seminary & University
Baltimore, Maryland

Claudia V. Camp
Texas Christian University
Fort Worth, Texas

Richard J. Clifford, S.J.
Weston Jesuit School of Theology
Cambridge, Massachusetts

James L. Crenshaw
Duke University
Durham, North Carolina

Alexander A. Di Lella, O.F.M.
The Catholic University of America
Washington, District of Columbia

Carole R. Fontaine
Andover Newton Theological School
Newton Centre, Massachusetts

Michael V. Fox
University of Wisconsin
Madison, Wisconsin

John S. Kselman, S.S.
Weston Jesuit School of Theology
Cambridge, Massachusetts

J. Clinton McCann
Eden Theological Seminary
St. Louis, Missouri

Leo G. Perdue
Brite Divinity School
Fort Worth, Texas

Choon-Leong Seow
Princeton Theological Seminary
Princeton, New Jersey

Raymond C. van Leeuwen
Eastern College
St. Davids, Pennsylvania

Claus Westermann
Heidelberg, Germany

R. N. Whybray
Ely, England

Addison G. Wright, S.S.
Trumbull, Connecticut

The Catholic Biblical Quarterly
Monograph Series (CBQMS)

1. Patrick W. Skehan, *Studies in Israelite Poetry and Wisdom* (CBQMS 1) $9.00 ($7.20 for CBA members) ISBN 0-915170-00-0 (LC 77-153511)

2. Aloysius M. Ambrozic, *The Hidden Kingdom: A Redactional-Critical Study of the References to the Kingdom of God in Mark's Gospel* (CBQMS 2) $9.00 ($7.20 for CBA members) ISBN 0-915170-01-9 (LC 72-89100)

3. Joseph Jensen, O.S.B., *The Use of tôrâ by Isaiah: His Debate with the Wisdom Tradition* (CBQMS 3) $3.00 ($2.40 for CBA members) ISBN 0-915170-02-7 (LC 73-83134)

4. George W. Coats, *From Canaan to Egypt: Structural and Theological Context for the Joseph Story* (CBQMS 4) $4.00 ($3.20 for CBA members) ISBN 0-915170-03-5 (LC 75-11382)

5. O. Lamar Cope, *Matthew: A Scribe Trained for the Kingdom of Heaven* (CBQMS 5) $4.50 ($3.60 for CBA members) ISBN 0-915170-04-3 (LC 75-36778)

6. Madeleine Boucher, *The Mysterious Parable: A Literary Study* (CBQMS 6) $2.50 ($2.00 for CBA members) ISBN 0-915170-05-1 (LC 76-51260)

7. Jay Braverman, Jerome's Commentary on Daniel: A Study of Comparative Jewish and Christian Interpretations of the Hebrew Bible (CBQMS 7) $4.00 ($3.20 for CBA members) ISBN 0-915170-06-X (LC 78-55726)

8. Maurya P. Horgan, *Pesharim: Qumran Interpretations of Biblical Books* (CBQMS 8) $6.00 ($4.80 for CBA members) ISBN 0-915170-07-8 (LC 78-12910)

9. Harold W. Attridge and Robert A. Oden, Jr., *Philo of Byblos,* The Phoenician History (CBQMS 9) $3.50 ($2.80 for CBA members) ISBN 0-915170-08-6 (LC 80-25781)

10. Paul J. Kobelski, *Melchizedek and Melchireš^c* (CBQMS 10) $4.50 ($3.60 for CBA members) ISBN 0-915170-09-4 (LC 80-28379)

11. Homer Heater, *A Septuagint Translation Technique in the Book of Job* (CBQMS 11) $4.00 ($3.20 for CBA members) ISBN 0-915170-10-8 (LC 81-10085)

12. Robert Doran, *Temple Propaganda: The Purpose and Character of 2 Maccabees* (CBQMS 12) $4.50 ($3.60 for CBA members) ISBN 0-915170-11-6 (LC 81-10084)

13. James Thompson, *The Beginnings of Christian Philosophy: The Epistle to the Hebrews* (CBQMS 13) $5.50 ($4.50 for CBA members) ISBN 0-915170-12-4 (LC 81-12295)

14. Thomas H. Tobin, S.J., *The Creation of Man: Philo and the History of Interpretation* (CBQMS 14) $6.00 ($4.80 for CBA members) ISBN 0-915170-13-2 (LC 82-19891)

15. Carolyn Osiek, *Rich and Poor in the Shepherd of Hermes* (CBQMS 15) $6.00 ($4.80 for CBA members) ISBN 0-915170-14-0 (LC 83-7385)

16. James C. VanderKam, *Enoch and the Growth of an Apocalyptic Tradition* (CBQMS 16) $6.50 ($5.20 for CBA members) ISBN 0-915170-15-9 (LC 83-10134)

17. Antony F. Campbell, S.J., *Of Prophets and Kings: A Late Ninth-Century Document (1 Samuel 1-2 Kings 10)* (CBQMS 17) $7.50 ($6.00 for CBA members) ISBN 0-915170-16-7 (LC 85-12791)

18. John C. Endres, S.J., *Biblical Interpretation in the Book of Jubilees* (CBQMS 18) $8.50 ($6.80 for CBA members) ISBN 0-915170-17-5 (LC 86-6845)

19. Sharon Pace Jeansonne, *The Old Greek Translation of Daniel 7-12* (CBQMS 19) $5.00 ($4.00 for CBA members) ISBN 0-915170-18-3 (LC 87-15865)

20. Lloyd M. Barré, *The Rhetoric of Political Persuasion: The Narrative Artistry and Political Intentions of 2 Kings 9-11* (CBQMS 20) $5.00 ($4.00 for CBA members) ISBN 0-915170-19-1 (LC 87-15878)

21. John J. Clabeaux, *A Lost Edition of the Letters of Paul: A Reassessment of the Text of the Pauline Corpus Attested by Marcion* (CBQMS 21) $8.50 ($6.80 for CBA members) ISBN 0-915170-20-5 (LC 88-28511)

22. Craig Koester, *The Dwelling of God: The Tabernacle in the Old Testament, Intertestamental Jewish Literature, and the New Testament* (CBQMS 22) $9.00 ($7.20 for CBA members) ISBN 0-915170-21-3 (LC 89-9853)

23. William Michael Soll, *Psalm 119: Matrix, Form, and Setting* (CBQMS 23) $9.00 ($7.20 for CBA members) ISBN 0-915170-22-1 (LC 90-27610)

24. Richard J. Clifford and John J. Collins (eds.), *Creation in the Biblical Traditions* (CBQMS 24) $7.00 ($5.60 for CBA members) ISBN 0-915170-23-X (LC 92-20268)

25. John E. Course, *Speech and Response: A Rhetorical Analysis of the Introductions to the Speeches of the Book of Job, Chaps. 4 - 24* (CBQMS 25) $8.50 ($6.80 for CBA members) ISBN 0-915170-24-8 (LC 94-26566)

26. Richard J. Clifford, *Creation Accounts in the Ancient Near East and in the Bible* (CBQMS 26) $9.00 ($7.20 for CBA members) ISBN 0-915170-25-6 (LC 94-26565)

27. John Paul Heil, *Blood and Water: The Death and Resurrection of Jesus in John 18 – 21* (CBQMS 27) $9.00 ($7.20 for CBA members) ISBN 0-91570-26-4 (LC 95-10479)

28. John Kaltner, *The Use of Arabic in Biblical Hebrew Lexicography* (CBQMS 28) $7.50 ($6.00 for CBA members) ISBN 0-91570-27-2 (LC 95-45182)

29. Michael L. Barré, S.S., *Wisdom, You Are My Sister: Studies in Honor of Roland E. Murphy, O.Carm., on the Occasion of His Eightieth Birthday* (CBQMS 29) $13.00 ($10.40 for CBA members) ISBN 0-91570-28-0 (LC 97-16060)

Order from:

The Catholic Biblical Association of America
The Catholic University of America
Washington, D.C. 20064